POLICY ANALYSIS IN THE CZECH REPUBLIC

International Library of Policy Analysis

Series editors: Iris Geva-May and Michael Howlett,
Simon Fraser University, Canada

This major new series brings together for the first time a detailed
examination of the theory and practice of policy analysis systems
at different levels of government and by non-governmental actors
in a specific country. It therefore provides a key addition to
research and teaching in comparative policy analysis and policy
studies more generally.

Each volume includes a history of the country's policy analysis which
offers a broad comparative overview with other countries as well as the
country in question. In doing so, the books in the series provide the
data and empirical case studies essential for instruction and for further
research in the area. They also include expert analysis of different
approaches to policy analysis and an assessment of their evolution and
operation.

Early volumes in the series will cover the following countries:

Australia • Brazil • China • Czech Republic • France • Germany •
India • Israel • Netherlands • New Zealand • Norway •
Russia • South Africa • Taiwan • UK • USA

and will build into an essential library of key reference works. The series
will be of interest to academics and students in public policy, public
administration and management, comparative politics and government,
public organisations and individual policy areas.
It will also interest people working in the countries in question
and internationally.

In association with the ICPA-Forum and *Journal of Comparative Policy Analysis*.
See more at http://goo.gl/raJUX

Policy Press
UNIVERSITY OF BRISTOL

POLICY ANALYSIS IN THE CZECH REPUBLIC

Edited by Arnošt Veselý,
Martin Nekola, Eva M. Hejzlarová

International Library of Policy Analysis, Vol 8

First published in Great Britain in 2016 by

Policy Press
University of Bristol
1-9 Old Park Hill
Bristol BS2 8BB
UK
+44 (0)117 954 5940
pp-info@bristol.ac.uk
www.policypress.co.uk

North America office:
Policy Press
c/o The University of Chicago Press
1427 East 60th Street
Chicago, IL 60637, USA
t: +1 773 702 7700
f: +1 773 702 9756
sales@press.uchicago.edu
www.press.uchicago.edu

British Library Cataloguing in Publication Data
A catalogue record for this book is available from the British Library.

Library of Congress Cataloging-in-Publication Data
A catalog record for this book has been requested.

ISBN 978 1 44731 814 9 hardcover

Cover design by Qube Design Associates, Bristol
Front cover: image kindly supplied by www.istock.com
Printed and bound in Great Britain by CPI Group (UK) Ltd, Croydon, CR0 4YY
Policy Press uses environmentally responsible print partners

Contents

List of tables, figures and boxes

Notes on contributors

Karel Čada is lecturer and researcher in the Institute of Sociological Studies at Charles University in Prague. His main research interests lie in interpretative policy analysis, discourse analysis, deliberative democracy, social inclusion and health policy. Among his latest publications is the paper 'Between clients and bureaucrats: an ambivalent position of NGOs in the social inclusion agenda in Czech statutory cities' (with K. Ptáčková, *Policy and Society*, 2014); 'Category making in discourses of health policy reforms: the case study of the Czech Republic' (*Asia Europe Journal*, 2014) and the chapter 'Social exclusion of the Roma and the Czech society' (in *The Gypsy Menace: Populism and the New Anti-Gypsy Politics*, 2012).

Ondřej Císař is associate professor in the Department of Sociology at Charles University and is also affiliated to the Institute of Sociology of the Academy of Sciences of the Czech Republic; he is editor-in-chief of the Czech edition of *Czech Sociological Review*. His main research interests lie in the fields of political mobilisation, social movements and political sociology. His recent publications include 'The emergence of a European social movement research field' (with M. Diani, *Routledge Handbook of European Sociology*, 2014), 'Promoting competition or cooperation? The impact of EU funding on Czech advocacy organizations' (with J. Navrátil, *Democratization*, 2014) and 'Social movements in political science' (*The Oxford Handbook of Social Movements*, 2015).

Eva M. Hejzlarová is lecturer and researcher in the Department of Public and Social Policy at Charles University in Prague. Her main research interests lie in interpretive policy analysis and marginalised groups. Among her latest publications are 'Policy analysis in the Czech Republic: positivist or postpositivist?' (*Central European Journal of Public Policy*, 2010) and '"Neviditelní" aktéři v policy analysis' ['Invisible' stakeholders in policy analysis] (*Sociální studia* [Social Studies], 2014).

Milan Hrubeš is a PhD student in the Faculty of Social Studies, Masaryk University, and a researcher in the International Institute of Political Science at Masaryk University. His research interests include political language analysis, framing analysis and political framing. Recent publications include, 'For rule of law, political plurality, and a just society: use of the legislative veto by President Václav Havel' (with V. Havlík and M. Pecina, *East European Politics and Societies and Cultures*, 2014) and *Analýza Policy* [Policy Analysis] (editor, 2011).

Vladimír Hulík is head of the Analytical Unit at the Ministry of Education, Youth and Sports of the Czech Republic. His research interests are focused on benchmarking and indicators of education systems (especially in the international context) and methods for output forecasting of education systems. Recent publications include 'Dopady demografického vývoje na vzdělávací soustavu v České Republice' [Impacts of the demographic development on the education system in the Czech Republic] (with K. Hulíková Tesárková, *Orbis scholae*, 2012); 'Míra účasti dětí na předškolním vzdělávání a faktory ovlivňující její regionální diferenciaci' [Participation rate in pre-primary education and key factors influencing its regional differentiation] (with L. Šídlo and K. Hulíková Tesárková, *Studia paedagogica*, 2008) and 'Úloha mezinárodních organizací ve vzdělávání' [The role of the international institutions in education] (in: *Vzdělávací politika v globálním kontextu* [Educational policy in a global context], 2006).

Klára Hulíková Tesárková is senior lecturer in the Department of Demography and Geodemography, Faculty of Science in Prague, Czech Republic. Her research focuses on demographic development and methodology (methods of mortality analysis) and applied demography (focused on education and life insurance). Her recent publications include 'Konvergenční a divergenční tendence v Evropě z hlediska úmrtnosti: Jaké je postavení Česka?' [Convergence and divergence tendencies in Europe from the mortality point of view: what is the situation of Czechia?] (with D. Kašpar, P. Zimmermann, *Geografie–Sborník ČGS*, 2015); 'Selected demographic methods of mortality analysis: approaches focused on adults and the oldest age-groups using primarily cross-sectional data' (LAP LAMBERT Academic Publishing, 2013) and 'DeRaS: software tool for modelling mortality intensities and life table construction' (with B. Burcin and D. Kománek, 2011).

Kateřina Merklová is a PhD candidate in the Department of Political Science, Faculty of Arts, Charles University in Prague. Her research interests lie in the areas of interpretive policy analysis, critical discourse analysis and gender studies. In her thesis, Kateřina studies processes of de/politicization and repoliticization related to selected public policy issues in the Czech Republic. Her recent publications include 'Politika soukromé expertízy' [Politics of private expertise], (*Acta Politologica*, 7, 2/2015, 156-176) and 'Construction of "no alternative" discourse and its "alternatives" after the outbreak of the crisis: The case of the Czech Republic (*International Conference on Public Policy*, Milano, 2015).

Vlastimil Nečas is assistant professor in the Department of Media Studies, Faculty of Social Sciences at Charles University in Prague. His research interests lie in political communication, agenda-setting research, media effects and framing analysis. Among his publications are 'Constitutional debate in the Czech Republic' (*Central European Journal of Communication*, 2009) and 'Media context of the Czech foreign policy' (with L. Vochovcová in: *Czech Foreign Policy in 2007--2009*, 2010).

Martin Nekola is lecturer and researcher in the Department of Public and Social Policy, Faculty of Social Sciences at Charles University in Prague. His research interests lie in policy work, drug policy, programme evaluation and theories of policy-making process. His recent publications are 'Regulating new psychoactive substances in the Czech Republic: policy analysis under urgency' (with J. Morávek, *Journal of Comparative Policy Analysis: Research and Practice*, 2015); 'Conceptualizing policy work as activity and field of research' (with J. Kohoutek and V. Novotný, *Central European Journal of Public Policy*, 2013) and 'Pragmatists, prohibitionists and preventionists in Czech drug policy' (*Central European Journal of Public Policy*, 2012).

Vilém Novotný is lecturer and researcher in the Department of Public and Social Policy at Charles University in Prague. His research interests lie in policy-politics relations, policy expertise of political parties, policy work, policy advisory systems, theories of policy-making process (especially the Multiple Streams Approach), development of study of public policy, and higher education. His recent publications include 'Multiple streams approach and political parties: modernization of Czech Social Democracy' (with M. Polášek, *Policy Sciences*, 2016), 'Czech study of public policy in the perspective of three dominant approaches' (*Central European Journal of Public Policy*, 2015), 'Conceptualizing Policy Work as Activity and Field of Research' (with J. Kohoutek and M. Nekola, *Central European Journal of Public Policy*, 2013).

Michel Perottino is associate professor and researcher in the Department of Political Science at Charles University in Prague. His research interests lie in political parties (theory, sociology, membership), French and Czech politics and the Czech political system. His recent publications are 'Le parti communiste tchèque entre continuité et rupture' [The Czech communist party between continuity and rupture] (in *Les partis de la gauche anticapitaliste en Europe*, 2011), 'Les évolutions de la fonction présidentielle tchèque' [Evolutions of the role of Czech president] (*Revue d'études comparatives Est-Ouest*, 2008) and *Francouzský politický systém* [The French political system] (2005).

Martin Polášek is lecturer and researcher in the Institute of Political Science at Charles University in Prague. His research interests lie in party organisation, intra-party processes and the theory of the welfare state. His latest publications are 'Revizionisté, tradicionalisté a progresivisté: programové debaty v československé sociální demokracii v letech 1924-1938' [Revisionists, traditionalists and progressives: programmatic debates in the Czechoslovak Social Democratic Party in the years 1924-1938] (2013), 'Mezi masovou a kartelovou stranou: Možnosti teorie při výkladu vývoje ČSSD a KSČM v letech 2000-2001' [Mass and cartel parties: sources of theory for interpreting the development of ČSSD and KSČM in 2000–2010] (with V. Novotný et al, 2012) and 'Studying welfare state from constructivist perspective: points of departure for the Czech case' (with V. Novotný, *Central European Journal of Public Policy*, 2011).

Martin Potůček is professor of public and social policy at Charles University in Prague, and head of the Centre for Social and Economic Strategies. His research focuses on processes of forming and implementing public and social policy in the Czech Republic and particularly the regulatory functions of the market, government and civic sector, on the European context and global dimension of public and social policy, and on the problems of public administration reform. He coordinates the comprehensive foresighting projects at the national as well as international level. He acted as an advisor to the Czech Prime Minister Vladimír Špidla (2002–04) and to the Czech Ministers of Labour and Social Affairs (1998–2006). He serves as an advisor to the Czech Prime Minister Bohuslav Sobotka and head of the Expert Committee for Pension Reform to the Czech government since 2014. His most important publications are *Not only the market* (1999), *Public policy in Central and Eastern Europe: theories, methods, practices* (with L. Leloup, G. Jenei, L. Váradi, 2003) and *Strategic governance and the Czech Republic* (2009).

Kateřina Ptáčková is a PhD candidate in the Institute of Sociology at Charles University in Prague. Her research interests include political sociology, policy analysis and decision making, civil society and the public sphere and democracy. Her latest publications are 'Professional curiosity engaged in policy sociology' (*Human Affairs*, 2012), 'Possibilities and limits of collaboration between science and NGOs in the Czech Republic' (with K. Čada, *Journal of Cleaner Production*, 2013) and 'Between clients and bureaucrats: an ambivalent position of NGOs in the social inclusion agenda in Czech statutory cities' (with K. Čada, *Policy and Society*, 2014).

Dan Ryšavý is assistant professor in the Department of Sociology, Andragogy and Cultural Anthropology, Philosophical Faculty, Palacky University Olomouc, Czech Republic. His research interests lie in topics of local government, political elites and economic sociology. His latest publications include 'Political professionalization of county councillors in Europe' (with D. Čermák, *Policy Making at the Second Tier of Local Government in Europe*, 2016), 'Career politicians a dozen years after regionalisation of the Czech Republic (2000-13)', *The Journal of Legislative Studies*, 2016, 'Size and local democracy: the case of Czech municipal representatives' (with J. Bernard, *Local Government Studies*, 2013), 'European mayors and councillors: similarities and differences' (in *Local Councillors in Europe*, 2013) and books *Na/O kraji* [*Regions in the Margins*] (with D. Čermák et al, 2015), *Zastupitelé českých měst a obcí v evropské perspektivě* [*The Czech town and municipal councillors in a European perspective*] (with P. Šaradín, 2011), 'Political professionalization of county councillors in Europe' (with D. Čermák, *Policy Making at the Second Tier of Local Government in Europe*, 2016).

Vojtěch Sedláček is senior consultant in Devoteam Consulting. Formerly, he was head of the Programme Management Office in Ministry of Interior, director of the Department of EU Funds in the Ministry of Interior and advisor to the Deputy Minister of the Interior of the Czech Republic.

Ivo Šlosarčík is professor of European Integration, Jean Monnet Chair in EU Law and director of the European Integration Studies Programme at Department of European Studies, Faculty of Social Sciences, Charles University in Prague. His research interests cover EU constitutionalism, compliance and enforcement of EU norms and EU justice and home affairs cooperation. His latest publications include *Ireland and Crisis* (2015), *Transformace kondicionality v Evropské unii* [Transformation of conditionality in the European Union] (2013) and *Instituce Evropské unie a Lisabonská smlouva* [EU institutions and the Lisbon Treaty] (edited with Z. Kasáková, 2013).

Libor Stejskal is research fellow in the Centre for Security Policy, Institute of Political Studies, Faculty of Social Sciences, Charles University in Prague. His research interests lie in security policy, human security, resilience and volunteering in the security sector. His recent publications are 'The hidden human security dimension of the Czech security policy' (with M. Balabán, A. Rašek in *National, European and Human Security: From Co-existence to Convergence*, 2012), 'The extended concept of security and the Czech security practice' (with M. Balabán, A. Rašek, *Central European Journal of Public Policy*, 2008) and 'The security dimension of the quality and sustainability of life' (in *Capacities of Governance in the Czech Republic*, 2008).

Tereza Stöckelová is a researcher in the Institute of Sociology of the Czech Academy of Sciences and assistant professor in the Department of General Anthropology, Charles University; she is an editor-in-chief of the English edition of *Sociologický časopis* [*Czech Sociological Review*]. Her work is situated in between sociology, social anthropology and science and technology studies (STS), drawing upon actor network theory and related material semiotic methodologies. She is interested in ethnographic investigation of academic practices in the context of current policy changes, science and society relations and medicine. Her latest publications include 'A tool for learning or a tool for cheating? The many-sided effects of a participatory student website in mass higher education' (*British Journal of Educational Technology*, 2015), 'Power at the Interfaces: The Contested Orderings of Academic Presents and Futures in a Social Science Department' (*Higher Education Policy*, 2014) and 'Immutable mobiles derailed: STS and the epistemic geopolitics of research assessment' (*Science, Technology & Human Values*, 2012).

Paulína Tabery is junior researcher and deputy head of department in the Public Opinion Research Centre, Institute of Sociology of the Academy of Sciences of the Czech Republic. Her field of professional interest lies in theories of public opinion formation, media and public opinion, public policy and public opinion. Her recent publications are 'První a druhý stupeň nastolování agendy (agenda-setting), rámcování (framing) a vypíchnutí (priming)' [Agenda setting, framing and priming] (in *Agenda-setting: teoretické přístupy* [Agenda-setting: theoretical approaches], 2008), 'Vnímání volební kampaně: příznivý, či nepříznivý dojem?'

[Perception of election campaign: positive or negative impression] (with G. Šamanová in: *Voliči a volby 2010* [Voters and elections 2010], 2012) and 'Sociologie veřejného mínění: Veřejné mínění jako sociální proces a komunikační koncept' [Sociology of public opinion: public opinion as social process and communication concept] (with J. Vinopal in: *Soudobá sociologie VI* [Contemporary sociology IV], 2014).

Tomáš Trampota is assistant professor in the Deparment of Media Studies in the Faculty of Social Sciences, Charles University Prague. His research interests focus on Czech media system and sociology of media. Among his key books are *Metody výzkumu médií* [Media research methods] (with M. Vojtěchovská, 2010) and *Zpravodajství* [News] (2006).

Arnošt Veselý is head and associate professor in the Department of Public and Social Policy, Faculty of Social Sciences, Charles University in Prague. He is also vice-head of the Institute of Sociological Studies and Senior Researcher at the Centre for Social and Economic Strategies in the same faculty. His main research interests include empirical analysis of policy work in public administration, accountability of public institutions, policy advisory systems and problem structuring in public policy. In terms of policy domains, he focuses upon educational policy. Apart from other research and policy analysis projects, he has been principal investigator of the project Policy Workers in the Czech Public Administration: Practices, Professional Values and Identity (Grant Agency of the Czech Republic). Together with Martin Nekola he edited and co-authored the first Czech policy analysis textbook *Analýza a tvorba veřejných politik: Principy, metody a praxe* [Methods of policy analysis and design]. He is also author of the book *Vymezení a strukturace problému ve veřejné politice* [Public policy problems delimitation and structuring].

Anna Zelinková is a PhD candidate in Department of Public and Social Policy, Faculty of Social Sciences, Charles University in Prague. Her research interest lies in education policy and her latest paper is 'Effects of age and length of professional experience on teachers' attitudes to curricular reform' (*Central European Journal of Public Policy*, 2012).

Acknowledgements

We are grateful to the series editors of the International Library of Policy Analysis – Iris Geva-May and Michael Howlett – for creating a platform for this book, their inspiring scholarship as well as their friendship and their ability to bring people together. In addition, we would like to thank the team at Policy Press for their dedication, help and support.

The volume brings together contributions from key Czech scholars as well as from practitioners working in the field, crossing the borders between disciplines and policy domains. We would like to thank all of them for sharing their insights and observations with a broader audience.

The discipline of democratic public policy in the Czech Republic emerged soon after the Velvet Revolution in 1989. Several of the 'founding-fathers' contributed to this volume. Regrettably, some of them are no longer with us. Miroslav Purkrábek, Josef Vavroušek, Jiří Musil and Jaroslav Kalous have laid the foundations for us, and we have built on what they started. Long before the argumentative turn, they taught us that policy analysis is much more than 'speaking truth to power'. It is also, and perhaps mainly, about communication, trust and good relationships. We dedicate this volume to their memory.

ONE

Policy analysis in the Czech Republic: the state of the art

Arnošt Veselý

Introduction

Although there is no clear equivalent for policy analysis in the Czech language, production and use of policy-relevant information has a long tradition there. Located in the geographic centre of Europe, the country's culture has been influenced by different traditions. It still has some traces of the Austro-Hungarian epoch (1867-18), independent Czechoslovakia (1918-38), the German Protectorate (1939-45), the short intermezzo of post-war democratic Czechoslovakia (1945-48) and the totalitarian experience under Soviet influence (1948-89), though with periods of relative liberalisation (the second half of the 1960s). These are mixed with the post-communist transformation after the fall of socialism in 1989. The year 1989 indeed started the construction of a new social order from a strange mixture of components of various origins (Sztompka, 1996, p 120). While the theory related to the practice of policy analysis has been strongly influenced by an extensive import of ideas from the USA, the UK, Germany and other countries, the result of blending quite different traditions has led in many respects to the idiosyncratic nature of Czech policy analysis.

This book provides the first comprehensive review of the historical development and current state of the art of policy analysis in the Czech Republic. It discusses what is unique about it and what it shares with other countries. The aim of this introductory chapter is to provide the reader with the basic concepts used throughout the book (policy, policy analysis, public policy and so on), describe the structure of the book as well as the key research topics and questions that are dealt with. First, the problems with translating 'policy analysis' and 'public policy' are discussed and the practical and theoretical consequences of this are noted. Second, four different possible meanings of policy analysis in the Czech discourse are discerned: (1) policy analysis as policy studies; (2) policy analysis as institutionalised methodological practice; (3) policy analysis as any type of policy advising based upon relevant knowledge; (4) policy analysis as policy work. Third, we describe the structure of the book and provide a brief outline of the individual chapters, basic core themes and questions covered in the book.

Doing policy analysis without policy: intricacies of language and their consequences

Before delving into a description of the development of policy analysis in the Czech Republic, it seems only appropriate to define what is actually meant by this term. There are virtually hundreds of different definitions of policy analysis, and even more definitions of the concept of 'policy' (for example Birkland, 2001; Hill, 2009). These are, however, not very informative for our purposes. This is because the Czech language, similar to most other languages, does not have a clear equivalent for the concept of 'policy'. While the English language has three connected but distinct terms related to different aspects of the policy-making process (politics, polity and policy), the Czech language has only one concept: *politika*. This concept might denote (Fiala and Schubert, 2000): (a) the process of making politics/policy in which different interests and approaches clash and become more or less successful by means of conflict or consensus (that is politics), (b) the institutional and normative aspect of politics/policy - the existing or demanded specific political order and the overall design and orientation of the society (that is polity), (c) the content of the policy-making process - laws and regulations, programmes and so on that may have a direct impact on citizens (that is, policy).

In everyday discourse, the Czech word *politika* seems to be associated more with politics than policy or polity. If you say that you are analysing *politika*, for instance, most people would probably think that you are studying disputes among politicians, struggles of political parties to get into power and suchlike. True, *politika* as policy is also present in public discourse. For instance, it is not uncommon to hear that 'his/her *politika* went wrong', 'we need a new employment *politika*' and so on. In these cases, *politika* clearly denotes policy, and when translated into English, it is also translated in this way.

These linguistic intricacies have very direct consequences. It is, for instance, not very useful to translate policy analysis into Czech as '*analýza politiky*' (analysis of *politika*). It would be too vague and could mean analysis of policy, politics or polity. For this reason, when Czech authors want to make it clear that they are writing about policy analysis in the Anglo-Saxon usage, they simply use policy analysis untranslated, or choose a longer expression. The first Czech policy analysis textbook (Veselý and Nekola, 2007), for instance, solved this problem by entitling the book *Metody analýzy a tvorby politik* (literally Methods of policy analysis and design). Adding these two words – methods and design – suggests to potential readers that the book is more about how to make and design *politika* (on the basis of analysis) than about how to analyse political parties, struggles for power and so on. The plural of 'policies', then, suggests not only that there are numerous public policies (in contrast to one *politika*) but also the prospective orientation; while numerous policies might be suggested for the future, the singular would imply the past (analysis of what already happened).

Non-existence of the concept of 'policy' has implications for other terms, especially for 'public policy' and 'policy-making process'. The term public policy is translated as *veřejná politika*, the term policy-making process usually as *proces tvorby politiky*. Although the concept of 'policy' in these phrases is translated into the otherwise multiple-meaning word *politika*, these expressions now seem to be rather well established, and the meaning of *politika* as 'policy' is generally assumed.[1] One of the reasons is that public policy was institutionalised as early as in 1993, when the department of Public and Social Policy in the Faculty of Social Sciences at Charles University in Prague was established. Consequently, there have been masters' programmes in public and social policy for more than 20 years (and also PhD programmes for about 18 years). There are now more than 500 graduates in 'Public and Social Policy'. The concept of public policy (*veřejná politika*) is part of official documents (such as accreditation), research grants and so on.[2]

Veřejná politika (public policy) currently has at least two different meanings in the Czech language (Potůček, 2005). First, it denotes a social practice - that is, the processes of policy making that actually take place in real life (for example, the ways a law or a strategy emerges and is subsequently implemented). Although arguably public policy as a social practice has a long tradition in the Czech lands (see Chapters Two and Three), it started to be described as public policy only very recently. Second, *veřejná politika* denotes the academic discipline that studies policy-making processes. Thus, in the former meaning of the term, public policy is an object of inquiry (*what* is studied), while in the latter meaning public policy is the subject of inquiry (the discipline that studies this object).

Of course, this may, and does, cause different misunderstandings because other disciplines usually use two different terms to denote themselves and their objects of study, respectively. For example, sociology is concerned with the study of society and demographics with the development of population structure. However, as for public policy, we might say, without being tautological, that 'public policy is concerned with public policy'. This is farther complicated by the paradoxical situation of the Czech Republic, where understanding of public policy as a discipline in fact *preceded* understanding of public policy as a social practice. When public policy was established as an academic discipline in the

---

[1] The question, however, is to what extent this applies to discourse outside academia and the public administration. It is our guess that the general public would still be quite puzzled by the terms veřejná politika or proces tvorby politiky, let alone policy analysis.

[2] From the very beginning the department at the Faculty of Social Policy as well as all the programmes it realised were labelled as 'Public and Social Policy'. The reason was that the first generation of scholars attempted to merge two traditions: American (where the concept of 'public policy' is used) and European (where in 1993 the term 'social policy' over 'public policy' was preferred). While the younger generations of policy scholars seem to take 'public policy' as a broader term encompassing social policy (and they thus consider including social policy in the title as redundant), for traditional purposes both the department and its programmes keep both 'public' and 'social' in their titles. Also, the label social policy might be more intelligible for prospective students.

Czech Republic, it was quite difficult to explain what the *object* of inquiry of this discipline would be. Only gradually did the concrete meanings of public policy start to be clarified, and with that, along with the intensive inflow of translation and usage of English-language scholarly texts and political documents by Czech scholars and practitioners, *veřejná politika* slowly began to be used in public discourse to denote the actual social practice, too.

Four meanings of policy analysis

The mere fact that in the Czech language there is no equivalent for policy does not mean, of course, that policy analysis does not exist in the Czech Republic. On the contrary, as is argued throughout the book, many things that are associated with policy analysis (such as providing advice to politicians on the basis of systematic, in-depth analysis of social problems and proposals for their possible solution) have a long tradition in the Czech lands. In our experience, in the current Czech discourse at least four different meanings of policy analysis might be encountered:

1 *policy analysis as policy studies*: policy analysis as the description and explanation of policy-making processes;
2 *policy analysis as institutionalised methodological practice*: policy analysis as a systematic approach, usually based upon a 'step-by-step' methodology and a set of techniques which help to provide useful advice to the client, especially policy makers; it can have either a traditional or an interpretive account;
3 *policy analysis as any type of policy advising based upon relevant knowledge*: policy analysis as any systematic cognitive activity that seeks to improve the policy-making process by providing relevant knowledge and information;
4 *policy analysis as policy work*: policy analysis as any activity that seeks to positively influence the policy-making process.

The first possible meaning of policy analysis can be well demonstrated by the first Czech book with policy analysis in the title. It was written jointly by the Czech political scientist Petr Fiala and the well-known German scholar Klaus Schubert. The book is entitled *Moderní analýza politiky. Uvedení do teorií a metody policy analysis* (literally Modern analysis of policy: introduction to theories and methods of policy analysis). While acknowledging that policy analysis includes both 'knowledge *of* policy' and 'knowledge *in* policy', the authors clearly focus upon the former. They understand policy analysis as one of the sub-disciplines of political science, and describe different theories and approaches to the study of the policy-making process (such as the policy cycle, policy networks, policy arenas). The book is strongly influenced by the political science background of the authors and the German tradition of policy analysis (focusing upon policy-making theories). In their understanding policy analysis is similar to what is in Anglo-Saxon countries often labelled as 'policy studies' or 'policy process research'.

The second possible meaning of policy analysis can also be well demonstrated using the example of another book, in this case the previously mentioned first policy analysis textbook edited by Veselý and Nekola (2007). This textbook was strongly influenced by the 'step-by-step policy analysis' books by Dunn (2003), Bardach (2000), Patton and Sawicki (1993), Weimer and Vining (2005) and others. The authors follow what is sometimes in the European context referred to as the 'American style' of policy analysis. They understand policy analysis as a practical activity with the aim to produce knowledge and methodology for use in real policy making (that is, knowledge *for* policy). The book consists of two parts. While the first part introduces the foundations of policy analysis, the second part, consisting of eight chapters (such as problem definition, setting goals and evaluation criteria, identification of possible solutions), describes various methods and techniques that can be used in producing knowledge relevant for the policy-making process (such as problem tree analysis, stakeholder analysis, cost-benefit analysis). As in other countries, the positivist paradigm of rational step-by-step policy analysis was criticised and in response several Czech scholars argued for, and started to practise, more interpretive policy analysis. Policy analysis as an institutionalised methodological practice thus nowadays can have either the form of a 'step-by-step' approach based upon predominantly rational techniques (hereafter referred to as 'traditional policy analysis'), or the form of interpretive policy analysis based upon the assumption that the social world can be interpreted in many different ways (henceforth 'interpretive policy analysis').

Both the first and second perspectives on policy analysis, as policy studies and as institutionalised methodological practice (either traditional or interpretive), have clear foreign origins. While the first is inspired by the German tradition, the second draws heavily upon the Anglo-Saxon (especially American) or European (French, Dutch) traditions of policy analysis, respectively. Both approaches are nowadays to a certain degree institutionalised in instruction and research (the first approach mainly at Masaryk University in Brno, the second particularly at Charles University in Prague).[3] We can thus assume that a not insignificant number of people in both academia and practice are now familiar with either the German or American/European tradition of policy analysis, and have some idea what policy analysis means in an international context.

Nevertheless, there is no doubt that in general only a minority of practitioners is familiar with either of the two meanings as previously discussed. Many of them simply *do* what could be labelled as policy analysis without actually knowing that their activities could be labelled as 'policy analysis'. If we restricted this book

---

[3]   Both books have been relatively influential in terms of readership. It is difficult to judge the real impact of these books. However, based upon our experience, we assume that while in academia both books are more or less equally used in public policy (and similar courses), in practice the textbook by Veselý and Nekola (2007) is used more, mostly because it provides practical methods and techniques. If this is really so, the American perspective is likely to be prevalent in practice. Nevertheless, this claim is based only upon our experience and anecdotal evidence we have and should be subject to rigorous research.

only to work done solely under the rubric of policy analysis, we would miss the bulk of work that closely adheres to the principles and ideas of policy analysis as it is practised and defined abroad. Therefore we can say that policy analysis in the Czech Republic can also have a third meaning: as any type of policy advising based upon relevant knowledge.

In this respect, it might be helpful the review the basic ideas which constitute policy analysis elsewhere. There are many competing definitions of policy analysis. Patton and Sawicki (1993, p 24) define policy analysis as 'a systematic evaluation of the technical and economic feasibility and political viability of alternative policies (or plans or programmes), strategies for implementation, and the consequences of policy adoption'. According to Weimer and Vining (2005, p 24) policy analysis denotes 'client-oriented advice relevant to public decisions and informed by social values'. Dunn (2003, pp 1-2) offers the following description:

> Policy analysis is a problem-solving discipline that draws on theories, methods, and substantive findings of the behavioural and social sciences, social professions, and social and political philosophy ... policy analysis is a process of multidisciplinary inquiry that creates, critically assesses, and communicates information that is useful for understanding and improving policies.'

While these and similar definitions stress different aspects of policy analysis, they overlap on several points. First, policy analysis deals with real-life problems and problem situations. Second, it attempts to produce relevant knowledge about these problems, based upon sound methodology and the best available evidence (though taking into account practical limitations, such as time constraints). Third, it strives to provide useful and relevant advice (based upon this knowledge) to clients, usually decision makers. As argued throughout the book, if policy analysis is understood in this broader sense as any type of policy advising based upon relevant knowledge then policy analysis clearly has a long tradition in the Czech lands (see Chapters Two and Three). The Czech social sciences have always had a strong practical orientation. The most famous Czech scholars and authors like Tomáš Garrigue Masaryk, Karel Čapek, Karel Engliš, Josef Macek, Inocenc Arnošt Bláha, Václav Havel have been interested in real-life problems, tried to understand them and propose possible solutions.[4] At the same time, many of these figures were quite active in political life. This is also true today.[5] As in many other countries, the Czech social sciences are sometimes blamed, often correctly, for being too self-centred and impractical. On the other hand, Czech universities

---

[4] This practical orientation could be demonstrated with even much older examples, such as John Amos Comenius, the 'father' of modern education.

[5] For instance, Professor Petr Fiala, mentioned earlier as co-author of the first Czech book with policy analysis in the title, served as Minister of Education and became a leader of the Civic Democratic Party.

have never been ivory towers, and have always played an important role in political life (see Chapter Seventeen). To sum up, policy-oriented research and analysis have always been strongly present in the Czech lands, though they have rarely been formally institutionalised in terms of establishment of institutions formally devoted to generating policy-relevant knowledge.[6] Consequently, much of this book is about policy analysis in this third meaning: about the systematic production of knowledge that can be usefully utilised in the policy-making process. This broad category ranges from policy research generated in academic institutions, think tanks or other similar institutions to ad hoc analyses from various actors (for example, consultancy companies).[7]

Recently, the fourth possible, and the most encompassing, meaning of policy analysis has begun to be discussed. Case studies included in the book edited by Hal Colebatch in 2006 demonstrated that relatively few policy analysts were given the tasks depicted by standard policy analysis textbooks (that is, the use of scientific methods and the rational assessment of possible alternatives). Instead, policy analysts devoted themselves to various activities that were quite distant from both traditional and interpretive policy analysis. It was among their tasks to design and implement projects, communicate with actors, moderate conflicts, manage organisations, and so on. The practice was simply much richer and more differentiated than the textbook account. For that reason, Colebatch (2006) began to use the terms 'policy work' and 'policy workers'. Although he never defined them precisely, it is clear from the context that policy work includes activities related to the analysis and making of public policy which require specific knowledge and skills (but not only strictly scientific or academic ones). Policy work lies in 'the exercise of professional judgment' rather than the application of scientific techniques (Colebatch and Radin, 2006, p 220).

The term 'policy worker' is more general than 'policy analyst'. While a policy analyst provides advice through the text of his analysis, a policy worker does not necessarily write any text. There is no standard position of 'policy analyst' in the Czech Republic, but no doubt there are a huge number of people who could be defined as policy workers. Without going too far in this direction (where a policy worker could in principle be any citizen who is somehow involved in the policy-making process), we consider this possible meaning of policy analysis as well, especially in Chapters Seven and Eight.

---

[6] Paradoxically, policy research was institutionalised to the greatest extent during socialism in terms of the so-called 'departmental institutions' (resortní ústavy), managed by particular ministries. However, while the number of staff in these institutions was enormous, the practical impact upon policy making was quite limited.

[7] The first policy analysis textbook (Veselý and Nekola, 2007) was originally organised in line with Dunn's (2003) book. Though Dunn's book is arguably the textbook that most successfully incorporates the real world of policy analysis, it soon became clear that simple 'translation' of Dunn into the Czech context is impossible. The demands of practice were found to be too different, and to write a truly practical book the authors were forced to introduce new concepts (such as 'policy documents'), and propose a different approach.

Overall structure of the book, core themes and questions

'Analysis of policy analysis' can be done in multiple ways, and from quite different perspectives. It can also cover quite different topics, ranging from theory of policy analysis to instruction to actual everyday practices. In this book we adopt quite a broad approach and we try to accommodate as many perspectives and themes as possible. We also cover all four of the possible meanings of policy analysis mentioned earlier. However, our aim was more than to produce a mere set of detached chapters. We aspire to also provide a more or less coherent 'macro-view' of policy analysis in the Czech Republic, which is impossible without setting common topics and clearly structuring the discussion.[8]

There are two lines on which this book is organised. First, the book is structured in accordance with the International Library of Policy Analysis (ILPA) library, which makes it possible to compare policy analysis in the Czech Republic with other countries. Following this introductory chapter, Part I focuses on the 'Styles and Methods of Public Policy Analysis' in the Czech Republic, describing the historical origins and development of both public policy and policy analysis, and their styles and methods. In *Chapter Two*, Martin Potůček sums up the development of public policy as a scientific discipline and object of research and instruction in the Czech Republic. This is presented within a historical context, examining different stages of the development of Czech social sciences even before it was formalised, and how it has been constituted since the early 1990s. It also takes into account the broader cultural, political and institutional context of the development of this field, including the role of various personalities. A characterisation is given of the main streams of research and instruction (with references to key literature, its authors and context). This is followed by a reflection on results and specification of development potentials.

In *Chapter Three*, Vilém Novotný picks up on the previous chapter and deals in greater detail with the development of policy analysis as science-based policy-related advising in the Czech Republic and the former Czechoslovakia. He describes the state of policy analysis in the Czech Republic using a historical overview of Czech policy analysis and explains it by means of the theoretical supply-demand model. He emphasises the demand side concerning the social and political factors influencing the development of policy analysis. First, the roots of Czech policy analysis are examined going back to the beginning of the 20th century and the foundation of the Czechoslovak Republic in 1918. Then, policy analysis during the communist regime is focused on. In the last section, the development of Czech policy analysis after the Velvet Revolution in 1989 and its contemporary state is considered.

---

[8] It should be noted that by a 'coherent macro-view' we do not mean a uniform perspective hiding controversies and ambiguities. On the contrary, our aim was to include authors from different backgrounds and schools of thought, with different views and experiences.

In *Chapter Four*, Eva M. Hejzlarová reflects different analytical styles used for classification of the work on policy analysts and workers in foreign literature with special focus on the two most prominent: the rational 'modern' style of the 1960s and 1970s, based on the quantification of economic costs and benefits, and the 'post-modern' analysis of the 1980s and 1990s, focused on the social construction of policy problems and a more interpretive approach. Using this background and original research, she unveils the dominant paradigm of policy analysis in the Czech Republic. Later on, the application of the Mayer, Els van Daalen, and Bots classification of six different styles is discussed under the condition of Czech policy analysis field.

Part II of the book examines 'Policy Analysis by Governments'. Besides policy analysis on the central, subnational and local levels, it also covers the influence of supranational institutions on Czech policy analysis. In *Chapter Five*, Martin Potůček, Vladimír Hulík, Klára Hulíková Tesárková and Libor Stejskal provide a broader perspective on policy analysis by examining the impact of supranational organisations on policy making in the Czech Republic. They deal with the direct influence of supranational organisations on national public policy making, focusing predominantly on the processes of problem identification and policy formulation. After a theoretical outline, three case studies from different policy fields are presented: social policy, educational policy and defence policy. Based on these case studies, a tentative assessment on the developmental trends, shortcomings and prospects of the relationship between supranational and national levels are offered.

In *Chapter Six*, Ivo Šlosarčík analyses the impact of European Union membership on the institutional and public law framework for policy making in the Czech Republic. Using the perspective of new institutionalism, he covers the shift from passive 'transplantation' of EU norms during the association and accession negotiations to active formulation of EU policies after the accession. The development of new Czech structures responsible for the EU agenda is also addressed, including institutional competition within the Czech administration. The limits of the Europeanisation of policy making in the Czech Republic are explained with a particular focus on the lack of stability of Czech administrative structures, the dominance of the domestic political context and the limited expertise and/or self-confidence of Czech policy makers.

In *Chapter Seven*, Arnošt Veselý and Martin Nekola deal with the profile and policy work of policy bureaucrats (PBs) in the Czech Republic ministries as the most prominent organisations of central public administration. Based on theoretical assumptions of policy work, their analysis draws on data from a survey among the officials of 11 ministries in 2013. Where applicable, results are contrasted with findings from an analogous survey on regional policy bureaucrats from 2012. First, the role of ministries in the overall governance system of the Czech Republic is described. Second, a profile of ministerial PBs in terms of age, education and previous experience is presented. Third, policy-related tasks are analysed and compared, with special focus on the relationship between analytical and communication tasks.

In *Chapter Eight*, Martin Nekola and Arnošt Veselý deal with the question of how policy work is done in the specific context of regional authorities. They provide a description of how policy research and analysis is generated and utilised and, in particular, what different analytical styles can be found among regional policy workers. Based upon the large-scale questionnaire survey carried out in all Czech regions except the capital city Prague at the end of 2012, the relationship among regional policy workers' tasks, activities and the types of problems they solve is examined. The authors analyse the day-to-day basis of regional bureaucrats' policy work and contrast it with ideal types, concluding that the way policy work is done differs significantly from 'Western' theoretical accounts and/or experience.

In *Chapter Nine*, Dan Ryšavý follows from the previous two chapters and analyses policy work within the context of local self-government. The first part briefly examines the relevant literature and the main sources on which the chapter is based. The following section deals with the context of public administration on the local level and its main determinants – a fragmented municipal structure, a fused model of public administration, its financing and the main local bodies responsible for carrying out public administration. The third part presents the basic socio-demographic and political profile of local decision makers and perceived influence of different bodies on decision making. The fourth part approaches local policy work through a description of mayoral time management and communication networks.

Part III studies the discipline's application by 'Internal Policy Advisory Councils, Consultants and Public Opinion'. In *Chapter Ten*, Kateřina Merklová and Kateřina Ptáčková analyse governmental and departmental advisory bodies as a part of the policy advisory system in the Czech Republic whose primary aim is to improve the situation in a related policy area through providing the government with relevant policy advice. Their analysis focuses on the formal framework of the advisory bodies and its impact on the nature of the policy they produce. Based on the analysis of the three selected advisory bodies, several internal paradoxes of the current institutional framework of the Czech advisory councils are identified and four main factors contributing to success or failure of the policy advisory bodies are suggested. These are a high level of uncertainty, a high level of centrality of the issue within the government's policy agenda, definition of the advisory body's activity and inclusion of knowledge other than scientific knowledge in the policy advice.

In *Chapter Eleven*, Paulína Tabery deals with the relationship between public opinion and public policy. The first part discusses the dominant role of opinion polls as a representation of public opinion, and their strengths and weaknesses. Further, this part also deals with the question of what policy makers consider to be public opinion and what the role of interest groups in this context is. The conclusion of this section is devoted to the question of the impact of public opinion on public policy and problems in its measurement. The second part focuses on the Czech Republic. Firstly, it introduces the history of public opinion research in this country. Further, it focuses on interest in politics and public affairs and people's preferences in different areas of public life which might be addressed by public policies. Finally, the relationship between public opinion and public policy is demonstrated using the example of building an anti-missile radar base.

In *Chapter Twelve*, Vojtěch Sedláček and Arnošt Veselý deal with the outsourcing of policy advice, focusing in particular on consulting companies providing policy analysis and advice on a commercial basis. First, they attempt to quantify the extent of outsourcing in the Czech ministries as the most important central public administration institutions. Then the types and roles of different commercial providers of policy advice are described, followed by discussion of why outsourcing happens and what are its possible consequences. Apart from statistical data, the authors draw upon more than ten years' experience from both consuming and providing outsourced policy analysis in the Czech central state administration as well as interviews from representatives of both demand and supply side.

Part IV turns towards 'Parties and Interest Groups' and examines policy analysis in political parties and nongovernmental organisations (NGOs). In *Chapter Thirteen*, Vilém Novotný, Martin Polášek and Michel Perottino deal with policy analysis in Czech political parties. They address the question of how the main Czech political parties (Social Democrats and Civic Democrats) use policy analysis to respond to increasing demands on their policy capacities in policy making. Thus, their main focus is on the parties' formal mechanisms and the organisational arrangements that produce the required policy-related expertise. In particular, they concentrate on the configuration of a party advisory system on the intra- and extra-party levels (expert committees, 'shadow' ministers, policy analysis units and so on). Based on Kuhne's typology of extra-party consultation, three sources of external policy expertise for political parties are distinguished (academic-based, lobbying and professional consultation).

In *Chapter Fourteen*, Karel Čada and Kateřina Ptáčková discuss the role of NGOs and other civil society actors in the policy-making process in the Czech Republic. In particular, they focus on the structure of the formal opportunities Czech NGOs have for participation in designing and implementing public policies, the capacities they have for gathering information and policy analysis production, and finally the strategies they have developed to exert their influence over public policies. It is argued that NGOs have become crucial actors in the implementation part of the policy process, employing widely varied forms of expertise and evidence-based policy making, with law, economics and the social sciences as the most frequently employed disciplines. However, in many areas the government has remained rather reluctant to accept NGOs as equally relevant actors in the initial stages of the policy process. The chapter concludes with a reflection on the consequences of the recent economic crisis on the Czech NGO sector. Besides the direct impacts in the form of budgetary cuts and austerity policies, the emergence of new grass-roots NGOs and activist groups has also been identified.

Part V on 'Academic and Advocacy-based Policy Analysis' addresses the media, think tanks, academics and policy analysis instruction. In *Chapter Fifteen*, Vlastimil

Nečas and Tomáš Trampota address the role of the news media in decision-making processes. The chapter is divided into two main sections dealing with different topics. In the first section, the authors employ the concept of political parallelism and deal with the development of the media system in the Czech Republic with an emphasis on its development within the democratisation of society after 1989 and the intersections of media and politics. The second part adopts the perspective of agenda-setting theory as the primary framework for analysing the political influence the media exert upon the public and describes selected characteristics of political communication in the Czech Republic

In *Chapter Sixteen*, Ondřej Císař and Milan Hrubeš map out the landscape of Czech think tanks. Their approach is based on two types of literature: empirical studies of think tanks and discursive institutionalism. Drawing on think tank studies, they categorise Czech think tanks as academic, contractual, advocacy based and party affiliated. Drawing on discursive institutionalism, they differentiate among four major policy discourses in the Czech Republic: liberal-conservative, social democratic, support for democracy, and international and foreign policy discourses. While the liberal-conservative discourse is most well developed, social democratic organisations present the exact opposite. Probably due to the general ideological and funding context, they are poorly resourced, not numerous and not densely connected to other partners.

In *Chapter Seventeen*, Tereza Stőckelová maps and discusses the key structural limits and incentives of policy-relevant knowledge production by academics in the Czech Republic. Firstly, she analyses current science and higher education policy arrangements (funding and evaluation) with implications for the production of social science expertise and interactions between science and society. Secondly, she focuses on economists who form the most clearly influential, though increasingly controversial, academic discipline regarding both the shaping of public policy and media discourses in the country. She offers a brief introduction to the role of economists in political and policy transformation in 1990 and two ethnographic studies of economists' engagement in expertise production and the shaping of public policies. It is argued that the pressing current issues related to academics' involvement in policy making are the diversity of expertise invited into the policy process and the possibilities to embed the production of policy-relevant expertise in individual academic careers.

In *Chapter Eighteen*, Arnošt Veselý, Eva M. Hejzlarová and Anna Zelinková examine the development and current state of academic public policy programmes in the Czech Republic and the role of policy analysis instruction in them. The chapter is based mostly upon an analysis of the publicly available list of study programmes accredited by the Ministry of Education, Youth and Sport, an internet search, email correspondence with public policy and policy analysis instructors, syllabus analyses as well as a quantitative analysis of masters' theses in the three main public policy programmes. After a brief introduction to the Czech higher education system, an overview of study programmes/fields in public policy and related fields is provided. Then the content of policy analysis courses is described.

The orientation of the three main public policy programmes is analysed using unique data on masters' theses. The chapter concludes with some preliminary findings regarding public policy/policy analysis instruction in the Czech Republic.

The book concludes with *Chapter Nineteen*, where Arnošt Veselý and Martin Nekola summarise the main findings from the chapters and discuss future prospects for policy analysis in the Czech Republic.

The second line of structuring concerns the cross-cutting themes that are covered throughout the book in different chapters. Each topic includes several questions which we try to answer in the conclusions. These themes and questions are as follows:

- The general standing of policy analysis in the broader context: How is policy analysis institutionalised? How is policy analysis embedded in other disciplines? How are policy analysis activities reflected in the general discourse? How is knowledge coming from policy analysis used and legitimised by different actors?
- Methods and approaches: What is the nature of current policy analysis in the Czech Republic? In what, if any respects does policy analysis in the Czech Republic resemble the 'textbook' model? To what extent are interpretive perspectives reflected in real policy making? Which methods are predominant in policy analysis? To what extent was the 'argumentative turn' in policy analysis realised in the Czech Republic?
- Czech policy analysis vis-à-vis development of policy analysis abroad: To what extent has policy analysis in the Czech Republic been inspired by foreign practices? Which tradition has been predominant? Is there anything particular about the policy analysis style in the Czech Republic as compared to neighbouring countries such as Germany or Poland? Which were the main cultural barriers in 'translating' the Anglo-Saxon concept(s) of policy analysis into the Czech context?
- Location and people: Where and by whom is policy analysis actually practised? Who are the people who perform policy analysis? What are the core 'policy work' activities of the most important policy actors? Are there any specific traditional and interpretive 'tribes' of policy analysts?

Acknowledgement
The chapter was written with the financial support of PRVOUK programme P17 'Sciences of Society, Politics, and Media under the Challenge of the Times'.

References
Bardach, E. (2000) *A Practical Guide for Policy Analysis: The Eightfold Path to More Effective Problem Solving*, New York: Seven Bridges Press.
Birkland, T.A. (2001) *An Introduction to the Policy Process: Theories, Concepts, and Models of Public Policy Making*, New York: M.E. Sharpe.

Colebatch, H.K. (ed) (2006) *The Work of Policy: An International Survey*, Lanham, MD: Lexington Books.

Colebatch, H.K. and Radin, B.A. (2006) 'Mapping the work of policy', in H.K. Colebatch (ed) *The Work of Policy: An International Survey*, Lanham, MD: Lexington Books, pp 1-19.

Dunn, W.N. (2003) *Public Policy Analysis: An Introduction* (3rd edn), Upper Saddle River, NJ: Prentice Hall.

Fiala, P. and Schubert, K. (2000) *Moderní analýza politiky. Uvedení do teorií a metod policy analysis* [Modern analysis of policy: introduction to theories and methods of policy analysis], Brno: Barrister & Principal.

Hill, M.J. (2009) *The Public Policy Process* (5th edn), Harlow: Pearson Longman.

Patton, C.V. and Sawicki, D.S. (1993) *Basic Methods of Policy Analysis and Planning* (2nd edn), Upper Saddle River, NJ: Prentice Hall.

Potůček, M. (ed) (2005) *Veřejná politika* [Public policy], Praha: Sociologické nakladatelství.

Sztompka, P. (1996) 'Looking back: the year 1989 as a cultural and civilizational break', *Communist and Post-Communist Studies*, 29(2): 115-29.

Veselý, A. and Nekola, M. (eds) (2007) *Analýza a tvorba veřejné politiky: přístupy, metody a praxe* [Methods of policies analysis and design], Praha: Sociologické nakladatelství.

Weimer, D.L. and Vining, A.R. (2005) *Policy Analysis: Concepts and Practice* (4th edn), Upper Saddle River, NJ: Prentice-Hall.

Part I

The styles and methods of public policy analysis in the Czech Republic

TWO

Public policy in the Czech Republic: historical development and its current state

Martin Potůček

Introduction

This chapter sums up the development of public policy as a scientific discipline and object of research and instruction in the Czech Republic. This is presented within a historical context, examining different stages of the development of Czech social sciences even before it was formalised, and the development of its being constituted since the early 1990s. It also takes into account the broader cultural, political and institutional context of the development of this field, including the role of various personalities. A characterisation is given of the main streams of research and instruction in the field (with reference to the key literature, its authors and context). This is followed by a reflection on results and specification of development potentials.

The early 20th century

Brilliant brains often beat generations of intellectual stereotypes. In the Czech social scientific environment there were thinkers who, by formulating problems and proposing solutions, laid the foundations for something that came to be called, decades later, *public and social policy*. As early as the 1870s, Albín Bráf carried out a brilliant analysis of working conditions in North Bohemia, and as Austro-Hungarian Minister of Agriculture he took part in shaping the economic and social policies of the day. Worthy contributions were doubtless made by the likes of Tomáš Garrigue Masaryk with his *Social Question* and *Humanitarian Ideals*, as well as his broad concept of democracy (Masaryk, 1972, 1990, 2000); Josef Macek (1935), who asserted himself as both a national economic expert with deep insight and a social policy theorist, convinced that the world needs to clarify the essence of economic prosperity and its conditions – not only material and technical but also moral and political; Ferdinand Peroutka with his characterisation of the problems of forming Czech statehood in the monograph *Building of a State* (Peroutka, 1991); and last but not least, Karel Čapek with his reflections on politics, public affairs, chronic deficits of citizenship and man as a *zóon politikon* in the context of Czech society (Čapek, 1993, pp 16-22). Interestingly, their contributions always coincided with critical episodes in the life of Czech national community, which was either working to achieve its full political emancipation or in the formative years of asserting it.

This period of forming public policy is best compared to a baby yet to be born, that makes itself heard although a name has yet to be given to it.

Is there light at the end of the tunnel?

Younger Czech experts, let alone their foreign colleagues, know little about communist-era social scientific studies. They naturally focus on the procedures and outcomes of Western science. At the same time, however, the present state of social sciences in the Czech Republic continues to be marked (in both a positive and negative sense) by their allegiance to the scientific, moral and partly also institutional legacy of communist rule.

To see the communist era in the former Czechoslovakia (1948-89) merely as the Dark Ages with the unchallenged rule of the Communist Party of Czechoslovakia is both anti-historical and lamentably distortive of the true nature of the concurrent social, economic, political and administrative processes. Generally speaking, not only did public policy issues figure in research, but some decision makers also had a tendency to apply public policy concepts in political practice.

The 1960s

The phenomenon of cultural and social transformation which occurred throughout the world in the 1960s, including in Czechoslovakia, has yet to be satisfactorily explained. The fact is that parallel political and civic anti–establishment movements originated and existed in the United States, Western Europe (notably in France and West Germany), and indeed also in the East. Czechoslovakia's short-lived, brutally interrupted political and economic liberalisation was a component part of this breakthrough, even though it had its own specific features.

Czechoslovakia's Prague Spring in 1968 was ideologically presaged above all by the work of expert teams which, although formed within official institutions, had begun to extricate themselves since the early 1960s from the highly ideological and intellectually sterile concepts of the official Marxist-Leninist doctrine (see Box 2.1).

Box 2.1: Examples of expert teams in the 1960s

Machonin's team, active in the Charles University Institute of Social and Political Sciences (the Institute of Marxism-Leninism until 1968) legitimised both solid research in the field of empirical social studies and the concept of society as an evolving, stratified body with differentiated interests of various classes and with inner tensions determined by the dynamic functional imbalance of its individual component parts.

Main output: Machonin, Pavel et al (1969) Československá společnost. *Sociologická analýza sociální stratifikace* [Czechoslovak society. A sociological analysis of social stratification], Bratislava: Epocha. See also Machonin (1970).

Richta's team, active in the Czechoslovak Academy of Sciences, outlined a comprehensive hypothesis of societal changes determined by the growing importance of knowledge and its application in the life of society. The team weaned itself off one of the Marxist-Leninist clichés about the base (material production) determining the superstructure (system of society's values and culture).

Main output: Richta, Radovan et al (1966) (reissued in 1967, 1969), *Civilizace na rozcestí: společenské a lidské souvislosti vědeckotechnické revoluce*, Praha: Svoboda. (Richta, Radovan et al (1969) *Civilization at the Crossroads: Societal and Human Implications of Scientific and Technical Revolution*, International Arts and Sciences Press.)

Ota Šik was director of the Czechoslovak Academy of Sciences' Economic Institute from 1961. Against the background of protracted crises and growing inefficiency of the centrally planned economy he studied – and proposed, within the politically constricted environment of one-party rule – a broader use of the regulatory potential of the market. He coined the phrase 'third road'.

Main output: Šik, Ota (1967a) *Plán a trh za socialismu*, Praha: Academia. (In English Ota Šik (1967b) *Plan and Market under Socialism*, Praha: Academia.)

Zdeněk Mlynář, in his capacity of staff employee of the Czechoslovak Academy of Sciences' Institute of State and Law in the 1960s, headed an interdisciplinary team dealing with the questions of development of the socialist political system. His main theme was extending possibilities for popular participation in the running of society. His team eventually recognised the need to pluralise the political system of the day.

Main output: Mlynář, Zdeněk (1964) *Stát a člověk: úvahy o politickém řízení za socialismu* [State and man: reflections on political management in socialism], Praha: Svobodné Slovo.

In addition to the outputs of these teams, in the late 1960s many other offshoots of freer scientific reflection on various public policy problems of the Czechoslovak society of the day sprang up. Significantly, these remarkable attempts to break through the rigid ruling ideology relied on the (temporary, situational and tactical) legitimacy of expertise, sought a multidisciplinary projection of new analyses, and were biased in favour of practical application of their findings (see Box 2.2).

Box 2.2: Prague Military Academy

A group of Prague Military Academy researchers (**Vojtěch Mencl, Miroslav Purkrábek, Zdeněk Novák, Milan Ždímal, Antonín Rašek** and others) laid the foundations for a new approach to military science and sociology. Many works by Western military experts were translated into Czech, dozens of theoretical papers were processed, and research was done on the problems of war and peace, the social status of servicemen and officers, their academic interests, leisure activities and so on. These efforts resulted in a memorandum demanding greater autonomy of the Warsaw Pact member states over military decisions. The text was one of the reasons why the Warsaw Pact occupation troops seized the Military Academy even before taking the Army General Headquarters and the Defence Ministry building on 21 August 1968.

Czechoslovakia's occupation led by the Soviet Union in 1968 and the subsequent 'normalisation' drive resulted in the dispersion of these teams and ruthless political purges. Due to massive external and internal emigration and examples of opportunistic accommodation or even aiding and abetting the new environment (the case of Radovan Richta; see Box 2.1), only modest enclaves survived, particularly in empirical research on fringe public policy issues, such as the functioning of sports clubs, the management of public enterprises, the relationship between public service personnel and clients and so on. They were only gradually allowed to extend the scope of their activities and gain more breathing space as late as the 1980s.[1]

This period of forming public policy is best compared to a stillborn baby.

The 1980s

The communist regime was not homogenous. Even the so-called 'society of real socialism' (including its political establishment) pursued differentiated interests. Moreover, scientists profited from the official Marxist-Leninist ideological proclamations about the management of society bearing a scientific character and being therefore based on the practical application of scientific findings.

In practice, research institutions were active not only within the Czechoslovak Academy of Sciences but also at universities (albeit with a very limited scope) and government-controlled research institutes reporting to the various government

---

[1] Refer to the thematic issue of Sociologický časopis (Czech sociological review), including a roundtable discussion of witnesses (Sociologický časopis, 2004).

ministries.[2] The non-profit organisations within the National Front (*Národní fronta*) also established their own research facilities. (I spent my novice years in the Department of Comprehensive Modelling of Sportpropag, an establishment run by the Czechoslovak Physical Training Association.)[3]

In the 1980s, the more pragmatic communist establishment circles around Prime Minister Lubomír Štrougal grew strong enough to programme social science research. They established a State Economic Research Programme masterminded by Professor Zdeněk Kolář (who had been 'scratched out' from the Communist Party ranks in the early 1970s). Not without reason, this programme was said to provide a livelihood to many politically suspected intellectuals. Consultative agencies were set up to procure public funds for research teams (such as the Pardubice Technology Centre of the Czechoslovak Scientific and Technological Society).

Public discussions were part of a slowly changing societal atmosphere. From the second half of the 1970s, the Sportpropag Department of Comprehensive Modelling, led by Miloš Zeman, was in existence.[4] Other possibilities were offered by the Czechoslovak Scientific and Technological Society and learned societies attached to the Czechoslovak Academy of Sciences, for example the Ecological Section of the Biological Society, which organised environmentally focused debates for people dissatisfied with the price society paid for maximising material production at the expense of the environment and human health. Economists were the main participants in the public debates organised by Václav Klaus at the Czechoslovak National Bank.[5] This chapter does not include an overview of the research activities organised by the then Forecasting Institute of the Academy of Sciences, although its staff was relatively free to outline issues and their solutions, and many of them later became public figures. Summary outputs of this institution (including practical recommendations to the party leadership) were subjected to consistent ideological censorship by its director, Waltr Komárek (see Box 2.3).

---

[2]   Construction and Architecture Research Institute, Living Standards Research Institute, Social Development and Labour Research Institute, Institute of Social Medicine and Organisation of Health Services, Institute of Scientific and Technical Research, Territorial Planning Institute, Research Institute of Engineering Technologies and Economics, Research Institute of Agricultural Economy, to name them all.

[3]   The National Front was an umbrella corporatist organisation. It was used by the Communist Party as an instrument of ideological surveillance, personnel and financial control of other puppet political parties and non-profit organisations.

[4]   This department was disbanded in the spring of 1984, for political reasons. It had published an anthology on the methodology of social sciences, which was openly critical of the condition and state of the pro-regime Czechoslovak science (Oddělení komplexního modelování Sportpropag, 1982/83). Its chief, Miloš Zeman, served as the Prime Minister of the Czech Republic (1998-2002), and was elected the Czech President in 2012.

[5]   Václav Klaus served as the Czech Prime Minister (1992-97) and as the Czech President (2003-12).

Box 2.3: Examples of expert teams in the 1980s

Yvonne Strecková and research on branches of human development

The workshop of this political economist in the Faculty of Law of Brno's Masaryk University (then J.E. Purkyně University) launched the professional careers of many contemporary professors of public economics and public administration. It was obvious that the specific features of the national economic branches that do not generate material estates but services, and especially changes in the delivery of public goods (education, healthcare, arts and culture, physical education and sports, and social care), cannot be properly investigated in terms of the classic Marxist political economy. The research programme she coordinated in the 1980s was called *Development of the socioeconomic complex of human development and perfection of its management system.*

Miroslav Purkrábek and associates (Lubomír Kružík, Ctibor Drbal, Jaromír Štěpán, Martin Potůček and others) and research on healthcare and the organisation of healthcare services

Professor Vilibald Bílek, director of the Institute of Social Medicine and Organisation of Health Services, did not see eye to eye with Health Minister Jaroslav Prokopec. This clash opened new vistas for critically oriented, sociologically, economically and legally supported research in the running, management and financing of the Czech healthcare system which resulted in an overall forecast of the development of healthcare, identifying various bottlenecks and developmental problems (Kružík and Potůček, 1985, p 97; Potůček, 1988a, p 175; 1988b, pp 375, 470, 522).

Martin Potůček's team studying the processes of cultivation and assertion of human potential in the process of societal reproduction

The development of human beings' capabilities vis-à-vis their living conditions was the topic of an interdisciplinary research project framed and sanctioned by the State Programme of Economic Research, conducted by a team of more than 20 experts from various institutions, operating mainly in the 'grey zone' of the social sciences of the day. The project developed and asserted an original concept of human potential with the ambition to suggest a change in public political practice mainly, but not only, in the field of human development – a concept akin to the human capital concept developed much later in the West. By analogy, the social participation concept was very close to the concept of social capital as applied later (Potůček, 1988c, p 175; 1989, p 325; 1991, p 115; 1992).

Josef Alan's team and the family policy concept

By the late 1980s, the slow process of emancipation of the social sciences from the straitjacket of political and ideological surveillance led to the formation of teams focusing on selected issues related to the functioning of social systems, their impact on people's lives, and the search for alternative solutions. A team led by Josef Alan was active in the Prague branch of the Research Institute of Social Development and Labour. His team formulated an alternative decentralised and individualised concept of family support. However, before it could be discussed in the structures of the then Federal Ministry of Labour and Social Affairs, the events of November 1989 changed everything (Alan, 1988).

These are but a few examples of the *sui generis* public policy research themes tackled in the Czechoslovakia of the late 1970s and 1980s. Many other topics of a similar character were tackled here, there and everywhere, and the list of their authors and outcomes is too vast to list here. A more detailed account of the development conditions and state of social studies of the period was provided by a roundtable organised by Sociologický časopis (see Sociologický časopis, 2004).

This period of forming public policy is best compared to advanced pregnancy.

Freedom at last

Since public policies had simmered under the lid of the totalitarian kettle, the Civic Forum (*Občanské fórum*) Programme Commission briefly savoured its moment of glory, from November 1989 to May 1990.[6] The experts tackling various research tasks, perfecting their tools and honing their craft in these discussions, albeit without hope of putting them into practice, had instantly seen a 'window of opportunity' open wide and furnished the newly born political entity with a wealth of programme documents, addressing miscellaneous spheres. Josef Vavroušek headed this commission until his appointment as the Federal Minister of the Environment, being succeeded by Daniel Kroupa. The commission formulated the Civic Forum's political manifesto for the first free elections in June 1990, edited (but not written, contrary to his later assertions) by Miloš Zeman (Koordinační centrum Občanského fóra, 1990).

Other programmatic documents also saw the light of day. Within a short period of five months, a draft reform of healthcare was outlined and published, even before the elections, by a Ministry of Health and Social Affairs Reform Task Group (SKUPR), made up of experts within the Civic Forum of Health Workers. This document served as the basis of the first moves to transform the Czech healthcare system after November 1989. As early as 1990, the Defence Ministry established its Military Institute of Social Research to study the social conditions of servicemen. In the same year, the Institute of Strategic Studies was established to prepare a reform of the armed forces.

After 1989, the field of social sciences was allowed to develop freely in the *lege artis* fashion. This was made easier by two principal circumstances: suddenly the personnel, political and ideological surveillance of the field of social sciences disappeared while new possibilities opened for the study and application of Western findings and making productive contacts with the West.[7]

---

[6] The Civic Forum (Občanské fórum) was a political movement which emerged spontaneously and peacefully took over power from the hands of the Czechoslovak Communist Party in the process called the 'Velvet Revolution' at the end of 1989.

[7] Until the collapse of the communist regime, the Czech social sciences, unlike their Polish or Hungarian counterparts, were effectively prevented from establishing any meaningful contacts and cooperation with Western partners.

The 1990s

Even though many public policy themes were explored in the Czech lands from the 1960s, there cannot really be any talk about public policy as a scientific field until the early 1990s. If we look around the world, we will see that its origins in the United States, the country that gave birth to this discipline, date from about the second half of the 1960s when, germinating within the realm of other scientific fields (most notably public administration and law), it slowly started its process of emancipation.

The event which finally initiated the establishment of this field in the Czech Republic was my study trip to the United States in the autumn of 1992, under the auspices of the Philadelphia-based Eisenhower Foundation. During this visit, I was able to study the current status of public policy in the USA. I visited key universities, think tanks, central research organisations and the US Association of Public Policy Schools, and also attended the annual conference of the American Public Policy Association.

Having returned to Czechoslovakia, which was just about to split in two states, the Czech Republic and Slovakia, I knew that many of the Czech social science research activities conducted thus far were in fact public policy research projects and public policy proposals without being perceived and described as such. They dealt with various political processes; in terms of methodology, they tended to rely on sociology and managerial science. But I was sure this field deserved expansion as it possessed huge untapped potential for academic development and practical application.

From the spring of 1990 I was active in the newly established Faculty of Social Sciences of Charles University in Prague. It was less rigid than other academic institutions, slowly shedding their 'real socialist' stereotypes. That was why I decided to implement my plans there. However, it was necessary to settle with the largely European-anchored Continental tradition of teaching social policy.[8] A narrow bias in favour of public policy would have hampered access to many useful sources of knowledge and methodological experience from practical research and instruction in this field. However, it was obvious at the same time that the strongest innovative impulses were coming from the United States. It was therefore decided to call the field *Public and Social Policy*, under the proviso that it would tap into findings from both the strong European and Czech cognitive traditions harking back to the early 20th century – see Engliš's slim but important volume, *Social Policy* (Engliš, 1916) – and new ideas coming from across the Atlantic Ocean.

A succession of necessary but difficult steps followed. It was crucial to prepare and implement a master's and doctoral study programme, to establish a systematic programme of research on public policy in the Czech Republic, and to adjust the organisational structure of the Faculty of Social Sciences. The first application for

---

[8]   I was strongly informed by this intellectual tradition during my master's studies within the European Social Policy Programme in the Department of Social Policy and Administration of the London School of Economics and Political Science in the academic year 1990/91.

accreditation of the master's level Public and Social Policy Programme, filed in the autumn of 1992, was dismissed by the Accreditation Commission of the Ministry of Education, Youth and Physical Training. It was rejected as something that would unduly widen the sum of accredited and established fields of study. However, one of the commission members, Ladislav Tondl, was keen to listen. Having studied the theory and methodology of science, philosophy, logic and sociology, he understood the importance of this field of science as well as its relevance for the practical tasks of the newly born Czech Republic. Having discussed the issue with him, the proposal was slightly reworked and a new application was filed; this application was passed by the relevant committee. Following a reorganisation of the faculty in 1993, the newly established Institute of Sociological Studies transformed its social policy department into the Department of Public and Social Policy (KVSP). This became the institutional core of instruction and research in the field. At the bachelor's level, the programme in Sociology and Social Policy was launched as soon as 1990. The first master's study hopefuls were admitted in the academic year 1993/94. An in-service master's study programme for professionals followed suit in the academic year 2007/08. The English version of the programme was launched in the academic year 2013/14. The accreditation of the doctoral programme in Public and Social Policy and the commencement of doctoral studies followed in the academic year 1996/97; its English version in 2012/13.

It is safe to say that the link between public policy and sociology, the union that owes its existence to my education as a sociologist and my presence in the Department of Sociology when the field was new, has left an indelible mark on the Czech public policy school. However, in addition to teaching social science matters, we were also able to use the relevant offer of other institutes within the Faculty (Economy, Political Science and European Studies). Instruction is based on courses in public policy, social policy, public administration, public economics and law; students later requested the inclusion of research in analytical and policy-making methods. Gradually the offer of special courses expanded in various fields of application. Public policy education in the United States inspired us to introduce obligatory internships in the public or civic sector and to ease the conditions of enrolment in master's and doctoral programmes. We consider practical experience in a profession close to our field and/or a measure of life experience plus interest in the given field equal to previous formal education within the same realm. Our master's programme accepts applicants with a full university education in other (not necessarily social science) fields; doctoral students need to document their previous career if coming from other fields of study, such as demography, law or security studies. Our programme has 415 master's graduates and another 131 students are in the pipeline, while 40 students have completed their doctoral study programmes, and 28 students are aiming to do so.[9]

---

[9]   Data from February 2014.

The late Miroslav Purkrábek took up the task of coordinating the research of public policies. In two three-year cycles, supported by the Grant Agency of the Czech Republic, he and his co-workers from the department and other invited experts developed a broadly based empirical research probe into the important aspects of formulating and implementing public policies in the Czech Republic in the 1990s as a political process on the central level. The outcomes of the period's only research were published by Charles University in Prague's Faculty of Social Sciences in ten anthologies in the *Public and Social Policy* series during 1994-99 (see Appendix). Czech public policy in social practice preferred economic development to the other spheres of society's life, especially the civic sector; it adhered to centralised management, while underestimating the role of expert analyses and underrating the role of the ethical and value-based foundations of societal life (Potůček, 1996, p 192). A leading Czech environmentalist, the late Josef Vavroušek, contributed to the development of the discipline, leaving the federal government after the 1992 elections and joining our department.

The first Czech textbook in the field was published after the commencement of master's level instruction by the Institute of Sociological Studies (Potůček et al, 1996).

This period of forming public policy is best compared to a child in his early years.

A new millennium begins

Contrary to the previous predictions, the Department of Public and Social Policy and its associates took another ten years to write the second Czech textbook (Potůček et al, 2005a). The book they produced was a continuation of an international public policy textbook for Central and Eastern Europe, published two years earlier with contributions by several members of the department (Jenei et al, 2003). However, the original English version was largely updated and adjusted to Czech usage. The textbook offered a more focused definition of our field.

Public policy shall be determined as the discipline that works through and applies the explanation frameworks of sociology, economics, political sciences, law, the theory of management, as well as other fields, for the sake of analysing and forecasting the processes of shaping and asserting public interests associated with the solution of differentiated social problems. Public policy is chiefly involved in the institutional mediation of these processes through the public, civic and commercial sector, in a way usable for political practice (Potůček et al, 2005a, p 21).

The Centre for Social and Economic Strategies (CESES) of the Charles University Faculty of Social Sciences, established in 2000, has created the preconditions for more intensive research of Czech public policy. Being an interdisciplinary centre of development of the theory and practice of summary forecasting of visions and strategies for the Czech state and society, it has provided fertile ground for interdisciplinary socio-scientific research and the development of its methodological dimension, pursuing the ambition of providing a relevant background for the strategic management of the country. CESES has since its inception produced a great number of research reports and summary studies, organised many conferences and promotional events, and successfully joined the European research space (see Box 2.4).

Box 2.4: Examples of CESES research projects

Visions and strategies for the development of Czech society

In this project we are preoccupied with the systematic identification and analysis of key questions of modernising Czech society, and its developmental barriers and development opportunities. CESES concentrates on generating partial and comprehensive visions and strategies for the social, economic and political development of the Czech Republic in a broader global, international, security and environmental context in relation to the assertion of these visions and strategies within the European Union. To this end, analyses and scenarios make it easier to articulate national interests with a view to the priorities of the Czech state. One component of the implementation of this project is the development of methods of investigating the possible futures and the application of tools of strategic management (Potůček et al, 2001, 2003a, 2005b, 2009).

Social and cultural cohesion in a differentiated society

This project is focused on the current state, changes and prospects for the development of the social and cultural cohesion of Czech society with the aim of suggesting a realistic strategy of boosting cohesion both on the macro level, that is state level, and on the mezzo and micro levels of society.

Systematic development of the methodology of foresighting

This involves the systematic monitoring, experimental verification, development and evaluation of internationally applied foresighting methods and processes, and the development of new methods as well as their inclusion in the complex of forecasting methodologies and the practice of examining the future development of the Czech Republic (Nováček et al, 2004; Potůček (ed), 2006; Potůček and Slintáková, 2005).

Comparative research on the non-profit sector

The second and third stages of the Johns Hopkins University project examined the basic parameters of the non-profit sectors in more than 20 countries. CESES, as the national coordinator, created a national report published in a third-stage bulletin at the end of 2007.

Europe's third sector policy

The research cooperation between eight 'old' EU member countries and the Czech Republic was aimed at analysing the impact of EU policies on the public policies of the various countries in regard to the third sector. In addition to working out a 'national chapter' for the Czech Republic, CESES also coordinated the provision of the case studies in third sector public policy on behalf of all participating countries.

Millennium Development Goals for the Czech Republic
The Czech Republic's National Report was jointly commissioned by the United Nations Development Programme (UNDP) Regional Centre for Europe and the Commonwealth of Independent States. It was conceived as part of a regional report including national reports for the Czech Republic, Hungary, Slovenia and Slovakia, together with regional comparisons. The purpose of these reports was to stimulate public interest in the UN Millennium Development Goals of these countries (Potůček et al, 2004).

Report on Human Development 2003
The aim of the project was to prepare, in conjunction with the International Labour Organization and the UNDP, a Report on Human Development 2003 in the Czech Republic and present it as a background text for a national conference on the social and economic development in the previous decade (Potůček et al, 2003b).

Obviously, the institutional affiliation of public policy research comprises not only the Department of Public and Social Policy and CESES of the Faculty of Social Sciences at Charles University in Prague, but also other universities (mainly public, such as Masaryk University in Brno) and different research institutes (namely the Research Institute of Labour and Social Affairs and the Institute of Health Policy and Economics), which have also been involved in the research on health and social services and corresponding policies.

This period of forming public policy is best compared to a person coming of age.

Other teaching institutions in the Czech Republic

Instruction in the field was gradually introduced by other Czech institutions of higher learning, namely at the Masaryk University in Brno. At its Faculty of Social Studies, the Department of Social Policy and Social Work has systematically developed its master's programme, followed by a doctoral study programme in Social Policy and Social Work since the 1990s. Since the academic year 2010/11, this department has also offered a master's programme in Public Policy and Human Resources. Another important stream of teaching and research there has been institutionalised at the Department of Political Science, which offers several courses in public policy studies (Novotný, 2012, p 195). The first Czech textbook on policy analysis originated there as well (Fiala and Schubert, 2000). The Faculty of Economics and Administration of the same university offers courses in public and social policy to master's and doctoral students in the field of Public Economics.

The University of Ostrava has included an obligatory public policy and administration course in its master's programme in Public Economics and Management, similar to Palacký University in Olomouc which included this course in its International Development study programme. Prague's Anglo-American University opened an English Public Policy master's programme in the academic year 2007/08.

International cooperation

Cooperation within the post-communist world began with establishing ties with the Budapest University of Economics, which was the first in the region to offer a master's course in Public Policy. With the support of the nongovernmental organisation, the Network of Institutes and Schools of Public Administration in Central and Eastern Europe (NISPAcee), but mainly through interaction with our colleagues from Hungary, the United States and Slovakia, the first textbook in this field was published, focused on the region's issues. Contacts have been forged since the early 1990s with our Slovak colleagues (mainly those active in the not-for-profit Institute of Public Affairs and in the recently established Institute of Public Policy of the Faculty of Social and Economic Sciences of Comenius University in Bratislava).

Cooperation with the United States has been chiefly developed through interaction with the School of Public Health of the University of California in Berkeley by means of research and teaching grants enabling talented researchers with a completed doctoral education to spent time at the university. Similar contacts have been made with the Carl Vinson Institute of Government in Athens, the University of Georgia, and George Mason University in Fairfax. Long-term cooperation has been established with many European institutions, including the Department of Social Policy and Applied Social Research at Oxford University in Britain, the Konstanz Universität and the Wissenschaftszentrum für Sozialforschung in Berlin, Germany, and the European Foundation for the Improvement of Living and Working Conditions in Dublin, Ireland.

Reflection on the current state of the field in the Czech Republic

Our field has transformed over the years into a form bearing certain telltale features. Let us mention above all the comprehensive analysis of problems, threats and development opportunities of the Czech Republic and its population, which can serve as the basis of identification of its strategic choices. Qualitative and quantitative methods are combined (research on the value orientations and activities of the general public and elites, analyses of national and international statistical data, proposals of systems of indicators, analyses of institutional frameworks and policy documents). This is associated with the perfection of the concept of strategic governance including the study of interference in the regulatory functions of the market, state and civic sectors (Potůček, 1999; Potůček et al, 2005a). A number of sector analyses and policy proposals have been made in the field of security, education, healthcare and so on. Special attention has been paid to the specific features of the civic sector (Frič, 2000, 2004, 2005; Frič and Goulli, 2001; Frič et al, 2004; Potůček et al, 2006). Considerable attention has lately been paid to developing the theoretical (Frič and Potůček, 2004; Mašková et al, 2007) and methodological (Potůček et al, 2004; Potůček, 2006; Veselý and Nekola, 2007; Veselý, 2009; Nekola et al, 2011) foundations of the field.

Young experts receive training, key research projects are being implemented, research papers are being published, the scholarly *Central European Journal of Public Policy* (CEJPP) has been published twice a year since 1997. The 'second generation' of Czech public policy researchers, analysts and teachers, recruited mainly from the discipline's graduates, has matured (Novotný and Hejzlarová, 2011; Novotný, 2012) The strength of this young generation of public policy scholars was evident from the composition of the Czech participants in the first International Conference on Public Policy in Grenoble in June 2013: most of them were below the age of 40.

Having entered the public domain, CESES has provided a wealth of points to ponder and implement for both political leaders and the broader scientific and general public. With a few rare exceptions, however, this interaction has thus far consisted largely of one-off projects (although some were top level and involved seminars with members of the government) that have so far had no lasting impact on the formation of real public policy.

It is safe to say, though, that the field of public policy has taken root in the Czech Republic. It is therefore quite legitimate to discuss its deficits and new developmental options.

I believe that the interaction between public policy and sociology, the two disciplines developed jointly at the Institute of Sociological Studies since 1993, has been robust, productive and inspiring. It asserts itself not only through the development of theoretical foundations and methodical instruments of the field but also in a wealth of specific empirical projects. The contributions of economics are apparent, above all in the application of its sub-disciplines such as Public Economics and Institutional Economics. Nevertheless, cooperation with economists, political scientists and specialists in Law and Public Administration has its limitations, chiefly in different approaches to interdisciplinary collaboration.

I am positive that the field has come of age, in spite of its numerous shortcomings and offers an ever more attractive environment for the assertion of the talents and energy of the up and coming generation of researchers, teachers and practitioners.

The upcoming stage of shaping public policies in the Czech Republic could be described as a period of early adulthood.

Acknowledgements

The chapter was written with the financial support of PRVOUK programme P17 'Sciences of Society, Politics, and Media under the Challenge of the Times'.

This is the updated version of Potůček (2007). My thanks go to my colleagues, Pavol Frič, Jiří Musil, Antonín Rašek, Jiří Remr, Věra Tomandlová and Arnošt Veselý for their valuable inputs and comments on the working version of the text.

References

Alan, J. (1988) *Koncepce rodinné politiky* [Conception of family policy], Praha: Výzkumný ústav sociálního rozvoje a práce.

Čapek, K. (1993) *O věcech obecných čili Zóon politikon* [Public matters, or the Zoon Politikon], Praha: Melantrich.

Engliš, K. (1916) *Sociální politika* [Social policy], Praha: F. Topič.

Fiala, P. and Schubert, K. (2000) *Moderní analýza politiky. Úvod do teorií a metod policy analysis* [Modern policy analysis], Brno: Barrister & Principal.

Frič, P. (2000) *Neziskové organizace a ovlivňování veřejné politiky* [Nonprofit organisations and influencing public policy], Praha: AGNES.

Frič, P. (2004) 'Political developments after 1989 and their impact on the nonprofit sector', in A. Zimmer and E. Priller (eds) *Future of Civil Society: Making Central European Non-Profit Organizations Work*, Berlin: VS Verlag für Sozialwissenschaften, 217-40.

Frič, P. (2005) 'The third sector and the policy process in the Czech Republic', *Third Sector European Policy Working Paper*, 6 June, London and Prague: LSE-CCS.

Frič, P. and Goulli, R. (2001) *Neziskový sektor v České republice* [Nonprofit sector in the Czech Republic], Praha: Eurolex.

Frič, P. and Potůček, M. (2004) 'Model vývoje české společnosti a její modernizace v globálním kontextu' [A model of Czech society's development and its modernisation in a global context], *Sociologický časopis/Czech Sociological Review*, 40(4): 415-31.

Frič, P., Goulli, R. and Vyskočilová, O. (2004) 'Small development within the bureaucracy interests: the nonprofit sector in the Czech Republic', in A. Zimmer and P. Eckhard (eds) *Future of Civil Society: Making Central European Non-Profit Organizations Work*, Berlin: VS Verlag für Sozialwissenschaften, 601-33.

Jenei, G., LeLoup, L.T., Potůček, M. and Váradi, L. (eds) (2003) *Public Policy in Central and Eastern Europe: Theories, Methods, Practices*, Bratislava: NISPAcee.

Koordinační centrum Občanského fóra (1990) *Volební program Občanského fóra* [Election programme of Civic Forum], Praha: Koordinační centrum Občanského fóra.

Kružík, L. and Potůček, M. (1985) 'Problémy tvorby souhrnné prognózy československého zdravotnictví' [Issues of synoptic prognosis of Czechoslovak healthcare], *Československé zdravotnictví*, 33(3): 97-107.

Macek, J. (1935) *Cesta z krize* [Way out of Crisis], Praha: Jan Leichter.

Machonin, P., Jungman, B., Linhart, J., Petrusek, M., Šafář, Z. and Roško, R. (1969) *Československá společnost. Sociologická analýza sociální stratifikace* [Czechoslovak society. Sociological analysis of social stratification], Bratislava: Epocha.

Masaryk, T.G. (1972) *Masaryk on Marx: An Abridged Edition of T.G. Masaryk, The Social Question: Philosophical And Sociological Foundations of Marxism*, Lewisburg, PA: Bucknell University Press.

Masaryk, T.G. (1990) *Ideály humanitní* [The ideals of humanity], Praha: Melantrich.

Masaryk, T.G. (2000) *Otázka sociální* [The social question], TGM writings, vol 9, 10), Prague: Masaryk Institute of the ASCR.

Mašková, M., Musil, J. and Potůček, M. (eds) (2007) *Strategické volby pro Českou republiku: teoretická východiska* [Strategic choices for the Czech Republic: a theoretical starting point], Praha: Sociologické nakladatelství.

Mlynář, Z. (1964) *Stát a člověk: úvahy o politickém řízení za socialismu* [State and man: reflections on political management in socialism], Praha: Svobodné Slovo.

Nekola, M., Geissler, H. and Mouralová, M. (eds) (2011) *Současné metodologické otázky veřejné politiky* [Contemporary methodological questions of public policy], Praha: Karolinum.

Nováček, P., Potůček, M. and Slintáková, B. (eds) (2004) 'The first Prague workshop on futures studies methodology', *CESES Papers*, Praha: CESES FSV UK.

Novotný, V. (2012) *Vývoj českého studia veřejných politik v evropském kontextu* [The development of the Czech study of public policy in the European context], Praha: Karolinum.

Novotný, V. and Hejzlarová, E. (2011) 'Lesk a bída české analýzy veřejných politik: vývoj a aktuální stav z pohledu vnějších vlivů' [Splendours and miseries of Czech policy analysis: its state and development in the perspective of external influences], *Politologická revue*, 17(1): 3-32.

Oddělení komplexního modelování Sportpropag (1982/83) *Metodologické problémy společenskovědního výzkumu budoucnosti* [Methodological issues of social science research of the future], Praha: Oddělení komplexního modelování Sportpropag.

Peroutka, F. (1991) *Budování státu I-IV* [Building of the state], Praha: Lidové noviny.

Potůček, M. (1988a) 'Možnosti a meze prognózování péče o zdraví' [Possibilities and limits of healthcare prognostication], *Československé zdravotnictví*, 36(2): 175-88.

Potůček, M. (1988b) 'K vývoji perspektivního plánování, prognózování a strategického řízení péče o zdraví v ČSSR I, II, III' [Perspectives of planning, prognostication and strategic management of healthcare in CSSR I, II, III], *Československé zdravotnictví*, 36(8-9,11,12): 375-79, 470-75, 522-32.

Potůček, M. (1988c) 'Lidský potenciál v rozvoji československé společnosti' [Human potential in the development of Czechoslovak society], *Politická ekonomie*, 36(2): 175-88.

Potůček, M. (1989) 'Lidský potenciál československé společnosti' [Human potential in Czechoslovak society], *Sociológia*, 21(3): 325-42.

Potůček, M. (1991) 'Pojetí lidského potenciálu' [The concept of human capital], *Psychologie v ekonomické praxi*, 26(3): 115-24.

Potůček, M. (1992) 'The concept of human potential and social policy', *Acta Universitatis Carolinae Oeconomica*, (1): 51-67.

Potůček, M. (1996) 'Jak se formovala veřejná politika v České republice po roce 1989' [Formation of public policy in the Czech Republic after 1989], in M. Potůček, M. Purkrabek, P. Háva (eds) *Analýza událostí veřejné politiky v České republice. II. díl* [Event Analysis in Public Policy in the Czech Republic], Řada Veřejná a sociální politika 3/1996, Praha: UK FSV, ISS, pp 177-92.

Potůček, M. (1999) *Not Only the Market*, Budapest: CEU Press.

Potůček, M. (ed) (2006) *Manuál prognostických metod* [Handbook of future studies methods], Praha: Sociologické nakladatelství.

Potůček, M. (2007) 'Czech public policy as a scientific discipline and object of research', *Central European Journal of Public Policy*, 1(1): 102-21.

Potůček, M. and Slintáková, B. (eds) (2005) 'The Second Prague Workshop on Futures Studies Methodology', *CESES Papers*, Praha: CESES FSV UK.

Potůček, M. et al (1996) *Veřejná politika* [Public policy], Praha: Institut sociologických studií FSV UK.

Potůček, M. et al (2001) *Vize rozvoje České republiky do roku 2015* [Vision of the development of the Czech Republic to 2015], Praha: Guttenberg.

Potůček, M. et al (2003a) *Putování českou budoucností* [Travelling in the Czech future], Praha: Guttenberg.

Potůček, M. et al (2003b) *Zpráva o lidském rozvoji. Česká republika 2003: Odkud přicházíme, co jsme, kam jdeme?* [Human Development Report. Czech Republic 2003], Praha: UNDP a Karlova univerzita.

Potůček, M. et al (2004) *Rozvojové íle tisíciletí: Česká republika* [Millenium Development Goals: the Czech Republic], Bratislava: UNDP.

Potůček, M. et al (2005a) *Veřejná politika* [Public policy], Praha: Sociologické nakladatelství.

Potůček, M. et al (2005b) *Jak jsme na tom. A co dál? Strategický audit ČR* [How are we. Standing and what next? A strategic audit of the Czech Republic], Praha: Sociologické nakladatelství.

Potůček, M. et al (2006) 'Literature review on civil society, citizenship and civic participation in the Czech Republic', *Studie CESES*, Prague: CESES.

Potůček, M. et al (2007) *Strategické vládnutí a Česká republika* [Strategic governance and the Czech Republic], Praha: Grada.

Potůček, M. et al (2009) *Strategic Governance and the Czech Republic*, Praha: Karolinum.

Richta, R. et al (1966) *Civilizace na rozcestí: společenské a lidské souvislosti vědeckotechnické revoluce,* Praha: Svoboda.

Richta, R. et al. (1969) *Civilization at the Crossroads: Social and Human Implications of the Scientific and Technological Revolution,* International Arts and Sciences Press.

Sociologický časopis (2004) 'Česká sociologie v letech 1965-1989. Kulatý stůl Sociologického časopisu'[Czech sociology in 1965-1989. Round table of Czech Sociological Review], *Sociologický časopis*, 40(5): 695-744.

Šik, O. (1967a) *Plán a trh za socialism* [Plan and market under socialism], Praha: Academia.

Šik, O. (1967b) *Plan and Market under Socialism*, Praha: Academia.

Veselý, A. (2009) *Vymezení a strukturace problému ve veřejné politice* [Problem delimitation in public policy analysis], Praha: Karolinum.

Veselý, A. and Nekola, M. (2007) *Analýza a tvorba veřejné politiky: přístupy, metody a praxe* [Policy analysis: approaches, methods and praxis], Praha: Sociologické nakladatelství.

Appendix: Volumes in the Public and Social Policy series, chronologically ordered (Prague, ISS FSV UK 1994–99)

Potůček, M., Purkrábek, M. and Vavroušek, J. (1994) *Zrod teorie veřejné politiky v České republice* [The Birth of Public Policy as a Theory in the Czech Republic], Praha: UK FSV, ISS.

Potůček, M., Purkrábek, M. and Háva, P. (1995) *Analýza událostí veřejné politiky v České republice. I. díl* [Event Analysis of Public Policy in the Czech Republic. Vol. I], Praha: UK FSV, ISS.

Potůček, M., Purkrábek, M. and Háva, P. (1996) *Analýza událostí veřejné politiky v České republice. II. díl* [Event Analysis of Public Policy in the Czech Republic. Vol. II], Praha: UK FSV, ISS.

Purkrábek, M. (1996) *Veřejná politika a její aktéři. Z poznatků empirických výzkumů občanů, lokálních reprezentantů a poslanců Parlamentu České republiky (1994-1996)* [Public Policy and its Actors. Evidence of Empirical Surveys on Citizens, Local Representatives and Members of Parliament in the Czech Republic (1994-1996)], Praha: UK FSV, ISS.

Ošanec, F. (1997) *Poskytování, financování a reformy zdravotní péče v pěti demokraciích (Rakousko, Německo, Nizozemsko, Kanada, Velká Británie)* [Provision, Financing, and Reforms of Health Care in the Five Democracies (Austria, Germany, the Netherlands, Canada, Great Britain)], Praha: UK FSV, ISS.

Purkrábek, M. (1997) *Rozhodování, financování a komunikace ve veřejné politice v České republice* [Decision Making, Financing, and Communication in Public Policy in the Czech Republic], Praha: UK FSV, ISS.

Sarvaš, Š. (1997) *Bezpečnost a armáda v moderní společnosti* [Security and Army in Modern Society], Praha: UK FSV, ISS.

Purkrábek, M. (1998) *Centrální politické rozhodování v České republice. Volume I. First Part of a Set of Expert Studies on the Second Stage of Analysis of Public Policy in 1997-1999 1. díl.* [Central Political Decision Making in the Czech Republic. Vol. 1], Praha: UK FSV, ISS.

Křížová, E. and Purkrábek, M. (1999) *Občané a centrální politické rozhodování v České republice. Výsledky výzkumu názorů občanů ČR v září 1998* [Citizens and Central Political Decision Making in the Czech Republic], Praha: UK FSV, ISS.

Purkrábek, M. (1999) *Centrální politické rozhodování* v České republice. *Volume II. Second Part of a Set of Expert Studies on the Second Stage of Analysis of Public Policy in 1997-1999 2. díl.* [Central Political Decision Making in the Czech Republic. Vol. 2], Praha: UK FSV, ISS.

THREE

Development of Czech policy analysis: social and political factors

Vilém Novotný

Introduction

Policy analysis[1] is one of the largest and most dynamically developing areas of the study of policy in Western democracies in recent years. This dynamic is caused not only by growing demands for solutions to acute social and political problems but also by attempts to understand the changing world and society we live in. The Czech Republic recently celebrated the twenty-fifth anniversary of the Velvet Revolution in 1989. Like liberal democracies in the West, the country went through many transitions and faced many problems during those 25 years, for example economic transformation, EU enlargement, the effects of globalisation and regionalisation, security threats after 9/11, the world economic crisis after 2008. Thus, one might expect the kinds of pressures that stimulated the quick development of science-based policy-related advising in the form of policy analysis in the Euro-Atlantic area to bring about a similar need for expert policy advice and policy research in the Czech Republic as well.

In this respect, I should ask about the contemporary state of Czech policy analysis and its development. I attempt to grasp the development of Czech policy analysis from science-based policy-related knowledge (until World War II) over professional policy-related work activities during the communist regime to the establishment of a specific academic (sub)discipline dealing with policy problem solving after 1989. The goal of this text is to try to define the nature and state of Czech policy analysis, primarily from the perspective of the demand and context factors (see below) behind its historical development. Here I emphasise this perspective because other chapters deal with other aspects and meanings of policy analysis. Based on a review of related literature and my own observations, my underlying assumption is that the development of policy analysis as science-based policy-related knowledge used for political advising is a result of the interaction between academic (sub)disciplines dealing with policy problem solving and their social and political environments. For conceptualisation I rely on approaches

---

[1] Here, I consider policy analysis in a broader Lasswellian (policy sciences) perspective as one part of the study of public policy that is knowledge in the policy process (problem solving) (Lasswell, 1951, 1970). In this broader sense of policy analysis as science-based policy-related advising (knowledge) we are close to the meaning of Veselý's third type of policy analysis (see Chapter One).

working with the supply-demand model discussed below. Applying these lenses, I subsequently draft a historical overview of the development of policy analysis in the Czech Republic, especially in the inter-war period, the communist regime and the renewed democracy after 1989. This is especially interesting in a country that went through so many political changes in the 20th century.

Conceptualising an explanation of the development of policy analysis

Conceptualising an explanation of the development of policy analysis as a result of the interaction between academic (sub)disciplines related to policy problem solving and their social and political environments, I found inspiration in the literature considering the development of the social sciences. For example, political science has elaborated this issue in detail (for example Easton et al, 1998; Easton et al, 2002; Klingemann, 2007) and may inspire the field of policy analysis because of its disciplinary proximity. Contemporary literature about the development of policy studies, including policy analysis, reveals surprisingly little plurality of opinions and approaches compared to other areas. The encyclopaedic syntheses (Moran et al, 2006; Peters and Pierre, 2006; Fisher et al, 2007) present a single dominant theoretical approach to the development of policy studies.

This dominant approach was formulated by Peter deLeon (1988, 2006; deLeon and Martell, 2006; deLeon and Vogenbeck, 2007; deLeon and Gallagher, 2011) using the example of the policy sciences. In the late 1980s, deLeon built his model on a relatively simple but powerful idea: the study of the development of a discipline should not focus solely on its internal dynamics, as had been normal until that time. Instead, the development should be perceived in its social, economic, political and cultural context. The development of a discipline is determined by the mutual interaction between these two elements. DeLeon used the economic 'supply-and-demand' metaphor to define this interaction. The supply side is represented by expert policy advice which is based on science and arises out of the academic setting. This specific activity is conducted by a profession which needs some development, namely the accumulation of knowledge, preparation of personnel, institutionalisation and methodology, in order to be able to provide relevant 'advice' – that is to define problems and propose their solutions. On the other hand, such science-based advice must be in 'demand' from the sociopolitical elite. Members of the elite must be willing to listen to and must require policy analysts' 'advice'. An important quality of the model lies in the fact that both entities are considered to be separate and relatively independent from each other (cf deLeon, 1988, pp 9 and 52–54).

Two key conditions should be fulfilled in order for the policy sciences, and especially policy analysis, to develop. Not only should the 'supply side' have sufficient capacities for the production of relevant advice and the 'demand side' be interested in this kind of advice, but these two entities should also be connected. According to deLeon, such a connection occurs during political events such as the War on Poverty, the Vietnam War, the Watergate scandal, the energy crisis of the 1970s, the end of the Cold War and the 9/11 terrorist attacks in the United States. In the Czech case we could talk, for example, about the Velvet Revolution (1989), the declaration of independence (1993), NATO membership (1999), the EU accession (2004) and the world economic crisis (2008). Situations like these represent opportunities for applying accumulated science-based policy-related knowledge to solve the new social and political problems that the ruling elite is facing. In other words, policy analysis produces necessary underlying information for political decision-making, in order to replace obsolete solutions with new ones (compare deLeon, 1988, pp 54–56). This model is perhaps somewhat too general, but this fact may be the reason for its success compared to alternative explanations (for example Radin, 2000) or personal accounts (for example Nelson, 1998). Similar factors are structured in more detail in a more elaborate model that John Trent and Michael Stein proposed in order to explain the development of political science in Canada (Trent, 1987; Stein, 1998; Trent and Stein, 2002).

Their 'interactive model of the development of the discipline' works with assumptions similar to deLeon's model. It also considers the state of the discipline as a result of interactions between its internal dynamics and environment. The distinctive characteristics of the discipline are determined by influences from both 'the indigenous, national environment and the international social science environment. The distinctive characteristics of the discipline may, in turn, impinge on the host society and its political system as well as on the store of international social science knowledge' (Trent, 1987, p 9). Trent names five key variables, which are mostly interdependent: national conditions and their degree of dependency; the educational and intellectual context; the internal characteristics of the discipline (its capacities); discipline development (its content); and discipline impact (Trent, 1987, p 19).

In this chapter, I am primarily interested in interactions between the (sub) discipline and its society or government (political regime and/or social and political factors). The given society and political regime impinge upon the discipline in several different ways. The capacity of the discipline - that is its human, economic and institutional resources - is determined both by national socioeconomic and political development and by varying degrees of culture transfer. The socioeconomic development of a given society influences the discipline through mediating variables, including the education system, the intellectual traditions and the choice of public priorities.

National socioeconomic development based on modernisation through national integration, industrialisation, the adoption of scientific rationalism, and specialisation within national and international markets entails expansion of the education system. In general, the wealthier a society, the better it will be able to afford higher degrees of academic institutionalisation and research dissemination which, combined with the power and international cultural influence of that society, will determine the levels of impact of its national disciplines on the international environment. The social conditions in a given society affect not only the capacity of a discipline but also its content. They include predispositions in the national culture, current perceptions of national needs and the present state of the economy. A discipline can only affect the domestic society and political regime if it has sufficient resources for responding to domestic demand. These resources lie primarily in an adequate amount of accumulated expertise and sufficient skills of the practitioners in the discipline. Nevertheless, the impact of a discipline depends most on three factors: the esteem in which it is held by elites, the desires of social scientists to influence society and potential structural blockages in the society. (Trent, 1987, p 19–21)

The above models reveal the substantial effect of demand on the development of policy analysis in a given country. In order to understand the situation of Czech policy analysis in this chapter, I will focus primarily on factors affecting the demand side. I am especially interested in institutional factors in the broad sense of the term and will attempt to sketch the effects of ideas and of the sociopolitical setting over time.

Development of policy analysis in the Czech Republic

I have outlined the ways of approaching the development of Czech policy analysis analytically. Unfortunately, there has been little investigation in this domain, and therefore we will have to limit our ambition to a kind of outline of assumed development. I am well aware of my subjective approach (which, however, is common in cases like this - see for example deLeon, 1988) and of the risk of bias involved in such a brief outline. However, I perceive this approach as a necessary trade-off for delving into a hitherto rather underdeveloped topic and as an acceptable way of stimulating discussion and further investigation.

Relatively few academic texts in the Czech setting have focused on the development of Czech policy analysis as a part of the study of public policy. The first pioneer attempt to sketch the development of public policy, especially public policy as a scientific discipline, in the Czech Republic was undertaken by Martin Potůček (2007; see also Chapter Two, this volume), one of the 'founding fathers' of the Czech study of public policy. In this vein Vilém Novotný dealt, in a comparative perspective, with the contextualisation of the Czech study of public policy within the European area (2006, 2007, 2008, 2012, 2015). A stronger emphasis on grasping the development and practice of Czech policy analysis is presented in the texts of Eva M. Hejzlarová and Vilém Novotný (Hejzlarová 2010; Novotný and Hejzlarová 2011; Chapter 4). Somewhat surprisingly, the development of Czech public policy has been rather neglected by Czech political science.[2] On the other hand, some orientation for understanding the development of Czech policy analysis is provided by other disciplines such as sociology (Česká sociologie v letech, 2004). This regrettable situation can also be generally explained by the fact that, so far, Czech policy scholars have focused on

---

[2] The development of Czech political science has been studied, among others, by Jan Holzer, Pavel Pšeja, David Šanc and Karel Kouba (see, for example, Kouba et al, 2015).

---

building, developing, stabilising and standardising the (sub)discipline. As a result, there has not been enough interest, energy and capacity for critical reflections on the policy disciplines' development and current state. Let us now proceed to outline the development of Czech policy analysis itself.

The roots of Czech policy analysis

I will begin by looking back and searching for the roots and the traditions of Czech policy analysis. Policy advice in the form of advisors to the political elite have existed in the Czech lands at least since the establishment of an independent Czech state. Moreover, from the late 19th century to the 1930s, there were favourable conditions for the development of bases of policy analysis. Czech society, along with other advanced European societies, was adopting the ideas of scientific rationalism, including the promotion of science as a privileged source of policy advice and a generally accepted authority of cognitive frames telling us what the world around us 'really' is like, what kind of problems it confronts us with and, in particular, how we can solve those problems. Besides this, the socioeconomic conditions in the Czech lands were favourable. The Czech nation and Czech society had become fully consolidated and acquired the reputation of the most industrialised region of former Austria-Hungary. Czech industry had also successfully penetrated international markets. This relative economic prosperity allowed the tertiary education system to expand beyond its traditional centre, Prague, during the period of the First Czechoslovak Republic.

Arguably, the importance of scientific evidence for governing the state and society as well as for solving social problems was accelerated with the establishment of independent Czechoslovakia and became increasingly relevant in the Czech lands during the era of President Tomáš Garrigue Masaryk. Two main streams of scholarly interest in the field of science-based policy-related knowledge can be distinguished. The first one followed the tradition of public administration and public law, stemming from the *Polizeywissenschaft* and transformed into the more juridically based science of the state (*Staatslehre*) at the end of the 19th century. This approach was represented by lawyers such as František Weyr and Zdeněk Neubauer (for example, Neubauer, 2006). The second stream was promoted by important national economists such as Albín Bráf, Alois Rašín, Karel Engliš and Josef Macek (see, for example, Engliš, 1916) who served in high-ranking public offices and influenced the operation of Czech policies and society.

A third sociological stream could also be added. This was not only represented by Masaryk himself, as a professor of sociology and the first President of Czechoslovakia (for example, Masaryk, 2000), but is it also necessary to pay special attention to Edvard Beneš, Czechoslovakia's Foreign Minister and the second President of Czechoslovakia, who promoted and pioneered the idea of science-based politics and policy making (for example, Beneš, 1999). It is interesting, yet hardly surprising given Masaryk's relations with the United States, that at least in its general features, this development corresponded with the expansion of science-based policy-related knowledge under the public administration movement in the US during the era of Theodore Roosevelt and Woodrow Wilson (see, for example, Easton et al, 2002).

Another favourable condition lay in the building of the Czechoslovak state, which required not only professionally educated public servants loyal to the democratic regime but also the preparation of underlying expert materials for the solving of important problems of inter-war Czechoslovakia such as uneven economic development (the Czech lands versus Slovakia and Ruthenia), ethnic conflicts (Czechs, Slovaks, Germans, Hungarians, Ruthenians and Poles) and social issues (urbanisation, industrialisation, city versus countryside, proletariat versus bourgeoisie and so on). In 1919, the first policy-related analytical body, the Social Institute of the Czechoslovak Republic was already established, as an umbrella organisation for social policy research and analysis. However, policy analytical capacity was concentrated mainly in public administration and universities, which were partially complemented by the activities of big corporations such as, for instance, Baťa.[3]

In this area, I can also observe an important transition from the concept of a traditional liberal state, which sought little intervention in the economy and society, to the concept of a proactive state which intervened in these matters, especially under the weight of the Great Depression, World War II and post-war reconstruction. Considering these circumstances, the development and increasing status of science-based policy-related knowledge after 1948 is hardly surprising.

Policy analysis under the communist regime

The development of Czech policy analysis under the communist regime from 1948 to 1989 saw an important qualitative departure from the past era, especially in terms of professional policy practice (policy work, see Colebatch, 2006) and the laying of the foundation of a scientific (sub)discipline which accompanied it. In this respect, more attention should be devoted to the role of 'scientific communism' in this field. In any case, this entire era in the history of Czech policy analysis can be seen as highly interesting from several points of view.

First, the topic of coexistence between policy analysis and the communist regime begs several questions about the relations between the discipline and political regimes (see Trent, 1987; Easton et al, 1998). Especially in the Czech context this issue is highly salient. It is generally assumed that political science and, more particularly, policy analysis, is closely associated with democratic regimes and their support.[4] For instance, Lasswell's concept of the policy sciences (which has its closest Czech equivalent in the concept of public policy as a scientific

---

[3] For example, the first economics research institute was established in Prague during the Nazi occupation (1939–45).

[4] For example, the concept of political science as Demokratiewissenschaft is debated in Germany and the Czech Republic.

discipline) explicitly distanced itself from non-democratic regimes (fascism and communism). This approach, which included policy analysis, was formulated as a means of advancing democracy and especially human dignity (see, for example, Lasswell, 1951, 1970). Interestingly, this primary goal of democracy, the advancement of human dignity, is theoretically not much different from the primary goal of communism.

As for the relations between the communist regime and policy analysis, I side with Trent's opinion that authoritarian or dictatorial regimes perceive the social sciences merely as a service provider, do not tolerate the critical feedback they create and provide, and restrain their international cultural communication (Trent, 1987, p 19). Thus, the role of policy analysis in non-democratic societies is usually limited to technocratic analysis. At the same time, we should pay attention to the fact that a similarly strong technocratic trend was present in Western liberal democracies of the 1970s and 1980s as well. No matter what the reasons for this technological fascination were, it is apparent that the communist regime did not need to develop alternative perspectives on governance in society because it relied on its own Marxist-Leninist ideology which clearly stated what was right and what was to be done. The mere role of science, and specifically science-based policy-related knowledge, was to fulfil and elaborate this task.

There were also other important reasons why the communist regime needed to develop this specific form of production of science-based policy-related knowledge. Here I must note that perhaps any political regime in a modern society necessitates certain policy analytical capacities in order to obtain underlying information and materials for political decision making and for solving social problems. However, in a liberal democratic society, this information is provided by other institutions as well - for example, free elections, the market and civil society actors. Since these institutions were strongly suppressed and regulated under the communist regime, the ruling communist elite had to gather information about people's and society's needs in another way (see, for example, Česká sociologie v letech, 2004, p 700), especially through scientific policy analysis. Thus, in a way, the communist regime needed and used science-based policy-related knowledge for its functioning by definition. This helps us understand the substantial institutionalisation of policy analytical capacity under communism, not only in terms of human and economic resources but, more importantly, in terms of institutions producing policy-related scientific evidence.

Under the communist regime, a relatively dense network of policy research departments was built in order to produce policy analysis, not only in the traditional areas of basic research such as academy of sciences and universities (for example, the Institutes of Economics and Forecasting, the Czechoslovak Academy of Sciences) but also in the different domains of public administration (departmental research institutes such as the Research Institute of Construction and Architecture, the Institute of Social Medicine and Health Care Organisation and the Research Institute of Social Development and Labour) and as research departments within national umbrella organisations of organised civil society (for example, the Sportpropag at the Czechoslovak Sports Federation).

The building of capacities for the production of scientific information and materials underlying decision making and policy making stood in a notable parallel to the transformation of the role of government in liberal democracies. Just like in the communist bloc, an interventionist concept of government began to prevail in liberal democracies after World War II with a view to preventing or mitigating social conflicts and economic crises. While Czechoslovakia was officially building socialism and, after 1960, communism, Western liberal democracies were creating the welfare state. Interestingly, despite their differences, both concepts required an increased supply of scientific information and underlying materials for policy making. In both blocs, science or scientific approaches were the privileged producers of this kind of knowledge. Science-based advice was seen as objective and 'scientific', enjoying substantial political prestige and legitimacy as well as respect in society. A technocratic approach based on quantitative methods and models, which were starting to dominate the social sciences, became established in both regimes.

The distinct relation between the dominant ideology and scientific knowledge seems to be more apparent in the case of refusal of critical feedback and suppression of the critical social role of scientific knowledge, for example in public opinion making. It would be rather extreme to marginalise the role of policy analysis as a mere servant to the Czechoslovak regime; indeed, policy analysis undoubtedly was a factor for changes in the regime. Recall the important influence of the Šik, Mlynář and Machonin teams on the Prague Spring reform process;[5] or the impact of some reports by research teams and institutions backed by reformist Lubomír Štrougal on the eve of the Velvet Revolution, including personalities like Miloš Zeman, Yvonne Strecková, Walter Komárek and many others from the '1990s generation', not only from the Institute of Forecasting, Czechoslovak Academy of Sciences (Klaus, Dlouhý, Ježek, Dyba and associates). In this respect the fact that this reformist mobilisation of scientific knowledge under the communist regime occurred during the economic stagnation in the 1960s and 1980s (see, for example, Pullmann, 2011) is also notable.

One question remains: could these reform activities have actually been realised? Again, we can assume that the normative frames represented by the Marxist-Leninist ideology and embodied in the leading role of the Communist Party dominated the cognitive frames produced by policy analysts, including the abovementioned reform teams. In other words, whenever scientific knowledge conflicted with the ideas of the dominant ideology and the Party, the former were put aside or discarded, as exemplified by Šik's economic reform proposals (Šik, 1990). This is one possible reason why both researchers and the general population were frustrated by the communist regime. On the one hand, evidence-based

---

5   During the Prague spring several analytical teams were created, led by distinguished scholars whose purpose was to analyse and propose policy content of the communist regime reforms.

government was the declared approach, but a normative, ideological approach prevailed whenever science encountered conflicts between ideology and reality (see, for example, Polášek and Novotný, 2011). On the other hand, it should be noted that the latter approach can work in democratic regimes as well (for example, see the ideological dominance in decision making on the war in Iraq under the George W. Bush administration). At the same time, we can assume that analytic reports that did not contravene the dominant normative frameworks had a stronger impact on political decision making, compared to similar documents in the West (see, for example, Česká sociologie v letech, 2004, pp 731–732).

Once again, restrictions on international cultural communication and collaboration, especially with the capitalist bloc, may shed light on some specifics of Czech policy analysis. Presumably, the broader social scientific coverage of policy analysis in the Czech lands - that is, the fact that it was inspired not only by statistics and economics (which dominated in the West) but also by sociology - was caused by limited academic communication and resulted in marginal compliance with international standards.

To sum up, policy analysis as evidence-based support for policy making which combined economic, sociological and other social sciences approaches was clearly present in the Czech lands under communism. From the scientific perspective, it lacked not only contact with the contemporary academic world, both in scholarly literature and in personal liaisons (Česká sociologie v letech, 2004, p 709), but also the background of a specific scientific discipline (Potůček, 2007, p 110), even though it is again disputable whether or not scientific communism represented an alternative framework. This, however, does not mean that research outputs were necessarily ideological or of low analytical quality. For example, surveys related to housing policy were organised in the 1950s and 18 large surveys related to the family and population policy took place between 1956 and 1965 (Česká sociologie v letech, 2004, p 700). Another example is the abovementioned expert teams of the 1960s and 1980s (for example, Mlynář, 1964; Šik, 1967; Machonin, 1969, and so on) which produced high quality research outputs.

Czech policy analysis after 1989

The Velvet Revolution at the end of 1989 and the resulting regime change brought about new opportunities for the development of policy analysis. A strongly evolved expert infrastructure for production of science-based policy-related knowledge already existed both in academia and in the public sector; formal political autonomy as well as freedom of research and an international scholarly communication were soon added to it. The transformation of the political regime to a liberal democracy removed the formal restrictions previously placed on production of this knowledge by the Marxist-Leninist ideology and the communist regime. Thus, policy analysis was able to begin transcending its technocratic dimension by actively participating in the building of a democratic regime. For example, policy experts joined various advisory committees of the leading Velvet Revolution force, Civic Forum, and helped to formulate its election manifesto in 1990. Moreover, such experts took up offices in post-communist politics at the federal and national levels. Besides Václav Klaus and Miloš Zeman, the two most important figures of this '1990s generation', many others served in key political offices during the 1990s (see above).

However, these great expectations for advancing policy analysis began to be fulfilled rather more slowly than expected. This is notable for at least two reasons. First, political events arising out of important systemic changes, such as the Czech Republic's independence, economic transformation, public administration reform (deconcentration and decentralisation), NATO membership, EU accession, world economic crisis and so on, required more and more science-based policy-related knowledge for policy and decision making.

Second, for the first time, Czech policy analysis was explicitly established as an academic (sub)discipline (built into disciplines such as public policy, social policy, political science, economics and sociology), able to rely on a rich intellectual tradition and existing research infrastructure. Michael Stein's (1998, p 170) typology of developmental stages would be perhaps more precise here. According to this typology, Czech policy analysis as an academic (sub)discipline already passed the first stage of 'legitimisation' when it was legitimised as a part of policy-related disciplines (for example, the master's programme in Public and Social Policy was accredited in 1993) and somewhat institutionalised (for example, the Department of Public and Social Policy was established at the Institute of Sociological Studies, Faculty of Social Sciences, Charles University in Prague, in 1993). Now it is between the second stage of full 'institutionalisation' and the third stage of 'practical political accommodation'. The second stage has seen the establishment of a 'core' of full-time professionals, autonomous university departments (for example, policy analysis is a part of study programmes taught by the Department of Public and Social Policy in Prague and by the Department of Social Policy and Social Work in Brno), research units (for example the Centre for Economic and Social Strategies – CESES), professional associations (some academicians were or continue to be members of the Czech Political Science Association), textbooks (for example, the first full-fledged textbook was published in 2007 (Veselý and Nekola, 2007)) and related journals (for example, the *Central European Journal of Public Policy* since 2007). The second stage is not yet fully complete. The third stage includes efforts to win direct political and policy relevance for the discipline. However, Czech policy analysis as an academic (sub)discipline has still failed to obtain corresponding relevance in the society.

Thus, Czech policy analysis is best described as rather 'underdeveloped' in so far as its development is impeded by the lack of acknowledgement and reflection it is given. This can be explained by at least several factors, as follows. Perhaps the most important obstacle was posed by ideological change, namely the quick rise of neoliberalism. This complicated the situation of promoters of professional policy analysis in that they had to distance themselves from the discredited communist regime's system of central planning and policy making, on one hand, and from the rising neoliberalism's almost hegemonic faith in self-regulation inspired by the concept of the 'invisible hand of the market'.

Another notable coincidence is that the change in the perception of the role of government occurred roughly during the same time period in both Eastern and Western countries. Under the pressure of the economic crises of the 1970s and other factors, liberal democracies had gradually departed from their proactive, interventionist concept of government. Instead, they started pursuing limited government intervention and activity and outsourcing some of their activities to the private and civic sectors. This trend in Western liberal democracies began to gain momentum in the late 1970s with the political change initiated by Ronald Reagan, Margaret Thatcher and Helmut Kohl. It continued to grow in the 1980s with their privatisation, rejection of planning, marketisation of public administration (New Public Management), outsourcing of expert capacities and so on. In the Czech lands, this approach began to take over immediately after the Velvet Revolution and enjoyed overwhelming dominance under the rule of Prime Minister Václav Klaus in the middle of the 1990s.

This had several negative consequences for Czech policy analysis. Not only were all attempts at in-depth policy analysis and planning rejected in the name of the free market, but the relevant capacities of government and public administration were intentionally restricted. Thus, the middle of the 1990s saw substantial destruction of important policy analytical capacities within the bodies of public administration and underfunding of Czech academic research and development, on one hand, and, on the other, public policy outsourcing to the private and civic sectors, which in turn competed for funding with academia. This trend seemed to have changed after the Social Democrats became a leading governmental party in 1998. But a possible paradigmatic change was overridden by the relatively late rise of New Public Management and echoes of a 'third way' in the Czech Republic at the same time. This reinforced the neoliberal conception of public administration and externalisation and these trends were fostered by right-wing governments after 2006.

Interestingly, as a result, a substantial portion of the production of such expertise for political decision-making shifted to a 'grey zone' of practical policy work in various analytic institutions, think tanks, interest groups, advisory and auditing firms, and PR agencies which unfortunately did not and do not have sufficient awareness of the academic underpinnings and methodology of policy analysis.[6] We could talk about a Czech variant of the 'hollow state'. Thus, a market arrangement for policy analysis production was created where the traditionally dominant internal policy capacity of the public administration was diminished. Moreover, no strong institutional links between the public administration and

---

[6] Little attention has been paid to this substantial transformation; however, there are initial empirical studies on this externalisation development (for example, Veselý, 2013). Nevertheless, a clear picture emerges when looking at the authors of regional development conceptions after 2000, of various analyses for ministries or individual political representatives, or of advisory reports for large public contracts (see Chapter Twelve).

public policy research institutes and universities have been established. Academic policy analysis expertise provided to the public administration has a mostly entrepreneurial nature related to individual academics. This development has been heavily supported by the system of public contracts that channels financial resources to external providers (see Chapter Four). However, it is important to note that this development has been uneven and has depended on policy sectors and time (see Vesely, 2012).

Another factor was that transformation from a planned to a market economy brought about stagnation and subsequent economic changes which in turn cut down the financial means available for the education system, science and research. It is interesting in this respect that the economic crisis of 2008 had similar consequences (increasingly harsh competition due to further cuts in social science budgets in favour of the natural sciences - see, for example, Prudký et al, 2010).[7] The choice of public priorities with a clear emphasis on economic issues was another negative factor. This is illustrated cogently by the words of Martin Potůček (2007, p 113) that practice of Czech public policy preferred the economic aspects of economic development over other areas of social life, especially the civic sector. The pursuit of economic goals relied on centralised government and, at the same time, undervalued the role of expert analysis and of the ethical and value foundation of social life.

Policy analysis as an academic (sub)discipline continues to fail to win sufficient respect from the Czech socioeconomic and political elite. This is paradoxical in a country where most of the democratic presidents have been associated with some kind of production of science-based policy-related knowledge (Masaryk, Beneš, Klaus and Zeman). Academic institutions have been unable to persuade the Czech elite about the career potential for university graduates trained in this (sub)discipline. This results not only in a relatively low number of students of public and social policy but also in the fact that professional education in policy analysis is not explicitly required for work in public administration.[8] Moreover, the Czech political elite has not fully acknowledged the usefulness of the (sub) discipline as a provider of analysis and answers to issues that policy makers (or other actors) have to face, including social welfare reforms, the pension system, the education system and so on. This might be confirmed by the substantial

---

[7] On the other hand, in 2005 relative economic prosperity made it possible for the Ministry of Education to launch a programme of Research Intents which provided an important source of institutional funding for public universities and expanded the analytical capacity of academia. For example, the programme helped establish the Institute for Research on Social Reproduction and Integration (IVRIS) and the Institute for Comparative Political Research (ISPO) at the Faculty of Social Studies, Masaryk University in Brno, and supported existing institutions such as the Centre for Economic and Social Strategies (CESES) at the Faculty of Social Sciences, Charles University in Prague.

[8] This started to change incrementally since circa 2010 when some public administration departments, especially these dealing with European structural funds, began to require public analysis skills and training from their employees.

influence of consultancy, auditing and PR firms on political decision making in the Czech Republic.[9]

On the other hand, academic policy analysts cannot be blamed for lack of engagement in addressing these important social and political problems (for example, Petr Matějů in tertiary education or Martin Potůček in pension reform). One substantial reason remains: academic policy analysis continues to fail to win respect in competition with other intellectual traditions, namely economics, law and to some extent sociology. For example, Czech right-wing governments established the National Economic Council (2009 and 2010) to fight against the impacts of the economic crisis, but all members of the Council were economists; moreover, they were all of a neoliberal orientation.

Similarly, the research of Hejzlarová on the Czech central public administration's demand for policy analysis (Hejzlarová, 2010; Novotný and Hejzlarová, 2011) shows that ministries articulated their needs with little accuracy or clarity and demanded underlying materials, rather than policy proposals. She finds that this is primarily caused by lack of know-how and an unstable political environment. Another cause is the fact that policy analysis has not so far been acknowledged as a specific discipline by ministry officials.

Conclusions

In the Czech Republic there is a quite well-established academic policy analysis (sub)discipline. But there are also many institutions and professionals dealing with public policy and its analysis as a consequence of market-based supply-demand arrangements based on public contracts. However, most of these professionals are, like Molière's Mr. Jourdain, 'speaking in prose'. They practise policy analysis but they do not know it. I could explain this by a low common consciousness about policy analysis as an academic (sub)discipline. Thus, it could be better to speak about policy work as a prevailing practice of analysis here rather than an academic (sub)discipline.

I believe that a full transformation of policy analysis into a largely recognised source of relevant knowledge for policy making (problem solving) might be fostered by a more stable political situation and growing demand for a standardised political scene in the Czech Republic. While vaguely formulated, these values represent, in my opinion, key conditions for the application of policy expertise. For example, there is no use for policy analysis if a ministry is headed by a different person every year and new ministers do not respect analytical reports commissioned by their predecessors. The potential for growth of the importance of policy analysis also depends on public servants' self-confidence, which might

---

9   Examples of positive deviance occurred during the administration of Prime Minister
     Miloš Zeman and especially Prime Minister Vladimír Špidla (2002–04) when the public
     administration's analytical infrastructure began to be reconstructed. For instance, the CESES
     at the Faculty of Social Sciences, Charles University in Prague was established in 2000 and
     the Institute for Health Economics and Policy (IZPE) existed from 2000 to 2006.

be boosted by the functioning Act on Civil Service as well as by the obligation to publicise full documentation for public research contracts. It would not be appropriate to draw generalisations about the nature of policy analysis in the Czech Republic unless additional research is conducted. This brings us to a few concluding remarks.

The subject matter of Czech policy analysis deserves more detailed research attention because policy analysis represents an important factor in understanding the way countries are governed. The above text also demonstrates that the development of Czech policy analysis is unique and offers issues that are intriguing not only from the Czech perspective but also from the European or global perspective on study of public policy. For example, it would be interesting to find out why Czech academic policy analysis has failed to win respect from the sociopolitical elite as a relevant producer of knowledge for policy making, or why this educational background has not come to be demanded for a public servant's career. It would certainly be engaging to compare Czech policy analysis diachronously, following Beryl Radin's (2000, 2013) example, and demonstrate the generational and regime-related differences between policy analysts' work under communism (the 1960s to 1980s) and democracy (at present). And, undoubtedly, researchers should pay attention to grasping the environment of the contemporary practice of policy analysis in the form of policy work and policy workers. It is the 'grey zone' of policy analysis which seems to be producing most expertise for policy making. These are only some of the possible topics of research into Czech policy analysis.

Acknowledgement

This chapter was supported by the Czech Science Foundation (GACR) under Grant no. 13-20962S 'Policy-Related Expertise in Czech Political Parties'.

References

Beneš, E. (1999) *Demokracie dnes a zítra* [Democracy: today and tomorrow] (8th edn), Praha: Společnost Edvarda Beneše.

Colebatch, H.K. (2006) 'What work makes policy?', *Policy Sciences*, 39(4): 309–21.

Česká sociologie v letech 1965 – 1989. Kulatý stůl Sociologického časopisu [Czech sociology in the years 1965–1989. Round table of the Sociological Journal] (2004), *Sociologický časopis*, 40(5): 695–744.

DeLeon, P. (1988) *Advice and Consent: The Development of the Policy Sciences*, New York: Russell Sage Foundation.

DeLeon, P. (2006) 'The historical roots of the field', in M. Moran, M. Rein and R.E. Goodin (eds) *The Oxford Handbook of Public Policy*, Oxford: Oxford University Press, pp 39–57.

DeLeon, P. and Gallagher, B. K. (2011) 'A contemporary reading of *Advice And Consent*', *Policy Studies Journal*, 39(S1): 27–39.

DeLeon, P. and Martell, C.R. (2006) 'The policy sciences: past, present, and future', in G.B. Peters and J. Pierre (eds) *Handbook of Public Policy*, London: Sage Publications, pp 31-47.

DeLeon, P. and Vogenbeck D.M. (2007) 'The policy sciences at the crossroads', in F. Fisher, G.J. Miller and M.S. Sidney (eds) *Handbook of Public Policy Analysis: Theory, Politics, and Methods*, Boca Raton, FL: CRC Press, Taylor & Francis Group, pp 3-14.

Easton, D., Gunnell, J.G. and Graziano, L. (eds) (2002) *The Development of Political Science: A Comparative Survey* (2nd edn), London and New York: Taylor & Francis eLibrary.

Easton, D., Gunnell, J.G. and Stein, M.B. (eds) (1998) *Regime and Discipline: Democracy and the Development of Political Science* (2nd edn), Ann Arbor, MI: The University of Michigan Press.

Engliš, K. (1916) *Sociální politika* [Social Policy], Praha: F. TOPIČ.

Fisher, F., Miller, G.J. and Sidney, M.S. (eds) (2007) *Handbook of Public Policy Analysis: Theory, Politics, and Methods*, Boca Raton, FL: CRC Press, Taylor & Francis Group.

Hejzlarová, E.M. (2010) 'Policy analysis in the Czech Republic: positivist or postpositivist?', *Central European Journal of Public Policy*, 4(2): 88-107.

Klingemann, H.-D. (ed) (2007) *The State of Political Science in Western Europe*, Oplnden: Barbara Burdich Publishers.

Kouba, K., Císař, O. and Navrátil, J. (2015) 'The Czech political science: a slow march towards relevance?', in B. Krauz-Mozer, M. Kułakowska, P. Borowiec and P. Ścigaj (eds) *Political Science in Europe at the Beginning of the 21st Century*, Kraków: Jagiellonian University Press, pp 63-85.

Lasswell, H.D. (1951) 'The policy orientation', in D. Lerner and H.D. Lasswell (eds) *The Policy Sciences*, Stanford, CA: Stanford University Press, pp 3–15.

Lasswell, H.D. (1970) 'The emerging conception of the policy sciences', *Policy Sciences*, 1(1): 3-14.

Machonin, P. (1970) 'Social Stratification in Contemporary Czechoslovakia', *American Journal of Sociology*, 75: 725-41.

Machonin, P., Rosmány, K. and Jirkal, J. (1969) *Československá společnost: Sociologická analýza sociální stratifikace* [Czechoslovak society: sociological analysis of social stratification], Bratislava: Epocha.

Masaryk, T.G. (2000) *Otázka sociální* [The social question] (6th edn), Praha: Masarykův ústav AV ČR.

Mlynář, Z. (1964) *Stát a člověk: Úvahy o politickém řízení za socialism* [The state and human being: essays on political organisation under socialism], Praha: Svobodné slovo.

Moran, M., Rein, M. and Goodin, R.E. (eds) (2006) *The Oxford Handbook of Public Policy*, Oxford: Oxford University Press.

Nelson, B.J. (1998) 'Public policy and administration: an overview', in R.E. Goodin and H.-D. Klingemann (eds) *A New Handbook of Political Science*, New York: Oxford University Press, pp 551-92.

Nebauer, Z. (2006) *Státověda a teorie politiky* [The science of the state and theory of the political] (3rd edn), Praha: Slon.

Novotný, V. (2006) 'Francouzská tradice studia veřejných politik: Možné inspirace' [French tradition of public policy studies: possible inspirations], in J. Němec and M. Šůstková (eds) *III. Kongres českých politologů*, Olomouc 8-10 September, Praha, Olomouc: Česká společnost pro politické vědy, pp 896–906.

Novotný, V. (2007) 'Nástin komparativního rámce pro studium veřejných politik na příkladech USA, Francie, SRN a ČR' [Toward a comparative framework for public policy studies: the cases of the USA, France, Germany and the Czech Republic], *Politologická revue*, 13(2): 143–54.

Novotný, V. (2008) 'Studium veřejných politik v komparativní perspektivě' [Study of public policy in comparative perspective], *Člověk [online]: časopis pro humanitní a společenské vědy*, 10. Available from http://clovek.ff.cuni.cz/view.php?cisloclanku=2008032504

Novotný, V. (2012) *Vývoj českého studia veřejných politik v evropském kontextu* [Development of Czech public policy studies in the European context], Praha: Karolinum.

Novotný, V. (2015) 'Czech study of public policy in the perspective of three dominant approaches', *Central European Journal of Public Policy*, 9(1): 8-48.

Novotný, V. and Hejzlarová, E.M. (2011) 'Lesk a bída české analýzy veřejných politik: vývoj a aktuální stav z pohledu vnějších vlivů' [Splendours and miseries of Czech policy analysis: its state and development from the perspective of external influences], *Politologická revue*, 17(1): 3-32.

Peters, G.B. and Pierre, J. (eds) (2006) *Handbook of Public Policy*, London: Sage Publications.

Polášek, M. and Novotný, V. (2011) 'Studying the welfare state from a constructivist perspective: points of departure for the Czech case', *Central European Journal of Public Policy*, 5(1): 96-117.

Potůček, M. (2007) 'Czech public policy as a scientific discipline and object of research', *Central European Journal of Public Policy*, 1(1): 102-21.

Prudký, L., Pabian, P. and Šima, K. (2010) *České vysoké školství: Na cestě k univerzálnímu vzdělávání 1989-2009* [Czech higher education: on the way to universal education 1989-2009], Praha: Grada.

Pullmann, M. (2011) *Konec experimentu: přestavba a pád komunismu v Československu* [End of an experiment: perestroyka and the fall of communism in Czechoslovakia], Dolní Břežany: Scriptorium.

Radin, B.A. (2000) *Beyond Machiavelli: Policy Analysis Comes of Age*, Washington, DC: Georgetown University Press.

Radin, Beryl A. (2013) 'Policy analysis reaches midlife', *Central European Journal of Public Policy*, 7(1): 8-27.

Stein, M.B. (1998) 'Major factors in the emergence of political science as a discipline in Western democracies: a comparative analysis of the United States, Britain, France, and Germany', in D. Easton, J.G. Gunnell and M.B. Stein (eds) *Regime and Discipline: Democracy and the Development of Political Science* (2nd edn), Ann Arbor, MI: University of Michigan Press, pp 169-95.

Šik, O. (1967) *Plán a trh za socialism* [Plan and market under socialism], Praha: Academia.

Šik, O. (1990) *Jarní probuzení: Iluze a skutečnost* [Spring awakening: illusion and reality], Praha: Mladá Fronta.

Trent, J.E. (1987) 'Factors influencing the development of political science in Canada: a case and a model', *International Political Science Review*, 8(1): 9-24.

Trent, J.E. and Stein, M. (2002) 'The impact of the state on the development of political science in Canada: a preliminary mapping', in D. Easton, J.G. Gunnell and L. Graziano (eds) *The Development of Political Science: A Comparative Survey* (2nd edn), London and New York: Taylor & Francis eLibrary, pp 59-92.

Veselý, A. (2012) 'Policy advisory system in the Czech Republic: from state monopoly to hollowing out?', Paper presented at the XXIInd World Congress of Political Science in Madrid.

Veselý, A. (2013) 'Externalization of policy advice: theory, methodology and evidence', *Policy and Society*, 32(3): 199-209.

Veselý, A. and Nekola, M. (eds) (2007) *Analýza a tvorba veřejné politiky: přístupy, metody a praxe* [Methods of policy analysis and design], Praha: SLON.

FOUR

Policy analysis styles and methods

Eva M. Hejzlarová

Introduction

In the Czech Republic, policy analysis is far from being an established discipline, which makes it difficult to delimit and structure the field. At the same time, there is a lack of reflection on policy analysis outputs and processes which makes it even more difficult to describe the policy analysis styles and methods. Even though many of the details described in previous publications on this topic are not achievable due to the low level of available knowledge, the content of this chapter is inspired by the related chapters of Dobuzinskis et al's (2007) book, *Policy Analysis in Canada*.

This chapter reflects the classification of analytical styles by various authors discussing the rational, 'modern' analysis of the 1960s and 1970s, which is based on the quantification of economic costs and benefits, and the 'postmodern' analysis of the 1980s and 1990s focused on the social construction of policy problems and a more interpretive approach (for example, Radin, 2000). Using this background and original research, we will try to unveil the dominant paradigms of policy analysis in the Czech Republic. Later we discuss the classification of Mayer, Els van Daalen, and Bots (2001), who distinguish six different styles of policy analysis and apply their ideas to the Czech setting.

Dominating paradigms of Czech policy analysis

Deriving from policy analysis textbooks (see Stokey and Zeckhauser, 1978; Behn and Vaupel, 1982; Hogwood and Gunn, 1984; Weimer and Vining, 2004), the early years of policy analysis were marked by a strong inclination toward quantitative methods and techniques adopted from economics, statistics, operational research and system analysis. In those days, policy analysis was supposed to be a scientific, rational and objective tool to find the best solutions and recommendations in public policy processes.

During the 1980s this approach (later labelled 'traditional') started to be criticised for distinct reasons:

- Its opponents claimed that quantitative analysis (for example cost-benefit analysis) often fails and does not lead to expected outcomes (Kosterlitz, 1991; deLeon, 1994, p 201).

- Others (Weiss, 1977a, 1977b; Booth, 1990; Shulock, 1999) raised doubts about the use of policy analysis as many of the recommendations did not have any (or had very little) influence on public policy decisions.
- The last set of arguments against policy analysis based on rationality and quantification claimed that these assumptions simply do not work as they fail to take into account the irrational context of politics and anticipate *rational* actors and stakeholders.

Through these objections two policy analysis streams developed: 'traditional' policy analysis, called 'positivist' or 'empiricist', based on quantitative techniques and the idea of an objective approach; and 'postpositivist' (or 'postmodern' and 'interpretative') policy analysis that stressed qualitative techniques and the subjectivity of both policy analysts and policy actors, and consequently the need to consider their values and points of view. This depiction is necessarily rough and many authors distinguish between these two streams and discuss the reasons why they developed from various positions.

DeLeon, for example, characterises the traditional positivist stream as aspiring to prediction and 'trying to extract and codify universal laws and their responding behaviors' (deLeon, 1998, p 148), with the latter resulting in understanding. Howlett and Ramesh distinguish the two lines by stressing the role of political actors – while positivists argue these have little influence on policy outcomes, postpositivists attribute great importance to them (Howlett and Ramesh, 1998, p 467).

As for interaction between the streams, there are authors (Lynn, 1999) who are reserved in acknowledging the contribution of the postpositivist school to the positivist one; there are also authors who claim that postpositivism is an entirely new paradigm that differs from positivism on all levels – ontological, epistemological and methodological (Guba and Lincoln, 2000, p 165) – and is not reconcilable with the latter; and, last but not least, there are authors who advocate a dialogue between these streams. The two streams have thus coexisted since the 1980s and the subsequent years of policy analysis history have been marked by the goal of intersection. Many authors (for example, deLeon, 1998; Durning, 1999) find the solution of the clash in the overlap that is iconically represented by Q-methodology.

The conflict that mainly US policy analysis passed through in the 1980s and 1990s and which resulted in two streams of positivist and postpositivist policy analysis also appeared in Czech policy analysis, though under different conditions. Czech policy analysis after 1990 did not experience an easy start as there was general mistrust toward planning, central decision making and, on the other hand, faith in the self-regulation inspired by the concept of the 'invisible hand of the market'. As Potůček claims:

> The Czech public policy in social practice preferred economic development to the other spheres of society's life, especially the civic

sector, adhered to centralised management, while underestimating the role of expert analyses and underrating the role of the ethical and value-based foundations of social life. (Potůček, 2007, p 113)

After the socialist period when political expertise was taken into consideration, the potential of policy analysis with all its promising features nearly disappeared. The early 1990s represents discontinuity, which makes our aim to locate Czech policy analysis even more difficult. A certain change toward higher acceptance of policy analysis occurred perhaps in the first decade of the new century. For more thorough insight into the specifics of Czech policy analysis development see Chapters Two and Three.

To observe the nature of the dominating Czech policy analysis paradigm, we use two analyses. The first one focuses on 42 public procurements launched as 'public contracts in research and development for the needs of state'[1] in 2005-09 by three Czech ministries, *Ministerstvo pro místní rozvoj* (the Ministry for Local Development; MMR), *Ministerstvo práce a sociálních věcí* (the Ministry of Labour and Social Affairs; MPSV) and *Ministerstvo vnitra* (the Ministry of the Interior, MV).[2] The findings, based on the contracts (or more precisely calls), were completed by interviews with the ministries' responsible officials. The second one analyses 62 public procurements by the same three ministries in the 2011-14 period until June 2014.[3] These two analyses help us both to approach the nature of Czech policy analysis paradigms and to describe potential change or development.

In order to operationalise the paradigm or paradigms, we decided to analyse the following analytical categories:

a. Demand of the client for quantitative methods versus demand for qualitative methods. This category was chosen because the distinction between the traditional positivist and postpositivist streams is most often based upon the distinction between quantitative and qualitative methods (deLeon, 1998). Some authors argue that this distinction is not accurate and suggest dividing the methods into (a) quantitative, (b) qualitative-positivist and (c) qualitative-interpretative (Yanow, 2007, p 407). Also Lin (1998) warns that leading with the distinction between positivist and postpositivist approaches according to methods used misses the point as the data gained either by qualitative or

---

[1]   According to Act No. 137/2006 and Act 130/2002, Coll. (resp. 211/2009).

[2]   The ministries were selected according to the following criteria: (1) number of public contracts, (2) amount of finances. The data were gathered via www.isvav.cz; originally the analysis covered 125 procurements but for the purposes of the chapter we only consider the procurements which are relevant for policy analysis. There were 12 procurements for MV, 8 for MMR and 22 for MPSV. For more details of the selection procedure see Hejzlarová (2010).

[3]   Due to legislative changes, the data were gathered from the MV and MMR websites (www.mvcr.cz/clanek/vyhlasene-verejne-zakazky.aspx; https://ezak.mmr.cz/), the MPSV website (www.mpsv.cz/VerZakM_list.php) and the e-marketplace (www.tenderarena.cz).

quantitative methods may be used in both frames. This objection is legitimate and therefore the public contract submissions were analysed not only based upon the use of methods but also with respect to the way the data were expected to be interpreted.

b. Application of quantitative and qualitative methods by the provider. Unfortunately, we were not able to apply this criterion to all the procurements.[4]

c. Demand of the client for considering subjectivity. This category may coincide with the first one as the distinction between qualitative and quantitative techniques is depicted as the difference between objective and subjective methods and their results. In this case they do not overlap as this category aims to focus on values and stakeholders with no respect to the way these are processed. The public contracts will be evaluated according to how much they take into account values and actors or require stakeholder analysis (Howlett and Ramesh, 1998) or, on the other hand, to what extent they operate with 'objective' techniques such as cost-benefit analysis and others (CEA [Cost-effectiveness analysis], CUA [Cost-utility analysis]).

d. Application of subjectivity/objectivity by the provider.

e. Policy analysis features. This is defined as occurrence of methods, heuristics or reflection in any stage of the policy analysis process. The range of features was delimited in relation to techniques mentioned in Czech policy analysis handbooks (Fiala and Schubert, 2000; Veselý and Nekola, 2007).

All these categories were applied to the procurements in the 2005–09 period; for the 2011–14 period only (a), (c) and (e) were applied.

As for the calls in the 2005–09 period, the analysis showed that they were not very specific. This fact may be illustrated by the finding that more than one-third of the calls had fewer than 900 characters, which means they consisted of some 12 lines (approximately 1300 characters was the average). In short, the submissions were very brief and very often they did not contain detailed requirements of the ministry.

Most of the calls did not have any signs either of demand for quantitative or qualitative methods or of considering subjectivity/objectivity. In three cases, the demanded methods were description or comparison, and in seven cases the ministry demanded quantitative methods. Three times the ministry demanded an objective approach; in the rest of the cases there was no special demand regarding this issue. The interim conclusion is that although the ministries usually do not create strict boundaries, if they do, the features tend to be rather positivist.

The analyses in 2005–09 were based on both quantitative and qualitative data in four cases, in three cases they used description and comparison as a method and in three cases the methods were not identified (the texts were probably just

---

[4] It was impossible to gather all the proposals as there was no legal requirement to publish them. The author dealt with the same problem with the winning proposals, respectively the outputs. The wording of Act 130/2002 makes the ministry the only possessor of the outputs and if the ministry denies access to the outputs there is no legal recourse.

compiled). The application of subjectivity and objectivity was also differentiated. Three of the analyses showed other than purely positivist features; they included stakeholders in their analysis and considered their attitudes. There was no explicitly positivist approach applying tools such as CBA [Cost-benefit analysis] or CEA. At the same time, there was an analysis that was very technical and based on statistics and mathematics. There were also two more analyses that were mainly statistical or descriptive-statistical.

The policy analysis features - that is the application of methods, heuristics, techniques - were very weak. There was only one analysis that conceived of different alternatives.

The analysis of both the required and offered expertise showed that client-ministries do not articulate their needs precisely and strongly (if there is any tendency then it is towards positivism) and they do not call for policy designs but rather for background papers. According to previous research, this was caused by a lack of know-how and an unstable political environment (Hejzlarová, 2010, p 99). Moreover, policy analysis as a specific field has not been established yet in the eyes of ministry employees. This all means that ministries did not shape policy analysis actively. As for provider-analysts, their outputs show neither specific methodological features (either positivist or postpositivist) nor policy analysis features. This means there is no predominant approach. The only typical characteristic is that every provider shapes the output in the way he or she is used to. However, an academic style is dominant.

The analysis of 62 public procurements in the 2011-14 period shows a slightly different picture. Before describing the most important differences, it is necessary to distinguish the two samples. Contrary to the first period where the sample covered a wide range of ministries' needs, the legislation which was in force in the second period differentiated between R&D needs that are organised under *Technologická agentura* (the Technology Agency in the Czech Republic; TAČR) and procurements that are more commonly applied and are run under ministries. The latter were the subject of our research. Therefore, it is obvious that public procurements from the 2011-14 period may show a more homogenous and more applied character.

First, the data show that the demand for policy analysis in the three ministries was increasing. In the first five-year period (2005-09), there were 42 procurements; in the second period, limited to 3.5 years, there were 62. At the same time, the distribution of procurements among the selected ministries was unbalanced, with 25 procurements for MMR, 33 for MPSV and only four for MV. This may be explained by the special role played by MMR and MPSV as key stakeholders in the EU funding infrastructure, which may carry a demand for both supporting activities and financial sources. At the same time, it may also indicate the different organisational cultures of various ministries, where in some outsourcing is more acceptable than in others (see Veselý 2012, 2013). As for the state of policy analysis styles and methods in the Czech Republic, this may also imply that both the production and development are uneven.

Second, the demand in 2011–14 is far more specific than in 2005–09. This is visible both in the increasing number of pages specifying the subject of the procurement and the language. The part related to demand specification may still be very short but the standard is about three pages of research questions, detailed descriptions of steps that should be taken and so forth. On the other hand, there are calls which are copy-pasted, which means that when there is a need for repeated activities (such as evaluations), once the pattern is set no special effort was being made to improve it.

Third, the calls in 2011–14 are more focused on policy analysis than the calls in 2005–09. Whereas in the preceding period the tasks related to a policy analysis approach were weak, 41 of the 62 procurements from 2011–14 carry some of the policy analysis features. About one-third of these are focused on evaluation; very often there is also a task to set up guidelines for a specific area, and feasibility studies are also rather common.

Concerning the demanded methods and some other indicators of policy analysis being positivist or post-positivist, the situation had not changed much. In 43 procurements methods were not mentioned, in nine cases statistical methods were demanded, and in eight cases both quantitative and qualitative methods were preferred. In the two remaining cases, where qualitative methods were requested this referred to the way of collecting data, not the way these should be analysed.

In the 52 procurements from 2011–14 we were not able to decide on the paradigmatic roots; in seven cases inclusion of stakeholders was demanded, which refers to a non-positivist policy analysis stream. In three cases the procurements called for statistical evidence, which in one case meant a task including a cost-benefit analysis which relates to the positivist approach as used in Western policy analysis.

The conclusion concerning the period of 2005–09 is that if we really wanted to decide the positivist/postpositivist puzzle the result would be 'slightly positivist' (with respect to the calls). The most fitting label for Czech policy analysis, then, is in any case 'underdeveloped' in the sense of a low level of acceptance and reflection that does not allow it to grow. The 2011–14 period indicates changes in terms of the volume of policy analysis that is demanded by ministries but when it comes to the dominating paradigm, the answer is still unsatisfactory as Czech policy analysis does not seem to be crystallised in the terms which are used to classify the development in Western countries. Respectively, it may be described as 'slightly positivist' in the methods and thoughts behind it (the idea of improvement, optimalisation, minimalisation of costs and so on) but not in a specific approach to policy analysis. Not all of the contracts show positivist features but these are also far from being called postpositivist. In these cases we decided to call it 'non-positivist', which indicates that the approach goes beyond the positivist perspective but still has not turned into a stand-alone approach. To conclude, Czech policy analysis has been developing but due to many reasons mentioned in Chapters Two, Three and Five its methods are specific.

Policy analysis styles in the Czech Republic

The classification of policy analysis styles by Mayer, Els van Daalen and Boots (2001) offers six approaches to policy analysis to distinguish the different functions policy analysis has. These are: a rational style, an argumentative style, a client advice style, a participatory style, a process style and an interactive style. Contrary to the authors, we will not be able to find examples of the application of all of them. The main problem is that the specific development of Czech policy analysis is not similar to the development in North America and Europe (as seen in Part One), moreover some processes and outputs are not public and it is extremely difficult to get to know them better (to learn more about these see Chapter Twelve).

From the six different styles identified by Mayer, Els van Daalen and Bots (2001) we will put a special focus on the rational/client advice style and interactive style. As far as we have been able to ascertain, the three remaining styles have not been significant in the Czech policy analysis landscape.

Rational and client advice style

The idea of a rational style is defined by a stress on knowledge approved by (scientific) quality criteria whereas the client advice style applies rather instrumental criteria of usability and its aim is to design and recommend. We decided to connect the two styles because, as both analyses and our experience show, these are combined very often, also because of the tradition of applied research in various policies before 1989 (see Chapters Two and Three).

The 'pure' rational analytical style is still common in the Czech Republic, as it is present in various research reports on politics and policies and it also dominated the analysed public procurements of 2005-09. When analysing these (Hejzlarová, 2010; Novotný and Hejzlarová, 2011) we noticed that many of the documents lacked an applied policy analysis approach with its stress on practical and policy-related information. Some of the analyses were full of definitions and theoretical background which could have been eliminated - verbose and lacking examples. Even the empirical evidence was sometimes missing, replaced by theoretical infilling. There were only a few analyses with a detailed policy design (in the best cases, the reports included a two or three page outline of policy tools at the very end). The analysis of procurements in 2011-14 showed a higher degree of provision of support for policy decisions (see above) and we could state that a combination of rational and advisory styles prevailed.

As for the scientific background applied within this rational-advisory analytical style, we may distinguish two main branches: sociology and economics. Moreover, there is a considerable stream of policy analysis; although it is not a proper academic discipline in the Czech Republic, some of its approaches (such as external evaluation) are doing well. The sociological heritage is well depicted in Chapter Two and visible also in the public procurements. Here, we will first stress economics, which we see as having a strong influence on policy analysis features in the Czech Republic; then we will focus on policy analysis. The purpose of this division is not only to describe the role of science but also to enable us to have a closer look at the specifics of the style.

The economic approach

Economics played a key role (and was said to play the key role) in the process of transformation in the 1990s (Potůček, 1997). A huge number of analyses are published by Česká národní banka (the Czech National Bank; the central bank of the Czech Republic), Český statistický úřad (the Czech Statistical Office) and many other institutions, either public or private. This economic stream can be defined by the use of statistical methods and a strong focus on financial issues. Economic assessment is also present in feasibility studies which form a part of some EU funding applications (the European Regional Development Fund and related Czech operational programmes); these have a strict procedure of elaboration.

The most visible example of the economic stream was the functioning of *Národní ekonomická rada vlády* (the National Economic Council; NERV; see also Chapters Ten and Seventeen), which was in 2009-13 the most cited advisory body. NERV worked in two periods: January 2009–September 2009 and summer 2010–August 2013 and had the special status of an independent government advisory body. Its aim was defined as 'to initiate and suggest the principles and features of the public sector economic reform in order to improve the state of public finances, competitiveness of the Czech economy and transparency of the public sector'. Although the task was formulated as highly ambitious, the operationalisation was achievable and it would have been an excellent example of policy analysis.

At the same time, the outputs of NERV were problematic. First, NERV was independent and was not included in the standard public administration procedures, which means that its outputs were usually only taken into consideration, not necessarily adopted. Second, members of NERV - that is economists (NERV consisted mainly of economists) from universities and academic research centres - were providing their expertise (almost) for free and 'in their free time' (web). This decision was probably made to relate to national revivalist enthusiasm and to show NERV as a group of unselfish experts willing to work for the benefit of the nation (literally: 'develop the right decisions for public budget development and for the future of all the citizens of the Czech Republic'). This target was hit but the decision also caused an unintentional effect: the members divided into two groups, one taking the challenges seriously and the other making use of NERV as good PR. Many NERV outputs were based on desk research performed by master's or PhD students invited to cooperate; in some cases the topic related to the research interests of the students, which made the outputs of high quality. Unfortunately (and not only in the case of students), some of the outputs consisted of one-source texts downloaded from the internet (see NERV, 2011). There was no procedure of peer review or external examination and the structure of the outputs was rather random. Even on the level of general consideration of what would be the topics of interest, there was no evidence-based debate or overall schedule of work – the members distributed the areas according to their individual decisions.

This short case study of NERV demonstrates not only the importance economics plays in Czech policy analysis. It also attracts our attention to the way it is (poorly) organised and reminds us of the missing or shallow roots that policy analysis has in the Czech Republic.

The policy analysis approach

The policy analysis stream does not have a long history in the Czech Republic. It is connected with the process of establishing public policy as an academic programme and policy analysis courses taught at universities (see Chapters Two and Eighteen) and, to a greater or lesser extent, with EU accession and democratic development. With respect to policy analysis, two areas are mentioned: evaluation and regulatory impact assessment (RIA).

In relation to the research of Veselý and Nekola presented in Chapter Seven, which depicts evaluation as a not very common analytical activity, we stress that evaluation stands out as very strong in the analysis of public contracts in ministries. As we saw in the first section of this chapter, evaluation took place in around a third of public procurements and is thus a dominant outsourced domain of policy analysis. In addition to the evaluation of the European Union fund operational programmes, which is the main subject of the procurements, there is also another strong branch of evaluation which focuses on development cooperation.

Evaluation in development cooperation has about a 20-year history. Evaluators connected to the former Development Centre of the Institute of International Relations and the Ministry of Foreign Affairs were provided training by the European Union, the United Nations Development Programme (UNDP), the Canadian International Development Agency and various donors. There have been challenges regarding a generally weak evaluation culture, which means that the meaning of evaluation and its aims and benefits were not recognised; therefore evaluators faced a certain mistrust. In 2010, evaluation in development cooperation was partially devolved to UNDP Bratislava (Slovakia). In addition to the policy analysis operations mentioned earlier, there is space to grow on the sides of both demand and supply. On the other hand, the Czech Ministry of Foreign Affairs plays a positive role as it responds to the evaluation findings and implements them. All the evaluations are publicly accessible on the websites of the Ministry.[5] A fairly high standard of evaluation was confirmed by the acceptance of the Czech Republic into the Organisation for Economic Co-Operation and Development (OECD) Development Cooperation Directorate (OECD-DAC) where the evaluation function was assessed. The Czech Republic was the first state from the group of 2004 EU enlargement countries to enter the committee.

---

[5] www.mzv.cz/jnp/cz/zahranicni_vztahy/rozvojova_spoluprace/dvoustranna_zrs_cr/evaluace/index.html

Contrary to the evaluation of Development Cooperation, which is driven by national and supranational organisations, the evaluation framework in the area of the EU operational programmes is set by Brussels. It is stated that a compulsory part of every operational programme is evaluation; even the use of the pre-structural funds like Phare and Community Programmes was dependent on establishing structures for evaluation (see Samková, 2003). This necessity established demand (and thus a material and practical framework) for evaluation as a policy analysis area. Evaluation is the only formalised part of the ideal six-fold-path of the policy analysis process, which means that the expectations towards it are high and the evaluation is understandably a source of disappointment when the expectations are not fulfilled.

Some insiders say with irony that the typical demand from the side of the ministry is 'we want to know everything about everything' and the typical research design for evaluation is a mix of desk research, focus groups, interviews and sometimes a case study. Methods like counterfactual analysis, qualitative comparative analysis, theory-based approaches and process tracing are being used as well but they are far from being standard.

This situation seems to have common features with the situation mentioned earlier in the area of public procurement. The demand is vague (although still improving) since investment in the education of bureaucrats is underestimated and suppliers follow their educational background and their more-or-less intuitive understanding of what evaluation is. This may lead to the situation described in a meta-evaluation of 16 evaluation reports from 2007-13 (Remr, 2014). This report points out that the evaluation findings are not supported by analyses, descriptions of methodology or literature and sources used, which means that the recommendations are untrustworthy, and in some cases the methods were not described properly (either in the sense of transparency or accuracy).

The other common feature is misunderstanding of the policy analysis findings. *Nejvyšší kontrolní úřad* (the Supreme Audit Office; NKÚ) announced that there have been some failures on the side of ministries when evaluation recommendations were not taken into account, which further influences (in a negative way) the environment in which evaluation is prepared (both the instructions and the outputs are defined in a vague way).

There are also some other problems. Monitoring is not tailored to the needs of evaluation, which makes the process more difficult and may lead to superficial evaluation outputs. The time for elaborating an evaluation is typically two or three months and the evaluation is driven mostly at the end of the intervention and not from the very beginning as it should be.

As for the positives, on the ESF website there is a forum where many (not all) evaluation reports can be found. Another very promising thing about evaluation is the existing and developing infrastructure. There is a working group for evaluation which comments on all the calls and evaluation reports. Its members come from various ministries and the academic sector (the cooperation between decision makers and academia in evaluation is poor). For both development evaluators and

EU fund evaluators there has also been high-quality annual training organised by the NGO Development Worldwide and the Czech Society for Evaluation. Lecturers come from the World Bank and International Program for Development Evaluation Training in Canada. Every year an evaluation conference is organised by Česká evaluační společnost (the Czech Society for Evaluation; ČES). ČES seems to be one of the important factors in the prospective development of the policy analysis field. Without an umbrella organisation it is impossible or more difficult to shape the area, to organise common education, to share experiences and to define the evaluation standards or the ethical codex. The existence of ČES is thus very promising and makes the area of evaluation the dark horse of the policy analysis race. At the same time the ČES has not yet been a key actor (due to the small number of members and the fragmented field of evaluation) and the progress may be thus limited.

These two streams – development cooperation and EU funds – of course do not cover the whole area of evaluation. Some kind of evaluation is a part of many other areas, either legislatively or on a voluntary basis. The legal framework supports, for example, the quality of social services and education; on a voluntary basis there are plenty of initiatives such as gender audits, healthcare certificates and many others.

Regulatory impact assessment is another area where a policy analysis approach is applied. RIA is a part of the legislative process in the Czech Republic, obligatory for all legislative documents introduced by the government since 2007. The process of assessment (mainly) by bureaucrats (but in some cases also NGOs) formally leads to a document which includes the formulation of the public policy problem that should be resolved, variants of solutions and impacts on various levels of societal life (including cost-benefit analysis). The final report is then approved by the government and goes to the Parliament or is declined. The aims of RIA are (among others) 'improving the quality of the Czech legislative system, increasing the transparency of the public administration performance, increasing the level of information of citizens and NGOs'.[6]

On a theoretical level, RIA offers a great opportunity for policy analysis; the evaluation of RIA (Vláda ČR, 2013) revealed that it is still more a formal process. The bureaucrats do not consult on the material with the public; the form of assessment is in many cases formal as those involved do not know how to deal with it; and there is a lack of data. However, an international comparison (Staroňová, 2010) shows that the process of RIA is facing various problems in the Central and Eastern European region and that the Czech Republic does not show up as a laggard.

---

[6] www.vlada.cz/cz/ppov/lrv/ria/uvod-87615/

The interactive style

Mayer et al state that the interactive style of policy analysis typically involves 'target groups and stakeholders [being] invited to structure problems or devise solutions in structured working meetings at which policy analysis techniques may be used' (Mayer et al, 2001, p 14). The special value of the interactive policy analysis style lies in the process which typically provides heterogeneous perspectives carried by various stakeholders and better information for both decision makers and citizens. Mayer et al also talk about the possibility of empowerment but they place it under the participatory style.

In the Czech Republic, the interactive style is present in the community planning of social services, which is a process defined by Law No. 108/2006 Coll., on social services. This process is continuously taking place on two levels, in the 13 regions and Prague and in many tens of municipalities (some estimates talk about 200, see Bernard, 2009), and its aim is to design social services in the area. For regions, community planning is obligatory; the municipalities are financially motivated to undergo the process as the system of financing prefers municipalities which have a community plan. The law defines three types of stakeholders: decision makers, social services providers and users.

As Bernard (2009) points out, the process of planning defined by the law on social services does not mean a transformation from directive planning to participatory planning. Instead, it has created the space to start planning the services. At the same time, the two dominant actors in the process are usually the municipality and the providers of social services. Users very rarely follow the meetings and serve mainly as a source of information. The question of representation is also persistent since providers often speak for users. Bernard concludes that the process of community planning of social services is *de jure* participatory – or interactive; but according to his findings, it is a space for providers rather than pressure groups.

In addition to the community planning of social services, there are also various strategic planning meetings, working groups and commissions. The experience of using techniques of public involvement has also been exported to some of the post-socialist and post-conflict states as a part of development cooperation.[7]

Conclusion

The main analytical divisions in this chapter were made through the topics of paradigms, styles and methods in the Czech Republic. Based on the features of these categories, we have tried to derive some more general characteristics of policy analysis in the Czech Republic.

The discussion about Czech policy analysis' dominant paradigms showed that it is extremely difficult to solve the puzzle using the positivist–postpositivist scale as

---

[7] www.mzv.cz/jnp/cz/zahranicni_vztahy/lidska_prava/prioritni_zeme_a_projekty_ transformacni/index.html

its development differs from the Western policy analysis which introduced these terms. Policy analysis in the Czech Republic has a short history and although it has been growing, it lacks some important features. These may include critical discussion about the nature of the knowledge, which is necessary for high-quality policy designs and good governance and low demand as a result both of low awareness of policy makers about policy analysis as a discipline and few financial resources at the same time. Nevertheless, we have concluded that outsourced policy analysis in 2005-09 had 'slightly positivist' features, which refers mainly to the general scientific methods that were demanded. The period of 2011-14 can be characterised by stronger pressure for useful advice and recommendations that would enable policy makers to create evidence-based policy. This direction is nevertheless not postpositivist.

With respect to policy analysis styles, we discussed the rational/client advice style and the interactive style. The remaining styles are either a part of a 'grey zone' of policy analysis which is not publicly accessible or does not exist. Regarding the rational/client advice style which seems to be dominant in Czech policy analysis, the influence of the economy and some features of economic-centred policy analysis production were shown. The central role which the economy plays in Czech society may lead us back to thoughts about a paradigm, but still the expertise does not fit into either the positivist or postpositivist boxes. The other important sources are policy analysis and especially the field of evaluation. This case shows the considerable influence of foreign institutions on Czech policy analysis (this topic is the subject of Chapter Five). As for the European Union, it initiated the organisational, financial and knowledge framework where policy analysis, in this special case evaluation, can be done. The unusually high share of public procurements based on evaluation can be explained only by the infrastructure and financial sources of the EU. Regulatory impact assessment was inspired by the OECD and the transfer of knowledge in evaluation of development cooperation has been made possible by the United Nations and other institutions.

As for methods used in policy analysis, there are a wide range of these: statistical methods for large-N surveys or econometrics, interviews and focus groups, case studies, counterfactual analyses and qualitative comparative analyses in evaluation, public hearings and so on. Unfortunately, not all these methods are used on a regular basis. Moreover, as our analysis showed, the use of methods is limited to two disciplines – sociology and economics – and policy analysis, or, to put it precisely, on their positivist component (the only exception is deliberative policy analysis). This means that policy analysis in the Czech Republic is growing in terms of its volume, and is increasingly taking the form of good advice (although slowly). It has various streams but still the main paradigms are positivist and 'non-positivist', which means it goes beyond positivism but is not postpositivist. As for explanations of the situation, we suggest the narrow academic background of policy analysis in the Czech Republic (policy analysis is taught mainly under public policy and the political sciences and does not make use of other disciplines such as public administration, organisational or development studies), and a slightly positivist demand from clients.

Acknowledgement

The chapter was written with the financial support of PRVOUK programme P17 'Sciences of Society, Politics, and Media under the Challenge of the Times'.

References

Behn, R.D. and Vaupel, J.W. (1982) *Quick Analysis for Busy Decision Makers*, New York: Basic Books.

Bernard, J. (2009) 'Participativní procesy v komunitním plánování sociálních služeb – vize a realita' [Participative processes in community social-services planning – vision and reality], in D. Čermák (ed) *Aplikace principů partnerství a participace v prostředí malých měst České republiky* [Application of the Partnership and Participation Principles in small towns of the Czech Republic], Praha: Sociologický ústav AV ČR, pp 63-81.

Booth, T. (1990) 'Researching policy analysis', *Knowledge: Creation, Diffusion, Utilization*, 12(1): 80-100.

DeLeon, P. (1994) 'Democracy and the policy sciences: aspirations and operations', *Policy Studies Journal*, 22(2): 200-212.

DeLeon, P. (1998) 'Models of policy discourse: insights versus prediction', *Policy Studies Journal*, 26(1): 147-61.

Dobuzinskis, L., Laycock, D.H. and Howlett, M. (2007) *Policy Analysis in Canada: The State of the Art*, Buffalo, NY: University of Toronto Press.

Durning, D. (1999) 'The transition from traditional to postpositivist policy analysis: a role for Q methodology', *Journal of Policy Analysis and Management*, 18(3): 389-410.

Fiala, P. and Schubert, K. (2000) *Moderní analýza politiky. Úvod do teorií a metod policy analysis* [Modern policy analysis. Introduction to theories and methods of policy analysis], Brno: Barrister & Principal.

Guba, E.G. and Lincoln, Y.S. (2000) 'Paradigmatic controversies, contradictions, and emerging confluences', in N.K. Denzin and Y.S. Lincoln (eds) *Handbook of Qualitative Research* (2nd edn), London: Sage Publications, pp 163-88.

Hejzlarová, E. (2010) 'Policy analysis in the Czech republic: positivist or postpositivist?', *Central European Journal of Public Policy* [online], 4(2): 88-107. Available from www.cejpp.eu/index.php/ojs/article/view/52

Hogwood, B. and Gunn, L. (1984) *Policy Analysis for the Real World*, London: Oxford University Press.

Howlett, M. and Ramesh, M. (1998) 'Policy subsystem configurations and policy change: operationalizing the postpositivist analysis of the politics of the policy process', *Policy Studies Journal*, 26(3): 466-81.

Kosterlitz, J. (1991) 'Educated guesswork', *National Journal*, 23(40): 2408-13.

Lin, A.C. (1998) 'Bridging positivists and interpretivist approaches to qualitative methods', *Policy Studies Journal*, 26(1): 162-80.

Lynn, L.E. (1999) 'A place at the table: policy analysis, its postpositive critics, and the future of practice', *Journal of Policy Analysis and Management*, 18(3): 411–24.

Mayer, I.S., Els van Daalen, C.E. and Bots, P.W.G. (2001) 'Perspectives on policy analyses: a framework for understanding and design', *Journal of Technology, Policy and Management*, 4(2): 169-91.

NERV Národní ekonomická rada vlády [National Economic Council] (2011) *Boj proti korupci: sborník textů pracovní skupiny pro boj proti korupci* [Fight against corruption: compilation of texts of the working group on the fight against corruption], Praha: Úřad vlády České republiky.

Novotný, V. and Hejzlarová, E.M. (2011) 'Lesk a bída české analýzy veřejných politik: vývoj a aktuální stav z pohledu vnějších vlivů' [Splendours and miseries of Czech policy analysis: its state and development in the perspective of external influences], *Politologická revue*, 17(1): 3-32.

Potůček, M. (1997) *Nejen trh* [Not only the market], Praha: Sociologické nakladatelství.

Potůček, M. (2007) 'Czech public policy as a scientific discipline and object of research', *Central European Journal of Public Policy* [online], 1(1): 102-21. Available from www.cejpp.eu/index.php/ojs/article/view/12

Radin, B.A. (2000) *Beyond Machiavelli: Policy Analysis Comes of Age*, Washington, DC: Georgetown University Press.

Remr, J. (2014) 'Peer – review evaluačních zpráv z oblasti strukturálních fondů' [Peer review of evaluation reports from the field of structural fonds], in *Česká evaluační společnost* [online]. Available from www.czecheval.cz/konference_2014_prez/f_prezentace_remr_02t.pdf

Samková, P. (2003) *Implementation of the EU Pre-Accession Aid in Czech Regions*, PhD thesis, Praha: Faculty of Social Sciences. Available from http://bit.ly/1sDpuBm

Shulock, N. (1999) 'The paradox of policy analysis: if it is not used, why do we produce so much of it?', *Journal of Policy Analysis and Management*, 18(2): 226-44.

Staroňová, K. (2010) 'Regulatory impact assessment: formal institutionalisation and practice', *Journal of Public Policy*, 30(1): 117-36.

Stokey, E. and Zeckhauser, R. (1978) *A Primer for Policy Analysis*, New York: W.W. Norton and Company Inc.

Veselý, A. (2012) 'Policy advisory system in the Czech Republic: From state monopoly to hollowing out?', Paper presented at the XXIInd World Congress of Political Science in Madrid.

Veselý, A. (2013) 'Externalization of policy advice: theory, methodology and evidence', *Policy and Society*, 32(3): 199-209.

Veselý, A. and Nekola, M. (eds) (2007) *Analýza a tvorba veřejné politiky: přístupy, metody a praxe* [Methods of policies analysis and design], Praha: Sociologické nakladatelství.

Vláda ČR (2013) *Závěrečná zpráva z Analýzy implementace a efektivnosti stávajícího nastavení procesu RIA v ČR* [Analysis of implementation and effectiveness of RIA in the Czech Republic: final report] [online], Praha: Vláda ČR, 2013. Available from http://bit.ly/1rU1XZ3

Weimer, D.L. and Vining, A.R. (2004) *Policy Analysis: Concepts and Practice* (4th edn), Upper Saddle River, NJ: Prentice-Hall.

Weiss, C.H. (1977a) 'Research for policy's sake: the enlightenment function of social research', *Policy Analysis*, 3(4): 531–45.

Weiss, C.H. (1977b) *Using Social Research in Public Policy Making*, Lexington, MA: Lexington Books.

Yanow, D. (2007) 'Qualitative-interpretive methods in policy research', in F. Fischer, G.J. Miller and M.S. Sidney (eds) *Handbook of Public Policy Analysis: Theory, Politics, and Methods*, New York: CRC Press, pp 405-16.

Part II

Policy analysis by governments

Policy analysis in the Czech Republic and the influence of supranational organisations

Martin Potůček, Vladimír Hulík, Klára Hulíková Tesárková, Libor Stejskal

Introduction

This chapter examines the impact of supranational organisations on policy making in the Czech Republic. The question to be answered is to what extent are national policy formulations influenced by international and national expertise – in the context of the direct influence of supranational organisations on national public policy making. We focus predominantly on the processes of problem identification and policy formulation; nevertheless, where necessary, implementation and evaluation of policies is taken into account as well.

After a theoretical outline, we present three case studies from different policy fields: social policy, educational po

licy and defence policy. All three policies consume a considerable part of the state budget.[1] They share the common feature of step-by-step adaptation of Czech politicians, civil servants, analysts, consultants, policy entrepreneurs, public and non-profit institutions to the need to identify and launch policies more ready to deal with (and make full use of) Europeanisation and globalisation. On the other hand, they differ in terms of both their content and the scale of the involvement of international actors and institutions on national policies. The European Union is the only institution which exercises considerable influence on all of them.

Even before the dramatic switch from a centralised state to a market economy and from an authoritarian political system to a political democracy in the 1990s, there was local scholarly expertise in policy analysis.[2] At the same time, there was a considerable deficit in understanding both the market's functioning and the democratic mediation of interests. Thus, support from outside prevailed during

---

[1] The share of the state budget allocated to the Ministry of Labour and Social Affairs represented 43%, to the Ministry of Education 11.6% and to the Defence Ministry 3.6% in 2013.

[2] Refer to Chapter Two, 'Public Policy in the Czech Republic: Historical Development and its Current State'.

the first decade after the fall of communism in 1989,[3] sometimes with little understanding of the specificities of national culture, character and institutional legacies. Since the beginning of the third millennium, the national analytical capacities have become more professional in understanding policy making in new political and economic settings, and in their international contexts.

Based on the three case studies, we offer a tentative assessment on the developmental trends, shortcomings and prospects of the earlier mentioned processes at the end of the chapter.

Theoretical outline

Our approach is based on governance theory, as 'it has tremendous potential in opening up alternative ways of looking at political institutions, domestic-global linkages, trans-national co-operation, and different forms of public-private exchange' (Pierre, 2000, p 241).

On another occasion, we developed and applied the holistic concept of governance, consisting of three mutually dependent dimensions (Potůček, 2008a, 2008b):

- Public policies are no longer a matter of a single decision of a national sovereign. Governance is executed at several levels, acting and interacting simultaneously (Dančák and Hloušek, 2007). We will take into consideration just two levels – the supranational and national ones.
- This research field cannot be reduced to the government and its activities. Other regulators should also be taken into account, namely the market and the civic sector (Potůček, 1999).
- Contemporary governance cannot put its entire stake in hierarchies; it is vitally dependent on horizontal links as well as on informal policy networks.

Decision makers have to respect institutional regulations (laws, standards). They have to take into consideration tough fiscal restrictions. They have at their disposal programmatic documents, such as policy goals, strategies, Green and White books, and benchmarks. Last but not least, they may (or may not) consider the advice of international and national policy analysts and consultants.

---

[3] Namely the EU's and OECD's (Organisation for Economic Co-operation and Development) technical assistance programmes (such as PHARE [Poland and Hungary: Assistance for Restructuring their Economies] and SIGMA [Support for Improvement in Governance and Management]) and the tailor-made programmes of American foundations.

Case studies

Impact of EU policies on Czech social policy

EU policies with national relevance

The history of post-communist candidate countries' preparation for EU accession[4] started with the launching of the Copenhagen criteria of accession (1993). These criteria were designed more as a technical (economic and political) instrument to be implemented from above than as an appropriate tool to steer people's living conditions in the candidate countries. Legal, economic and political issues prevailed.

Candidate countries were asked to reform their national economies to be able to compete, and be compatible with market economies. They had to build robust and reliable institutions of political democracy, and adjust their legal and administrative systems to the *acquis communautaire*.

On the other hand, genuine social goals were at the very bottom of the then list of priorities – limited to the preservation of individual human rights and the building of a loosely defined framework for social policy making. Most national social policies in the post-communist candidate countries in the beginning and middle of the 1990s consisted of the withdrawal of the state and the improvement of efficiency by the privatisation and marketisation of services. These steps were to be completed by the reduction of the coverage and standards of all social benefits except social assistance, a well-targeted safety net for the poor (Ferge, 2001).

The 1999 elections brought about a majority of left-of-centre political parties in the European Parliament. The European Council launched the Lisbon Strategy in 2000. It opened up new political initiatives, stressing the importance of human resources, social cohesion and quality of life. The Czech Republic was asked to accept the Lisbon Strategy after the 2002 Barcelona Summit, when the preparation of the new member states to enter the EU, until then organised within the logic of the Copenhagen criteria, had just been completed. Fully fledged participation in the Lisbon Strategy started only with the country's accession to the EU in May 2004. Thus, social policy moved to the top of the EU political agenda of enlargement as late as one decade after setting up the Copenhagen criteria of accession.

The 2004 elections changed the political map of the European Parliament by giving the majority to right-of-centre political parties. In 2005 the New European Commission under Chairman José Barroso redefined the Lisbon Strategy by prioritising economic growth, education, research and development, and fighting unemployment. The Czech government reacted by preparing the National Lisbon

---

[4]   The first wave of countries consisted of the Czech Republic, Estonia, Hungary, Latvia, Lithuania, Poland, Slovakia and Slovenia. They joined the EU on 1 May 2004.

Programme 2005–08 (Office, 2005). Significantly, it consisted of three parts only: macroeconomic, microeconomic and employment.

The Czech scholarly community discussed the nature and implementation potential of the Lisbon Strategy in general and in the Czech Republic in particular. The whole spectrum of positions has occurred. Some economists (such as Václav Klaus, the long-term Chairman of the Civic Democratic Party, Czech Prime Minister from 1992 to 1997 and the Czech President between 2002 and 2013) have challenged the inclusion of social cohesion, environmental goals and the sustainable development concept. Even the scholars, who in principle agreed with the structure of the Lisbon Strategy goals and the usefulness of such a programmatic effort, have found it quite difficult to see it as a realistic document, namely its ambitious part that endeavours to make the EU 'the most competitive and dynamic knowledge-based economy in the world by 2010'.

Technical assistance

The influence of the European Union in supporting and mediating modernisation can be identified in various fields. Well worth noting was the EU's assistance in institution and capacity building (for example the PHARE and SIGMA projects), specifically designed modernisation efforts – reform of public administration, regulatory reform, training of professionals (including civil servants), implementation of new methods of public management and administration, collaboration in the field of education and so on.

National Action Plans of Social Inclusion (NAPSIs)

The European Commission asked all the candidate countries' governments to elaborate Joint Inclusion Memoranda in order to identify key problems and policy measures to combat poverty and social exclusion in 2002. The Czech version was approved by the representatives of the European Commission and the Czech government two years later (Ministry, 2004).

The National Action Plan for Social Inclusion 2004–06 followed suit (Ministry, 2005). Though called a plan, it was simply a summary of programmes, plans and measures that had either already been implemented or were about to be launched. The new measures in favour of the disadvantaged and fighting poverty and social exclusion were set out in the programming document on tapping money from the European Structural Funds. The weak point of the document was the lack of explicit goals, poorly defined responsibility for implementation, and missing links to the budgetary process. Significantly, the Ministry of Finance did not participate in the preparation of this document (Beránková, 2004; Potůček, 2004; Atkinson et al, 2005). The second National Action Plan on Social Inclusion for 2006–08 (Ministry, 2006) and the third National Report on Strategies for Social Protection and Social Inclusion 2008–10 (Ministry, 2008) were elaborated, with specific attention paid to selected policy fields and a more sophisticated methodology, but with similar negligible real life policy impact.

Various authors have described the process of 'Europeanisation' (Featherstone and Radaelli, 2003); some positive effects of this process could also be recognised.[5] The actors participating in NAPSIs were gradually honing their craft as to both the methods at their disposal and thematic cultivation of problems within this category. The plans brought about increasing public awareness of 'newly emerging' social problems. They legitimised some until then neglected social problems, namely the problem of rising homelessness (Hradecká and Hradecký, 1996).

The Open Method of Coordination (OMC)

The EU policies toward social policy making in member states relied predominantly on 'soft' instruments, such as the Open Method of Coordination.[6] In the Czech case, operational and tactical tasks, short-term interests, lack of time and professional blindness severely limited the effects of its application (Potůček, 2012). Although the OMC was apparently toothless when it came to influencing strategic social policy choices, the elements of its positive, though incremental, impact on the overall culture of political discourse and decision making (such as the rising activism of non-profit services, advocacy organisations and epistemic communities) should not be neglected.

National initiatives

The elaboration of 'The Social Doctrine of the Czech Republic' (Sociální doktrína České republiky, 2002) represents an interesting example of the activity of a national epistemic community. Its aim was to build a broad national consensus concerning the future orientation, goals, priorities and corresponding instruments of Czech social policy. Five preparatory conferences in 1998-2000 were a 'joint venture' of the academic community concentrated around the non-profit Socioklub, the Ministry of Labour and Social Affairs and the Senate (the Upper House of the Czech Parliament). The document, elaborated by a group of nine academicians from various fields and with various political affiliations, was mentioned in the coalition agreement statement of the political parties in power in July 2002, as the starting point for the further development of government social policy and its priorities and approaches. Nevertheless, until its resignation in 2004, the government failed to find sufficient capacity and motivation for the

---

[5] Refer to Chapter Six for more detail.

[6] The Open Method of Coordination (OMC) is a form of EU soft law, a process of policy making which does not lead to binding EU legislative measures or require member states to change their law. It aims to spread best practices and achieve greater convergence towards the main EU goals.

consequent implementation steps: social policy decisions mostly stemmed from either urgent problems or strong demands articulated by various pressure groups.

Other examples of concerted national efforts to analyse and design policies were two attempts to prepare consistent proposals for pension reform. A public discussion about pension reform was initiated by experts from international financial institutions, namely the International Monetary Fund and the World Bank, who strongly recommended that the country opt for compulsory private co-insurance. This new type of old-age insurance would complement the pay-as-you-go public scheme that would gradually lose its importance in the total amount of redistributed resources. Another stimulus was the EU Green Paper on 'Confronting Demographic Change: A New Solidarity between the Generations' (Commission, 2005) Consecutive governments established cross-party task forces for pension reform in 2004-05 and again in 2010-11 in order to simulate the consequences of alternative pension reform options and thus contribute to rational discussion of the representatives of different ideological views. Nevertheless, neither of these attempts to reach a political consensus has materialised in successful pension reform implementation. The first attempt ended up in the House of Commons, which refused to pass the corresponding bill. The second attempt was a Pyrrhic victory, as the law establishing a fully funded private second pillar of pension system came into power in 2013, but it gained only negligible public support. The new coalition government decided to abolish it completely by 2015.

Conclusion: social policy

The EU's role in shaping certain domestic policy fields, namely social policy, should not be overestimated. The obvious discrepancy between the Copenhagen criteria of accession, covering a very limited part of the social welfare agenda and implemented in 1993, and the Lisbon Strategy, laid out as an explicit and balanced public policy programme for the candidate countries as late as 2002 and politically and administratively executed only since 2004, opened a considerable space for other, more active and influential international actors, namely the World Bank and International Monetary Fund led by the Washington Consensus' neoliberal ideology of the 1990s (Potůček, 2004). The European Union's political weakness created a sharp sociopolitical tension: the Czech Republic joined the EU with its health, social and employment policies not developed enough to cope with the demands of this strategic policy document.

The European Union did not communicate with the country in a single voice. One of its two Janus faces spoke about further trade liberalisation (including services of general interest), fiscal discipline, flexible labour markets, the need to make the European economy the most competitive in the world, whereas the EU's other Janus face spoke about social justice, social rights, the fight against poverty and social exclusion.

The impact of supranational institutions on Czech educational policy

Making changes in education policy is a long process. Education systems typically have an internal inertia which works against efforts to change the system. After 1989, Czech policy makers tried to set up and implement new ideas and build a competitive education system for a market-oriented economy. During the time of the transformation of Czech society in the 1990s, there was a strong demand for policy recommendations from internationally respected organisations for transformation of the education system. Based on the analysis of political documents adopted during 1990-2012, it is possible to consider these three: the Organisation for Economic Co-Operation and Development (OECD), the European Union and the IEA.[7]

These recommendations are expected to be adopted and adapted to the national conditions because the opinions of experts from supranational institutions constitute much stronger arguments for the Czech political representation than the opinions of national experts. The ideal approach is that the recommendations of supranational institutions pass through discussions between national experts and government institutions. There are many national expert groups in the Czech Republic which are involved in the education policy analysis process. Some of them have an academic background (that is the Education Policy Centre[8]), some of them were established as think tanks (that is ISEA[9]) and some of them are interested groups of experts from educational institutions (that is EDUin[10]) or associations of educational institutions (that is SKAV[11]). These groups are involved in discussions about the direction of education policy and sometimes also in the creation of national policy documents.

OECD analyses of education policy

The analytical work of the OECD in the field of education policies can be divided into two types. The first is through reviews of national education policies and the second works on the basis of the review of a selected education area in several member states (*thematic review*). In the first, the country is the object of the analysis, while in the second the theme of education policy is taken as the key factor.

The recommendations of the OECD experts are usually taken seriously. These recommendations make up an institutional framework that enables national experts to participate in the process of policy making and provides a discussion platform on the future direction of national policies for civil servants, (in)dependent experts and the scholarly community. The role of experts and the scholarly community

---

[7]   The International Association for the Evaluation of Educational Achievement, www.iea.nl

[8]   Faculty of Education, Charles University in Prague, www.strediskovzdelavacipolitiky.info

[9]   Institute for Social and Economic Analyses, www.isea-cz.org

[10]   A public benefit association, www.eduin.cz

[11]   Standing Conference of Educational Associations, www.skav.cz

in the policy-making process is relatively strong within this framework; usually a group of national experts is mandated to transform the recommendations into a policy document.

The first request of the Czech Republic for an OECD review was sent in 1990 and the work was done between the years 1990 and 1993. The review was focused on national tertiary education policies and although those recommendations were highly appreciated by national analysts and policy makers and marked as key factors for further development of the Czech higher education sector, most of the results have never been incorporated into the strategic documents (Pabian, 2007). Other levels of the Czech education system were reviewed by the OECD experts in 1995-96 and in 1999. Some of the recommendations resulting from those evaluations were included in the *National Programme for the Development of Education in the Czech Republic: White Paper* (Kotásek, 2001, p 7), especially in the areas of finance, access to tertiary education, adult education, quality assurance, educational staff and so on. In 2005-08, the OECD compiled the *Thematic Review of Tertiary Education*, in which the Czech Republic participated. For many experts and policy makers it was a surprise that the OECD experts' recommendations were almost the same as in 1992. This may reflect the persistent weaknesses of the Czech higher education system (Pabian, 2007). Some recommendations were incorporated into the *White Paper on Tertiary Education* (Matějů et al, 2009), but only within the narrow specific view of participating national experts. This White Paper has never had strong support: firstly, there has never been a broad consensus even among policy makers or national experts, and secondly, representatives of public universities play a key role in tertiary sector governance in the Czech Republic. It is undisputed that it is difficult to enforce any reforms that could weaken the privileged position of public universities in the tertiary sector and in the decision-making processes dealing with them (Pabian, 2007). The adoption of both OECD recommendations on tertiary education, which were incorporated into the policy documents, was influenced by this factor.

OECD and IEA surveys

The OECD and IEA surveys in many areas of education are a special case of the influence of supranational institutions on Czech education policy. Due to the lack of data in some areas (especially in the area of key competencies), these surveys are the only relevant source of information on these issues. Some of the problems of the Czech education system were revealed by the poor results of Czech pupils and students in these tests. Only then did Czech policy makers begin to be seriously interested in the problematic areas. For example, the deteriorating results of 15-year-old pupils in PISA[12] (OECD), pupils of the eighth grade of basic school

---

[12] Programme for International Student Assessment, www.oecd.org/pisa/aboutpisa/

in TIMSS[13] (IEA) and pupils of the fourth grade of basic school in PIRLS[14] (IEA) in the 2000s were among the reasons that after 14 years of preparation the state school-leaving examination at secondary schools was launched in 2011 and new testing of pupils in the fifth and ninth grades of basic school was prepared by the Czech School Inspectorate.

The EU's influence on educational policy

The real influence of the European Union on Czech education policy started to appear in 2002, when the Czech Republic (as acandidate country at that time) became a full member of the EU expert and policy maker working groups. Since the adoption of the Lisbon Strategy in 2000, the EU has used the Open Method of Coordination to steer EU education policy. Although education policy has never been among the EU's common policies, education is perceived as a key factor for employment growth.

The OMC, although not mandatory, is based on the assumption that the EU member states should adopt the European goals in their national policies. In practice, it leads to the Europeanisation of national education policies through facilitated coordination (Bulmer and Radaelli, 2004, p 7). It would seem that the OMC is an ideal platform for European governance, but this is not an accurate perspective. It is very difficult to include independent experts, who often have a critical view of the analyses prepared by the European Commission and the common European goals, within the European working networks. A similar issue can be found in the Czech policy-making process – usually there is no time or will to invite national experts to the consultations and transfer of the European recommendations or goals into Czech national strategies. The implementation process is, in the majority of cases, limited to government institutions. Consultation with national experts takes place in problematic cases only.

For the period 2000-10 a set of five European benchmarks was adopted in the field of education in the 'Education and Training 2010' programme (Council, 2003, p 2). In accordance with these benchmarks, the Czech Ministry of Education, Youth and Sports focused on lifelong learning because it was the area where the Czech Republic had achieved the worst results compared to other EU member states and to the European average performance. As a result, the initiatives in the field of lifelong learning were adopted at the national level.

In 2007, at the European level it was already quite clear that in four of the five stated benchmarks it would not be possible to achieve the adopted target values. Therefore, the Council of Ministers of Education, Youth and Culture gave a mandate to the European Commission to prepare a new strategy (including a new set of benchmarks) which should be targeted on the period 2011-20: the 'Education and Training 2020 (ET 2020)' programme, which was adopted in

---

[13] Trends in International Mathematics and Science Study, www.iea.nl/timss_2011.html

[14] Progress in International Reading Literacy Study, www.iea.nl/pirls_2011.html

2009 during the Czech Presidency of the EU. At the same time, a new ten-year economic strategy, 'Europe 2020', was launched in 2010, following the Lisbon Strategy. Two benchmarks from ET 2020 were included in the headline targets of the Europe 2020 strategy: reducing the early school leaving drop-out rate (from the current 15% to 10%) and increasing the share of the population aged 30-34 having completed tertiary education from 31% to at least 40% (European Commission, 2010, p 9). Based on the Europe 2020 strategy, the EU member states should adopt their own national reform programmes (NRP), which should be coherent with the EU headline targets and updated annually. In response to the NRP and their annual updates, the Council of the European Union gives country-specific recommendations.

The two mentioned EU headline targets are included in the Czech NRP, which is updated and approved annually by the Czech government. For 2013, the national targets were set at 5.5% for the early school leavers' drop-out rate[15] and 32% for completion of tertiary education (Office, 2013, p 9). Generally, in the field of education the Council recommended that the Czech government focus on increasing the availability of affordable and quality pre-school childcare in 2012 (Council, 2012, p 15). In 2013 the Council recommended taking action in the area of compulsory education (a comprehensive evaluation framework, supporting schools with low ranking educational outcomes), higher education (accreditation, funding) and funding of research institutions (Council, 2013, p 10). These recommendations are reflected in the updated Czech NRP as well as in the forthcoming strategic document that should incorporate all existing documents directly focused on education (Educational Policy Strategy of the Czech Republic to 2020[16]).

It must be stated here that it is somewhat difficult not to reflect the recommendations of the Commission or the Council in the national policy-making process, although these recommendations are not always in line with national priorities. Countries that do not accept the recommendations may be labelled as a 'bad example'. This negative assessment of course worsens the position of member states in further negotiations on the priorities of education policy in the EU.

Conclusion: educational policy

We can say that the analytical capacity of supranational institutions is quite well used for policy recommendations in the field of education because education is perceived as one of the key factors for successful development of a knowledge-based economy. The policy analysis documents of the OECD and the EU have

---

[15] Early school leavers – persons aged 18 to 24 who have finished no more than a lower secondary education and are not involved in further education or training as a percentage of the total population aged 18 to 24.

[16] In Czech: www.vzdelavani2020.cz/clanek/12/aktualni-dokumenty.html

---

a relatively strong impact on policy making in the Czech Republic. While the recommendations of the OECD are mostly widely discussed among educational professionals, and national experts and the scholarly community are usually involved in transforming recommendations into national policy documents, recommendations of the EU are generally accepted at the government level and they are often not discussed at all.

Impact of supranational institutions on Czech defence policy

Paradox of the small allies' defence policy

Defence policy traditionally differs from other public policies in its potentiality. Most of its implementation in Europe consists of preparing for something that is actually never going to happen. Only recently has this 'missing' peacetime purpose been complemented with crisis management operations, supplanting the defence of one's own territory.

The defence policy of the Czech Republic as a small or midsize, non-neutral European country is deeply paradoxical. Its concept of national defence has been reforged into the concept of collective defence. Most European states simply cannot maintain the capabilities to defend themselves solely using their own resources and manpower; in principle they share the burden of defence with allies.[17] The allied framework is predominantly represented by the North Atlantic Treaty Organization (NATO) since 1949 and to a much lesser extent by the European Union since the Lisbon Treaty of 2007. At the same time, this allied model of defence does not restrict full national sovereignty over the defence policy of any member state – in its goals, priorities, doctrine and, surprisingly, armaments and operations as well. Curiously enough, countries are basically not limited in doing what they want and can afford to build their armed forces, transform them and deploy them in legitimate international operations, and on the other hand in practice they have submitted their core task of self-defence to the command of the international organisation (NATO).

This disconnectedness has inevitably influenced the ways in which supranational expertise impacts on national policy making in the Czech Republic. Disregard the fact that NATO and the EU are actually international governmental organisations, with a very limited purely 'supranational' element.

From the Warsaw Pact into NATO and the EU

The pre-1989 Czechoslovak defence policy was formed within the Warsaw Pact (1955–91). This intergovernmental organisation was run by the Soviet hegemony,

---

[17]   There are only a few exceptions of those who at least aim at defence sovereignty and self-sufficiency: Finland and Switzerland among small states, and France and the United Kingdom among the big ones.

authoritarian and directive, not in a multilateral mode of operation. So, the flow of expertise was Soviet-controlled, unilateral and one-directional in questions of strategy, doctrine, operational planning, armament and military technology development.

When communism collapsed, the Cold War ended and the Warsaw Pact was dismantled, Czechoslovakia's sovereign defence policy was marked with gradually growing participation in international crisis management operations (the UN's Desert Storm 1990-91 in Iraq, peace enforcement missions in former Yugoslavia, led by the UN from 1992 to 1995 and NATO starting in 1996). A unique challenge took place in 1992 as the federation and its armed forces had to be divided into new states with two separate militaries. Then the armed forces of the Czech Republic went through a permanent transformation in the 1990s, consisting mostly of reductions in manpower and weaponry.

For the Czech political representation, NATO membership was the only viable prospect for future defence. NATO's Partnership for Peace programme and Study on Enlargement (1995) set up the accession agenda of 'NATO standards'. Five criteria were political (democracy, a market economy, a good neighbourhood, human rights and civilian control over the military), and only one military (minimum interoperability). The process accelerated in 1997 when the Czech Republic was invited to join the Alliance. Seven areas of standards had to be met (1997-99) with the support of intensively mobilised expertise:

- political (wide majority support for membership);
- institutional (adaptation of the public administration);
- legislative (NATO legal acquis, amendment to Constitution);
- defence (planning, interoperability, infrastructure for Allied reinforcement);
- resources (financial and human);
- information security;
- public support.

To achieve this, routine institutional structures within the ministries of Foreign Affairs and Defence had to be augmented with temporary expert committees. NATO accession brought about new permanent expert structures: the Security Council (BRS) with several committees and the National Security Authority to safeguard classified information protection (Borkovec, 2014).

On the military level, Czechs were concerned with adapting the armed forces, still manned with conscripts and equipped with obsolete weapons systems, to sufficient interoperability. Most of this was done through the 'learning by doing' method as the Czech troops were deployed in large numbers on NATO-led missions to Bosnia, Croatia, Kosovo, and later Afghanistan and Iraq.

The Czech Republic's accession to the European Union in 2004 was not significant as the EU at that point was a marginal actor in both security and defence. The high ambitions declared in the European Security Strategy of 2003 and in the Lisbon Treaty of 2007 were not supported by adequately robust policies. Despite the Czech reservations regarding the EU's relevance for defence, the country put great effort into forming the EU Battle Group in 2009, with lesser contributions to Common Security and Defence Policy (CSDP) operations.

Forms of supranational dissemination of expertise

Being a member of the Alliance since 1999 has naturally had a deep impact on Prague's defence policy formation and implementation. The guidance and steering 'from above' continues to be manifold, implicit and explicit, direct and indirect.

The reform of the armed forces in 2001-03, an ambitious modernisation project to recast their profile into smaller, mobile, fully professional and fully interoperable forces, was a milestone in the permanent transition of the Czech military. However, this project was not motivated, or directed by any request from the Alliance. NATO never prescribes what a member state must do with its forces and resources. The overall shape, structure, size and equipment of the national military rest solely upon the member state's sovereign choice, competence, responsibility and affluence. Similarly, documents like *Long-term Vision of Defence* (2008) or the *White Paper on Defence of the Czech Republic* (2011) display only a loose, declaratory link to NATO's key policy document, the Alliance's strategic concept (the last one adopted in 2010). Nevertheless, in regular cycles NATO staff formulate specific targets identifying the contribution each ally is expected to make towards the overall capabilities of the Alliance. NATO expertise is also available upon request by any ally to provide recommendations on what lines of capability development would provide the greatest benefit to the Alliance.

The following categories, ordered from tacit to voiced, may be utilised to trace the flows of expertise between the national and supranational levels:

- socialisation;
- standardisation;
- certification;
- NATO defence planning process.

Socialisation refers here to the 'soft' process of moving people within the national defence establishment toward sharing, accepting and disseminating the values and skills from the international governmental organisation, here mostly NATO. Gheciu (2005) found that this cultural interchange took the form of teaching and persuasion at least during the accession process. NATO representatives assumed the role of educators; Czech politicians, diplomats and officials were students, adopting the set of liberal democratic norms and also navigating into the lifeworld of shared values and Western security culture. However, this process can also be denoted as self-socialisation, as NATO interacted only with decision makers, with limited intensity, and let the Czech elites and experts persuade the domestic public on their own, with the modest but sophisticated support of NATO public diplomacy. In 1999 NATO's Secretary General George Robertson assessed that the Czech armed forces still had a lot of work to overcome communist-inherited habits and attitudes (Gheciu, 2005, p 987). Nowadays the Alliance culture is a fully internalised routine within the Czech defence establishment, creating a large enough pool of 'NATO-positive' officers and civilian experts to maintain the enduring goodwill of the domestic political representation and public.

Inside the NATO HQ (headquarters), the Czech experts are concentrated within the national delegation; the military is also represented in the international military staff and in the NATO Command Structure. These national representatives are usually posted for two to three years; the rotation distributes the income benefits of foreign deployment among larger numbers of personnel. Hence, the concentration and continuity of expertise and knowledge is limited, if not undermined repeatedly. However enthusiastic, short-term rotated interns cannot attain the same level of experience as freelancers hired by NATO HQ (international staff and international military staff). The bad news for the Alliance is that its pool of independent experts is shrinking due to budget cutbacks, and their contracts are shortened (no longer eight or ten year contracts).

Standardisation is the least visible, often neglected form of supranational expertise. 'Standards' in general were the adaptive instrument in the process of accession. Due to their particular technical meanings, they present an on–the-ground, explicit tool for routine cooperation. NATO standardisation covers an extensive scope of technologies, techniques and procedures – from classified information management, training, procurement, requirements for weapons and arms, and so on. The standards developed by Alliance structures and agencies have to be followed by member states' militaries and public administration bodies, and by private suppliers and contractors. The impact of standardisation is ubiquitous in the Czech Republic, since for example standards for classified information protection are used routinely not only by everyone who interacts with the Ministry of Defence and the armed forces, but the ministries of Foreign Affairs and the Interior as well.

Certification is a tool enhancing interoperability on the tactical level. The member states' units from battalion level above need to undergo the CREVAL (ground forces) and TACEVAL (tactical air force) certification before deployment in NATO operations. In the Czech army, the mechanised battalions have passed CREVAL certification repeatedly.

The *NATO Defence Planning Process* (NDPP) is the most pronounced and prominent vehicle of expertise. Its major purpose is to coordinate the member states' contributions to the Alliance's total pool of forces and capabilities. Generally the NDPP consists of five steps:

1 Establishing political guidance.
2 Determination of total requirements needed, and their breakdown into minimum capability requirements.
3 Apportionment of requirements to member states in the form of capability targets.

4 Facilitation of implementation.
5 Review of results, capability review.

Supranational expertise is first present in the second step – that is, determining the minimum capability requirements, or in other words what capabilities NATO countries must generate collectively in order to meet the Alliance's level of ambition. Then the third step – that is setting the capability targets (former force goals) – takes place, in which the NATO staffs proposes the targets for each member state. Quite often the member states refuse some of the proposed targets; then the Defence Planning and Policy Committee decides whether the target is or is not 'a reasonable challenge' for that particular ally. It is important to say that the member state in question has no vote in this case. In the fifth step member states are requested to submit their replies to the Defence Planning Capability Survey (former Defence Planning Questionnaire). These national replies are evaluated by experts from the NATO staff who then elaborate an assessment from NATO's perspective of individual nations' capability development plans and other contributions to the Alliance's efforts. The assessment also includes an indication, again from the NATO perspective, of where the major shortfalls are and what the focus of National Capability Development Plans should be. This is essentially the only institutionalised NATO feedback on national defence efforts which is regularly brought to the attention of defence ministers (Stejskal, 2013, pp 72-73).

In 2013, the Czech Republic accepted all 44 capability targets, including the provision of supersonic fighters and teams for post-conflict reconstruction. It had also faced questioning by international staff experts about some of its intentions, which were broadly not coherent with NATO's interests. For instance, the Czech plan to purchase anti-ground precision-guided munitions only for light combat aircraft and basically only for training purposes (since the use of these aircraft in operations outside of national territory is highly unlikely) was questioned as the required heavier aircraft had not yet been fitted for operational use of such munition. In another example from 2007-08, NATO recommended abandoning a number of rescue battalions which were not deployable outside the national territory, and reinvesting the freed resources in development of capabilities usable in NATO operations. In this case the Czechs followed the advice (Stejskal, 2013, pp 79-80).

Besides the regular design of the NDPP, a substantial part of defence policy (and relevant expertise) is articulated through 'initiatives', mostly launched based on diverse political motives. They consume a huge amount of the political and expert energy of the Alliance, like the 'NATO Response Force' concept launched at the 2002 Prague Summit or more recent initiatives 'Connected Forces' and 'Smart Defence'. These initiatives undergo a process from glorious political initiation through becoming a flagship of joint endeavour, to attracting less attention and, in some cases, fading away.

Institutions facilitating national expertise

The ministries of Defence and Foreign Affairs are the primary organisations facilitating the penetration of supranational expertise. Most of the routine expert exchange belongs to the Defence Policy and Strategy Division (SOPS) and Division of Capabilities Development and Planning (SRPS) of the General Staff. Interestingly enough, the University of Defence does not play any visible role. Outside the public administration several academic think tanks and non-governmental organisations constitute the security and defence community, which provides independent expertise, public diplomacy, dialogue and, sometimes, consultancy in the field of defence policy. The impact of this non-state expert community is limited and varies in time according to the actual openness and receptivity of the government. Even think tanks with close ties to the defence establishment do not record any remarkable success in policy formulation.

Conclusion: defence policy

The reception of supranational expertise is subject to change. This can be illustrated by the altered attitude of the Czech political elite and defence establishment towards the EU CSDP. The acceptance and will to participate in the CSDP is currently much greater due to the settled division of labour between NATO and the EU and progressive sharing of standards for capabilities planning and development in NATO and the EU. The Czech Republic supports the civilian dimension of the CSDP, deeper integration and equal access to the European defence market.

From the military point of view, during the last two decades the Czech armed forces gained full ability to participate in Allied missions. This excellent tactical experience is, however, matched with eroded experience at the operational and strategic level of warfare (Spišák, 2011). This dichotomy is present in most comparable NATO and EU countries.

Due to sustained national sovereignty over defence planning and force development, membership in such strong organisations as NATO and the EU cannot guarantee efficiency and transparency in the national defence sector. The Czech Republic has gone through decades of resource wasting and corruption because even international commitments do not prevent chaos, abuse, the lack of vision and ideas in domestic policy. The result has been a drastically decreased defence budget in the last few years followed by erosion of armed forces' capabilities.

The Alliance has almost no instruments to enforce fulfilment of the member states' commitments. In this respect, the Czech Republic has become a partially atrophied but still reliable partner. Unlike some other Allies, Czechs generally have retained the culture of transparency and consultations prior to any decision on changing or reducing their contribution to collective efforts. However, this approach of resolution more in words than in actions cannot stop the gradual cannibalising of the Alliance's overall capabilities.

Conclusions

Our analysis revealed interesting facets of the incorporation of Czech national policy-making processes into supranational contexts. Since we paid attention to just three policy fields in a time span of 25 years, there is not much space left for generalisations. Nevertheless, some tentative conclusions can be submitted for further scholarly discussion.

The concept of governance represented our theoretical starting point of reference (Pierre, 2000, p 241; Potůček, 2008a, 2008b). Both the supranational and national levels of governance proved to be relevant (Dančák and Hloušek, 2007), even though with various explanatory potentials for the different policies in question. Interestingly enough, supranational organisations played a more influential role in times of political ruptures (for example, the switch from an authoritarian to a democratic political system and from a command to a market economy) or when significant events happened or robust structural changes were prepared (such as joining NATO or the EU). National decision makers regained some of their previous political power in politically, economically or socially more stable periods - namely when the country became a full member of NATO in 1999 and of the EU in 2004.

Analysis of the interplay between the government, market and civic sector as regulators (Potůček, 1999) revealed the dominant regulatory power of the national government; the civic sector institutions influenced the policy processes only occasionally and accidentally. The role of networking was raised in characterising some grassroot programmatic initiatives, explicitly in the sectors of education and social policy. Since all three case studies dealt predominantly with the public sector, the regulatory power of the market was mentioned only in the context of socially pathological forms of regulation such as incidences of corruption in the defence sector, enabled due to inadequate laws and unethical behaviour of civil servants. The government proved to be both the leading actor, and the dominant institutional vehicle of policy changes. A more accurate conceptualisation of the role of the European Union in national policy making was coined by concepts such as 'facilitated coordination' (with its instrument, the Open Method of Coordination) and 'cultural interchange'. By the same token, the concept of 'socialisation' (Gheciu, 2005) was applied to analyse the process of moving people within the national defence establishment toward sharing, accepting and disseminating the values and norms maintained within NATO.

The influence of supranational expertise in setting specific agendas in national policy making may be illustrated using the issues of life-long learning and testing of pupils in the fifth and ninth grades of basic school in the educational policy field; politicians were awakened by poor national outcomes whereas previously they had not taken the warning voices of national experts seriously. In general, educational policies were considerably influenced by supranational expertise. In social policy less so: a mixture of supranational and national expertise was typical in this area (such as in pension reform or in fighting homelessness). Defence policy represented a special case as neither international nor national expertise had any direct impact on it.

The role of national experts and institutions in policy analysis and design should not be overestimated. Decision makers were sometimes prepared to listen to experts' advice and recommendations; sometimes they seemed to be completely deaf. Robust scientific expertise as a basis for evidence-based public policies was more an exception than a rule in post-1989 Czech policy making.[18]

Our research exercise cannot give conclusive answers for obvious reasons. There are other interesting policy fields such as economic policy, health policy and labour market policy which might deserve research attention, and their exploration might contribute to a deeper understanding of the studied processes. Comparative analysis with the developments in other countries experiencing similar structural changes to the Czech Republic might shed light on these issues as well.

Acknowledgement

The chapter was written with the financial support of PRVOUK programme P17 'Sciences of Society, Politics, and Media under the Challenge of the Times' and with the financial support of the project 'Adaptation of the Security System of the Czech Republic to Changing Economic, Social, Demographic, and Geopolitical Realities' (VG20132015112).

References

Atkinkson, A.B., Cantillon, B., Marlier, E. and Nolan, B. (2005) *Taking Forward the EU Social Inclusion Process*, Independent report commissioned by the Luxembourg Presidency of the Council of the European Union [online]. Available from www.researchgate.net/publication/247697970_Taking_Forward_the_EU_Social_Inclusion_Process

Beránková, K. (2004) 'Národní akční plán sociálního začleňování' [National Action Plan of Social Inclusion 2004–2006], *Práce a sociální politika*, MPSV.

Borkovec, Z. (2014) 'Proces vstupu ČR do NATO a jeho vliv na utváření bezpečnostního systému ČR' [The process of accession to NATO and its influence on shaping the Czech Republic security system], *Vojenské rozhledy/ Czech Military Review*, 23(1): 8-21.

Bulmer, S.J. and Radaelli, C.M. (2004) 'The Europeanisation of national policy?', *Queen's Papers on Europeanization*, No 1/2004 [online]. Available from www.qub. ac.uk/schools/SchoolofPoliticsInternationalStudiesandPhilosophy/FileStore/ EuropeanisationFiles/Filetoupload,38405,en.pdf

---

[18] A similar conclusion was drawn in the analysis of the development of strategic governance in the Czech Republic (Potůček, 2009).

Commission of the European Communities (2005) *Green Paper: Confronting Demographic Change: A New Solidarity Between the Generations* [online], Brussels: Commission of the European Communities. Available from http://ec.europa. eu/comm/employment_social/news/2005/mar/comm2005-94_en.pdf

Council (2003) *Council Conclusions of 5/6 May 2003 on Reference Levels of European Average Performance in Education and Training (Benchmarks)* [online], Brussels, 7 May, 8981/03 EDUC 83. Available from http://eur-lex.europa.eu/LexUriServ/ LexUriServ.do?uri=OJ:C:2003:134:0003:0004:EN:PDF

Council (2012) *Council Recommendation on the National Reform Programme 2012 of the Czech Republic and Delivering a Council Opinion on the Convergence Programme of the Czech Republic, 2012-2015* [online], Brussels, 6 July. Available from http://register. consilium.europa.eu/doc/srv?l=EN&t=PDF&gc=true&sc=false&f=ST%20 11248%202012%20INIT&r=http%3A%2F%2Fregister.consilium.europa. eu%2Fpd%2Fen%2F12%2Fst11%2Fst11248.en12.pdf

Council (2013) *Council Recommendation on the Czech Republic's 2013 National Reform Programme and Delivering a Council Opinion on the Czech Republic's 2013 Convergence Programme for 2012-2016* [online], Brussels, 19 July. Available from http://register.consilium.europa.eu/doc/srv?l=EN&t=PDF&gc=true&sc=f alse&f=ST%2010626%202013%20REV%201&r=http%3A%2F%2Fregister. consilium.europa.eu%2Fpd%2Fen%2F13%2Fst10%2Fst10626-re01.en13.pdf

Dančák, B. and Hloušek, V. (eds) (2007) *Víceúrovňové vládnutí v Evropě: zkušenosti, problémy a výzvy* [Multi-level governance in Europe: experiences, issues and challanges], Brno, Masarykova univerzita.

European Commission (2010) *Europe 2020: A Strategy for Smart, Sustainable and Inclusive Growth* [online], Communication from the Commission, Brussels, 3 March. Available from http://ec.europa.eu/eu2020/pdf/COMPLET%20 EN%20BARROSO%20%20%20007%20-%20Europe%202020%20-%20 EN%20version.pdf

Featherstone, K. and Radaelli, C.M. (eds) (2003) *The Politics of Europeanization*, Oxford: Oxford University Press.

Ferge, Z. (2001) 'Welfare and "ill-fare" systems in Central-Eastern Europe', in R. Sykes, B. Palier and P. Prior (eds) *Globalization and European Welfare States: Challenges and Change*, Basingstoke: Palgrave MacMillan, pp 127-52.

Gheciu, A. (2005) 'Security institutions as agents of socialization? NATO and the "New Europe"', *International Organization*, 59(4): 973-1012.

Hradecká, V. and Hradecký, I. (1996) *Bezdomovství – extrémní vyloučení* [Homelessness - extreme expulsion], Praha: Naděje.

Kotásek, J. (ed) (2001) *National Programme for the Development of Education in the Czech Republic: White Paper*, Prague: Institute for Information on Education.

Matějů, P., Ježek, F., Münich, D., Slovák, J., Straková, J., Václavík, D., Weidnerová, S. and Zrzavý, J. (2009) *White Paper on Tertiary Education*, Prague: Ministry of Education, Youth and Sports.

Ministry of Labour and Social Affairs (2004) *Joint Inclusion Memorandum*, Prague: Ministry of Labour and Social Affairs.

Ministry of Labour and Social Affairs (2005) *National Action Plan on Social Inclusion 2004–2006* [online], Prague: Ministry of Labour and Social Affairs. Available from www.mpsv.cz/files/clanky/1103/NAPSI_eng.pdf

Ministry of Labour and Social Affairs (2006) *Národní akční plan sociálního začleňování 2006–2008* [National Action Plan on Social Inclusion 2006–2008] [online], Prague: Ministry of Labour and Social Affairs. Available from www.mpsv.cz/files/clanky/9118/Narodni_zprava_2006-8.pdf (in Czech).

Ministry of Labour and Social Affairs (2008) *National Report on Strategies for Social Protection and Social Inclusion 2008-2010* [online], Prague: Ministry of Labour and Social Affairs. Available from www.mpsv.cz/files/clanky/5830/zprava_aj.pdf

Office of the Government of the Czech Republic (2005) *National Lisbon Programme 2005–2008* [online], Prague: Office of the Government of the Czech Republic. Available from www.mfcr.cz/cps/rde/xchg/mfcr/hs.xsl/cardiff_report.html

Office of the Government of the Czech Republic (2013) *National Reform Programme of the Czech Republic 2013: Growth – Competitiveness – Prosperity* [online], Office of the Government of the Czech Republic. Available from www.vlada.cz/assets/evropske-zalezitosti/dokumenty/NPR-2013-v-PDF-_AJ_.pdf

Pabian, P. (2007) 'Doporučení OECD z roku 1992 a jejich realizace v české vysokoškolské politice' [OECD recommendations of 1992 and their implementation in Czech higher education policy], *Aula – revue pro vysokoškolskou a vědní politiku*, 15(1): 67-78.

Pierre, J. (ed.) (2000) *Debating Governance. Authority, Steering, and Democracy*, Oxford: Oxford University Press.

Potůček, M. (1999) *Not only the Market. The Role of the Market, Government, and Civic Sector in the Development of Postcommunist Societies*, Budapest: CEU Press.

Potůček, M. (2004) 'Accession and social policy: the case of the Czech Republic', *Journal of European Social Policy*, 14(3): 253-66.

Potůček, M. (ed.) (2008a) *Capacities of Governance in the Czech Republic* (1st edn), Praha: Matfyzpress.

Potůček, M. (2008b) 'The concept of the neo-Weberian state confronted by the multi-dimensional concept of governance', *NISPAcee Journal of Public Administration and Public Policy*, 1(2): 83-94.

Potůček, M. (2012) 'Discourses on social rights in the Czech Republic', in A. Evers and A.M. Guillemard (eds) *Social Policy and Citizenship: The Changing Landscape*, New York: Oxford University Press, pp 335-58.

'Sociální doktrína České republiky' [Social doctrine of the Czech Republic], *Sociální politika*, 28(1-2): 7-11. Available in English from www.martinpotucek.cz; available in Czech from www.sds.cz/docs/prectete/e_kolekt/soc_dokt.htm

Spišák, J. (2011) 'Operational art in the armed forces of the Czech Republic and vision of its development', *Obrana a strategie/Defence & Strategy*, 2011(1): 101-10.

Stejskal, J. (2013) 'Obranné plánování NATO (neustále) v tranzici', *Vojenské rozhledy/Czech Military Review*, 22(3): 71-80.

SIX

Europeanised policy making in the Czech Republic and its limits

Ivo Šlosarčík

Introduction

This chapter, primarily from the perspective of new institutionalism, analyses the impact of European Union membership on the institutional and public law framework for policy making in the Czech Republic. In particular, it covers the shift from passive 'transplantation' of EU norms during the association and accession negotiations to active formulation of EU policies after the accession and the development of new Czech structures responsible for the EU agenda, including institutional competition within the Czech administration. It also explains the limits of the Europeanisation of policy making in the Czech Republic, for instance due to the lack of stability of Czech administrative structures, the dominance of the domestic political context and the limited expertise and/or self-confidence of Czech policy makers.

This chapter first maps the transformation of policy making in the Czech Republic during the pre-accession period. Afterwards, the analysis shifts to the institutional aspects of policy making after the accession to the EU and the last segment of the text focuses on three short case studies (the 2003-04 European Convention, 2009 Czech Presidency and 2010-13 Eurozone crisis) to demonstrate selected aspects of the Europeanisation of Czech policy making in practice. The chapter covers the situation in the Czech Republic until the end of 2013. Therefore, the analysis does not deal with the activities of the new government led by the social democratic leader Bohuslav Sobotka inaugurated in January 2014.

Asymmetric Europeanisation before EU accession

The Czech accession process to the EU was relatively straightforward. The Czech Republic applied for EU membership in 1996, the accession negotiations started in 1998 and were finalised at the Copenhagen summit in December 2002. After ratification of the accession treaty signed in Athens in 2003, the Czech state joined the European Union on 1 May 2004.

Due to the character of the accession negotiations (screening of Czech legislation, regular evaluation by the European Commission) the Europeanisation of Czech policy making commenced several years before the EU accession. During this period, policy making in the Czech Republic was framed in a specific way due to the asymmetrical character of Czech-EU relations. The accession process concentrated on norm transfer from the EU to the Czech Republic and the capacity of Czech institutions to implement and apply the EU acquis. During the accession process, there was relatively limited space for future EU members to negotiate (temporary) derogations from the duty to apply the EU acquis or adapt it (Inglis, 2004).

Therefore, the Europeanisation of Czech policy making in the pre-accession years focused on the implementation of the EU acquis in the Czech Republic and practical issues linked with communication between the Czech negotiating team and its EU counterpart(s). Significantly less attention was given to building up the Czech capacity to formulate and pursue its policy priorities within the EU. Consequently, the dominant impact of Europeanisation in the pre-accession period was constraints on autonomous policy making in the Czech Republic that were not compensated with possibilities to 'export' Czech policy preferences to the EU level.

From an institutional perspective, the Ministry of Foreign Affairs (MFA) played a central role. The Deputy Minister for Foreign Affairs, Pavel Telička, acted both as the chief negotiator for Czech accession to the EU and State Secretary for EU Affairs, vested with responsibility for coordination of the EU agenda in the Czech Republic. Using its expertise in diplomatic negotiations, the MFA built a relatively robust apparatus dealing with EU affairs.[1] Later, the leading position of the MFA was further strengthened by the fact that it was given a key communication role in the information campaign before the Czech accession referendum in 2003.

In the pre-accession period, the Prime Minister kept a relatively low profile in the EU policy-making area, at least compared with his role in the domestic policy-making process. A ministerial post with responsibility for EU affairs, integrated into the Prime Minister's apparatus, was created in 1998 but when its first holder, Egon Lánský, resigned in November 1999, the position remained vacant. Hence, a potential centre of coordination of EU affairs affiliated with the Prime Minister disappeared before it could develop into a competitor of the MFA. Several horizontal bodies, responsible for coordination between different ministries and other governmental agencies were also established.[2] However, they did not threaten the dominance of the MFA in EU-related policy making since the Minister of Foreign Affairs chaired the working level of these bodies (Marek and Baun, 2010, p 73).

Another institution whose role was diminished by the Europeanisation of policy making in the pre-accession period was the Parliament of the Czech Republic. Since the Czech Parliament lacked both expertise in EU affairs and direct communication

---

[1]   The MFA's units dealing with the EU agenda included the EU Relations Coordination Department (oddělení pro koordinaci vztahů s EU – OKEU), Department of European Union and Western Europe (oddělení Evropské unie a západní Evropy – EUZE) and Communication Strategy Department (oddělení komunikační strategie – OKS) (Šlosarčík and Weiss, 2007, pp 294-295).

[2]   The Governmental Committee for European Integration (Vládní výbor pro evropskou integraci) was established in 1994. In 2001, the committee was transformed into the Governmental Council for European Integration with broader coordination competencies.

channels with the EU institutions, the executive power successfully exploited these parliamentary weaknesses to reduce the role of the Czech Parliament as the agenda setter and final legislator. Instead, the parliamentary role shifted towards that of a formal legislator only that was obliged to implement the EU acquis under the direction and supervision of the EU-focused segments of the executive branch.

Another change in the Czech administration with the potential to influence EU-related policy making concerned the stability and qualification of the Czech civil service. Several years before the expected accession to the EU, the government approved a scheme for mandatory education of civil servants dealing (even potentially) with the EU agenda.[3] Even more important was the requirement of the EU that the Czech Republic should adopt legislation stabilising its civil service and protecting it from undue political interference.[4] A Civil Service Act was indeed adopted in 2002 but its application was postponed several times beyond the time horizon of the Czech accession to the EU.[5]

To sum up, in the pre-accession period, the key impact of Europeanisation on Czech policy making was a reduction in the sphere of policy-making autonomy of Czech institutions and a focus on norm import from the EU. At the same time, the accession process contributed to the emergence of 'islets of excellence' within the Czech civil service, socialised with their EU counterparts (Schimmelfennig and Sedelmeier, 2008, p 95). Simultaneously, the balance of power shifted towards the executive branch at the expense of the legislative one; and towards the MFA within the executive branch itself.

Europeanised policy making after accession: institutional structure

The transformation of Europeanised policy making in the Czech Republic after its accession to the EU can be described as a shift from 'policy taker' to 'policy maker'. While the post-accession Czech Republic continued to import a significant number of the EU norms into its domestic regulatory regime and its autonomous policy making remained constrained by the requirements of EU law, the post-accession Czech Republic gained the potential to influence the substance of the EU regulatory framework. This new dimension of the Europeanisation of Czech policy making required the building of domestic capacities to formulate

---

[3]   Usnesení vlády ČR č. 841/1999 a č. 965/2003 Sb. [Governmental regulations number 841/1999 and 965/2003 Coll.].

[4]   In particular, new legislation was expected to clarify division between 'political' and 'expert' posts within civil service where only appointment of holders of the former category of positions were expected to depend on the electoral results.

[5]   Zákon č. 218/2002 Sb., o službě státních zaměstnanců ve správních úřadech a o odměňování těchto zaměstnanců a ostatních zaměstnanců ve správních úřadech (služební zákon) (Civil Service Act). Originally, the act was expected to be effective from 1 May 2004 (that is, from the date of Czech accession to the EU) but its implementation was postponed in 2003 (by act number 281/2003 Coll.) until 2005 and then again by acts number 626/2004 Coll., number 531/2006 Coll., number 381/2008 Coll. and act number 445/2011 Coll.

Czech priorities as well as the ability to communicate Czech positions within the EU policy-making procedures.

The most visible challenge concerned the position of the MFA in the domestic policy-making process. While the centrality of the MFA's role was justifiable in the pre-accession period, due to the external character of the accession negotiations and the MFA's expertise in international treaty-making, post-accession coordination tasks were much less compatible with the MFA's institutional strengths. The bulk of the EU agenda deals with policy issues managed domestically by bodies other than the MFA that lack specific policy expertise going beyond general negotiation skills within the EU institutions. Only a limited number of issues, such as Common Foreign and Security Policy (CFSP), enlargement and development policy, correspond to the traditional foreign policy agenda vested in the MFA. This discrepancy creates a risk of the MFA turning into only a 'mail-box' responsible for communication between the EU institutions and the domestic sectorial ministries but with questionable added value for the substance of the respective policy. In addition to this structural weakness, the post-accession MFA suffered from a 'brain-drain' when many of its key experts opted for newly opened positions in the EU institutions.

This challenge was not unique for the Czech Republic. A variety of policy coordination models developed in the EU states. While the MFA retained its central role in some EU states (Denmark, Hungary, Latvia, Portugal, Spain), in others the coordination task was located in the offices of the Prime Minister (Estonia, Italy, Lithuania), the ministries of economy/finance (Germany, Greece) or an interdepartmental body with shared responsibilities (Poland, Austria, Sweden, United Kingdom, France) (Kassim, 2013, pp 285-6).

However, no coordination model for Europeanised policy making in the EU states dominates and 'the EU impact has not produced administrative convergence between the member states' (Kassim, 2013, p 284; Laffan 2008, p 133; Bursens 2008, p 119). Therefore, the post-accession Czech Republic could not simply transplant a model provided externally. The search for an optimal policy-making model was further complicated by the coalition character of governments in the Czech Republic. Since 1993, every Czech government has been of a coalition (or de facto coalition) character.[6] Usually, a junior coalition party has held the post of the Minister of Foreign Affairs while the leading political party has occupied the position of Prime Minister (see Table 6.1). Consequently, any attempt to

---

6   The following governments can be described as 'de facto coalitions'. First, the single-party (Social Democratic) minority government led by Miloš Zeman in the years 1998-2002 that was supported by the major centre-right party, the Civic Democrats, within the framework of an 'opposition agreement', officially called Agreement Establishing a Stable Political Environment in the Czech Republic (Smlouva o vytvoření stabilního politického prostředí v České republice), between the Social Democrats and the Civic Democratic Party that distributed key governmental and parliamentary positions between representatives of those two parties. Second, the relatively short-term 'caretaker' governments of 1997-98, 2009-10 and 2013-14 that were composed primarily of non-partisan experts and/or civil servants but with the political support of key political parties in the Parliament.

transfer EU-related competencies from the MFA to other governmental bodies, in particular to the Prime Minister's Office, has been interpreted by the junior coalition member not as a reform motivated by policy-making efficiency but as an attempt to shift the power balance within the governmental coalition. On several occasions, these tensions have led to the establishment of parallel structures within the civil service – most visibly in 2011-13 when the post of state secretary for EU affairs with responsibility for coordination of the EU-related policy agenda existed both within the MFA (Jiří Schneider) and the Office of the Government (Vojtěch Belling).

Table 6.1: Party affiliations of Czech prime ministers (PM), ministers of foreign affairs (MFA) and EU ministers during the years 1993-2014

	PM	MFA	EU minister
1993-97	Václav Klaus (ODS)[a]	Jiří Zieleniec (ODS)	-
1997-98	Josef Tošovský[b] (-)	Jaroslav Šedivý (-)	-
1998-2002	Miloš Zeman (SD)	Jan Kavan (SD)	Egon Lánský (SD)
2002-04	Václav Špidla (SD)	Cyril Svoboda (Chr.D)	-
2004-05	Jiří Gross (SD)	Cyril Svoboda (Chr.D)	-
2005-06	Jiří Paroubek (SD)	Cyril Svoboda (Chr.D)	-
2006	Mirek Topolánek (ODS)	Alexander Vondra (ODS)	-
2006-09	Mirek Topolánek (ODS)	Karel Schwarzenberg (Green Party)	Alexandr Vondra (ODS)
2009-10	Jan Fischer[c] (-)	Jan Kohout[d] (-)	Štefan Füle (-) Juraj Chmiel (-)
2010-13	Petr Nečas (ODS)	Karel Schwarzenberg (TOP09)	-
2013-14	Jiří Rusnok[e] (-)	Jan Kohout (-)	-
	Bohuslav Sobotka (SD)	Lubomír Zaorálek (SD)	-

Notes: [a] ODS: Civic Democratic Party (Občanská demokratická strana); (-): no political party membership; SD: Czech Social Democratic Party (Česká strana sociálně demokratická); Chr.D: Christian and Democratic Union – Czechoslovak People's Party (Křesťanská a demokratická unie – Československá strana lidová); TOP09: Tradition, Responsibility and Prosperity 2009 (Tradice, Odpovědnost, Prosperita 09).
[b] Caretaker government, appointed by President Václav Havel, composed primarily of non-party members but supported by the majority of parliamentary parties.
[c] Caretaker government, appointed by President Václav Klaus, composed primarily of non-party members but supported by the majority of parliamentary parties.
[d] Jan Kohout was a member of the Social Democratic party but he suspended his party membership during his participation in Fisher's and Rusnok's governments.
[e] Caretaker government, appointed by President Miloš Zeman. The government failed to get a vote of confidence in the Parliament and was replaced with a government led by the Social Democratic leader Bohuslav Sobotka.

In general, the trend in the post-accession period has been a gradual strengthening of the position of the Prime Minister and his governmental office. The preparations for the Presidency of the European Council and the Council of the EU, held by the Czech Republic in the first half of 2009, led to the establishment of the post of Deputy Prime Minister for EU Affairs,[7] as well as to the formation of an autonomous bureaucratic section for presidency coordination within the Office of the Government (Beneš and Karlas, 2008, p 69; Tomalová, 2008). However,

---

[7]   The post of Deputy Prime Minister for European Affairs was originally held by Alexandr Vondra and, after the resignation of the government in the middle of the EU Presidency, by the diplomats Štefan Fülle and Juraj Chmiel (with the title of Minister for European Affairs).

the MFA remained the key platform for Czech Presidency activities in the CFSP (the 2009 Presidency operated in the pre-Lisbon Treaty regime, that is with the rotating Presidency of the Foreign Affairs Council) and maintained its autonomous EU and European sections (Beneš and Braun, 2010, pp 72-3).

After the end of the EU Presidency, the ministerial post for EU affairs was abolished (in July 2010) but the new Prime Minister Petr Nečas maintained the high profile of the Office of the Government in EU-related policy making. The presidency-focused section was transformed into a general European affairs section with general policy coordination responsibilities (Beneš and Braun, 2011, p 70). The post of State Secretary (*státní tajemník*) for EU Affairs was created, despite the opposition of the MFA, within the Office of the Government in August 2011; the MFA reciprocated by appointing its own State Secretary for EU Affairs in September 2011. Although both state secretaries avoided direct open confrontation, a tension between the Prime Minister's apparatus and the MFA emerged regarding many issues, such as the (non)accession to the Fiscal Compact (Beneš and Braun, 2012, p 77). Disagreements between the Office of the Government and the MFA also existed regarding the representation of the Czech Republic in the General Affairs Council (GAC)[8] and during debates about the key strategic policy document on Czech priorities in the EU adopted in May 2013 (Beneš and Braun, 2012, pp 77-9).[9] The institutional framework for policy making was further blurred by the activities of the President of the Republic (Václav Klaus in 2003-13 and Miloš Zeman since 2013) whose formal constitutional competencies in EU affairs are relatively modest but whose influence in policy making has reached beyond the limits indicated by a simple reading of the Czech constitutional text (Šlosarčík, 2007).

In spite of the turbulent development during the first year in the European Union, the institutional framework for EU-related policy making in the Czech Republic seemed to be relatively stable by 2013. Its key elements are listed below.

The Office of the Government (*Úřad vlády*), politically and institutionally affiliated primarily with the Prime Minister, hosts the State Secretary for European Affairs who chairs the Section for European Affairs composed of four departments.[10] They are responsible for the preparation of Czech positions for the European Council as well as for more general analytical tasks and information

---

[8]   In principle, the question was whether the Czech Republic should be represented at the FAC by the Minister of Foreign Affairs (who is a cabinet minister) or by the State Secretary for European Affairs from the Office of the Government (who is a senior civil servant).

[9]   Czech Strategy in the European Union – Active Policy for Growth and a Competitive Europe (Strategie působení ČR v EU – Aktivní politika pro konkurencechopnou Evropu), 15 May 2013.

[10] European Policies Coordination Department (OKE – odbor koordinace evropských politik), Strategies and Institutional Department (OKI – odbor koncepční a institucionální), European Affairs Information Department (OEZ – odbor informvání o evropských záležitostech) and EU Economic Policy Coordination Unit (OKH – oddělení koordinace hospodářských politik EU).

activities connected with the EU. No position of Minister for EU Affairs exists; the State Secretary for European Affairs is a senior civil servant directly responsible to the prime ministers.[11]

As of 2013, the MFA has an 'unchallenged' key policy-making role in the agenda of the Common Foreign and Security Policy of the EU. In other policy areas, the MFA 'competes' with the corresponding departments of other Czech institutions, in particular with the Office of the Government regarding institutional and general EU policy coordination issues and/or the 'European units' at individual ministries in sectorial policy making.[12] The 'European Section' of the MFA covers both the bilateral relations with EU states and the 'exclusive' EU agenda.[13] The EU's Common Foreign and Security Policy issues are managed by a specific CFSP Department established within the 'Multilateral and Security Section' that also deals with international security policy outside the EU framework, such as NATO and OSCE (Organization for Security and Co-operation in Europe) cooperation, the international fight against terrorism and democratic transformation policy. Direct procedural responsibility for the EU law agenda, including the representation before the Court of Justice of the EU, is vested in a specific department within the broader legal and consular section. A specific department, established outside other sections of the MFA, is responsible for general analytical tasks, including those connected with the EU.

'European' units or departments have been established (without a homogeneous format and/or terminology) within every ministry or other central administrative body in the Czech Republic. A two-level horizontal coordination mechanism, the Committee for the European Union (*Výbor pro Evropskou unii*), was established, with responsibility for the preparation of common Czech executive positions for the European Council, the Council of the EU and COREPER (Committee of Permanent Representatives). The ministerial level of the committee (*Výbor na úrovni členů*) is presided over by the Prime Minister and involves all ministers

---

[11] In May 2014, other changes are expected in the EU Section of the Office of the Government, focused primarily on strengthening the economic governance in the EU.

[12] As of 2013, the Department of General EU Affairs (odbor pro všeobecné záležitosti EU – EUGA) is responsible for the institutional agenda, including the EU rotating presidency, and the European Policy Department (odbor evropských politik – EUPO) covers the sectorial agenda, including the Common Agricultural Policy, internal market, trade policy, environmental issues, transport and energy policies and the EU 2020 Strategy. The competition was even more intense in the past. Until the end of 2009, the MFA also had a Secretariat for the EU Presidency. In the first post-accession years (until 2007), a Department for Internal Market and Sectoral Policies (odbor vnitřního trhu a sektorových politik – OVTSP), Department of Agricultural and Trade Policy (odbor obchodní politiky a zemědělství – OPZE) and Department of Internal and External Relations of the Member States of the EU (odbor vnějších a vnitřních vztahů členských zemí Evropské unie – OVVZ) existed within the MFA, with a clear overlap of competencies with the Ministries of Industry and Trade and the Ministry of Agriculture.

[13] As already mentioned, within the European Section, two departments deal specifically with EU affairs: the EUPO and EUGA.

and representatives of several other key institutions (the Office of the President of the Republic, the Czech National Bank, the Czech Statistical Office). The working level of the committee is composed primarily of the deputy ministers responsible for the EU agenda. Its chairmanship has been transferred between different actors several times in the post-accession years; in 2013 the working level of the Council was chaired by the State Secretary for European Affairs.[14]

The institutional position of the President of the Republic in the EU agenda is relatively vague. His opinions are heard within the Committee for the European Union but the President does not have veto power there. The President's weakness in formulating a 'positive' EU agenda is underlined by the modest personnel and analytical capacity of the presidential office, compared to relatively robust teams at the Office of the Government, the MFA and other ministries. Therefore, the presidential capacity to influence EU-related policy making is primarily a 'negative' one, using his general constitutional prerogatives which limit the activity of the government and the Parliament, such as presidential vetoes of legislation (even that implementing the EU rules) or referrals to the Constitutional Court. The President also appoints members of the Governing Board (*Bankovní rada*) of the Czech National Bank, thus influencing, at least indirectly, the position of Czech central bankers on the Eurozone agenda.

As mentioned in the section on the pre-accession period, the Parliament of the Czech Republic was weakened by the Europeanisation of Czech policy making. The government was originally only obliged to inform the Parliament 'regularly and in advance' about issues connected with Czech membership in the EU. During the ratification of the Lisbon Treaty, the Parliament used its constitutional competences to suspend the ratification process to force the government to accept further extension of parliamentary powers in general EU policy making. Therefore, in 2013 the government is obliged to respect a parliamentary veto over the most serious decisions in the European Council (for example use of the passerelle clause in the CFSP or simplified amendment of the treaties) or the Council of the EU (for example activation of the flexibility clause).[15] The Parliament is also empowered (using the apparatus of the MFA) to trigger an annulment action before the Court of Justice of the EU for violation of the subsidiarity principle by EU legislation.[16] Last but not least, the Lisbon Treaty has directly strengthened the position of the Czech Parliament by creating a direct communication channel between national parliaments and the European

---

[14] The working level of the Council of the EU was originally (until 2007) chaired by the Minister of Foreign Affairs (or the Deputy Minister), later by the Minister for European Affairs and finally by the State Secretary for European Affairs.

[15] Rules of Procedure of the Assembly of Deputies, article 109j.

[16] Rules of Procedure of the Assembly of Deputies, articles 109d–109h.

Commission.[17] At the same time, the Parliament has built its own autonomous analytical structure (*Parlamentní institut*) independent from the executive power. In spite of all the changes mentioned earlier, the parliamentary role in post-accession policy making remains a 'negative one' - that is, constraining the freedom of action of the Czech government at the EU level.

Czech accession to the EU has also influenced the judiciary, albeit with relatively modest intensity. The autonomy of Czech courts to interpret Czech law has been limited by the obligation of the Czech judiciary to apply the EU norms, including the interpretations provided by the case law of the Court of Justice of the European Union in Luxemburg. On the other hand, by virtue of EU membership, Czech courts were provided with the capacity to ignore those Czech laws colliding with directly applicable EU norms and with the possibility to bypass more senior courts via preliminary questions sent to the EU Court (Kühn and Bobek, 2010; Šlosarčík, 2013).

The practice of Europeanised policy making after accession

The Convention on the Future of Europe and the 'kindergarten' of post-enlargement policy making

The Convention on the Future of Europe (2002-03) was an institutional experiment aimed at transparency and reduction of the democratic deficit in the EU treaty making process. The Convention was held before the EU enlargement in 2004 but the candidate countries were invited to participate in the Convention's work. For the Czech Republic, it was the first occasion to express its preferences on the future development of the EU, in contrast to simply adapting to the existing EU acquis in the accession process.

The Czech political elite was split regarding its preferred vision of the future of European integration. With the objective of avoiding the marginalisation of any relevant political opinion, the Czech Republic opted for a decentralised and virtually non-coordinated format of its representation within the Convention. The Czech Republic was entitled to send six representatives (three full members and three deputy members) to the Convention, two-thirds of them representing the legislative branch and the rest the government. The final format of the Czech representation was a compromise aspiring to provide space for all significant approaches to European integration in the Czech political debate. The executive power was represented by the Deputy Minister of Foreign Affairs, Jan Kohout, the Assembly of Deputies by Jan Zahradil and the Senate by Josef Zieleniec. Hence, all three major EU-related ideological groups in the Czech polity – the centre-left Euro-federalist (Kohout), centre-right Euro-federalist (Zieleniec) and

---

[17] Article 12 TEU, in combination with Protocol Number 1 on the Role of National Parliaments in the European Union and Protocol Number 2 on the Application of the Principles of Subsidiarity and Proportionality, attached to the Lisbon Treaty.

centre-right Eurosceptic (Zahradil) were represented at the Convention, including the political views of the then opposition.

However, the impact of the Convention on Czech policy making after enlargement was only limited. Virtually no coordination between Czech representatives emerged afterwards. Consequently, Czech representatives at the Convention presented radically different views; for example, Mr. Zahradil signed the dissenting report to the draft Constitution for Europe Treaty adopted by the Convention. Consequently, the Convention's follow-up leading to the adoption of the Treaty establishing a Constitution for Europe in 2004 and, after the French and Dutch referenda in 2005, the Lisbon Treaty in 2007, excluded the political opposition from the decision-making process; the opposition reciprocated by challenging the Lisbon Treaty before the Constitutional Court. Therefore, the Convention experience serves primarily as an example of a failed attempt at a broader and more inclusive approach to policy making in the Czech Republic.

The Czech 2009 Presidency as a catalyst for the Europeanisation of policy making

In the pre-Lisbon Treaty European Union, the rotating presidency of the European Council and the Council of the EU was a key element of the EU policy cycle. The presidency enhanced the visibility of a member state both inside and outside the (pre-Lisbon Treaty) European Union. At the same time, the rotating presidency tested the administrative capacity of the presidency state as well as the capacity of its politicians to act on the EU level (Karlas, 2008).

The Czech Presidency was scheduled for the first half of 2009. As already mentioned earlier in this chapter, the Presidency was used as justification for a power shift of the EU agenda from the MFA to the Prime Minister's Office. The most important challenge for Czech policy makers, however, was the expectation of a more active role in policy making at the EU level during the Presidency, both from the strategic (setting presidency priorities) and tactical (facilitating negotiations within the Council and representing the EU externally) perspectives. The Czech centre-right government with strong Eurosceptic tones, which was in power from 2007 to 2009, opted for a low-profile Presidency with relatively narrowly defined priorities (Drulák, 2008), focused on the removal of the remaining barriers within the internal market and the Eastern dimension of EU foreign policy (Král et al, 2009, pp 42-56). In contrast to the Convention period, the role of the parliamentary opposition was only marginal and there was no 'toleration' agreement between the government and the opposition concluded for the Presidency period (Beneš and Karlas, 2010, p 71).

However, the Presidency agenda was modified (or even 'hijacked') by unexpected events during the Czech Presidency, in particular by a gas dispute between Russia and Ukraine in January 2009 that caused a gas supply crisis in a substantial number of EU states. Therefore, a substantial segment of the Presidency activities shifted from strategic tasks to crisis management from the very beginning of 2009. Further, a relatively unimportant skirmish between the government and the opposition in March 2009 resulted in a parliamentary vote of no confidence in Topolánek's government and its consequent resignation in the middle of the Czech Presidency. A caretaker government, led by the former chairman of the Czech Statistical Office, was appointed for the rest of the Presidency. The Presidency, without strong political leadership, then moved to a 'survival' mode. A commentary on the performance of the Czech Presidency thus posed the ironic but legitimate question of whether the Czech Presidency was more a 'crisis management' or a 'management crisis' (Král et al, 2009, p 68).

Hence, the Czech Republic used the potential offered by the 2009 Presidency to a limited extent only. However, the Presidency demonstrated the crucial importance of the domestic political environment for Europeanised policy making as well as the interconnection with external events outside Czech control, such as the delayed ratification of the Lisbon Treaty, the forthcoming EP elections and political crises outside the EU.

The Eurozone crisis as the ultimate test of Europeanised Czech policy making

Due to a transition regime in the accession treaty, the Czech Republic did not join the Eurozone immediately after its EU accession in 2004. However, no permanent opt-out from monetary integration has been negotiated by the Czech Republic. Therefore, the Czech authorities have been obliged to take active steps towards compliance with the Eurozone convergence criteria and, ultimately, to replace the national currency with the euro.

In the years following accession, the government's strategic policy documents indeed contained an indicative date for Eurozone accession. With the arrival of new, more Eurosceptic, governments, those target dates disappeared (Šlosarčík et al, 2011, pp 101-2). Later, a referendum on Eurozone accession was even contemplated, regardless of its potential conflict with EU law.[18] The reasons behind this development are rooted in both Czech institutional design and the Eurozone crisis of 2010-13.

The Czech institutional framework for monetary and fiscal policies, albeit also Europeanised, is significantly different from that applicable in other policy areas. In addition to the obvious role of the Office of the Government and the MFA, the Czech National Bank (*Česká národní banka*) and the Ministry of Finance are strong actors in this area. Furthermore, the President of the Republic has a strong role, due to his exclusive competence to appoint members of the central bank's board. During the 2010-13 Eurozone crisis, the Prime Minister was the

---

[18] The accession treaty, technically, does not provide any space for a referendum on Eurozone accession since the Czech Republic only has a temporary exemption from the Eurozone rules. However, Prime Minister Petr Nečas, supporting the referendum idea, argued that the Eurozone project the Czech Republic agreed to join in the Accession Treaty (signed in 2003) is significantly different from the Eurozone in 2013; thus the Czech Republic might not be bound by its promise dating back to the year 2003 due to a fundamental change of circumstances.

leader of the Civic Democratic party, representatives of the second coalition party (TOP09) chaired the MFA and the Ministry of Finance while the central bank's board was filled with persons appointed by President Václav Klaus, the most prominent critic of the Eurozone project among Czech politicians. This combination provided for a potentially explosive mix of actors and processes.

At the EU level, the public finance crisis in several Eurozone countries (Greece, Ireland, Portugal, Italy, Spain, Cyprus) led to a profound transformation of the Eurozone rules. The transformation contained its short-term 'crisis management' element in the form of financial assistance to problematic Eurozone states as well as strengthening of long-term economic governance in the Eurozone. The catalogue of new Eurozone rules varied regarding innovativeness, legal form and inclusivity of non-Eurozone EU members. What the new initiatives shared was a significant element of improvisation, unpredictability and a rather cavalier approach to interpretation of the pre-crisis EU law (Louis, 2010; Ruffert, 2011; De Gregorio Merino, 2012).

The behaviour of the Czech Republic during the Eurozone crisis can be summarised as refusal to participate in those new EU initiatives where Czech absence did not block the initiative itself. Therefore, the Czech Republic did not block creation of the European Financial Stability Mechanism (EFSM), the reform of the Stability and Growth Pact ('six-pack') or the fast-track amendment of the Lisbon Treaty that inserted a 'bail-out' paragraph into article 136 Treaty on the Functioning of the European Union. At the same time, the Czech representation chose not to participate in the Euro Plus Pact and the Fiscal Compact, although they were opened to non-Eurozone states.

However, the internal formation of the Czech position was far more contested than the external perspective indicates. The MFA preferred a more inclusive approach than the Office of the Government, fearing diplomatic isolation of the Czech Republic in other policy areas, in particular the potential spill-over into debates on the 2014-20 financial perspective. For instance, two analyses of the Fiscal Compact prepared by the Office of the Government in 2012 stressed its legal shortcomings and ambivalences while the policy document prepared by the MFA found no significant problems related to compatibility of the Fiscal Compact with the Czech legal order and/or EU law (Francová et al, 2012). Paradoxically, the centre-right coalition government agreed in general terms with the content and objective of the majority of new EU initiatives. Therefore, while rejecting the Europeanised format of strengthened fiscal control over EU states, the Czech government pursued a fiscal policy of austerity inspired by the new Eurozone governance and even contemplated the establishment of a fiscal brake in the Czech Republic, similar to those required by new EU initiatives.

The Czech approach to Eurozone accession and new tools for Eurozone governance thus can be described as examples of minimalism in Europeanised policy making. In these areas, Czech elites opted for the least ambitious policy threshold acceptable to other EU partners. The reasons behind this policy style are primarily the lack of self-confidence of the Czech political representation to pursue Czech priorities at the EU level, particularly within the vague and unpredictable regulatory framework formed during the Eurozone crisis. In this regard, the Czech Republic differed significantly from several other EU states outside the Eurozone, such as Poland. Secondly, the institutional design and continuing opt-out from the Eurozone enabled the Czech Republic to pursue its policy minimalism without triggering significant political pressure from other EU states; in this regard, the Czech Republic's position particularly differed from Slovakia where reluctance to ratify an amendment of the European Financial Stability Facility in 2011 led to a political crisis and early elections due to criticism from the rest of the Eurozone.

Conclusion

The Europeanisation of Czech policy making started several years before the EU accession, within the framework of the association regime and the accession talks. The first phase of the Europeanisation of Czech policy making was an asymmetric process focused on the capacity to implement and apply existing EU norms while the capacity to identify the Czech Republic's own policy priorities was neglected. The second element of Europeanisation, the bottom-up process of formulation and pursuit of Czech policy preferences at the EU level, developed only later, when the negotiations leading to the adoption of the Lisbon Treaty, the 2009 Czech Presidency and the Eurozone crisis provided the most significant learning experiences for Czech policy makers but also demonstrated the limits of the Europeanisation of policy making in the Czech Republic.

Two phases of the Europeanisation of Czech policy making were reflected in the domestic institutional structure. In the pre-accession phase, the MFA was the winner in the transformation process, primarily at the expense of the Office of the Government and the Parliament. After the accession to the EU, the Prime Minister gradually regained his traditional prominence in the policy-making process, including the Europeanised elements. However, the institutional shift and fine-tuning was driven primarily by the coalition character of the government (the party affiliations of the Prime Minister and Minister of Foreign Affairs) and the EU-framed agenda (the Presidency, the Eurozone crisis), not by domestic policy-making considerations.

This chapter also mapped the factors limiting the Europeanisation of Czech policy making. The first was a lack of expertise and self-confidence in dealing with the complex and non-predictable EU agenda, beyond everyday EU business, that led Czech policy makers to resort to 'policy minimalism' during the Eurozone crisis. Another factor limiting the Europeanisation of Czech policy making has been the activities of domestic actors excluded from direct 'positive' policy making within the EU sphere, such as the President or the parliamentary opposition, who have used their domestic constitutional competencies immune from EU influence, such as referrals to the constitutional court or votes of non-confidence in the government, to constrain governmental activities within the EU sphere.

Acknowledgement

The chapter was written with the financial support of PRVOUK programme P17 'Sciences of Society, Politics, and Media under the Challenge of the Times'.

References

Beneš, V. and Braun, M. (2010) 'Evropský rozměr české zahraniční politiky' [European dimension of Czech foreign policy], in M. Kořán (ed) *Česká zahraniční politika v roce 2009* [Czech foreign policy in 2009], Praha: Ústav mezinárodních vztahů, pp 61-90.

Beneš, V. and Braun, M. (2011) 'Evropský rozměr české zahraniční politiky' [European dimension of Czech foreign policy], in M. Kořán (ed) *Česká zahraniční politika v roce 2010* [Czech foreign policy in 2010], Praha: Ústav mezinárodních vztahů, pp 57-91.

Beneš, V. and Braun, M. (2012) 'Evropský rozměr české zahraniční politiky' [European dimension of Czech foreign policy], in M. Kořán and O. Ditrych (eds) *Česká zahraniční politika v roce 2011* [Czech foreign policy in 2011], Praha: Ústav mezinárodních vztahů, pp 67-94.

Beneš, V. and Karlas, J. (2008) 'Evropský rozměr české zahraniční politiky' [European dimension of Czech foreign policy], in M. Kořán (ed) *Česká zahraniční politika v roce 2007* [Czech foreign policy in 2007], Praha: Ústav mezinárodních vztahů, pp 61-91.

Beneš, V. and Karlas, J. (2010) 'The Czech presidency', *Journal of Common Market Studies*, 48 (Annual Review): 69-80.

Bursens, P. (2008) 'State structures', in P. Graziano and M. Vink (eds) *Europeanization. New Research Agenda*, Houndmills: Palgrave, pp 115-27.

De Gregorio Merino, A. (2012) 'Legal developments in the economic and monetary union during the debt crisis: the mechanism of financial assistance', *Common Market Law Review*, 49(5): 1613-46.

Drulák, P. (2008) 'Možnosti nízkoprofilového předsednictví' [Potential of a low profile presidency], in J. Karlas (ed) *Jak Předsedat Evropské unii. Návrh priorit předsednictví ČR v Radě EU v roce 2009* [How to preside over the European Union. Proposal of priorities for Czech EU Council presidency in 2009], Praha: Ústav mezinárodních vztahů, pp 136-43.

Francová, J., Palán, J. and Ficner, F. (2012) 'Komentář k návrhu Smlouvy o stabilitě, koordinaci a správě v hospodářské a měnové unii' [Commentary on the proposal of a treaty on stability, coordination and governance in the Economic and Monetary Union], in L. Pítrová (ed) *Fiskální pakt: Právní a ekonomické souvislosti a důsledky přijetí Smlouvy o stabilitě, koordinaci a správě v hospodářské a měnové unii* [Fiscal compact: legal and economic consequences of adoption of treaty on stability, coordination and governance in the Economic and Monetary Union], Praha: Karolinum, pp 153-82.

Inglis, K. (2004) 'The accession treaty and its transitional arrangements: a twilight zone for the new members of the Union', in C. Hillion (ed) *EU Enlargement. A Legal Approach*, Oxford: Hart Publishing, pp 77-110.

Karlas, J. (2008) 'Předsednictví Rady EU – funkce, cíle, forma a vliv' [EU Council presidency - function, objectives, form and influence], in J. Karlas (ed) *Jak předsedat Evropské unii. Návrh priorit předsednicví ČR v Radě EU v roce 2009* [How to preside over the European Union. Proposal of priorities for Czech EU Council presidency in 2009], Praha: Ústav mezinárodních vztahů, pp 17-32.

Kassim, H. (2013) 'Europeanization and member state institutions', in S. Bulmer and C. Lequesne (eds) *The Member States of the European Union* (2nd edn), Oxford: Oxford University Press, pp 279-312.

Král, D., Bartovic, V. and Řiháčková, V. (2009) *The 2009 Czech EU Presidency: Contested Leadership at a Time of Crisis*, Stockholm: SIEPS.

Kühn, Z. and Bobek, M. (2010) 'What about that "incoming tide"? The application of EU law in Czech Republic', in A. Lazowski (ed) *The Application of EU Law in the New Member States*, Hague: Asser Press, pp 325-55.

Laffan, B. (2008) 'Core executives', in P. Graziano and M. Vink (eds) *Europeanization. New Research Agenda*, Houndmills: Palgrave, pp 128-40.

Louis, J.V. (2010) 'The no-bailout clause and rescue packages', *Common Market Law Review*, 47(4): 971-86.

Marek, D. and Baun, M. (2010) *Česká republika a Evropská unie* [Czech Republic and European Union], Brno: Barrister & Principal.

Ruffert, M. (2011) 'The European debt crisis and European Union law', *Common Market Law Review*, 48(6): 1777-806.

Schimmelfennig, F. and Sedelmeier, U. (2008) 'Candidate countries and conditionality', in P. Graziano and M. Vink (eds) *Europeanization. New Research Agenda*, Houndmills: Palgrave, pp 88-101.

Šlosarčík, I. (2007) 'The President of the Czech Republic and the European integration: the constitutional framework and the constitutional practice', *EU-CONSENT Annual Working Paper*, Köln, pp 1-16.

Šlosarčík, I. (2013) 'Czech Republic 2009-2012: on unconstitutional amendment of the constitution, limits of EU law and direct presidential elections', *European Public Law*, 19(3): 435-47.

Šlosarčík, I. and Weiss, T. (2007) 'Česká republika a EU. Zvykání si v nové roli' [Czech Republic and European Union. Adaptation to a new role], in L. Rovná, Z. Kasáková and J. Váška (eds) *Evropská unie v členských státech a členské státy v Evropské unii* [European Union in member states and member states in European Union], Praha: VIP Books, pp 287-309.

Šlosarčík, I., Kasáková, Z., Váška, J. and Weiss, T. (2011) 'Fragmentation and coexistence of Leitbilder in the Czech Republic', in G. Brincker, M. Jopp and L. Rovná (eds) *Leitbilder for the Future of the European Union*, Baden-Baden: Nomos, pp 74-119.

Tomalová, E. (2008) 'Koordinační mechanismus předsednictví ČR v Radě EU' [Coordination mechanism for Czech EU Council presidency], in J. Karlas (ed) *Jak předsedat Evropské unii. Návrh priorit předsednicví ČR v Radě EU v roce 2009* [How to preside over the European Union. Proposal of priorities for Czech EU Council presidency in 2009], Praha: Ústav mezinárodních vztahů, pp 120-35.

SEVEN

Policy analysis and policy work in the central public administration

Arnošt Veselý, Martin Nekola

Introduction

Ministries are somewhat enigmatic institutions for many people. Ministerial officials are usually guarded from ordinary citizens by reception clerks who reject all unauthorised visitors. Information on what concrete tasks are undertaken in a given ministry and which members of staff are responsible for them is often restricted. Not surprisingly, then, research on what ministerial officials do is rather limited. This is especially true for countries such as the Czech Republic where until recently only very little and rather anecdotal evidence was available (Drulák et al, 2003; Scherpereel, 2004).

In this chapter we open the black box of the Czech ministries and we try to describe the ministerial policy bureaucrats and what they do.[1] We draw especially on a survey organised by the authors of this chapter between April and July 2013. Eleven ministries out of 14 agreed to participate in the survey. A total of 1351 complete questionnaires were obtained, and the response rate was 29.4% (see Veselý, 2013 for an in-depth description of the methodology of this research).[2] Of course, the empirical evidence can always be analysed and interpreted against

---

[1] Various authors use different labels for people involved in policy design and policy making. Melsiner (1975) wrote about 'bureaucratic policy analysts', Page and Jenkins (2005) used the term 'policy bureaucracy' and 'policy bureaucrats', Howlett sometimes uses the term 'public sector analysts' (Howlett, 2009), while in more recent articles he follows Colebatch (2006) and calls them 'policy workers' (Howlett et al 2014). With the exception of referring to the particular work of other authors, where we use their labels, in this chapter we use 'policy bureaucrats' (abbreviated as 'PBs'; ministerial policy bureaucrats – 'MPBs' and regional policy bureaucrats – 'RPBs'). For further discussion, see Veselý (2013).

[2] We used negative criteria for inclusion in the sample frame. First the list of all public officials working for the ministries/regional offices was created and then from this full list those fulfilling the criteria for non-inclusion were excluded. Those who focused on the inner functioning of the office only were also excluded: that is those persons working in secretariats and departments responsible for management of the regional offices: financial/economic, investment and IT departments, business licensing authorities, technical maintenance and drivers. The reason for this procedure is that in the Czech Republic no such position as 'policy analyst' (or similar) exists and it was unclear who a priori counts as a 'policy worker'. So we aimed at all officials who are at least partly involved in any type of policy-related work.

different 'baselines'. In this chapter we take as a point of reference similar research conducted in the Czech Regional Authorities (*kraje*) between September and November 2012 (N = 783, response rate of 32.4%; see Chapter Eight for a description of this survey).

The Central Public Administration of the Czech Republic

The organisation and functioning of the central state administration is defined by Act number 2/1969 Collection, on the Establishment of Ministries and Other Central Bodies of State Administration of the Czech Republic as modified by later amendments. This so-called Competence Act (CA) currently establishes 14 ministries and 11 other bodies of central state administration (such as the Office of the Government and the Czech Statistical Office). The central state administration also includes various administrative bodies with nationwide responsibilities, subordinated to one of the ministries, which are not mentioned in the law (for example the Czech Trade Inspection Authority and the Central Land Office). In this chapter we will focus upon the ministries because they are arguably the most important institutions in terms of policy analysis and policy work in general. In contrast to most other central organisations, they prepare legislation and policy proposals, and they are also responsible for coordinating the policy work within the central public administration.

The Czech Republic is the only European Union country which at the moment of this writing lacks an effective civil service law, even though its creation and implementation had been a condition for Czech accession to the EU.[3] The nature of ministries' work is thus defined in the Competence Act mentioned earlier and partly also in the Labour Code. While the text of the CA is relatively brief and abstract, it does prescribe a highly diverse array of responsibilities for the different ministries. They are for instance obliged to coordinate the individual bodies of public administration, prepare conceptual and strategic documents for their policy domains, prepare and table draft laws, provide information and methodological guidance, negotiate agreements, direct government inspection in specific areas and so on.

Profile of policy bureaucrats in ministries

Table 7.1 shows a comparison between ministerial (MPBs) and regional policy bureaucrats (RPBs) according to a series of parameters. Although most of the differences are statistically significant, they vary in magnitude. What stands out at first sight is the difference in gender ratio: equal numbers of men and women work in Czech ministries, while the majority in regional offices are women (62%).

---

[3]   The Civil Service Act was approved by the Parliament as Act number 218/2002 Coll.; however, its coming into force has been postponed several times, and has never been effective.

Table 7.1: A profile of ministerial and regional officials

Variable	Ministries			Regional offices			Labels
	N	Mean	SD	N	Mean	SD	
Gender**	1343	0.50	0.50	783	0.62	0.49	0 = male 1 = female
Age**	1337	43.43	12.43	783	41.38	10.81	Respondent's age
Education**	1349	4.80	0.97	783	4.60	1.01	1 = primary + lower secondary (without GCSE) 2 = secondary, vocational, with GCSE 3 = secondary, general, with GCSE 4 = tertiary, bachelor's degree or lower 5 = tertiary, master's degree 6 = tertiary, doctorate
Years spent in public administration**	1348	11.95	9.70	783	10.32	7.77	How many years have you been working in public administration? each of 1-30 individually, more than 30
Years spent with present employer	1346	2.73	0.99	783	2.70	0.90	1 = less than 1 year 2 = 1-5 years 3 = 6-10 years 4 = more than 10 years
Plans to stay with present employer (years)**	1007	3.27	1.21	537	3.79	1.16	How many more years do you intend to remain in your job with your present employer 1 = less than 1 year 2 = 1-2 years 3 = 3-5 years 4 = 6-10 years 5 = more than 10 years
Prior work experience							
Academia**	1349	0.08	0.271	783	0.05	0.212	0 = no, 1 = yes
Ministries**	1349	0.12	0.330	783	0.04	0.204	0 = no, 1 = yes
Bodies of central government other than ministry**	1349	0.24	0.430	783	0.07	0.262	0 = no, 1 = yes
Regional (or district) offices**	1349	0.06	0.232	783	0.22	0.417	0 = no, 1 = yes
Other bodies of regional government**	1349	0.04	0.189	783	0.06	0.242	0 = no, 1 = yes
NGO sector	1349	0.06	0.244	783	0.06	0.233	0 = no, 1 = yes
Business sector**	1349	0.43	0.495	783	0.25	0.433	0 = no, 1 = yes
Foreign/international bodies of public administration**	1349	0.03	0.163	783	0.00	0.051	0 = no, 1 = yes
No prior work experience	1349	0.15	0.355	783	0.13	0.331	0 = no, 1 = yes

Note: $*p \leq 0.05$; $**p \leq 0.01$; independent t-test (2 tailed).

MPBs are on average two years older than RPBs, which could be due to the fact that regional offices are historically much younger institutions than ministries, and when they came into being in 2000 they not only took over the staff of the abolished lower administrative level offices (*okresní úřady*), but also recruited a significant share of fresh, mostly young, workers. In general, in ministries there is a large group of officials at pre-retirement or retirement age but the age structure of ministerial staff is weaker in the middle generation.

Both MPBs and RPBs are generally well educated, with more than 90% of MPBs having at least a bachelor's degree. There are more workers with doctorates in the ministries (13%) than in the regions (6%). Both these numbers are quite high, given the total number of PhDs in the Czech workforce. Undoubtedly, the generally high levels of education among PBs are caused by the fact that a university degree is a typical job requirement; it remains difficult to interpret the high proportion of officials with a PhD degree.

The surveys also included a question about the number of years spent in the civil service. Since the MPBs are generally older, it is not surprising that they have also worked as civil servants for more years. Nevertheless, MPBs and RPBs have on average spent the same number of years at the present ministry or regional office respectively. Further analysis revealed a higher variance of this parameter among MPBs, with larger groups of those who have been at the ministry for less than six years or more than ten years. This suggests the existence of at least two typical categories of ministerial workers in terms of their history in the present institution: long-serving 'veterans' and a large group of relative 'freshmen'. The middle group of officials who have worked at the ministry for six to ten years is relatively small, compared to the regional level.

In general, the jobs of ministerial officials are more precarious – that is, affected by higher levels of fluctuation – than jobs in the regional offices. This interpretation is further supported by data about individual plans to stay with the present employer. On average, MPBs are planning to stay fewer years, with as many as 7% planning to leave in less than a year, and only 22% of MPBs maintaining a long-term perspective of more than ten years (compared to 39% of RPBs). This may be caused by several factors. First, due to the absence of an effective Civil Service Act or other obstacles, young people may find few prospects in their ministerial jobs. Also, because all the ministries are located in Prague with its rather abundant job opportunities, a large group of young MPBs may consider public service merely as a start-up job bridging the time between university and a more desirable stage of their professional career. In contrast, since there are fewer opportunities for highly qualified workers in the regional capitals, a regional office job may represent one of the few stable career prospects for people with a university degree (or even a PhD).

Another question concerned the officials' prior career histories. As hypothesised, MPBs are somewhat more likely than RPBs to have an academic job on their resume. Not surprisingly, MPBs are more likely to have prior work experience in central government administration. The two levels of government have equal percentages of officials without prior work experience (who came straight from university) or with experience from the NGO sector. Surprisingly, a relatively high number of MPBs have experience in the business sector (43%, compared to 25% of RPBs). This finding is difficult to interpret and contradicts the common stereotype of 'career bureaucrats' who join the ranks of the civil service immediately after university and remain completely untouched by business experience.

Policy work in ministries

Tasks and activities

The work of ministries goes far beyond the 'mere' drafting of regulations and the administration of diverse forms and documents. Indeed, empirical evidence from other countries suggests that ministerial MPBs are no longer (if they ever were) just bureaucrats stamping and circulating documents. In fact, they 'have numerous tasks including formal analysis, writing reports, managing the demands of the governmental process and above all, interacting with other players involved in the issue' (Colebatch et al, 2010, p 15). The work of PBs at both central and regional levels includes drafting legislation, writing policy papers, implementing various programmes and projects, monitoring the work of lower-level bodies, formulating official positions on various issues. This is an immensely heterogeneous mix of tasks (Radin, 2013).

In this chapter, we are primarily interested in the two categories of tasks which are most relevant from the perspective of this book. The first concerns analytical activities typical for 'traditional' policy analysis, such as problem definition, identification of alternative solutions, evaluation of such options and recommendations on what (or what not) to do (for example Dunn, 2004; see also Chapter One). Traditional policy analysis is based on the assumption that what politicians (or policy makers in general) need for making a decision is a piece of frank and faithful advice derived from systematic analysis and based on the best available evidence. The main idea of this rational account can be expressed by the motto, 'speaking truth to power', in which truth stands for maximum objectiveness. As explained in Chapter One, in the Czech Republic, as in other Central and Eastern European (CEE) countries, policy analysis is barely established as a discipline, and the term policy analysis can have different meanings. Nevertheless, we assume that the actual work of ministerial (and regional) PBs in the Czech Republic also includes those tasks that can be subsumed under traditional policy analysis – that is, gathering data and relevant information, defining problems, identifying alternative solutions, selecting options and formulating recommendations.

The other type of tasks on which we focus in this chapter consists of communication and negotiation with other actors. As many authors have noted, merely 'speaking truth to power' often does not result in better policy choices.[4] The policy process is typically not so much about 'finding the truth' but also about finding a consensus, or reconciling different interests, values and beliefs. In the words of Robert Hoppe (1999), 'making sense together' is at least as important as rational and objective policy advice. In this respect, many authors argue that it is increasingly important to communicate with other actors in public administration and beyond, while tasks such as data analysis or cost-benefit evaluation of policy options are receiving less attention (Colebatch and Radin, 2006).

Our data enables us to analyse to what extent the Czech PBs are analysts and/ or communicators.[5] Table 7.2 shows the proportion of different bureaucratic tasks done in ministries and regional offices measured by simple and rather broad multiple choice questions (that is, check all that apply). The most common task for both MPBs and RPBs is communication with other bodies of public administration and with non-state organisations (from the business or Non-governmental organization [NGO] sectors). The second most common are routine administrative tasks which are reported by more than half of PBs. Approximately half of MPBs are somehow involved in analyses for decision making (problem analyses, needs assessments, economic analyses, policy recommendations) and preparing the conceptual and strategic policy documents of the ministry. On the contrary, only about one-fifth of PBs are involved in budgeting and providing advice for the political leadership of the ministry.

Only a few tasks are undertaken to the same extent by both MPBs and RPBs, including budgeting and communication with other bodies of the public sector or with NGOs, and also the preparation of conceptual/strategic policy documents. In all other aspects, ministerial and regional bureaucratic work differs. More MPBs seem to be involved in routine administration on one hand, but they also participate in more analytical tasks on the other. Given the number of RPBs involved in administrative tasks, we can conclude that there are more workers doing policy analysis to some extent at ministries than at regional offices. Also, the central administration requires more people to work on legal analyses than the regional one. There, as expected, tasks related to policy implementation (management, monitoring, direct communication with the public) outdo those at the ministerial level. However, it is surprising that more regional than ministerial

---

[4] Traditional policy analysis has also been criticised from epistemological perspectives. However, for the purpose of the present discussion, we take the liberty of leaving the questions about the nature of 'objective knowledge' aside.

[5] First, the respondents were presented with a list of tasks and asked whether or not they were personally involved in each of them (Table 7.2). This was a dichotomous (yes/no), multiple-choice question (respondents were free to tick as many options as they wanted). Inspired by Canadian surveys, the second item consisted of a set of question measuring the frequency of involvement in each type of activities (Table 7.3). The wording of the questions was identical for MPBs and RPBs, with only a few minor exceptions. Apart from these exceptions, all items are directly and fully comparable.

Table 7.2: Tasks undertaken by policy bureaucrats

Variable	Ministries			Regional offices		
	N	Mean	SD	N	Mean	SD
Communication with other bodies of public administration and with non-state organisations (from the business or NGO sectors)	1351	0.66	0.475	783	0.67	0.469
Routine administrative tasks[**]	1351	0.60	0.491	783	0.51	0.500
Analyses for decision making (problem analyses, needs assessments, economic analyses, policy recommendations)[**]	1351	0.50	0.500	783	0.41	0.492
Preparing conceptual and strategic policy documents of the ministry/region[*]	1351	0.46	0.499	783	0.45	0.498
Methodological guidance, training or lecturing[**]	1351	0.35	0.477	783	0.49	0.500
Direction and monitoring (of lower-level bodies or concrete programmes)[**]	1351	0.33	0.469	783	0.39	0.487
Direct communication with citizens[**]	1351	0.29	0.453	783	0.43	0.496
Administrative tasks[**]	1351	0.25	0.433	783	0.44	0.497
Legal analyses[**]	1351	0.22	0.415	783	0.10	0.298
Budgeting	1351	0.18	0.388	783	0.21	0.406
Advice for political leadership of the ministry/political bodies of the region[**]	1351	0.16	0.369	783	0.22	0.414

Note: [*]$p \leq 0.05$; [**] $p \leq 0.01$; independent t-test (2 tailed); ordered according to frequencies of tasks in ministries.
Multiple choice, dichotomous variable where 0 = NO and 1 = YES.
Activities with significantly higher scores are shaded.

PBs are, to some extent, involved in advising political leaders, apparently pointing to more direct politico-administrative relations at the regional level.

Table 7.3 provides a more detailed picture of policy work activities, reporting answers to the question 'How often do you deal with any of the following activities?' Both MPBs and RPBs spent most of their working time on activities that come under the rubric of traditional policy analysis – that is, identification of possible solutions, problem identification, collection of data and information and evaluation of possible solutions. MPBs are somewhat less, but still quite substantially, involved in consultations and communications with other actors, especially with other public administration institutions. The least frequent are

Table 7.3: Policy work activities

Variable	Ministries				Regional offices			
	N	Mean	SD	% never	N	Mean	SD	% never
Identification of possible solutions[**]	1316	4.54	1.29	2.3	783	3.41	1.56	2.5
Problem identification[**]	1321	4.47	1.36	3.0	783	3.33	1.56	3.2
Collection of data and information[**]	1320	4.34	1.60	6.8	783	3.22	1.46	9.5
Evaluation of possible solutions[**]	1312	4.34	1.33	3.0	783	3.38	1.56	3.0
Consultations/negotiations with bodies of central state administration[**]	1306	3.06	1.44	16.4	783	2.21	0.98	24.4
Consultations/negotiations with other stakeholders[**]	1284	2.90	1.50	20.9	783	2.54	1.30	24.4
Consultations with the public	1297	2.54	1.69	39.8	783	2.53	1.60	35.2
Implementation of policies and programmes[**]	1268	2.44	1.62	37.0	783	2.91	1.56	21.8
Consultations/negotiations with bodies of regional administration[**]	1299	1.97	1.27	48.5	783	2.39	1.14	26.2
Research[**]	1247	1.69	1.20	59.8	783	1.51	0.87	65.1
Consultations/negotiations with elected politicians outside the ministry (MPs)/with elected politicians[**]	1269	1.40	0.75	67.8	783	2.02	1.26	49.0

Note: $*p \leq 0.05$; $**p \leq 0.01$; independent t-test (2 tailed); ordered according to frequencies of tasks in ministries

Labels: 1 = never, 2 = several times a year, 3 = several times a quarter, 4 = several times a month, 5 = several times a week, 6 = daily.

activities involving research and consultations/negotiations with elected politicians outside the ministry.

PBs do not significantly differ in the extent they consult with the public. All other activities display clear differences. MPBs more often undertake data collection, research, problem identification and identification of possible solutions. Thus, as expected, MPBs are more often involved in analytical activities and research than RPBs. However, in absolute terms, MPBs do not display high levels of 'research capacities' (see below). Confirming the findings from Table 7.2, MPBs are not only less frequently involved in implementation, but also consult or negotiate with elected politicians significantly less than RPBs.

To conclude, we can see that the most frequent activities such as problem identification, collection of data and identification of possible solutions come under the umbrella of traditional policy analysis. Consultation with various stakeholders and the general public is less frequent but these tasks are done by the majority of PBs. In contrast to the widespread conception of ministerial officials as mere bureaucrats doing routine and stereotyped paperwork, the data shows quite a different picture. Though in the Czech Republic policy analysis is *not* institutionalised as a systematic methodological practice, the generic activities that constitute policy analysis are almost universally common.

However, this should not be overstated and misinterpreted as a sign of strong policy capacities of the ministries. As indicated by the non-use of analytical methods and expert or scientific evidence (see below), the reality is far from 'speaking truth to power' on the basis of systematic, rigorous and in-depth analysis. This is also documented by the fact that as much as 65% of MPBs stated they were never involved in research tasks, while only 5% of MPBs dealt with them daily or several times a week.

Task-specialists or multi-taskers?

Another interesting question is to what extent the policy-analytical activities are complementary to or mutually exclusive with activities such as negotiation and communication. This question reflects the more general question of whether distinct policy-analytical styles can be found in practice, or whether the styles overlap. The classical but still prevalent theories of bureaucracies assume that in public administration there is a clearly defined division of labour with specialisation and training required for assigned tasks. On the contrary, the tables suggest that this division between the worlds occupied either by skilled rational analysts or different kinds of mediators, facilitators or communicators with advanced communication skills is rather artificial. If this is so, there should be some correlation between theoretically distinct types of activities such as analysis and consultation/negotiation.

In order to test that hypothesis, we have reduced policy-relevant activities to two internally consistent composite variables. The first variable, labelled 'policy analysis' includes collection of data and information, problem identification, identification of possible solutions and evaluation of possible solutions (Cronbach's $\alpha = 0.90$). The second variable, referred to as 'consultancy', includes consultations or negotiations with bodies of the central state administration, with bodies of the regional administration, with elected politicians or with other stakeholders and consultations with the public (Cronbach's $\alpha = 0.63$). The value of each composite variable was defined as the average of the frequencies of the different activities on the scale where 1 equals never and 6 equals daily.

Table 7.4 gives more information on the frequency of both policy analysis and consultancy in the two samples generally, and for each ministry specifically. It is immediately apparent that both MPBs and RPBs are involved in policy analysis much more frequently than in consultancy. As for the distribution of both types of activities among ministries, the highest intensity of policy analysis is exhibited by the ministries of Foreign Affairs, Defence and Transportation, and the lowest levels by Labour and Social Affairs, Justice, and Education, Youth and Sports. It should be noted that these results do not suggest that some ministries are 'better' than others because they tell us nothing about the complexity and quality of their policy-analytical efforts. However, possible structural differences between the ministries cannot be ruled out, and it would certainly be interesting to examine more thoroughly why MPBs in 'welfare ministries' - that is, those responsible

Table 7.4: Involvement in policy analysis and consultancy by organisation

	Policy analysis			Consultancy		
	N	Mean	SD	N	Mean	SD
Foreign Affairs	58	4.78	1.00	53	2.56	0.83
Defence	219	4.64	1.08	218	1.96	0.72
Transportation	102	4.51	1.13	101	2.59	0.91
Finance	122	4.42	1.07	123	2.27	0.77
Environment	78	4.41	1.16	68	2.31	0.77
Culture	140	4.37	1.25	141	2.44	0.94
Industry and Trade	79	4.37	1.14	64	2.40	0.79
Health	124	4.36	1.24	126	2.51	0.89
Education, Youth and Sports	80	4.33	1.12	80	2.51	0.88
Justice	103	4.29	1.23	103	2.33	0.80
Labour and Social Affairs	174	4.26	1.11	175	2.43	0.74
Ministries total	**1279**	**4.43**	**1.15**	**1252**	**2.35**	**0.84**
Regional offices total	**783**	**3.33**	**1.40**	**783**	**2.33**	**0.60**

for public services such as healthcare, education and social welfare - exhibit the lowest intensity of policy analysis and, at the same time, slightly above average involvement in consultancy.

As indicated by individual-level correlations between policy analysis and consultancy in Table 7.5, there is clearly a strong *positive* association between these two activities. Thus, officials involved in policy analysis are also more likely to undertake consultancy. This is in sharp contrast with the hypothesis that these two activities are at odds. Quite the opposite is the case – they seem to be highly complementary. A comparison among ministries, however, reveals large differences in the strength of the relationship between PBs' involvement in policy analysis and consultancy, with the highest levels of correlation measured for the ministries of Foreign Affairs, Transportation, Environment, and Industry and Trade. This suggests that welfare ministries might exhibit higher levels of specialisation in terms of policy analysis and consultancy than the other ministries. It also indicates the often overlooked fact that the nature of policy work differs between policy domains, for example between the so-called 'power' and welfare ministries.

Congruence of perceived roles and actual tasks

The interesting thing is not only what PBs actually do but also how they perceive their roles, and with which role they identify most. This is especially interesting because, as explained in Chapter One, there is no such position as 'policy analyst'.

Table 7.5: Correlation between analytical and brokering tasks

	Pearson's r	N
Foreign Affairs	0.447**	53
Transportation	0.415**	100
Environment	0.388**	66
Industry and Trade	0.360**	63
Defence	0.328**	215
Culture	0.321**	140
Justice	0.302**	103
Labour and Social Affairs	0.264**	173
Education, Youth and Sports	0.182	79
Finance	0.175	122
Health	0.085	124
Ministries	0.257**	1237
Regional offices	0.529**	783
Combined dataset	0.352**	2020

Note: *$p \leq 0.05$, **$p \leq 0.01$.

In the survey, therefore, we asked ministerial officials the following question: 'According to your opinion, which word best characterises your role in the ministry?' Respondents were allowed to choose one of nine possible roles, or to use an open question. As shown in Table 7.6, the role by far the most MPBs particularly identify with is 'clerk'. This is followed by 'manager' and 'lawyer'.

Table 7.6: Congruence between perceived role and actual tasks

	%	Average on analytical tasks scale	Average on communication tasks scale
Clerk	44.8	4.29	2.39
Manager	14.9	4.58	2.49
Lawyer	14.0	4.47	2.39
Analyst	7.8	4.60	2.23
Economist	5.4	4.54	2.05
Advisor	2.0	4.64	2.58
Planner	1.6	4.26	1.94
Statistician	0.8	4.18	1.85
Researcher	0.4	5.13	2.30
Other, please, specify	8.2	4.46	2.25

Note: *$p \leq 0.05$, **$p \leq 0.01$.

About 8% of MPBs view themselves mostly as 'analysts'. This might seem low, but taking into account the lack of such an official position in the public administration, this is a relatively high proportion of people.

When we combine the perceived roles with actual tasks, we see surprisingly little variation. The PBs that report the most analytical tasks see themselves as researchers, analysts or advisors. Yet the difference is not substantial and all other categories – including clerks and lawyers – show a high degree of analytical activities. As for communication tasks, they are typical mostly for the people who see themselves as advisors or managers. On the other hand, this type of task is relatively less common among statisticians and planners. Somewhat surprisingly, people who see themselves as 'statisticians' report the lowest value of both analytical and communication tasks. However, again the differences between these types are far from huge.

We can conclude that in the Czech ministries categories of policy workers are not set and predefined. There is no clear category of policy analysts, at least not in ministerial offices. A large proportion of PBs did not identify with either role and were looking for other terms that would describe their roles.

Analytical methods and sources of information

Last but not least, another aspect of bureaucratic policy work at ministries is usage of different (analytical and other) methods and sources of information. Respondents were provided with a multiple-choice list of the ten most common methods identified in Czech policy analysis textbooks and qualitative interviews during preparation of the questionnaire. They were also provided with an option 'Other methods' and 'Not use any analytical method at all' (only about 3% of the sample chose the first option and 24% selected the second option).

Analysis of the methods used show a mixed picture in terms of 'hard' and more technical methods and 'soft' and participatory techniques (see Table 7.7). The most frequent methods are risk analysis and brainstorming/brainwriting, followed by impact analysis and future scenarios. Cost-benefit analysis and statistical modelling are used to the same degree as the problem tree heuristic. Focus group, operational research and the Delphi method are rather at the periphery of policy workers' interest.

In general, MPBs in defence, labour and social affairs and finance use all the listed methods more frequently than others but, for example, cost-benefit methods are also favoured in transport. On the other side of the spectrum are policy workers in foreign affairs and environment with the lowest usage of almost all methods. Also, most MPBs who do not use any analytical method come from culture, justice and health, followed by environment. However, there are no domain-specific (groups of) methods used exclusively in one domain. This evidence contradicts the 'lumpiness' thesis that variability in applied policy analysis techniques in Canada can be traced back to the fundamental task or mission of each agency or issue type (Howlett et al, 2014). In the Czech Republic, variability

Table 7.7: Policy work methods used

Method	Responses		% of Cases
	N	%	
Risk analysis	700	22	69
Brainstorming or brainwriting	667	21	65
Impact analysis (RIA, EIA ...)	412	13	40
Future scenarios	405	13	40
Cost-benefit etc	253	8	25
Problem tree	230	7	23
Statistical modelling	186	6	18
Focus group	118	4	12
Operation research methods	108	3	11
Delphi method	64	2	6
Total	3143	100	308

Note: multiple choice variable; N = 1022 (without respondents who do not use any method).
Source: own calculations.

is actually higher among ministries than among individual methods, suggesting a more important role of organisational culture rather than the particularities of substantive tasks and issues.

One may also ask if the usage of methods is evenly distributed among MPBs or 'accumulated' in a few 'multi-method' individuals. Mostly, one, two or three methods are used by individual policy workers (15%, 17% and 17% respectively). Only 11% use four methods and 16% of policy workers use five or more methods. Most of these multi-method policy workers come from defence and finance.

The second inquiry aimed at the different sources of information used for policy work in ministries. It is often argued that the quality of policy making depends on good evidence. However, there is ongoing debate on what exactly constitutes useful and policy-relevant evidence. Is it the result of rigorous empirical research and analysis, the professional knowledge of service providers, technical knowledge of programme managers, political knowledge of stakeholders or experiential knowledge of service users? In a constantly changing political and institutional context, policy bureaucrats no longer have a monopoly over policy advice. Instead, they must be able to weave together a diverse array of information, research and analysis from alternative sources (Parsons, 2004; Head, 2010, 2013).

The results in Table 7.8 indicate that MPBs rely heavily on internal sources, with a strong emphasis on their own experience and consultations with other bureaucrats. They also often use technical and/or evaluation reports and consult with domestic experts. Other sources are used rather occasionally. Interestingly, the above unconfirmed lumpiness thesis is supported when viewed from the perspective of utilisation of different sources of information. On average, MPBs in

Table 7.8: Utilisation of different sources of information

Sources of information	Mean	SD
Personal experience	3.41	0.75
Consultations inside public administration	3.10	0.79
Technical/evaluation reports	2.43	0.96
Consultations with domestic experts	2.42	0.84
Domestic professional/scholarly literature	2.38	0.89
Budgetary data	2.21	0.99
Foreign professional/scholarly literature	1.84	0.83
Information from non-governmental actors	1.80	0.77
Consultations with foreign experts	1.56	0.69

Source: own calculations.
Note: Frequency of utilisation on the scale 1 = never, 2 = occasionally, 3 = often, 4 = very often; differences are significant at 0.01 level.

finance utilise budgetary data more than in other domains and are less dependent upon personal experience. Similarly, the use of foreign sources of information (together with personal experience) surpasses domestic sources in foreign affairs. On the contrary, MPBs in transport and the environment count on domestic experts, while for the latter, budgetary data and consultation inside the public administration are not used often. Information from non-governmental actors is prominent for industry and trade, but rather unimportant for justice. To conclude, the particularities of substantive tasks and issues seem to be related to the rate of utilisation of different information sources in policy work rather than differences in policy analytical capacity.

Conclusions

Our analysis revealed that MPBs are highly educated, but not necessarily with enough relevant experience. Jobs in ministries also do not seem to provide sufficient stability and long-term prospects. Consequently, though we have not directly measured policy capacity in ministries, we can argue that it is not likely to be of sufficient quality.

Our analysis of policy work has been led by the hypothesis that in current public administration negotiation, communication and networking have become more and more prevalent, but that this can be at odds with involvement in traditional policy analysis. Our data strongly rejects this hypothesis. Most officials are multitaskers. It is not by accident that several respondents used the open question asking them to describe their work activities, commenting that they felt like "Ferdy the Ant – work of all kinds". 'Ferdy the Ant' is a hero from the famous books by Czech writer Ondřej Sekora. Ferdy is an extraordinary ant with a lot of diverse experience and challenges, which he is able to solve with manifold abilities and skills. In Czech discourse, Ferdy the Ant is a synonym for a person who has to, and is able to, do many quite diverse things.

The 'Ferdy phenomenon', as we could call it, seems to be less pronounced in ministries than regional offices. This might be caused by the fact that regional offices are on average smaller than ministries, and there is thus a lower capacity to specialise in particular tasks such as analysis. It is also true that in ministries with a higher number of employees (such as the Ministry of Education, Youth and Sports and the Ministry of Finance) the correlation between policy analysis and consultancy is lower than in smaller ministries such as the Ministry of Culture or the Ministry of Transportation). However, there is no clear linear trend. For instance, the Ministry of Health, where the correlation is the lowest, is a relatively small ministry.

In any event, policy analytical activities and consultancy seem to be rather complementary, although the data available do not allow a definite explanation of this relationship. We can hypothesise that the line between different groups of officials is drawn along the *intensity* of their work, rather than its *content*. The actual tasks undertaken by any given MPB or RPB may somewhat deviate from their official job description. Like any other institution, the public administration is occupied both by people who live for their work, strive to be active and efficient and work extra hours when necessary, and by others who work to earn their living and do not seek any special engagement. Based on our data, we would also assume that in order to do the job of policy analysis thoroughly, one needs to spend some extra time consulting and negotiating. In other words, those who honestly strive to identify problems and recommend solutions find it necessary to consult on their opinions with those stakeholders who are most affected by these problems. This explanation at the individual level may be completed by that at the organisational level. As suggested by this analysis of methods and utilisation of information sources, there seem to be at least two different organisational cultures at the ministries. The first one supports a systematic approach to policy work in general and policy analysis in particular, no matter what substantive issue is dealt with. The second one relies on intuition and the beaten track of how policy is/ should be done. There is no doubt that in both types, the Ferdy phenomenon is present. But in the first case, we can imagine trained and skilled workers dealing with non-routine tasks, applying different analytical methods and using different sources of policy-relevant knowledge to some extent, depending on the nature of the problem to be solved. In the second case, policy bureaucrats are not using systematic methods and rely heavily on internal sources of information. Their methodological toolbox is very limited and they are unable to accommodate different types of policy problems.

Finally, the findings of our analysis also feed back into the theoretical framework. The nature of the work in public administration seems to depend on a number of additional factors that tend to be overlooked. Besides macro-structural factors such as decentralisation, multilevel governance and the growing role of networking, we have identified a number of mezzo- and micro-factors such as size of the bureau, age of the institution, policy domain (health, social affairs and so on) and employment opportunities in the region. There is also a specifically Czech factor: the precarious employment situation of MPBs due to the ineffective Civil Service Act. The fact that our data was collected in 2013 – that is, before the Act came into effect – gives us the opportunity to make a comparison in the future to see the difference such a regulatory framework would make.

Acknowledgements

The chapter was written with the financial support of the PRVOUK programme P17 'Sciences of Society, Politics, and Media under the Challenge of the Times' and of the Grant Agency of the Czech Republic – project 'Policy Workers in the Czech Public Administration: Practices, Professional Values and Identity' (GA ČR P404/12/0725).

References

Colebatch, H.K., Hoppe, R. and Noordegraaf, M. (eds) (2010) *Working for Policy*, Amsterdam: Amsterdam University Press.

Colebatch, H.K. and Radin, B.A. (2006) 'Mapping the work of policy', in H.K. Colebatch (ed) *The Work of Policy: An International Survey*, Lanham, MD: Lexington Books, 217-26.

Colebatch, H.K. (ed) (2006) *The Work of Policy: An International Survey*, Lanham, MD: Lexington Books.

Drulák, P., Česal, J. and Hampl, S. (2003) 'Interactions and identities of Czech civil servants on their way to the EU', *Journal of European Public Policy*, 10(4): 637-54.

Dunn, W.N. (2004) *Public Policy Analysis: An Introduction* (3rd edn), Upper Saddle River, NJ: Prentice Hall.

Head, B.W. (2010) 'Reconsidering evidence-based policy: key issues and challenges', *Policy and Society*, 29(2): 77-94.

Head, B.W. (2013) 'Evidence-based policymaking – speaking truth to power? Evidence-based policymaking', *Australian Journal of Public Administration*, 72(4): 397-403.

Hoppe, R. (1999) 'Policy analysis, science and politics: from "speaking truth to power" to "making sense together"', *Science and Public Policy*, 26(3): 201-10.

Howlett, M. (2009) 'Policy advice in multi-level governance systems: sub-national policy analysts and analysis', *International Review of Public Administration*, 13(3): 1-16.

Howlett, M., Tan, S.L., Migone, A., Wellstead, A. and Evans, B. (2014) 'The distribution of analytical techniques in policy advisory systems: policy formulation and the tools of policy appraisal', *Public Policy and Administration*, 29(4): 271-91.

Meltsner, A.J. (1975) 'Bureaucratic policy analysts', *Bureaucratic Policy Analysts*, 1(1): 115-31.

Page, E. and Jenkins, W.I. (2005) *Policy Bureaucracy: Government with a Cast of Thousands*, Oxford: Oxford University Press.

Parsons, W. (2004) 'Not just steering but weaving: relevant knowledge and the craft of building policy capacity and coherence', *Australian Journal of Public Administration*, 63(1): 43–57.

Radin, B. (2013) 'Policy analysis reaches mid life', *Central European Journal of Public Policy*, 7(1): 8–27.

Scherpereel, J.A. (2004) 'Renewing the socialist past or moving toward the European administrative space? Inside Czech and Slovak ministries', *Administration & Society*, 36(5): 553–93.

Veselý, A. (2013) 'Conducting large-*N* surveys on policy work in bureaucracies: some methodological challenges and implications from the Czech Republic', *Central European Journal of Public Policy*, 7(2): 88–113.

EIGHT

Policy analysis in subnational governments

Martin Nekola, Arnošt Veselý

Introduction

In multilevel systems, subnational governments control many important areas of policy making. Not surprisingly, as a consequence they require a lot of personnel, including so-called policy bureaucrats (PBs). It is argued that, compared to the national level, subnational PBs are more commonly engaged in 'street-level' advice, oriented towards day-to-day firefighting and implementation of public programmes and policies. This chapter focuses on PBs at regional authorities in the Czech Republic. It starts with a brief and general introduction to the distribution of competencies between regions and other levels of government. Then we examine the profile of Czech regional public bureaucrats including demographics, education, training and work experience. The next part deals with questions of how policy work is actually done in this specific context (that is, how policy knowledge is generated and utilised) and, in particular, what different tasks are done and which methods and sources of information are used by regional policy workers. Based upon a large-scale questionnaire survey carried out in all Czech regions except the capital city of Prague at the end of 2012 (N = 783), the paper thus provides a descriptive analysis of the relationship among the tasks, activities and methods regional policy bureaucrats use.

Subnational governments in the Czech Republic

Since 2000, the regional self-government of the Czech Republic has been formed by 13 regions (*kraje*).[1] A so-called joint model of public administration has been established, meaning that regions (and municipalities) also exercise some tasks of the state administration in addition to their own competencies and independent powers. These tasks can be delegated to regional authorities in cases provided for by an Act of Parliament. Regions are public law corporations and they re-established a regional level of governance in the Czech public administration as part of a complex reform undertaken after the fall of the previous regime in 1989 (see Baun and Marek, 2006). During this reform, more than 70 districts (*okresy*) were replaced with 204 municipalities which took over most of their

---

[1] The fourteenth 'region' is the capital city, Prague, which is governed on the basis of its own laws and was not included in the research.

administrative tasks (see Chapter Nine). The rest of the functions went to the regions with the aim to pursue universal development of their territories and to protect public interests. The regions have quite a lot of discretion in policy making and implementation within their jurisdictions, especially in regional development, health and social care, land use planning, transportation, tourism, environment, agriculture, education and sport. Also, they play an important role in the coordination of different actors (from different sectors – business and civic – and levels of government – from supranational to municipal) and their interests within a given territory.

The regions are governed by a Board of Councillors (*rada*, similar to a government) and a Regional Council (*zastupitelstvo*, similar to a Legislative Assembly), the latter elected in fully democratic regional elections. Their administrative bodies, the so-called regional authorities (*krajské úřady*), constitute the important organisational context of subnational policy work. They perform tasks within the sphere of their independent powers set by the elected bodies of the region (the Regional Council and the Regional Assembly) and of the delegated powers set by the state administration.

Methodology

This chapter presents the results of a large-scale questionnaire survey carried out in all Czech regions except the capital city of Prague at the end of 2012. Data was collected by self-administered online interviews (computer-aided web interview) from a sample of public officials at regional authorities. The sampling procedure was based on complete lists of workers, including job positions and contact information, published on their websites. A total of 2615 public officials were included in the final selection based on information on their functions or job positions.

Persons working at secretariats and departments responsible for public administration (financial/economic, investment and IT departments, business licensing authorities and so on), except their managers, were excluded. However, some sections or positions at these secretariats/departments which clearly did not perform secretarial or public administration tasks (judging by their name or job description) were included. Thus, public officials working in certain departments were not excluded from the sample across the board, but after consideration of the specific organisational structure of each government office. Similarly, officials working in those departments that were usually included in the sample were only selected based on the name or job description of each section. Since sections at the different regional government offices were not named in a unified fashion, we could not proceed automatically and exclude certain sections across the board. Instead, we considered not only the section's name but also the job description of its employees. As a result, sections or employees whose jobs were not expected to consist of analytical or strategic activities (for example, those concerned with school accounting, road economics or the building code) were excluded.

From the total number of 2615 email contacts, we received 783 fully completed questionnaires – that is, the overall response rate was 32% (200 questionnaires returned as invalid). The quantitative survey was accompanied by in-depth semi-structured interviews with 18 mid-level officials.

Subnational policy work

Profile of regional policy bureaucrats

As for the demographic profile of regional PBs, they are predominantly females and quite young, with more than 60% under 45 years old. They are well educated, the majority of them having tertiary education. A master's degree is predominant (70%); however quite a large number of PBs have PhDs (6%). Given the nature of regions' jurisdiction, it is not surprising that social sciences and humanities, together with social work, are the major fields of education among PBs. These are followed by natural and formal sciences (20%), engineering and architecture (17%). All the sociodemographic characteristics used are presented in Table 8.1. As for job position and work experience (see Table 8.2), the majority of our sample consists of low-level policy bureaucrats – that is official or official-specialists (62%). Managers and heads of subdivisions are similarly represented (about 12%) and are followed by heads of divisions. Representation of other positions including

Table 8.1: Socio-demographic characteristics of regional public bureaucrats

Sociodemographic characteristics		N	%
Sex	Male	300	38
	Female	483	62
Age	18–29 years	141	18
	30–44 years	330	42
	45–59 years	284	36
	60+ years	28	4
Education level	Primary	1	0
	Secondary with GCSE, professional	82	11
	Secondary with GCSE, general	7	1
	Secondary with GCSE, lyceum	1	0
	Post-secondary	15	2
	Tertiary, bachelor's degree	79	10
	Tertiary, master's degree	550	70
	Tertiary, doctoral degree	48	6
Field of education	Science, mathematics, information science	135	20
	Engineering, architecture	115	17
	Life sciences and veterinary medicine	70	10
	Healthcare, medicine, pharmacy	12	2
	Social sciences and humanities, social work	344	50
	Culture and arts	5	1
	Military science	13	2
	Other	57	8

Source: own calculations.

Table 8.2: Job position and work experience

		N	%
Job position	Official	257	33
	Official-specialist	228	29
	Manager/supervisor	91	12
	Economist	16	2
	Lawyer	13	2
	Head of subdivision	97	12
	Head of division	60	8
	Other	15	3
Work for the regional authority	Less than 1 year	57	7
	1-5 years	298	38
	6-10 years	247	32
	More than 10 years	181	23

Source: own calculations.

economists and lawyers is quite marginal (6%) which was determined by the sampling procedure. Experienced policy bureaucrats predominate within the sample with about 55% working for the regional authority for more than six years.

Subject areas of regional policy work

Only one-fifth of the respondents in the sample perform the delegated competencies of state administration only (state officers). A similar number of policy bureaucrats are engaged solely in regional agendas and the rest of the respondents combine both state and regional (autonomous) administration. State administration is carried out mainly by workers in the lower positions of officers and specialists while managers are more often involved in regional administration. This is related to the fact that many of them are managing projects financed by different EU regional policy funds (the Regional Development Fund, European Social Fund and Cohesion Fund) which fall within the competence of the regions.

As for the subject areas, the sample consisted of PBs with experience mainly in environmental issues, education, health and social services and regional development.[2] Areas such as transportation, urban planning, tourism and security are much less well represented. More than one-fifth of respondents indicated 'other area', which mainly covers agendas related to EU funds, public procurements and culture. While 'state officers' have been working predominantly in one area only, regional policy bureaucrats have more often been involved in two or three areas in the course of their work for the regional authority.

---

[2] The question asked for both previous and current involvement – 'In what area(s) have you been involved while working for the Regional Authority?'

Specialists and generalists within four subject areas

This brings us to the question about the proportion of policy specialists and generalists within the sample of regional PBs. There are two generally acknowledged ways to gain expertise in an area and thus become an expert with high *technical skills* (Meltsner, 1976). The first one is formal education and/ or training in the given subject. However it is also possible to gain expertise through practice – that is, working on similar types of issues or staying in the same department for some time. In this sense, Page and Jenkins (2005, p 39) discern interdepartmental mobility (moving among different positions within a given department) and job mobility (moving among different departments within a given subject area), both contributing to practical specialisation.

Analysis of the four most frequent subject areas – environment, education, health and social services and regional development – reveals that the proportion of workers with tertiary education relevant for the given subject area is highly variable across the areas – from two-thirds in environment to over one-third in regional development and health and social care to one-quarter in education. The overall picture changes when we add practitioners, that is workers without relevant tertiary education but with practical experience of more than five years in the given subject area. Most of these practitioners work in education and health and social care, less in regional development and environment (see Table 8.3).

Table 8.3: Proportion of specialists in four subject areas

Subject areas	Proportion of specialists based on their ...		Total (%)
	education[a] (%)	long-term practice[b] (%)	
Environment	66	22	88
Health and social care	36	32	68
Education	26	35	61
Regional development	37	23	60

Source: own calculations.
Note: [a]PBs with tertiary education in relevant fields of study; [b]PBs with practical experience of more than five years in the given subject area but without tertiary education in relevant fields of study.

It seems that environmental agendas at the regional level are highly technical and require educated specialists with relevant educational backgrounds. In other areas the proportion of educated workers and workers with extensive practical experience is more balanced and in educational agendas practitioners are even more involved than workers with relevant educational backgrounds.

Overall, specialists with technical training in the subject or long-term experience in the given policy field predominated in these four subject areas. The prevailing background of generalists is social sciences (for example, economics and management, business or public administration, law) and humanities (philosophy).

When compared to generalists, it is not surprising that specialists prevail at lower positions. They are expected to deal with more technical than procedural issues and to be involved mainly in implementation. However, the vast majority of middle and top officials, who are expected to more likely be generalists, can also be considered specialists based on their education or long-term practice. The only exception is the position of manager. Managers are split in half between technicians and generalists (see Table 8.4). We can conclude that if some mobility of policy workers in these four subject areas is present it takes place mainly among different positions within a given department or among different departments within a given subject area. Only a small proportion of workers have experience in two (20%) or more subject areas (13%) and are contemplating leaving their organisation within five years (29%). In this respect, Czech regional policy workers differ from the mobility patterns identified at the governmental level by Page and Jenkins (2005) and at the regional level by Wellstead et al (2009).

Table 8.4: Proportion of specialists in different positions within four selected areas

Position	Specialists (%) (N = 548)
Manager	51
Official	79
Official-specialist	81
Head of subdivision	92
Head of division	97

Source: own calculations.

What do regional policy workers do?

The job content of policy workers is quite diverse at the regional level.[3] However, most of them have in common one important task: to communicate with other bodies of public administration and with non-state organisations. This is the most frequently mentioned task, leaving behind all other tasks including routine administration. Surprisingly, almost a half of the respondents are involved in (methodical) training or lecturing. All tasks are summarised in Table 8.5.

All workers in the selected departments of regional authorities are involved in policy making to some extent. Thus, there are no 'bureaucrats only' in the sample

---

[3]   And similarly at the national level – see Chapter Seven.

Table 8.5: Tasks undertaken by regional policy workers (multiple responses)

Tasks	Responses		% of cases
	N	%	
Communication with other bodies of the public administration and with non-state organisations	527	15	67
Routine administrative tasks	403	12	52
Methodical, training or lecture activities	385	11	49
Making conceptual and strategic policy documents for the region	351	10	45
Administrative tasks	347	10	44
Direct communication with citizens	340	10	43
Making analyses for decision-making	321	9	41
Management and control	302	9	39
Providing advice for political units of the region	172	5	22
Budgeting	163	5	21
Other	124	4	16
Legal analyses	77	2	10

Source: own calculations.

– that is respondents working solely on (routine) administrative tasks. However, we can expect that the proportion of individual tasks will differ for different positions within the regional public administration (see Table 8.6).

When we return to the earlier discussion on the different roles of PBs, it is clear that although they are specialists, middle and top officials have to manage much more complex and varied tasks. Their policy work is multidimensional in nature (see also Howlett and Wellstead, 2011) and requires not only technical, but also political and managerial skills. This is supported by their answers to the question about what educational training would be helpful for them. Middle and top officials most significantly differ from other workers in their call for courses on policy design and implementation, strategic management and planning, risk management, organisational management and leadership.

In contrast, lower-level officials are significantly less involved in tasks not directly related to their expertise, such as legal analysis or budgeting, and are not in close contact with politicians. Clearly, only a minority of them is also involved in policy analysis and design. Policy work at this level consists mainly of communication with other public administration bodies and stakeholders, administrative tasks and direct contact with citizens. Significantly, communication with and/or involvement of the public was considered to be the most helpful course for official-specialists (together with time management). It is also interesting that

Table 8.6: Tasks by positions (adj. residuals and % of positive answers within each position)

Tasks	Official	Official-specialist	Manager	Head of	
				subdivision	division
Making conceptual and strategic policy documents for the region	-3.6 37%	-1.9 41%	-4.7 23%	7.1 79%	6.3 85%
Making analyses for decision making	-3.7 33%	-3.6 32%	-1.8 33%	6.5 72%	6.5 82%
Legal analyses	-1.5 7%	-1.4 7%	-2.8 1%	1.7 13%	6.1 30%
Budgeting	-4.9 10%	-4.3 11%	-0.1 20%	5.9 42%	8.7 63%
Communication with other public administration bodies and with non-state organisations	-3.6 60%	1.4 72%	-2.2 58%	3.7 85%	2 80%
Providing advice for political units of the region	-4 14%	-3.8 14%	-2.5 12%	6.4 47%	8.6 67%
Management and control	-3.5 30%	-2.9 31%	-0.8 35%	5.6 65%	5.1 70%
Methodical, training or lecture activities	-2.2 44%	-1.6 45%	-2.9 35%	4.4 70%	4.7 78%
Administrative tasks	0.4 46%	3.3 54%	-8.7 2%	0.8 49%	3.3 65%
Direct communication with citizens	1 47%	1,1 47%	-6.4 13%	1.9 54%	1.7 55%
Routine administrative tasks	0.8 54%	0.8 54%	-3 37%	0.8 56%	-0.1 52%

Source: own calculations.
Note: Differences are statistically significant (Pearson Chi-Square, $p<0.05$).

almost one-third of officials stated that no educational activity would be helpful for them.

At a more general level, only about 3% of respondents spent more than 90% of their working time dealing with operational tasks only.[4] However, operational tasks occupy a significant part of the working time of regional PBs. The median in the whole sample is 30% of working time and one-quarter of respondents spend more than half of their working time on regular operational tasks. If we add the time spent on immediate fire-fighting (median 20%) we can say that the

---

[4] Respondents were asked to estimate in percentages how much of their working time they spend dealing with strategic tasks (ongoing for more than a year), tactical tasks (ongoing for 6–12 months), operational tasks (ongoing up to 6 months), immediate 'fire-fighting' and other tasks.

almost universal picture of bureaucrats overburdened by day-to-day short-term tasks (Howlett, 2009, p 9) is also not far from the truth in the Czech regional administration. As shown also in Table 8.6, routine administration permeates the whole bureaucracy regardless of position. Both tactical and strategic tasks are in the minority at the regional authorities, with a median of 10% of working time. On the other hand, there certainly are individuals concentrating on mid- to long-term horizons.

However, questions still remain regarding what in particular regional policy workers do during working time and whether some distinct clusters of activities related to specific policy-making/analysis phases can be found. Identification and assessment of possible solutions for policy problems seem to be the most common policy-related activities of regional policy workers. More than half of them are somehow involved in such activities at least once per month. Also, the problem-oriented nature of policy work is underlined by the third most frequent activity: problem identification (median value 'Once per quarter of a year'). A similar proportion of regional policy workers is involved in actual implementation of policy programmes. In contrast, evaluation activities, either formative or summative, are very rare at the regional level. Most policy workers participate in evaluations once a year or less and experience from the regional authorities suggests that such evaluations are rather formal and instead of impact evaluation focus on the monitoring of programme data.

As for cross-sectional activities – that is, not specific to a certain phase – regional policy workers relatively often collect data and information and prepare reports for decision makers. However, they are not effectively involved in research activities and their policy work rests heavily upon personal experience and consultation with other bureaucrats (see Figure 8.1). Further analysis reveals a picture of regional policy workers confined within their organisations. Only a small number of policy workers consult outsiders on a regular basis; be it the general public, other stakeholders and interest groups, elected politicians and even other bodies of public administration. Quite the opposite, they acquire most of the information necessary for their work from internal sources such as colleagues, technical reports, strategic and conceptual documents of the region, and budgets and other financial data. Information from other stakeholders from both the for-profit and non-profit sectors is not utilised, just as scientific and professional advice, especially foreign advice, is not used. The data suggests that evidence-based or evidence-informed policy is very limited at the regional level.

Sources of information and analytical methods

So far, we can see two main 'worlds' of regional policy work. The prevailing one of rather technical activities focuses on dealing with problem definition on the one hand and implementation of chosen solutions on the other. The second includes a less frequent group of activities consisting of different types of consultations and negotiations, primarily inside the public administration and

Figure 8.1: Types of information used by regional policy workers

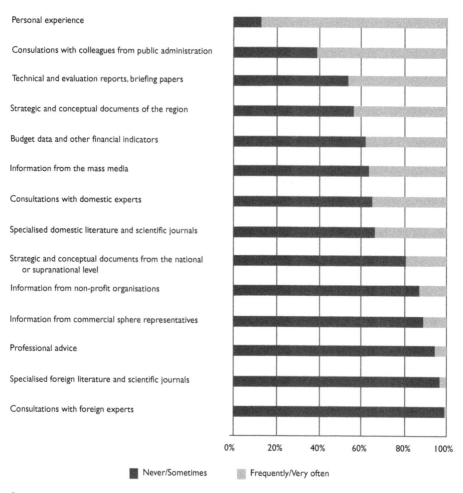

Personal experience

Consultations with colleagues from public administration

Technical and evaluation reports, briefing papers

Strategic and conceptual documents of the region

Budget data and other financial indicators

Information from the mass media

Consultations with domestic experts

Specialised domestic literature and scientific journals

Strategic and conceptual documents from the national or supranational level

Information from non-profit organisations

Information from commercial sphere representatives

Professional advice

Specialised foreign literature and scientific journals

Consultations with foreign experts

0%   20%   40%   60%   80%   100%

■ Never/Sometimes   ▨ Frequently/Very often

Source: own calculations.

with other stakeholders or the general public. Evaluation and research are the only residual activities done either formally or externally (if at all). To assemble a complete picture of the analytical styles of regional policy bureaucrats, an analysis of sources of information and analytical methods has to be done.

There are many sources that inform policy making in general: politics, ideology and values, perceived public opinion, or pragmatic constraints such as funding and research (Ritter, 2009, p 70). As indicated above, regional policy bureaucrats rely on personal experience most of all. They also often draw upon their colleagues' experience and information written in official policy documents and the mass media. Research evidence and expertise is acquired almost exclusively from domestic sources: either from experts or scientific literature and journals. Surprisingly, only one-fifth of respondents work with higher-level strategies and even fewer PBs use information from for-profit and non-profit organisations. Foreign expertise is almost not used. Thus, PBs draw from their personal experience and especially from consultations with and the experience of colleagues. Moreover, strategic documents represent important sources of information and direction.

As for analytical methods and techniques, most regional policy bureaucrats make do without any method at all (41%). Soft methods such as brainstorming or future scenarios (36%, resp. 22%) are most often used followed by problem tree analysis (13%). A small number of PBs also apply methods of financial analysis such as cost-benefit or cost-utility (15%). A special case is impact analysis, which is an umbrella term for several formal and systematic policy tools intended to examine and measure the likely benefits, costs and effects of new regulations (RIA [Regulatory Impact Assessment]), strategies (SEA [Strategic Environmental Assessment]), construction (EIA [Environmental Impact Assessment]) and so on. This is rather a set of different methods and techniques some of which are directly implemented into the Czech Republic's legal system. For regional authorities, EIA and SEA are the most relevant and almost one-fifth of respondents reported participation in these processes (see Table 8.7).

When considering different positions, we can see that the work of mid- and top-level officials is not only multi-task but also 'multi-method'. With some exceptions, they show the largest share of workers using almost all the listed methods and techniques. Also, a large number of officials and official-specialists do not use any analytical methods and thus are not analysts in the traditional sense.

Conclusions

This chapter deals with the ways policy work is done by public bureaucrats at the regional level in the Czech Republic. In particular, it focuses on who regional policy bureaucrats are and what they actually do - that is tasks, activities and methods used. As expected, regional policy bureaucrats are predominantly specialists involved mainly in communication with other administrative bodies, routine administrative activities and at lower positions with direct over-the-counter communication with citizens. However, besides these rather operational tasks, the bulk of policy bureaucrats are involved to a greater or lesser extent in tactical and strategic tasks related to sectoral regional policies or overall development of the region.

At first glance, we can also identify the types of policy work such as problem appraisal, implementation, strategic brokerage and evaluation known from relevant literature. However, deeper analysis shows that the way policy work is done differs significantly from theoretical accounts (Radin, 2000; Mayer et al, 2004) or foreign experience (Howlett and Wellstead, 2011; Hoppe and Jeliazkova, 2006; Colebatch et al, 2010). We can hardly speak about either rational or postmodern styles of policy work in a situation where rigorous research and evaluation are practically

Table 8.7: Analytical methods by positions (adjusted residuals and percentages of positive answers within each position)

Analytical methods/ techniques	Official	Official-specialist	Manager	Head of	
				subdivision	division
Scenarios	-2.7	-2.1	1.5	1.9	4.1
	17%	18%	29%	30%	43%
Cost-benefit etc	-4.7	-4.1	4.7	2.1	7.0
	6%	7%	31%	22%	45%
Brainstorming/brainwriting	-3.5	-3.7	3.1	4.3	3.2
	28%	26%	51%	56%	55%
Problem tree	-	-	-	-	-
	11%	10%	15%	21%	17%
Delphi or other expert methods	-2.3	0.5	1.2	-0.4	2.1
	1%	3%	4%	2%	7%
Impact analysis (RIA, EIA etc)	-1.6	0.7	-3.1	1.5	3.5
	15%	20%	7%	24%	35%
Other	-2.2	-0.7	0.9	2.7	0.7
	5%	7%	10%	14%	10%
Do not use any	4.3	2.3	-1.9	-3.5	-4.8
	52%	47%	32%	25%	12%

Source: own calculations.
Note: Differences are statistically significant (Pearson Chi-Square, $p<0.05$) with exception of the problem tree technique.

missing on one side and participation of or interaction with stakeholders outside regional authorities are very limited on the other.

Instead, there seems to be a majority of bureaucratic routinists performing rather formal duties and agendas and depending on their practical knowledge (based either on their own experience or internal sources). They coordinate their activities within the bureau, negotiate with other bodies and implement adopted policies. However, this does not mean that there are no actual policy advisory capacities at the regional level. First of all, considering the broader scope of the survey (including all bureaucrats in given areas), a high proportion of routinists can be expected. Secondly, some of the regional authorities make extensive use of external expertise and policy advisory capacities.[5] And finally, there definitely are policy workers at the regional level applying different analytical styles. At

[5]   The marginal proportion of those who use 'professional advice' can be explained by misapprehension of the term. We can assume that consultation with experts and partly also technical/evaluation reports are external policy advice. Extensive use of external advice in some regions is based on evidence from qualitative interviews and document analysis.

the middle and top levels, we can see workers with either relevant education or practical experience (or both) who are engaged in complex and multidimensional policy work. At least some of them have to apply different analytical styles in order to advise strategically, to be able to design and recommend policies and to manage and mediate the whole policy process.

At lower levels, a smaller proportion of workers deal with non-routine tasks, apply analytical methods (rather informal with the exception of impact assessment) and use different sources of policy-relevant knowledge. They are neither impartial researchers nor policy analysts in the traditional (rational) sense. More likely, they try to cope with the practical problems related to policy implementation on the one hand and more conceptual tasks on the other.

In this chapter, we have tried to go beyond a mere description of policy work done at the regional level and indicate significant relationships among the tasks, activities and methods used by different groups of policy bureaucrats. Due to a potential self-selection bias, the results cannot simply be generalised to the entire population of regional policy bureaucrats in the Czech Republic. However, we believe that they provide insight into the actual day-to-day policy work done at regional authorities and food for thought and discussion. It is also clear that further analysis in this area is needed to fully grasp the possible analytical styles of these policy bureaucrats.

Acknowledgements
The chapter was written with the financial support of the PRVOUK programme P17 'Sciences of Society, Politics, and Media under the Challenge of the Times' and of the Grant Agency of the Czech Republic – project 'Policy Workers in the Czech Public Administration: Practices, Professional Values and Identity' (GA CŘ P404/12/0725).

References
Baun, M. and Marek, D. (2006) 'Regional policy and decentralization in the Czech Republic', *Regional & Federal Studies*, 16(4): 409–28.

Colebatch, H., Hoppe, R. and Noordegraaf, M. (eds) (2010) *Working for Policy*, Amsterdam: Amsterdam University Press.

Hoppe, R. and Jeliazkova, M. (2006) 'How policy workers define their job: a Netherlands case study', in H. Colebatch (ed) *The Work of Policy: An International Survey*, Lanham, MD: Lexington Books, pp 35-60.

Howlett, M. (2009) 'A profile of B.C. provincial policy analysts: trouble-shooters or planners?', *Canadian Political Science Review*, 3(3): 50-68.

Howlett, M. and Wellstead, A.M. (2011) 'Policy analysts in the bureaucracy revisited: the nature of professional policy work in contemporary government', *Politics & Policy*, 39(4): 613–33.

Mayer, I.S., van Daalen, C.E. and Bots, P.W. (2004) 'Perspectives on policy analyses: a framework for understanding and design', *International Journal of Technology, Policy and Management*, 4(2): 169-91.

Meltsner, A.J. (1976) *Policy Analysts in the Bureaucracy*, Berkeley, CA: University of California Press.

Page, E.C. and Jenkins, B. (2005) *Policy Bureaucracy: Governing with a Cast of Thousands*, Oxford: Oxford University Press.

Radin, B. (2000) *Beyond Machiavelli: Policy Analysis Comes of Age*, Washington, DC: Georgetown University Press.

Ritter, A. (2009) 'How do drug policy makers access research evidence?', *International Journal of Drug Policy*, 20(1): 70-75.

Wellstead, A.M., Stedman, R.C. and Lindquist, E.A. (2009) 'The nature of regional policy work in Canada's federal public service', *Canadian Political Science Review*, 3(1): 1-23.

NINE

Policy work at the local level

Dan Ryšavý

Introduction

After the communist regime collapsed in 1989, the rebirth of local government in 1990 was an integral part of the transition from the *ancien régime* to a democratic political order. The second face of the development of public administration applied at the local level was more complicated; this was the delegation by law of a portion of state administration to the municipalities. The Czech Republic thus returned to a fused model of territorial administration, in which the same local bodies are entrusted with the execution of both local self-government and state administrative competences (Illner, 2011, p 525). The practical operation of this model runs up against a clash between two organisational logics and two value orientations – local democracy and autonomy on the one hand, and effectiveness and efficacy on the other. This tension cannot be avoided even in policy work at the local level.

This chapter intentionally focuses more on *policy work* at the local level (see Colebatch et al, 2010) rather than *policy analysis* in its different meanings. A quarter-century of efforts at reinstituting self-government and a dozen years after the most recent phase in the reform of public administration in the field of delegated competences is not a particularly long period, for example for the establishment of decision-making patterns among local political leaders. The tension noted above illustrates the need to stress a combination of different perspectives and to consider the context, which is described by the distinction between *output-based* and *activity-based* accounts of policy work (Colebatch et al, 2010, p 17). While the state administration is more focused on *results*, an important element of local self-government and autonomy is *experience*. Finally, the emphasis on description of the profile and opinions of decision makers also corresponds to the current state of research on public policies on the local level. In his conclusion to a co-authored monograph dealing with local government and local development in rural communities Josef Bernard stated: 'Czech political science still lacks any work which focuses in depth on the area of analysis of the specific policies of local governments and their impacts' (Bernard et al, 2011, p 206).

The first section briefly examines the relevant literature and the main sources on which the chapter is based. The following section deals with the context of public administration on the local level and its main determinants: fragmented municipal structure, a fused model of public administration, its financing and the main local bodies responsible for carrying out public administration. The third section presents the basic sociodemographic and political profile of local decision makers and the perceived influence of different bodies on decision making. The fourth section approaches local policy work through a description of mayoral time management and communication networks.

Sources of knowledge on local governance and policy work at the local level

Sources of information on local governance and policy work at the local level can be divided into four groups. The first consists of reports by national experts published in international handbooks and surveys (for example Brusis, 2010; Illner, 2010a, 2010b, 2011). The second consists of applied research results, which are usually initiated by the central authorities of the state such as ministries of finance, of the interior or of local development in connection with the preparation for or the results of the different phases of the reform of public administration and its modernisation (for example Galvasová et al, 2007; Vysoká škola ekonomická, 2009; Plaček et al, 2013). The third consists of domestic thematic collections, collective monographs and articles in professional journals which emerged thanks to the support for basic research projects from institutions such as the Czech Science Agency (for example Vajdová et al, 2006; Grospič et al, 2007; Ochrana et al, 2007; Bernard et al, 2011). The fourth includes doctoral and other graduate theses that deepen knowledge in specific topics (Klusáček, 2008; Havlík, 2013; Nunvářová, 2014).

In terms of methods, these works most often make use of analysis of documents (for example, developments in legislation), secondary analysis of statistical data (for example, cost-benefit analysis) and more or less structured interviews with key actors. In the last case, researchers most often turn to mayors who act as local experts and speak 'for the municipality'. Studies that distinguish between the opinions of different types of mayors (for example Bernard et al, 2011) or include interviews with the officials of local governments (for example Havlík, 2013; Nunvářová, 2014) are the exception rather than the rule.

This chapter makes repeated use of data from international comparative surveys of representatives of cities and municipalities in the Czech Republic. Those representatives have been of interest to social scientists since the early 1990s, for example the *Local Democracy and Innovation* project (LDI) (see Baldersheim et al, 1996, 2003). Later the Czech Republic took part in two of three cross-national research projects on comparative urban and local governance: a comparative study of mayors (POLLEADER project, see Bäck et al, 2006) and local councillors (MAELG project, see Egner et al, 2013). Thanks to these we know much more not only about the recruitment and career patterns of local politicians but also about their attitudes towards democracy, role perceptions and so on. To a certain extent, these studies also make it possible to describe changes in these characteristics over time. International comparative studies are limited by the fact that most of them survey the representatives of medium and large cities. For this reason, this chapter makes use of the outputs of national studies in order to include the perspectives and behaviours of the representatives of smaller communities (such as Bernard et al, 2011). However, the last angle of the 'local power triangle', the chief executive officers, has not been surveyed comparatively in the Czech Republic since the early 1990s when 84 of them were included in the first survey of the LDI project.

Context of public administration at the municipal level

The right of municipalities to local government is enshrined in the Constitution of the Czech Republic, according to which municipalities are the basic self-governing territorial units and counties (regional government) the higher self-governing units (Article 99 of Act Number 1/1993 Collection of Laws). Legislation concerning municipalities is further regulated by Act Number 128/2000 Collection of Laws on Municipalities (the Municipal Order). Dozens of other laws further regulate municipal administration in various ways. Along with individual steps taken as part of the reform of public administration, the functions of municipalities have gradually changed over time. Among the most important of these changes was the establishment of the counties in 2000, the abolition of regional offices at the end of 2002, and the differentiation of municipalities according to the amount of state administration delegated by the state to the municipal bodies on the same date.

Public administration at the local level is significantly affected by the size of the municipalities. There has traditionally been a high level of municipal fragmentation in the Czech Republic. Moreover, there was a wave of dissolution of the previously imposed municipalities in the first five years after the renewal of political freedom in 1989. Recently, more than half of municipalities have a population of less than 500 and only slightly more than one-tenth of the most populated exceed 2000. However, more than half of inhabitants live in towns with more than 10,000 people (see Table 9.1).

Table 9.1: Size structure of municipalities and population distribution

	Size groups of municipalities						
	<500	500-1999	2.000-9.999	10,000-49,999	50,000-99,999	>100,000	Total
Number	3473	2098	551	110	16	5	6253
% of population	8.0	18.9	21.0	20.5	10.8	20.9	100

Source: Czech Statistical Office (2013).

Municipal fragmentation is closely related to the other characteristics of public administration at the local level, such as the integrated model of territorial public administration, public financing and the type and number of collective organs established in a particular municipality.

Integrated model of public administration: independent and delegated competences

The functions of municipalities are divided into those that are independently granted by law and those delegated by the state administration. However, both of them are exercised through the same executive organs. Regardless of the large differences in the size of municipalities, their independent powers (such as the adoption of strategies of municipal development, the establishment of organisations to meet the objectives of the municipality, the management of municipal property, the approval of municipal regulations, and so on) are identical for all size categories of the municipalities with the exception of the City of Prague and some two dozen statutory cities that already have or are entitled to divide their territory into city districts with their own elected bodies. In addition to their role in self-government, municipalities also have various responsibilities in the area of state administration which have been transferred to them by the state. All local leaders have to deal with authorities in the fields of housing, public health, social welfare, fire-fighting services, water treatment, transport and communications, education, culture, maintenance of public order and so on.

The complexity of public administration in the Czech Republic at the local level is clearly illustrated by the distinct division between municipalities according to the range of activities of state administration delegated to them. All municipalities administer some basic delegated functions. In addition, since 2003 there are 388 municipalities of the second type with an authorised municipal office and 205 municipalities of the third type with extended powers. Offices in these two types of municipalities perform delegated functions for the citizens residing within their administrative area. Moreover, municipalities with registry offices (1230) and a building authority (618) further complicate the hierarchical structure of territorial administration.

Financing

The revenue of the municipalities is determined by the state, mainly through the tax assignment system, which has changed several times over the last two decades and has long been a highly political issue (see for example Provazníková, 2009; Kruntorádová and Jüptner, 2012). The biggest share is made up by the taxes that are centrally collected and distributed (VAT, personal income tax, corporate income tax). Property tax plays a much smaller role. However, this is the only tax which municipalities can set, within limits set by the law, through their own decision-making procedures. Delegated functions are financed from state grants. Other sources of income for municipalities include local fees, capital income and so on. All in all, size has the strongest effect on municipal income.

The mayors surveyed in 1997 regardless of the size of the municipality they represented considered 'too little discretion for municipal authorities in determining local income' as the most important problem (Baldersheim, 2003). Also, other research projects conducted among mayors, such as POLLEADER (see Bäck et al, 2006) and 'The Mayors of Small Municipalities' (Bernard et al, 2011), indicate that raising funds from external sources ranked among their main priorities.

Municipal organs

The form and number of organs established by a municipality is also influenced by the size of the municipality. The town council, elected for a four-year term of office, may consist of 5 to 55 members (with the exception of the City of Prague, which also has the status of a county). The specific number of representatives in the town council is determined by the council itself within the limits set by law. In total, every four years around 2% of the adult population stands for election and approximately 60,000 elected local councillors in more than 6000 municipalities get the opportunity to gain experience with the process of local decision making. Other citizens may participate in the work by serving on committees and commissions that have initiative and control functions.

From among its members the town council elects the mayor and vice-mayor (or vice-mayors) of the municipality. If the council has 15 or more members, it also elects other members of an executive board. Compared with collective bodies (council, board) a mayor has relatively few competencies, primarily that of representing the municipality externally. However, the executive boards are elected only in approximately one-fifth of all municipalities. Mayors of the rest, usually smaller municipalities, are endowed with most of the competencies of the board.

The administrative tasks of a municipality are carried out by the municipal office headed by the mayor and also including the vice-mayor(s), a secretary of the municipal office and other employees (Illner, 2011, p 512). The total number of secretaries is around 600 because municipalities without an authorised municipal office or without extended competences can decide if they wish to establish a position of chief administrative officer or not. According to the Czech Statistical Office, at the end of 2013, two-thirds of the municipalities or municipal districts employed fewer than 10 people, while the 50 largest municipal authorities had more than 250 employees (see Table 9.2).

Table 9.2: Number of employees of municipalities and city districts

Municipalities/city districts	Number of employees of municipalities and city districts								Total
	0	1-5	6-9	10-24	25-99	100-249	250+	No answer[a]	
Number	22	2928	1085	1048	424	140	53	604	6304
%	<1	46	17	17	7	2	1	10	100

Source: Czech Statistical Office.

Note: [a] It can be assumed that the one-tenth of municipalities for which the Czech Statistical Office did not have data were municipalities with very few or no employees. The Czech Statistical Office was ranked in the forefront of organisations that burdened municipal governments with unnecessary questions, a claim with which half of the mayors of municipalities with populations of below 1000 who were surveyed in 2007 agreed (Galvasová et al, 2007, p 45). The number of employees does not include organisations established by municipalities.

The relationship between the size of the municipality and the number of employees was well documented in research by Galvasová et al (2007). None of the municipalities with fewer than 500 residents had more than five employees. The most common employees of the smallest municipalities were accountants, followed by cleaning staff and maintenance workers and finally administrative workers. Administrative tasks in the smallest communities are therefore usually dealt with by the mayor.

Consolidation or cooperation between municipalities?

Many well-known arguments against the existence of small local government (for example Keating, 1995) have been used mainly by central organs in favour of amalgamation in the Czech Republic (Illner, 2010a, 2010b). However, there has not been significant movement towards mergers of small municipalities. The administrative merging of municipalities is also currently politically impossible (Illner, 2010b), and economic pressures have also failed to have this effect. An example would be the radical change in the system of taxation at the beginning of the new millennium. The result was a strengthening of the effect of size on municipal income. The smallest municipalities received four to six times less money per capita than the largest cities. However, the system of tax distribution was significantly changed twice to make the disparity between municipalities of different sizes less significant, among other things due to pressure from two interest groups, the Union of Towns and Municipalities of the Czech Republic and the Association of Local Governments.

From a functional point of view, the fragmentation of municipalities is dealt with by the abovementioned differentiation between municipalities according to the extent of transferred responsibilities. In the field of independent powers many municipalities make use of various opportunities for mutual cooperation, such as obtaining financial resources from the state budget or from EU structural funds. While the idea of merging municipalities is usually rejected by the representatives of small towns, and they are rather sceptical when evaluating reforms in public administration, they perceive the potential of inter-municipal cooperation in solving the problems of small towns to be positive (Vajdová et al, 2006; Klusáček, 2008). Nonetheless, Illner (2010b) claims that the scarcity and unpredictability of financial means are the main obstacles to municipalities forming voluntary unions. The Czech Ministry of the Interior in 2005 promised financial rewards for municipalities participating in the newly introduced so-called *communities of municipalities* that 'would take over and perform some of the independent responsibilities of their members. Hence, the foundations of a new, simplified territorial matrix of municipal government would be created' (Illner, 2011, p 524). Existing proposals, however, have so far not moved forward. In particular, small municipalities also take advantage of the opportunities offered by the Local Action Groups (LAG) implementing the 'Leader' approach, which, in addition, to bringing together communities also reaches out to private entities and non-profit organisations (European Communities, 2006).[1]

Who governs and who influences local leaders?

Profile of local decision makers

After the renewal of local democracy and free elections, men, middle-aged groups, highly educated people and citizens in white-collar occupations became overrepresented in the elected municipal bodies in the Czech Republic, as they are in many political systems (Offerdal et al, 1996, p 117). The highest proportions of university-educated mayors were found in the East and Central European countries (Steyvers and Reynaert, 2006), and councillors in Czech municipalities surveyed later were also above the median level in the same characteristic (Verhelst et al, 2013).

This bias in the sociodemographic profile of local politicians is correlated with size. As for mayors, smaller municipalities are more often led by women than bigger ones. Moreover, women are significantly more underrepresented in the executive boards than in local councils. In the case of education, the proportion of university-educated mayors of larger cities has long remained around three-quarters but small municipalities are usually led by mayors who have completed only secondary education (see Bernard et al, 2011; Ryšavý and Šaradín, 2011).

The level of professionalisation of local politicians is another characteristic that is strongly affected by the size of the municipality. In the approximately 25000 municipalities with no more than 500 or 600 inhabitants, not even the function of the mayor has been paid as full-time work. In most of the rest of the municipalities only the position of mayor is full-time. Only in a few dozen of the largest cities are there 4-10 full-time politicians, mostly members of executive boards.

The activities of political parties are also related to the size of each municipality because of the low level of party membership and the low level of organisational penetration, especially into smaller communities (Linek and Pecháček, 2007). The vast majority of the smallest municipalities are represented by independent candidates who run either individually or on local independent lists (see Kostelecký, 2007). Representatives of small municipalities often distance themselves from 'politicking', which they associate with parliamentary and party politics (Jüptner, 2008). Even bigger cities in the Czech Republic are not run by members of political parties as often as in many other European countries. In contrast to this, the project POLLEADER showed a high index of the importance of political parties in the Czech Republic (Fallend et al, 2006). In communities with active

---

[1]   According to the National Network of Local Action Groups, there were 180 LAG in the Czech Republic in April 2014 and these operate in 92% of all municipalities in the Czech Republic; 75% of municipalities in the Czech Republic participate in the decision-making process of LAG either directly or through voluntary associations of municipalities (http://nsmascr.cz/).

political parties, municipal leaders often hold functions in local or regional party organisations (see Ryšavý and Šaradín, 2011; Verhelst et al, 2013).

The size of a municipality also has an impact on the willingness of citizens to run in local elections. Larger municipalities are able to generate a greater number of people interested in working in the council. Councillors in smaller municipalities are less willing to stand for re-election even though their chance of repeated success is very high. In larger towns the opposite is true (Ryšavý and Bernard, 2013).

Influence on local decision making

Since the first research on local government, the elected councils have been considered to have the greatest influence on decision making about important matters concerning towns and villages. Two-thirds of mayors and chief executive officers surveyed in LDI considered them to have 'very much influence'. As shown in Figure 9.1, mayors underestimated their own influence at the beginning of the 1990s. Ten years later they assessed their influence to be comparable to that of the entire executive board. The extreme growth in the perceived influence of chief executive officers in 2003 can be explained by the context of the reform in public administration. After the abolition of the district offices, chief executive officers (CEOs) had to deal with functions delegated to cities with extended powers and they hired more subordinates. At that time, mayors considered 'lack of clear objectives in administrative reform' to be the strongest barrier to the improvement of productivity in local authorities (POLLEADER, 2003).

Figure 9.1: Influence on local decision-making from the mayors' perspective

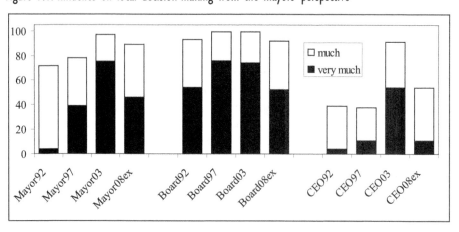

Sources: Answers of mayors - LDI I (1992); LDI II (1997); POLLEADER (2003); and members of executive boards - MAELG (2008). All respondents were from municipalities with more than 10,000 inhabitants.

Note: The lower proportions of 'very much influence' attributed to members of the executive boards in 2008 could be affected by the slight difference in the rating scales as translated into Czech.

The elected officials and CEOs make up the circle of the most influential people and institutions of local self-government. However, the *heads of departments* in the municipality, who are in addition responsible for implementing the policies adopted, seem also to have a lesser but still apparent influence on agenda setting. The influence attributed to the *presidents of council committees, party leaders and the party groups in the council* seems rather to lie in the possibility of pre-negotiating issues which are ultimately decided collectively by the council.

A portion of the local politicians also attach considerable influence to *regional and higher levels of government, local businessmen, local MPs or ministers*. The role of regional government (counties) is, to say the least, ambiguous. After the abolition of district offices in 2003, mayors often turned to the regional offices for technical or methodological assistance. In the programming period 2007-13, the leaders of counties started to contribute significantly to the distribution of money from European structural funds (Baun and Marek, 2008). In addition to the counties, local MPs and ministers can also help open the path to grants and other financial resources for municipalities. This phenomenon has sometimes earned its own name: it is referred to as 'pork barrel', 'small houses' or 'building parliamentary memorials'.

When the mayors of Czech cities were asked as part of the project POLLEADER to evaluate useful sources of information and whom to turn to for advice, they reported *consultants* and *other mayors* more often than the other mayors surveyed in 17 European countries. A possible explanation for reliance on other mayors is the previously mentioned reform of public administration. These 'other mayors' could then be representatives of cities with a similar status or mayors of cities falling within the parameters of cities with extended powers, with whom it was necessary to consult in order to carry out the delegated competencies.

The significance of the utility of consultants can to some extent be explained by other sources of information whose usefulness mayors mentioned, including their own experience and education. No mayor can be trained in all the fields relevant to their role as the representatives of their city. As the mayor of a small town said in one interview: 'Here you are always being asked questions. People simply know that you are the mayor and basically anything goes here – even things which have nothing to do with the performance of my work – so people just come to me'. From the research of Bernard et al (2011) it appears that in small rural communities the role of local experts can be filled by members of the council with whom the mayor consults often on matters which fall entirely within his competence.

Local policy work through the lens of time management and communication networks

Throughout this chapter, the role of the size of municipalities as one of the most important factors determining the form of local government and public administration on a local level has been highlighted. The aim of this section of the chapter is to clarify local policy work by comparing the time-management strategies of mayors of small towns and larger cities. Here again, this is derived from the research findings of POLLEADER (2003) and 'Mayors of Small Municipalities' (Bernard et al, 2011). The first of these encompasses the responses of the mayors of cities with more than 10,000 inhabitants, which are home to more than half of the population of the Czech Republic. The second incorporates the responses of mayors of towns with up to 2000 inhabitants, that is a category into which nine out of the ten municipalities in the country fall.

Mayors declared that their most time-consuming activities are meetings with citizens, their groups and organisations (see Table 9.3). Half of them devoted more than five hours a week to individual preparation for the duties of mayor. In the case of mayors of small towns other issues such as administrative tasks and fundraising came to the fore at the expense of these two activities. In larger cities such activities were carried out by employees of the offices with which the mayors were in contact. Especially in the case of non-professionalised mayors (those who do not receive a full-time salary), we can see how difficult it is for them to devote time to all the necessary matters. Mayors who hold other jobs more often limit the activities which, according to their responses, are most time-consuming (such as administrative tasks and meetings with citizens). The greatest difference is the in managing municipal employees, which is understandable because there are only a small number of officers and other employees in offices with non-professionalised mayors (see Table 9.4).

Research on the obligations burdening the performance of public administration showed that

> the majority of the mayors from the small municipalities found as the most burdening and difficult the competences which demand either highly specialised professional knowledge (for example juristic protection of children, making special expert decisions), or the competences which could be connected with unpleasant or even neighbour's conflicts. (Klusáček, 2008, p 7)

However, mayors carefully evaluated which spheres of activity should be transferred to a higher level of government. Even more of them complained of a lack of methodological guidance, and that they themselves are required to provide large amounts of information to higher levels of government, but do not get back the necessary information in sufficient quantity and quality (see Galvasová et al, 2007). In another study, mayors of small municipalities identified the complicated bureaucracy associated with grant applications as the most serious of nine potential impediments to promoting development in their communities (Bernard et al, 2011).

It is also possible to get a good view of the functioning of local administration in different sized municipalities through knowing with whom and how often key players such as mayors communicate. Nine out of ten mayors interviewed for the

Table 9.3: Time management of town mayors (median and percentage of more than five hours per week)

	Median	>5 hours (%)
Meetings with citizens, groups, etc	10 hours	68
Individual preparation for the duties of mayor	6 hours	51
Meetings with administrative staff	4 hours	29
Meetings with council and executive boards	4 hours	22
Ceremonial and representative functions in the town hall	4 hours	12
Field visits in the city	3 hours	17
Public debates and conferences outside the town hall	2 hours	12
Meetings with authorities from the region, national government	2 hours	7
Meetings with authorities from other cities	2 hours	4
Political party meetings	2 hours	3

Source: POLLEADER (2003)
Note: N = 76. Question: 'How many hours do you on average spend each week in the following activities?'

Table 9.4: Time management of mayors of small towns according to their status (median category and percentage of more than five hours per week)

	Full-time		Non-professionalised	
	Median	>5 hours (%)	Median	>5 hours (%)
Administrative tasks*	6-10	57	1-5	30
Meetings with citizens, groups, etc.	6-10	53	1-5	27
Managing municipal employees	6-10	54	1-5	21
Fundraising**	1-5	37	1-5	23
Preparation for council or board meetings	1-5	37	1-5	20
Dealing with state and regional authorities	1-5	28	1-5	16
Dealing with firms working for municipality	1-5	27	1-5	16
Meetings with authorities from other cities	1-5	5	<1	5

Source and note: The mayors of small municipalities (2011); N = 209 (109 full-time, 100 non-professionalised). Question: 'How much time do you spend, on average, on the following activities?'
Notes: *Dealing with the administrative requirements of state and regional authorities. ** Seeking and administering grants or other additional financial resources for the municipality

project POLLEADER said that they met on a daily basis with the municipality's chief executive officer. After the CEO, in order came ordinary citizens (53% of daily communication), heads of departments in the municipality (36%) and members of the executive board (33%). These were followed by private business lobbyists (25%), leaders of the mayors' own parties (20%) and other employees in the municipality (16%). After that came journalists, representatives of public agencies at the local level, different local councillors, representatives of other cities, regional and national politicians, union representatives, leaders of voluntary organisations and so on. Three-quarters of the mayors of small municipalities said that they are in daily contact with individual citizens. In second place, with a large gap, appeared individual councillors (35% in daily contact) and third were representatives of local associations (21%). Mayors communicate less frequently with representatives and employees of higher levels of public administration, other mayors and local businessmen.

In other words, in big cities the core is made up of the communications network of local executive authorities, which in municipalities without executive boards is embodied in the mayor. Communication with citizens in small villages is virtually unavoidable. The method of communication with ordinary citizens in major cities unfortunately was not specified in the research. The declared frequency of contacts between mayors and the business community is consistent with the finding that it is not only Czech mayors, but the vast majority of European mayors who perceived their main task to be to attract economic activity to their city (see Magnier et al, 2006). By contrast, most mayors of small municipalities perceive influencing the economic development of their communities to be beyond their power. This corresponds to relatively weak relationships and limited communications with economic actors and a greater focus on the development of civic participation and community activities (Bernard et al, 2011, p 77).

Conclusion

According to the Act on Municipalities (Number 128/2000 Collection of Laws), a municipality attends to the general development of its territory and to the needs of its citizens; in the fulfilment of its tasks it also protects the public interest. It should make an effort to foster conditions for the development of social services and the satisfaction of the needs of its citizens. This includes, in particular, meeting the needs for housing, the protection and development of healthcare, transport and communications, information, education and training, general cultural development, and the protection of public order. The Czech Republic does so in a context characterised by: (a) dual functions exercised by municipalities – independent and delegated – in a fused model; (b) a key role of collective organs (councils and executive boards) in local self-government; (c) mayors entitled to relatively low competencies if the executive board is an elected body; (d) a hierarchy of municipalities distinguished according to the scope of competences delegated by state administration to them; and (e) state support for inter-municipal cooperation (see Bernard et al, 2011, p 51).

Local administration at the local level is strongly affected by a high level of territorial fragmentation that places the Czech Republic at the European extreme with Cyprus, France and Slovakia (see for example Swianiewicz, 2003; Loughlin et al, 2011, Appendix 1). The wave of separation of previously merged municipalities after 1989 was one of the most distinctive aspects of the renewal of self-government in the Czech Republic, reversing for a time the long-term trend towards an increase in the average size of municipalities. Local autonomy is still highly valued. The large variation in the sizes of municipalities results in a state in which concrete local policy work in the Czech context can on the one hand consist of integration into structures of multilevel governance facilitated by the Europeanisation of the administrative structure of big cities (Havlík, 2013), while, on the other hand, mayors carry a 'policy *patch*work' on their shoulders, covering everything from providing information or making decisions on operating snow blowers in the winter, all of which fall outside of the performance of the mayor's proper job (Klusáček, 2008, p 125).

To sum up, the main characteristic of policy work at the local level in the Czech Republic is its great variability. According to J.S. Mill (2005), every town, regardless of size, ought to have its own municipal council. On the other hand, he states that a mere village has no claim to municipal representation because such small places rarely have a sufficient population to provide a competent municipal council. His justification was the low calibre of people who almost always make up such councils. In the Czech Republic, in the vast majority of municipalities staffing local authorities is not a problem. The greatest or eternal problem is reconciling the principle of local democracy and effective administration with the proper model of local governance.

Acknowledgements

This chapter was written within the framework of the project 'The Professionalisation of Local and County Politicians in the Czech Republic'. It was funded by the Fund for the Support of Scientific Activity, Philosophical Faculty, Palacky University Olomouc (FF_30_2012_004).

References

Bäck, H., Heinelt, H. and Magnier, M. (eds) (2006) *The European Mayor. Political Leaders in the Changing Context of Local Democracy*, Wiesbaden: VS Verlag für Sozialwissenschaften.

Baldersheim, H. (2003) 'Towards normalisation of local democracy in East-Central Europe. A developmental approach to institutional reform', in H. Baldersheim, M. Illner and H. Wollmann (eds) *Local Democracy in Post-Communist Europe*, Opladen: Leske+Budrich, pp 241-61.

Baldersheim, H., Illner, M., Offerdal, A., Rose, L. and Swianiewicz, P. (eds) (1996) *Local Democracy and the Processes of Transformation in East-Central Europe*, Boulder, CO: Westview Press.

Baldersheim, H., Illner, M. and Wollmann, H. (eds) (2003) *Local Democracy in Post-Communist Europe*, Opladen: Leske+Budrich.

Baun, M. and Marek, D. (2008) 'EU cohesion policy and sub-national authorities in the new members', *Contemporary European Studies*, 2008(2): 5-20.

Bernard, J., Kostelecký, T., Illner, M. and Vobecká, J. (2011) *Samospráva venkovských obcí a místní rozvoj* [Local government in rural municipalities and local development], Praha: Sociologické nakladatelství.

Brusis, M. (2010) 'The Czech Republic', in M.J. Goldsmith and E.C. Page (eds) *Changing Government Relations in Europe*, London: Routledge, pp 30-46.

Colebatch, H., Hoppe, R. and Noordegraaf, M. (eds) (2010) *Working for Policy*, Amsterdam: Amsterdam University Press.

Czech Statistical Office (2013) *Small Lexicon of Municipalities of the Czech Republic 2013* [online], Prague: Czech Statistical Office. Available from www.czso.cz/csu/2013edicniplan.nsf/engpubl/1302-13-eng_r_2013

Egner, B., Sweeting, D. and Klok, P.-J. (eds) (2013) *Local Councillors in Europe*, Wiesbaden: Springer VS.

European Communities (2006) *The Leader Approach. A Basic Guide* [online], Luxembourg: Office for Official Publications of the European Communities. Available from http://ec.europa.eu/agriculture/publi/fact/leader/2006_en.pdf

Fallend, F., Ignits, G. and Swianiewicz, P. (2006) 'Divided loyalties? Mayors between party representation and local community interests', in H. Bäck, H. Heinelt and A. Magnier (eds) *The European Mayor: The Role and Position of Political Leaders in European Cities in Transformation*, Opladen: Verlag fur Sozialwissenschaften, pp 245-70.

Galvasová, I., Kadečka, S., Binek, J., Galvas, M., Halásek, D., Toušek, V. and Chabičovská, K. (2007) *Identifikace kompetencí zatěžujících výkon veřejné správy se zvláštním přihlédnutím k malým obcím. Závěrečná výzkumná zpráva* [Identification of competencies burdening performance of public administration with particular attention to small municipalities. Final research report] [online], Brno: GAREP. Available from www.mvcr.cz/clanek/identifikace-kompetenci-zatezujicich-vykon-verejne-spravy-se-zvlastnim-prihlednutim-k-malym-obcim-1-etapa.aspx

Grospič, J., Louda, T. and Vostrá, L. (eds) (2007) *Územní samospráva v České republice a Evropě* [Territorial self-government in the Czech Republic and Europe], Plzeň: Aleš Čeněk.

Havlík, V. (2013) *Města jako partner v procesu vládnutí. Případ českých a německých měst* [Cities as a partner in the process of governance. The case of Czech and German cities], Brno: MUNI PRESS.

Illner, M. (2010a) 'The voluntary union of municipalities: bottom-up territorial consolidation in the Czech Republic?', in P. Swianiewicz (ed) *Territorial Consolidation Reforms in Europe*, Budapest: Open Society Institute, Local Government and Public Service Reform Initiative, pp 219-35.

Illner, M. (2010b) 'Top-down or bottom-up? Coping with territorial fragmentation in the Czech Republic', in H. Baldersheim and L.E. Rose (eds) *Territorial Choice. The Politics of Boundaries and Borders*, Houndmills, Basingstoke: Palgrave Macmillan, pp 214-33.

Illner, M. (2011) 'The Czech Republic: local government in the years after the reform', in J. Loughlin, F. Hendriks and A. Lidström (eds) *The Oxford Handbook of Local and Regional Democracy in Europe*, Oxford: Oxford University Press, pp 505-27.

Jüptner, P. (2008) 'Local lists in the Czech Republic', in M. Reiser and E. Holtmann (eds) *Farewell to the Party Model? Independent Local Lists in East and West European Countries*, Wiesbaden: VS Verlag für Sozialwissenschaften, pp 21-37.

Keating, M. (1995) 'Size, efficiency and democracy: consolidation, fragmentation and public choice', in D. Judge, G. Stoker and H. Wollman (eds) *Theories of Urban Politics*, London: Sage Publications, pp 117-34.

Klusáček, P. (2008) *Problematika malých obcí v České republice s ohledem na chod a efektivitu správy. Disertační práce* [The issue of small municipalities in the Czech Republic with regard to the operation and management efficiency. Dissertation theses], Brno: PřF MU Brno.

Kostelecký, T. (2007) 'Political parties and their role in local politics in the post-communist Czech Republic', in F. Lazin, M. Evans, V. Hoffmann-Martinot and H. Wollmann (eds) *Local Government Reforms in Countries in Transition*, Lanham, MD: Lexington Books, pp 121-39.

Kruntorádová, I. and Jüptner, P. (2012) 'Finanční aspekty autonomie českých municipalit v postojích politických aktérů' [Financial aspects of the autonomy of Czech municipalities in the attitudes of political actors], *Politologický časopis*, 2012(4), pp 341-58.

Linek, L. and Pecháček, Š. (2007) 'Low membership in Czech political parties: party strategy or structural determinants?', *Journal of Communist Studies and Transition Politics*, 23(2): 259-75.

Loughlin, J., Hendriks, F. and Lidström, A. (eds) (2011) *The Oxford Handbook of Local and Regional Democracy in Europe*, Oxford: Oxford University Press.

Magnier, A., Navarro, C. and Russo, P. (2006) 'Urban systems as growth machines? Mayors' governing networks against global indeterminacy', in H. Bäck, H. Heinelt and A. Magnier (eds) *The European Mayor. Political Leaders in the Changing Context of Local Democracy*, Wiesbaden: VS Verlag für Sozialwissenschaften, pp 353-76.

Mill, J.S. (2005) *Considerations on Representative Government* [online], Ann Arbor, MI: University of Michigan Library. Available from http://name.umdl.umich.edu/ABX0154.0001.001

Nunvářová, S. (2014) *Moderní přístupy k řízení územní veřejné správy* [Modern approaches to the management of local public administration], PhD thesis, Brno: Faculty of Economics and Administration, Masaryk University Brno.

Ochrana, F., Fantová Šumpíková, M., Pavel, J., Nemec, J., Klazar, S., Meričková, B. and Rousek, P. (2007) *Efektivnost zabezpečení vybraných veřejných služeb na úrovni obcí.* [The effectiveness of the security of chosen public services at the municipal level] [online], Praha: VŠE, Oeconomica. Available from http://kvf.vse.cz/storage/1212656291_sb_kniha_ochrana.pdf

Offerdal, A., Hanšpach, D., Kowalczyk, A. and Patočka, J. (1996) 'The new local elite', in H. Baldersheim, M. Illner, A. Offerdal, L. Rose and P. Swianiewicz (eds) *Local Democracy and the Processes of Transformation in East-Central Europe*, Boulder, CO: Westview Press, pp 105-40.

Plaček, M., Půček, M. and Šimčíková, A. (2013) 'The utilization of benchmarking for strategic and project management of municipalities in the Czech Republic', *International Journal of Business and Social Science*, 4(16): 18-23.

Provazníková, R. (2009) *Financování měst, obcí a regionů. Teorie a praxe* [Financing municipalities and regions. Theory and practice] (2nd edn), Praha: GRADA.

Ryšavý, D. and Bernard J. (2013) 'Size and local democracy: the case of Czech municipal representatives', *Local Government Studies*, 39(6): 833-52.

Ryšavý, D. and Šaradín, P. (2011) *Zastupitelé českých měst a obcí v evropské perspektivě* [Czech municipal councillors in the European perspective], Praha: Sociologické nakladatelství.

Steyvers, K. and Reynaert, H. (2006) '"From the few are chosen the few"... on the social background of European mayors', in H. Bäck, H., Heinelt and A. Magnier (eds) *The European Mayor. Political Leaders in the Changing Context of Local Democracy*, Wiesbaden: VS Verlag für Sozialwissenschaften, pp 43-73.

Swianiewicz, P. (2003) 'How beautiful is bigger? In search of the optimal size for local democracy', in H. Baldersheim, M. Illner and H. Wollmann (eds) *Local Democracy in Post-Communist Europe*, Opladen: Leske + Budrich, pp 289-300.

Vajdová, Z., Čermák, D. and Illner, M. (eds) (2006) *Autonomie a spolupráce: důsledky ustavení obecního zřízení v roce 1990* [Autonomy and cooperation: implications of the establishment of a municipal government in 1990], Praha: Sociologický ústav AV ČR.

Verhelst, T., Reynaert, H. and Steyvers, K. (2013) 'Political recruitment and career development of local councillors in Europe', in B. Egner, D. Sweeting and P.-J. Klok (eds) *Local Councillors in Europe*, Wiesbaden: Springer VS, pp 27-49.

Vysoká škola ekonomická (2009) *Analýza financování výkonu státní správy a samosprávy územních samosprávných celků, která poskytne relevantní množství dat pro přípravu nového zákona o RUD. Závěrečná zpráva výzkumného úkolu pro Ministerstvo financí ČR* [Analysis of funding the state administration and local government of the territorial units that provide relevant quantities of data for the preparation of a new law on budgetary allotment of taxes act. Final report of the research project for the Ministry of Finance] [online], Praha: Vysoká škola ekonomická. Available from http://kreg.vse.cz/wp-content/uploads/2010/01/Zprava-pro-MF-CR.pdf

Datasets:

LDI I (1992) *Local Democracy and Innovation.*

LDI II (1997) *Local Democracy and Innovation.*

MAELG (2008) *Municipal Assemblies in European Local Governance. The Mayors of small municipalities* (2011).

POLLEADER (2003) *Political Leaders in European Cities.*

Part III

Internal policy advisory councils, consultants and public opinion

TEN

Policy advisory councils: governmental and departmental advisory bodies

Kateřina Merklová, Kateřina Ptáčková

Introduction

Following the development of decision making in the Western democracies (see Radaelli 1998; Brown 2008, 2009; Robert, 2010; Fobé et al, 2013) characterised by shifts from traditional state-centred, hierarchical models towards more horizontal decentralised *governance* patterns (Craft, 2014, p 42; Howlett, 2011, p 248), governmental and departmental advisory bodies have recently been acknowledged as inherent components of the policy-making process in the Czech Republic. These councils and committees are set up primarily to provide the government with expert advice in a wide range of public policy areas in order to boost their policy (analytical) capacity (see Howlett, 2009). They include varying numbers of representatives of government (decision makers), bureaucrats, representatives of various public or private institutions and appointed 'independent' experts. They are very heterogeneous in terms of their size, scope, mission, resources, composition, influence and accountability to government. Moreover, all these aspects within most of the bodies evolve substantially over time due to changes in the composition of the government, duration of its term, its priorities and its stability as well as the government's willingness to take advice from the existing or newly set up advisory bodies and to cooperate with them. Given the extreme political instability of the Czech Republic, the level of dynamics within some of them is very high.

We can identify several reasons for involvement of these bodies in the policy-making process. Above all, increasing complexity of policy making with respect to engagement in supranational, transnational and international policy networks; a developing knowledge society; and a drift towards evidence-based policy making and scientification of politics (and politicisation of science) have contributed to the emphasis on knowledge and policy advice in contemporary policy making that has also been reflected in the Czech Republic. However, advisory councils and committees have a surprisingly long tradition in Czech policy making. Under communist rule, there was a well-established state policy advisory system at the central level as well as many bodies directly governed by the ministries which were supposed to provide policy advice within the limits of the official ideology

(Veselý, 2012, p 3).[1] Besides these, some cases of relatively independent advisory bodies appointed by the government in that era are also known.

In the Czech parliamentary system, government ministries are traditionally in a relatively stronger position than the Prime Minister. Strong departmentalism, which is believed to be one of the legacies of the communist era, was reproduced again during the EU accession process of 1998–2004 (Kabele and Linek, 2006) and still prevails. Referring to the locational dimension of the policy advisory system (PAS) (Halligan, 1995; Howlett, 2011; Craft and Howlett, 2012, 2013; Veselý, 2012), in the current Czech setting the ministries have retained their policy advice capacities in terms of well-trained civil servants ('direct internal policy advisory system') as well as relatively autonomous institutions, organisations and agencies gathering and analysing data of diverse sorts ('distant internal policy advisory system'). In addition to these two categories, there are bodies independent of the government and public service that provide the government with policy advice on a voluntary basis and on their own initiative ('external policy advisory system') (for applied terminology see Veselý, 2012).[2] The system of external advisory bodies constitutes an organisational framework for the representation of various social interests and an inclusive policy-making process.

In the 'marketplace for policy ideas and information' (Howlett, 2011; Craft and Howlett, 2012), the Czech governmental advisory bodies are located (organisationally) on the border between the external and internal policy advisory systems, acting as 'suppliers' as well as 'brokers' of policy advice. The main proposition of this chapter is that there is more than one legitimate way in which the government sets up its advisory bodies and, consequently (referring to the content dimension of the PAS), there are various kinds of policy advice the advisory bodies provide the government with as well as different roles they play in the policy-making process. Our analysis is based on the assumption that the role of the advisory bodies and the nature of the policy they produce are to some degree determined by their formal framework. We argue that the degree of determination may be higher in the Czech Republic than in well-established democracies with a strong tradition of inclusive democratic discussion. In particular, this is because officially prescribed guidelines may often be the only way to ensure minority protection in the absence of generally accepted and followed informal rules of democratic practice. Moreover, in the Czech policy-making process, there is traditionally a particularly strong emphasis upon the legal status of policy actors (Veselý, 2012, p 3).

---

[1] In the communist era, a parallel system of Soviet policy advisers was imposed on the government administration (Kaplan, 1993).

[2] Advisory councils and committees represent a significant, though not exclusive, source of advice to decision makers. There is a range of other actors that provide the government with knowledge and policy advice and are engaged in the policy-making process in the Czech Republic – among others, nongovernmental organisations (NGOs), the advisory base of political parties, private consulting firms and academia. Many of these actors are discussed in other chapters of this book.

We analysed the advisory council system in the Czech Republic by applying a twofold qualitative approach. First, we focused on three key elements of their formal framework: (1) membership and balance; (2) mode of appointment; and (3) decision-making systems within the councils. To address these objectives we carried out an extensive content analysis of relevant documents (mainly statutes, rules of procedure and research reports). Second, to examine the kind and the nature of policy advice the councils provide as well as their role and influence in the policy-making process we conducted 30 in-depth, semi-structured interviews with council members, members of the wider policy community, decision makers and high-ranking officials. The collected data were triangulated with content analysis of meeting reports, minutes, stenographic reports from parliamentary sessions, parliamentary committee and government reports, and so on as well as transcripts of press conferences, speeches and public statements of various issue-relevant decision makers and council members. In addition, reflections on the personal experience of one of the authors as a former member of several advisory committees represented an important source of information and understanding of advisory councils in the Czech Republic.

The first section of the chapter briefly outlines the contemporary state of the Czech policy advisory council system. The second section analyses the formal framework of that system with a special emphasis on three aspects: membership and balance, mode of appointment and decision-making systems. The final section is devoted to selected case studies of three advisory bodies from the recent past.

The current state of the policy advisory council system in the Czech Republic

In 2013, there were 26 standing advisory and working committees and councils at the governmental level.[3] Of these, 14 worked directly under the Office of the Government;[4] the other 12 were established and organised by particular government departments.[5] Depending on its composition, policy priorities, resources and stability, the government (or, with varying degree of independence, governmental departments) endowed the committees and councils with diverse tasks and objectives. In general, their main aim is to improve the situation in a related policy area through providing the government with relevant information

---

[3] Besides the government advisory and working committees, there are hundreds of departmental advisory committees organised by single departments. There is no publicly accessible information, and the departments themselves are not entirely sure either, about their numbers, tasks and membership.

[4] They focused on issues such as the EU, the economy, state security, corruption, legislation, the Roma community, human rights, national minorities, NGOs, drug policy, people with disabilities, the information society and research and development.

[5] They focused on issues such as energy policy, healthcare, economic and social consensus, safety, ageing, floods and sustainable development.

(see the concept of evidence-based policy making in Howlett, 2009).[6] Moreover, the advisory committees and councils formulate and express their opinions with respect to government bills and policy proposals. They may also, of their own initiative, identify or point out potential problems and formulate their own policy proposals. While they have certain (limited) resources for producing their own studies and analysis, they usually do not conduct inquiries and investigations. Besides these, their objectives may be rather process-oriented. They may initiate or facilitate cooperation among relevant actors within a policy community.

Their influence (see Fobé et al, 2013, pp 234-236) or impact (see Robert, 2008, pp 323-325) in the policy-making process differs significantly (compare Weible, 2008, pp 619-621). In terms of direct influence of their advice on a policy programme, some of them draw up recommendations and policy proposals which are almost entirely accepted by the government, while others stand in opposition to the government instead and exert their influence mainly through the news media and public discussion. There are also quite significant differences in terms of available resources granted by the government to enhance the capacity of the committees and their advice. Advisory committees are engaged mostly in the initial stages of the policy-making process (agenda-setting and formulation) as well as in policy evaluation. They are less often involved in policy implementation.[7]

To partially deal with the diversity of governmental advisory councils, we can divide them according to a few criteria. First, with regard to method of establishment, we can distinguish between statutory, (relatively) permanent and ad hoc groups. Second, concerning their institutional affiliation, we differentiate governmental, departmental and interdepartmental groups. Moreover, as outlined in the introduction, according to the degree of independence from and accountability to the government, we can identify three categories: predominantly external groups, predominantly internal groups and a hybrid category that represents an overlap and dynamism between these two. Last but not least, considering the nature of representation of the members and related balance provisions, that is ensuring or protecting the public interest in advisory committees either by representing and pursuing the 'interest of the public'/'public interest' or by balancing competing direct interests (Brown, 2008, 2009), we can divide those with committee members into experts in terms of their professional competence; and representatives in terms of their political interests.

Formal frameworks and guidelines of advisory bodies

An advisory body's formal framework determines, at least to some extent, its institutional purpose and the ways it can be used by various actors to pursue

---

[6] Based on an analysis of binding guidelines.

[7] Their role within the implementation stage is mostly limited to funding NGOs' educational, social inclusion, and drug prevention activities; however, there are also several legally binding decisions that the committees are supposed to take on behalf of the government.

their strategic interests. Its official guidelines may both determine the level of responsiveness of a given governmental policy to expert opinions and interest group preferences, and a government official's ability to ensure that his or her policy intentions will be carried out effectively (McCubbins et al, 1987). Despite an inevitable gap between the formal framework and actual operations, the guidelines 'provide a normative backdrop that potentially shapes how advisory committee members go about their tasks' and offer insight into 'how agency administrators and other public officials understand the concept of representation and its role in government advisory committees' (Brown, 2009, p 94; see also Robert, 2010, pp 23-25).

There is no generally binding legislative framework governing the operation of the governmental committees in the Czech Republic.[8] With only two exceptions, all the committees were established by an ad hoc Government Resolution.[9] Their activities are governed by *statutes* and *rules of procedure*. Approved by the government on an ad hoc basis, the *statutes* define a committee's responsibilities, composition, the role of its chair and other members, the mode of setting up working subgroups, the forms of potential external cooperation, and so on. *Rules of procedure* are, in the vast majority of cases, approved by the advisory committees themselves. They define, sometimes in elaborate detail, the operational level - for example, the form, frequency and course of meetings; the form and content of minutes; the voting procedure; the form of subgroup meetings; and the form of information to be publicised.

Neither in the founding government resolutions nor in the statutes and rules of procedure are the specific role and general objectives of the governmental advisory committees conclusively defined. Unlike in the case of the UK or US, the binding documents do not refer explicitly to any general principles (compare for example with the neo-corporatist logic of Fobé et al, 2013), such as (some sort of) balance, partnership, diversity, representation of the target groups, degree of independence, public interest or public good. Nor do they discuss the issue of disclosure of interests. In several cases, a general reference to expertise as the basis of a committee's work is made. Thus, in order to understand the Czech government's idea of its advisory committees, it is necessary to focus on particular aspects of their institutional arrangements and mutual in/coherences. In the following section, we will discuss three significant features of the committees' formal frameworks: types of membership and balance, mode of member appointment, and forms of decision making.

---

[8]   Unlike in the case of government administration in the US (Federal Advisory Committee Act 1972), the UK (the role of the Commissioner for Public Appointments created by the Public Appointments Order in Council 1995 on 23 November 1995) or Australia (Australian Public Service Act 1999).

[9]   The Research and Development Council and the Government Legislative Council were established by a single Act.

Membership and balance provision

Balance provision, the protection of the public interest within advisory committees, may be ensured by several different means, of which Brown (2008, 2009) points out two that are currently employed in US practice. Committee members are either obliged to represent and pursue the 'interests of the public'/'public interests' or the public interest is protected by a balance of competing direct interests. Representative members are distinguished from expert members, with the latter appointed on the basis of their individual qualifications. While the advice from representative members is expected to reflect their particular group bias, experts are supposed to present their individual best judgement. Consequently, different approaches to ensure a balance between these two groups are applied. 'With regard to experts, the task would be to solicit a balance of scientific disciplines; in the case of representatives, it would be to ensure a balance of political interests' (Brown, 2009, p 100). With reference to many studies in science and technology, Brown opposes this dichotomy between expert judgements and popular will, or science and politics, arguing that they are based on simplified liberal-rationalist assumptions and a narrow interest-based model of representation. He suggests overcoming these distinctions through a fundamental change in the model of balance and representation. The candidates' 'points of view' should be assessed in terms of both social and professional perspectives.

In the case of the Czech Republic, neither of these approaches towards balance provision is applied universally and consistently. None of the government resolutions establishing the governmental advisory bodies specifies any provisions with regard to the balance issue; any intention to achieve it; or any expectations towards various types of members. Similarly, the committees' statutes and guidelines are lacking in explicit or implicit definitions of interest balance. Nor is it possible to identify any balance-related intentions when looking at their membership.

Drawing from the formal statutes, we can identify a high level of diversity in the committees' membership. There is an unintended mixture of 'independent experts' and various types of representatives (representatives of government; representatives of non-governmental institutions, for example Chambers of Commerce or Trade Unions; and representatives of abstract entities such as civil society or national minorities).[10] With only a few exceptions, the membership structure is rather unpremeditated, based on ad hoc decisions that do not reflect any concept of public interest. The members are neither selected deliberately with the aim of reflecting the entire diversity of interests, nor to stand for the

---

[10] Three advisory committees consist exclusively of members of government. Two committees are formed by representatives of particular government bodies. Half of the committees comprise no members other than these bodies' representatives and/or members of the government. Members representing an abstract entity or subgroup constitute a majority in two committees, a minority in eight. 'Independent experts' are the only members in three other committees, a majority in one and a small minority in six.

whole variety of expertise (for example scientific disciplines) in a particular area. Moreover, the analysis of the interviews with members revealed that, in terms of the distinction between the members supposed to speak for a particular interest and those supposed to express a view based on his or her expert knowledge, their self-perceptions differ significantly even within one single committee and often do not correspond with the formally declared roles.

Mode of member appointment

The entire process of member selection is open to the public only to a very limited extent. At the same time, committee members are not selected deliberately and openly by the government itself from among like-minded people only. All committee chairs are appointed and dismissed by the government and, with only one exception, they are members of the government. Other committee members are either appointed by the government on the basis of a proposal made by the chair or appointed directly by the chair. In many cases, membership of a particular person results directly from the statute (on the basis of their position in a particular institution). In fact, such membership results from direct government decisions as the statutes are approved by the government. In the case of 'independent experts' and representatives of social groups and other entities (around one-third of all the members) the government gives up control over these nominations in favour of committee chairs.

The question related to both these modes of appointment is based on the criteria by which these members are chosen. In the statutes, the criteria that the members must meet are restricted to 'being an independent expert' or representing a particular entity/institution. There are no rules or recommendations concerning these members' ages or gender balance, diversity or political preferences and affiliations. There are no officially defined procedures of selection and appointment. No one except for the chair is officially entitled to make recommendations. Free positions in the committees are neither advertised nor open to potential candidates, for example through official registers.[11]

Committee members are usually appointed for a four-year term. There are either no restrictions in terms of reappointment, or a single member may serve for no more than two consecutive terms. However, exceptions to this limit are not rare and the procedures do not exclude the possibility of replacing a member with another person from the same organisation. Moreover, as there is no official procedure for member appointment, the leaving member's recommendation on their successor is followed quite frequently. Due to all these conditions, the committees are relatively closed and their membership is likely to be stable in the long term.

---

[11] For examples of this mechanism, consult UK Public Appointments (http://publicappointments.cabinetoffice.gov.uk/) or NSW Boards and Committees Registers (www.boards.dpc.nsw.gov.au/online-registration).

Decision making

The course of committee meetings is specified by the formal documents in terms of recording, taking minutes, the quorum, members' right to have alternatives, presence of guests and the chair's role (presiding over meetings, establishing the agenda). Common decisions, advice and recommendations are formulated exclusively on the basis of majority voting. Since the voting is usually transparent, every member of the committee can see how the others vote. However, the meetings are not public unless it is decided otherwise and minutes are limited to information about the voting ratio.[12] Although the voting is very often unanimous, consensus as a preferable way to achieve a decision is not mentioned and no minority reports or dissenting statements are formally institutionalised. While a minority opinion can be included in the minutes upon request, there is no binding rule demanding alternative opinions on an issue to be reflected in the final advice provided to the government. The voting procedure plays an important symbolic role in constructing the 'democratic' nature of the committees and it significantly limits the risk of not finding a common position. However, as there is no clear idea of constituency and the membership structure is often rather accidental, the legitimacy of the voting procedure is questionable. Hence under the current institutional arrangement, the role of voting has primarily symbolic meaning.

Surprisingly, there are no rules for discussions as a part of the committees' toolbox and one of their most common modes of work. Moreover, discussion is not even mentioned in the proceedings. Similarly, the manner of chairing (for example the opportunities for members to contribute to the discussion) is not defined formally. In practice, the discussion procedure at committee meetings is relatively well institutionalised. However, this procedure can be changed significantly and arbitrarily by the chair. If this happens there are no formally set rules or principles the opposing minority can call on. The procedural protection of minorities within the committee meetings is weak.

Case studies of selected advisory bodies in the Czech Republic

The last section of the chapter discusses in detail three selected advisory bodies engaged in Czech policy making after 2000. Our intention is to present a diverse sample (small-N) in terms of the institutional affiliation of the advisory bodies (governmental, departmental, interdepartmental) as well as the methods of their establishment (statutory, (relatively) permanent, ad hoc) simultaneously. Our sample selection represents three types of cases: intense cases that are rich in information and demonstrate the phenomenon intensely but not extremely;

---

[12] It is theoretically possible for non-members to participate in a meeting, follow voting and even influence the agenda. However, there are no criteria on which decisions about cooperation with external subjects is taken, no procedures on how the 'guest' or 'associate' status can be gained and no criteria the applicant has to fulfil.

politically important cases that attract desired attention (or avoid attracting undesired attention) for their explicit engagement in policy making (Miles and Huberman, 1994, p 28; Punch, 2006, p 51); and (3) cases that are, with regard to their policy area and members, networked and interconnected.

The National Economic Council of the Government

The National Economic Council of the Government (NERV) was a governmental advisory body which consisted of ten renowned Czech economists.[13] The Council was set up in January 2009 by the right-wing Prime Minister Mirek Topolánek in order to help the government deal with the global economic crisis. Its task was to assess the impact of the crisis on the Czech economy and subsequently draw up proposals to cushion its effects. Within two months, the Council drafted a range of recommendations, mostly austerity measures, and 14 of them were subsequently adopted by the government. The entire Council was engaged in the initial phases of the policy process, and a few members were involved in implementation by actively advocating and promoting their recommendations in the media and persuading the public of the 'unavoidable necessity' of these measures (Stöckelová, 2012.[14] Apart from the favourable political circumstances (uncertainty) caused paradoxically by the economic crisis, the coherence of the body, its narrow agenda and the pace of implementation contributed to the NERV's considerable direct influence in the policy-making process.

The appointment of the members was based exclusively on Prime Minister Topolánek's decision and did not follow any explicit balance provision. Expertise in economics (both in academic and professional terms) was regarded as the main qualification. The Prime Minister introduced the members as 'experts who are engaged in business, the banking and financial sectors as well as in academia'.[15] The appointment process raised controversy particularly due to the lack of transparency (as pointed out by members themselves) and the absence of diversity of world views within the Council. While one member perceived his appointment as a kind of personal honour, another accepted it so that he 'could transform the claims of the Confederation of Industry of the Czech Republic into policies'.[16] The uncertainty in terms of member accountability and representation did not prevent the government (and some of the members themselves) from presenting

---

[13] The number of members varied between 10 and 15.

[14] In the period from August 2010 to July 2011, members of the council held eight workshops open to the public, four public events at universities, tens of press conferences as well as hundreds of media appearances.

[15] Premiér jmenoval členy Národní ekonomické rady vlády [The members of the National Economic Council appointed by the PM], Press Release, Office of the Government of the Czech Republic, 8 January 2009, www.vlada.cz/cz/media-centrum/predstavujeme/premier-jmenoval-cleny-narodni-ekonomicke-rady-vlady-51464/

[16] See footnote 15.

the Council as an 'expert' or scientific body, based on its links with academia (Chapter Seventeen). The scientific character of its operation was even stressed by the decision-making procedure that sought the full consent of all participants; otherwise the Council would not express its opinion on the issue (as, for example, regarding the accession of the Czech Republic to the Eurozone). This procedure, quite exceptional among the Czech advisory committees, aimed to raise the level of legitimacy of the advice by declaring that there was no uncertainty regarding its appropriateness and effect.

The time period of 2009–13 was marked with political instability (the fall of the Topolánek government, the appointment of the caretaker government, the general election of 2010, the new centre-right government, the dissolution of the governmental coalition and one of its political parties).[17] In spite of that, the NERV remained stable in terms of its mode of operation, procedures and membership. Nevertheless, the scope of its agenda expanded considerably, from tasks related to the economic crisis at the beginning to many other areas under the new government. Consequently, the Council was structured into six separate working groups (on public finance, pension reform, anti-corruption, European affairs, competitiveness and business innovation, and healthcare funding). These groups comprised tens of external collaborators who volunteered in the formulation of recommendations and policy proposals.

In this late phase, the Council was well institutionalised within the Office of the Government; its secretary was appointed under a full-time contract and the government departments were obliged to provide data to the Council. On the other hand, the NERV's role was restricted to agenda setting and formulation of recommendations which were not binding. Its agenda was defined in three ways: first, by the government; second, on the members' initiative; and finally, by various government departments which asked for comments on and consultations on their own proposals. Thus, the Council's advice might have had an indirect impact on policy making by this very activity. However, representatives of the departments were rarely involved in the formulation of recommendations. This created, in some cases, a discrepancy between expert knowledge (produced exclusively by economists, and thus mono-disciplinary) and procedural knowledge, manifested in the inability to introduce proposals that could be built into the existing legal framework.

In assessing the role and the influence of the NERV, we see its main role in the initial phases of the policy cycle. Moreover, its members were more or less (depending on individual motivation) engaged in advocacy, promotion and diffusion of the governmental policies in particular policy communities as well as among the general public. Some of the members considered this task one of the main objectives of the Council. Others expressed their disillusionment regarding the limited implementation of the NERV's recommendations.

---

[17] The activity of the NERV was suspended before the general election in September 2009 and restored by the new prime minister in August 2010.

The Bezděk Committee

The Bezděk Committee, an interdepartmental advisory body, took part in the preparation of a pension reform. Despite the controversy related to the redistribution effects of pensions, this policy area requires consensual decision making, widely accepted solutions (in political as well as social terms) and long-term stability. Inspired by the Swedish Working Group on Pensions of 1991, the Bezděk Committee was established by the social democratic Prime Minister Vladimir Špidla in 2004. It ended its mission in June 2005 by releasing a final report that failed to have a considerable impact on the pension system. However, several years later the committee's activity was restored. Although chaired by the same person, the second Bezděk Committee differed significantly in its membership structure as well as the advice provided.[18]

The main objective of the first Bezděk Committee was to gather all relevant actors and analyse their explicit positions on the existing pension system. Regarding the balance provision, representation of the widest possible range of interests was sought. Moreover, special emphasis on transparency of the whole process was supposed to increase the level of mutual confidence and encourage cooperative and consensual decision making.

The committee consisted of two subcommittees: the *Group of Experts*, comprising two members nominated by each political party represented in the Chamber of Deputies plus one nominated by the Prime Minister, one by the Minister of Finance, and one by the Minister of Labour and Social Affairs; and the *Executive Group*, consisting of the chair, Vladimír Bezděk, an economic expert of the Czech National Bank, and officials from the Ministry of Labour and Social Affairs, the Ministry of Finance and one or two nominees from each political party.

The main task of the Executive Group was to compare the reform drafts of all political parties submitted by the Group of Experts according to a deliberatively agreed common set of criteria, to apply those criteria to the existing pension system and to assess its development and sustainability. Apart from the political parties, the submission of drafts was open to all interested organisations and individuals.[19] Therefore, neither the experts nor the Executive Group did any research on their own. The final report did not emphasise any proposal as an ideal alternative to the status quo. On the contrary, the first Bezděk Committee referred to the political nature and arbitrariness of a final decision. The intention to arrive at a consensus accepted by the entire range of participating actors was not explicitly expressed; nevertheless the entire activity of the first Bezděk Committee was considered the first stage of a consensual reform process.

---

[18] In order to avoid any confusion, we distinguish between the so-called 'first Bezděk Committee' and 'second Bezděk Committee' in this chapter. However, rather than seeing them separately, we prefer to understand them together as one committee with a high level of dynamism within it.

[19] For example, the Czech Confederation of Trade Unions and the private ING Pension Fund took this opportunity and submitted their drafts.

Under the leverage of the forthcoming general elections, decision makers did not reach any agreement on further progress and thus the first Bezděk Committee itself exerted only limited influence on the reform. However, it played a significant role in the initial stage of the policy-making process not just immediately but also, as will be explained below, when the reform process was re-initiated five years later. It framed the expert and public discussion in terms of the unsustainability of the status quo and delimited further discussions which used the widely accepted set of assessment criteria. Besides this, the coordinated approach and the parties' willingness to participate contributed to the good reputation of the first Bezděk Committee.

In 2009 the caretaker government decided to set up a second Bezděk Committee in order to draw up a reform programme based on expert opinions of the members. The initial cooperative, public-friendly mode of operation was transformed into a rather rationalistic, expert-based one. The nominees of the political parties were replaced with 'experts' designated by the chair and mostly recruited from within the expert community involved in the pension fund business. However, the selection process was not transparent and the membership did not explicitly claim representation of interests; on the contrary, in their discussions members 'aimed to put their employers' interests aside'. The rest of the committee comprised representatives of the government, the Ministry of Finance and the Ministry of Labour and Social Affairs. These high-ranking officials provided the committee with knowledge with regard to the feasibility of its proposals (technical and financial) and their compatibility with the existing legal framework. Nevertheless, similar to the NERV, decision makers were not actively involved in the formulation of recommendations and ultimately a gap between the expert and the political level of the policy-making process emerged and affected implementation of the recommendations.

Concerning membership in the second Bezděk Committee, we cannot identify an explicit definition of any form of balance provision. However, based on the in-depth interviews, the members themselves were able to identify some balance patterns within the body, such as a tripartite organisation (representatives of trade unions, the government and employers) and representation of all relevant actors within the policy community (a few pension funds, financial and pension consultants, clients, the government, the Ministry of Finance and the Ministry of Labour and Social Affairs).

Six months after its re-establishment, the second Bezděk Committee issued a final report introducing two alternative sets of recommendations, one of which was drawn up by just one dissenting member. This ambiguity along with an unstable post-election situation contributed to the indifferent positions of all political parties on the final recommendations of the second Bezděk Committee.

Immediately after the election in 2010, the new government declared a commitment to carry out the reform of the pension system as one of its policy priorities. However, neither of the two alternatives described in the final report was emphasised. A few of those members (including Bezděk) who advocated the majority opinion joined the abovementioned National Economic Council and continued in the preparation of the reform proposal in the Working Group on the Pension System Reform. Even though this proposal was repeatedly recommended and endorsed by the NERV, the government decided on a different policy programme to comply with the long-term political preferences of the most powerful right-wing coalition party.

The authors of the White Paper on Tertiary Education

The authors of the White Paper on Tertiary Education, classified as a departmental policy council, drew up a blueprint for higher education reform: the White Paper on Tertiary Education in the Czech Republic (White Paper). Unlike the previous advisory bodies, its members were not designated and officially appointed by the government. The initial intention of the Ministry of Education, Youth and Sports was to bring the Czech higher education policy community together and ensure the cooperation and engagement of all relevant actors in drawing up the reform proposal. Such an un–institutionalised approach was supposed to reconcile different interests and expert opinions. Under the ministry's leadership, the community was supposed to prepare the most profound and widely accepted reform of higher education since 1990. At the beginning, the group totalled about 30 experts (selected by the deputy minister) with various institutional backgrounds and perspectives on the higher education system. For the first time, the reform was not initiated by Czech universities but by the government and 'independent' experts (Pabian et al, 2011, p 115).

However, the initial inclusive approach progressively switched to a rather exclusive one. While the participants decreased to the final number of eight, crucial veto players (Prague-based universities, students, representative bodies of the entire academic community) boycotted the joint meetings and consequently left the group. Respondents in our interviews indicated various reasons: a lack of time, disappointment with meeting practices and a growing divergence of opinions on the reform. At the same time (or as a result), the basic principles of the White Paper crystallised into a reform proposal derived from neoliberal world views and the model of a knowledge economy, seeking convergence with a number of Western European higher education systems that had already adopted this course. Quite contrary to the initial intention of the government, there was more and more controversy surrounding the White Paper. Finally, a massive wave of protests was organised by students, academics and several ad hoc initiatives. Ultimately, in politically turbulent times characterised by three appointments (and resignations) of the Minister of Education in a very short period of time, the White Paper lost support even within the government coalition.

In general, the authors of the White Paper represented a body of experts with predominantly scientific backgrounds. The majority of members had long careers in academia and had held high offices in university governance. The rest of the group represented researchers focusing on higher education policy in the long term, including the deputy minister as the chair and a group member. He therefore acted both as a renowned independent sociologist and higher education expert, and as a high-level official and political nominee. On the one hand, this double identity could be perceived as an effort to bridge the gap between the expert and political levels of policy making, as we identified in the context of the previous two advisory bodies. On the other hand, it could undermine the independence of the group and its scientific legitimacy. In this case, we can observe a multidimensionality of members' identities. It is not apparent whether the members acted as representatives of particular interests (and whose interests those should be) or whether they were supposed to express their opinions based on their scientific knowledge and their understanding of the public interest.

The policy programme outlined in the White Paper drew from three sources. First, extensive long-term research on various aspects of higher education in the Czech Republic was produced by the authors and their research teams. Second, discussions within the group of authors and, to a limited extent, between the authors and the rest of the policy community had an agenda-setting impact on the final content. Finally, a considerable part of the White Paper followed the recommendations of the Organisation for Economic Co-Operation and Development (OECD) formulated in the 'Country Note' resulting from its Thematic Reviews of Tertiary Education.[20] In this context, we can see one of the roles of the Council as an agent of a wider transnational community aiming to converge Czech higher education with Western European models and propagating the policy paradigms and transnational policies suggested by the OECD.

The decision-making procedures within the group of the authors of the White Paper corresponded to the expert, scientific nature of the body. In case of any divergence of opinions, an argument based on stronger evidence prevailed. Such a practice strengthened the research-based kind of advice, leading to consensual types of recommendations and open acceptance by all the members. Besides, the Country Note also served as a crucial source of arguments and advocacy for the White Paper. Therefore, one could consider the Country Note not only as a model example of convergence with but also as a source of legitimacy for the reform. According to its advocates, the external (transnational) assessment of Czech higher education 'lacks the particular interests' present in domestic policy analysis.

Although no reform of higher education has yet been introduced, the White Paper has played a considerable role in agenda setting and framing the policy debate. It prevails as a reference (positive as well as negative), inspiration or policy model in any debate on higher education in the Czech Republic up to the present time. Nevertheless, one cannot overestimate the agenda-setting effect of the

---

[20] The thematic review was carried out between 2004 and 2006. The project involved 24 participating countries.

document. The right-wing political parties adopted some of its basic principles[21] many years ago under significant influence from the OECD review on Czech higher education carried out in 1992,[22] the New Public Management approach and the market-oriented model of higher education well established in Western Europe. Thus, in many respects, the Country Note not only normatively and ideologically resonated with their existing agenda, but its reiteration a few years later strengthened their positions and legitimised them through the advice of independent experts, the authors of the White Paper.

Conclusions

This analysis of advisory committees' guidelines has shown that some aspects of their formal framework are very detailed while others are vague or completely missing. The latter refers particularly to the process of member appointment, committee discussions, member accountability to a broader community and participation of the public in committee meetings. Moreover, even if we consider the various objectives and roles of the committees in the policy-making process, the formal framework seems to comprise several internal paradoxes.

First, the legal frameworks of the advisory bodies articulate neither explicitly, nor implicitly any balance provision, the protection of the public interest within advisory committees. However, in practice, we can identify some attempts to deliberately create some kind of balance of interests. Second, the guidelines supply neither any strong evidence of the government's reflection on the difference between experts and representatives nor any conception of what kind of representation members stand for. The 'representative' members are generally expected to represent a certain institution and simultaneously act as experts. However, 'expert' members are not always supposed to represent particular interests. On the contrary, they are rather labelled and supposed to act as 'independent' of any interests. Third, there is a paradox between the unpremeditated and often rather incidental composition, on one hand, and the mode of decision-making, on the other, as the decisions of the vast majority of the committees are taken by majority voting only. Finally, the committees are supposed to play advisory as well as coordinating roles in the policy-making process and thus complement conventional procedures of political decision making. However, this objective has no legal basis. The committees can be successful only if they are closely attached to the government, either through the presence of deputy ministers or through giving the chair a sufficiently strong position within the government. Hence, the internal advisory bodies have considerable capacity for assuring both

---

[21] For example, the most significant right-wing party of the time, the Civic Democratic Party, adopted the Australian model of tuition fees (HECS [Higher Education Contribution Scheme]). Since then, the proposal has been persistently (but unsuccessfully) advocated by its leaders, in the Country Note and finally in the White Paper.

[22] In principle, the examiners' report, the *Country Note*, repeated most of the recommendations from 1992 (Pabian, 2007, p 75; File et al 2006, p 67).

---

coordination of the policy community and implementation of advice. However, the relative separation of the advisory and political systems in the case of external bodies hinders the advisory, let alone the coordinating function. This gap may be bridged if the committee's agenda is backed by a strong and personally devoted chair and/or by an explicit government priority; nevertheless, the capacity of such a body is limited. Particularly in this context, we can notice variations in terms of agenda and membership, with some committees lacking any relevant impact on the given public policies and others being far from 'advisory only' (Brown, 2008).

Apart from their policy advisory role, the councils and committees may play different roles in which advice may not be the primary objective. Being endowed with epistemic authority, they may carry out instrumental (see different notion of 'instrumental' in Weible, 2008), legitimising as well as substantiating functions with regard to preferences in political contestation (Boswell, 2008, 2009; compare Weible, 2008; Robert, 2008). Selectivity in the process of the adoption of policy advice might imply a tendency to use it strategically in case 'certain knowledge is brought to bear on the choice of means to attain previously chosen ends' (Weingart, 1999, p 154). In fact, the current institutional framework of the advisory council system in the Czech Republic gives the government broad leeway for employing the advice highly selectively, neglecting the advice which contradicts government aims. However at the same time, the governmental decision can be presented as the product of broad expert consensus.

This analysis of three selected advisory bodies proved a high level of dynamism in terms of structure, membership and agendas within each of them, which was reflected in the role they played in the policy-making process. At some point, they were supposed to ensure coordination among a wide range of actors and to provide the government with a sort of consensual knowledge that takes into account diverse rationales of various policy actors. However, at other times, they instead followed the rationalistic logic of policy making supposing that the scientific authority on which their expert recommendations were based could be translated into a policy programme. We believe that political instability in the Czech Republic is one factor that might have contributed to this course.

Our cases necessarily focus only on a very small part of the advisory body system and leave out a range of other bodies (neither less relevant nor less interesting). Their analysis could expose new, and in some cases dissimilar rationalities. However, we identify a few factors that might contribute to success or failure of the policy advisory bodies in their primary intention – to provide policy advice in a relevant policy area: first, a high level of uncertainty which is understood both as a systemic, permanent decision-making condition emerging from networked governance and as temporary (shocks, crisis) uncertainty about an issue area that stimulates actors lacking strong preconceived views to demand a particular type of information (Haas, 1992; see also Radaelli, 1999); second, a high level of centrality of the issue within the government's policy agenda and the problem specification (time for production of advice and concreteness of the question for policy advice); third, the definition of the advisory body's activity, political support as well as the role and initiative of particular members and especially the chairs that Fobé et al call 'facilitators of advice production' (Fobé et al, 2013, p 234); fourth, inclusion of other than scientific knowledge in the policy advice through the participation of heterogeneous actors in the core of advisory bodies, who introduce different kinds of knowledge, for example related to technical feasibility or political support and acceptability.

While the advisory bodies exerted only limited direct influence on the policy-making process – in other words, little of their advice was accepted by the government and introduced – their indirect impact was relatively strong, particularly through cooperation with departmental officials and the news media, which paid close attention to their activities. Moreover, the network of persons engaged in the advisory councils in the Czech Republic is narrow and membership in more than one body is not rare (related issues such as conflict of interests or workload are unresolved). Given the absence of both a common legislative framework and a systematic approach to governing the operation and coordination of the advisory bodies in the Czech Republic, the personal overlaps of their members may facilitate the flow of information, data and arguments within the relatively closed advisory community and encourage the indirect influence of the bodies and their advice in the policy-making process. Consequently, this privileged community of expertise plays a significant role in agenda setting and in the shaping and framing of the public discourse on the reform of particular policies in the Czech Republic.

Acknowledgements

Katerina Ptackova's work on this chapter was done under the research project supported by Czech Science Foundation 'Social Dynamics Acceleration: Uncertainty, Hierarchical/Flat Governance Structures, and History Interiorisation' (grant no. P404/11/2098). Kateřina Merklová's work on this chapter was funded under Charles University Specific Research in 2013 (VG106/2013).

References

Boswell, C. (2008) 'The political functions of expert knowledge: knowledge and legitimization in European Union immigration policy', *Journal of European Public Policy*, 15(4): 471-88.

Boswell, C. (2009) *The Political Uses of Expert Knowledge. Immigration Policy and Social Research*, Cambridge: Cambridge University Press.

Brown, M.B. (2008) 'Fairly balanced: the politics of representation on government advisory committees', *Political Research Quarterly*, 61(4): 547-60.

Brown, M.B. (2009) *Science in Democracy: Expertise, Institutions, and Representation*, Cambridge, MA: MIT Press.

Craft, J. (2014) 'Policy advice and new political order', in C. Conteh and I. Roberge (eds) *Canadian Public Administration in the 21st Century*, London: CRC Press, Taylor & Francis, pp 41–59.

Craft, J. and Howlett, M. (2012) 'Policy formulation, governance shifts and policy influence: location and content in policy advisory systems', *Journal of Public Policy*, 32(02): 79-98.

Craft, J. and Howlett, M. (2013) 'The dual dynamics of policy advisory systems: the impact of externalization and politicization on policy advice', *Policy and Society*, 32(3): 187-97.

File, J., Weko, T., Hauptman, A., Kristensen, B. and Herlitschka, S. (2006) *Tertiary Review Czech Republic - Country Note*, OECD.

Fobé, E., Brans, M., Vancoppenolle, D. and Van Damme, J. (2013) 'Institutionalized advisory systems: an analysis of member satisfaction of advice production and use across 9 strategic advisory councils in Flanders (Belgium)', *Policy and Society*, 32(3), 225-40.

Haas, P.M. (1992) 'Introduction: epistemic communities and international policy coordination', *International Organization*, 46(1): 1-35.

Halligan, J. (1995) 'Policy advice and the public service', in B.G. Peters and D.T. Savoie (eds) *Governance in a Changing Environment*, Montreal: McGill-Queen's University Press, pp 138-72.

Howlett, M. (2009) 'Policy analytical capacity and evidence-based policy-making: lessons from Canada', *Canadian Public Administration*, 52(2): 153-75.

Howlett, M. (2011) 'Public managers as the missing variable in policy studies: an empirical investigation using Canadian data', *Review of Policy Research*, 28(3): 247-63.

Kabele, J. and Linek, L. (2006) *The paradox of the Czech Way of Coping with the EU Accession: The Case of Legislative Planning*, Prague: Faculty of Social Sciences, Charles University in Prague.

Kaplan, K. (1993) *Sovětští poradci v Československu 1949–1956* [The Soviet advisors in Czechoslovakia 1949-1956], Praha: Ústav pro soudobé dějiny AV ČR.

McCubbins, M.D., Noll, R.G. and Weingast, B.R. (1987) 'Administrative procedures as instruments of political control', *Journal of Law, Economics & Organization*, 3(2): 243-77.

Miles, M.B. and Huberman, A.M. (1994) *Qualitative Data Analysis* (2nd edn), Thousand Oaks, CA: Sage.

Pabian, P. (2007) 'Doporučení OECD z roku 1992 a jejich realizace v české vysokoškolské politice' [1992 OECD policy recommendations and their implementation in Czech higher education], *Aula*, 15(1): 67-78.

Pabian, P., Šima, K. and Kynčilová, L. (2011) 'Humbolt goes to the labour market: how academic higher education fuels labour market success in the Czech Republic', *Journal of Education and Work*, 24(1-2): 95-118.

Punch, K.F. (2006) *Developing Effective Research Proposals* (2nd edn), London: Sage.

Radaelli, C.M. (1998) 'Networks of expertise and policy change in Italy', *South European Society and Politics*, 3(2): 1-22.

Radaelli. C.M. (1999) 'The public policy of the European Union: whither politics of expertise?', *Journal of European Public Policy*, 6(5): 757-74.

Robert, C. (2008) 'Expertise et action publique', in O. Borraz and V. Guiraudon (eds) *Politiques publiques*, 1, Paris: Presses de Science Po, pp 309–35.

Robert, C. (2010) 'Les groupes d'experts dans le gouvernement de l'Union européenne. Bilans et perspectives de recherche', *Politique européenne*, 32: 7-38.

Stöckelová, T. (2012) *Nebezpečné známosti. O vztahu sociálních věd a společnosti* [Dangerous liaisons: on the relation of social sciences and society], Praha: Sociologické nakladatelství.

Veselý, A. (2012) 'Policy advisory system in the Czech Republic: from state monopoly to hollowing out?', Paper presented at the XXII Congress of Political Science Conference, Madrid, 8-12 July.

Weible, C.M. (2008) 'Expert-based information and policy subsystems. A review and synthesis', *Policy Studies Journal*, 36(4): 615-35.

Weingart, P. (1999) 'Scientific expertise and political accountability: paradoxes of science in politics', *Science and Public Policy*, 26(3): 151-61.

ELEVEN

Public opinion and public policy in the Czech Republic

Paulína Tabery

> Debates about the impact of public opinion on public policy are organized around a 'should' and an 'is'. (Burstein, 2014, p 45)

Deliberations on the relationship between public opinion and public policy most often focus on the influence of the former on the latter, from either the normative or analytical perspective. Although certainly the most attractive and interesting issue, the relationship between the two is reciprocal and their mutual interaction is highly complex. The many layers of the relationship are best demonstrated by the efforts to define the two concepts and describe their mutual interaction accordingly.

Definitions of public policy and public opinion

In the field of social sciences, one would be hard put to find more elusive concepts with so many definitions. Klein and Marmor (2006, p 892) call public policy 'a chameleon concept', claiming that each of the disciplines and sub-disciplines dealing with the concept has its own definitions and research methods. Similarly, Cochran et al (2009) claim that there is no definite, comprehensive and universally accepted definition. Both groups of researchers present their own definitions of public policy: for Klein and Marmor (2006, p 892), it is 'what governments do and neglect to do', whereas Cochran et al (2009, p 2) define public policy as 'an intentional course of action followed by a government institution or official for resolving an issue of public concern'. Both of these definitions are rather general and only hint at possible interaction with public opinion, but they both restrict the concept to government's deliberate actions (and, importantly, inaction). When looking at policy as a process expressed by the four stages of the policy cycle model (problem recognition or issue selection, policy formulation and decision making, implementation, and finally evaluation and termination – Jann and Wegrich, 2007), it becomes clear that each of these stages offers the possibility to interact with public opinion.

The definition of public opinion is similarly elusive. Donsbach and Traugott (2008, p 1) call it a 'nebulous concept', referring to its diverse perceptions and multiple definitions, resulting from the fact that various social researchers focus on different aspects of the phenomenon (Herbst, 1993). Considering that the concept is largely interdisciplinary, and each discipline approaches it differently, notions for defining public opinion fall into four categories: aggregation, a majoritarian approach, a discursive or consensual approach and a fiction or reification approach (Herbst, 1993, pp 44-46).

Aggregation refers to what we know as opinion polls - that is, an aggregated expression of individual attitudes, evaluated by a standard method. *The majoritarian approach* is partially based on aggregation, but not all opinions are assigned equal weight. Those expressed by a majority of respondents are ultimately considered more important than those expressed by a minority. *The discursive approach* includes definitions focusing on public opinion as a communication process, claiming that people's opinions are not formed and modified independently but are the result of social processes and communication stimuli found within a person's milieu and obtained from the media. The last approach does not perceive public opinion as an authentic entity, but claims it is a *fiction* that merely reflects the attitudes of the elite and the media. As such, it is highly susceptible to manipulation by those actors who use it to promote their own interests and activities (Herbst, 1993, pp 44-46). However, the last approach should not be confused with what Peters (1995, pp 14-18) calls 'the imagined public', pointing out that in today's complex societies, public opinion is largely a mediated representation. Nevertheless, even though a substantial part of the public opinion formation process takes place on a symbolic level, Peters (1995, p 16) points out that 'the imagined public is not, however, *imaginary*' (italics original); on the contrary, such mediated representation may turn public opinion into a highly relevant actor. Moreover, individual and group opinion is still formed through everyday personal interactions, which in turn affect and transform the symbolic level (for more on public opinion as a process, see Davison, 1958; Price and Roberts, 1987; Noelle-Neumann, 1993; Crespi, 1997; Glynn et al, 2004).

Public opinion as opinion polls

It is therefore obvious that both public policy and public opinion definitions provide a vast space for both concepts to interact. However, opinion polls are currently the most widely accepted representation of public opinion. Donsbach and Traugott (2008, p 3) claim that modern political systems have been transformed through two major factors: television and opinion polls. Polls have come to embody the cornerstone of democracy, since they made 'the will of people, measurable and thus available for political decision-making on an almost daily basis, be it political leaders or the electorate' (Donsbach and Traugott, 2008, p 3).

Since the beginnings of empirical research in the public opinion field, equating public opinion with opinion polls has been met with certain reservations. Some researchers object to this approach from a theoretical standpoint, doubting that such a method is capable of capturing the nature of public opinion and evaluating the concept correctly (Blumer, 1948; Bourdieu, 1979). If public opinion is indeed a social process in which communication plays a major role, how accurate can aggregating individual opinions be? Other opponents point out the weaknesses of the survey research methods, resulting in survey errors which occur during poll preparation, data collection and processing; or in survey-related effects that are not errors per se but cannot be avoided, such as question wording, question order and context within a questionnaire. All of the earlier have an impact on poll results (Weisberg, 2008). Despite these reservations, opinion polls remain a useful representation of public opinion for policy analysis and offer a standard, reliable and representative measurement method. It is important to keep in mind that any alternative methods have identical or even greater drawbacks (Manza and Brooks, 2012; see also Herbst, 1993).

Another important issue is the way the quantified survey results are applied and/or utilised in public space. Herbst (1993) points out that numbers enjoy a privileged position in modern, rationally oriented societies, and quantified opinion is thus considered somehow more convincing. Herbst therefore distinguishes between the *symbolic* and *instrumental role* of opinion polls, where the symbolic role is related to rhetoric and an attitude of power within public discourse, and the instrumental role refers to research fulfilling people's need to be informed. Through opinion polls, various actors may thus not only obtain information regarding the support of their position and activities, but may also utilise them strategically.

In both of these roles, opinion polls have become an indispensable, highly influential political tool. On the one hand, they have changed the nature of the entire political game: political marketing has now become essential, and election campaigns are organised based on pre-election surveys (Mancini, 1999; Stanyer, 2007); opinion polls have even managed to become events in their own right (Mancini, 1999). On the other hand, opinion polls provide policy makers with insight into citizens' needs and priorities, and their opinions on various areas, policies, government activities and the results of such policies. The instrumental role of opinion polls is therefore crucial for understanding the relationship between public opinion and public policy. Rather than researching political preferences, it is more important to establish the way opinion polls are utilised in creating and implementing policies, and the way public opinion is perceived by various actors, especially policy makers themselves.

Public opinion as perceived by policy makers

In her research, Herbst (1998, 2002) arrived at some fairly surprising conclusions: based on in-depth interviews with the legislative staff of the state of Illinois, she found out that policy managers often imagine public opinion as that presented by interest groups or the mass media. Considering that in analysing the policy process, researchers usually strictly distinguish between public opinion on one side and interest groups and especially media content on the other, such a conceptual overlap is highly unusual. However, it may indicate that theoretical approaches and concepts may be different from the way certain phenomena are perceived in everyday life. In any case, the mass media provide legislators with immediate, daily feedback which, in their opinion, shapes the entire discourse, and interest groups are in turn capable of in-depth discussions on a given subject and providing specific suggestions and observations. Opinion polls are taken with a certain degree of reserve, which stems from two primary causes. First, more attention is often paid to pre-election polls than to issue polls that deal with a subject the staff are currently working on. Second, objections are sometimes raised against surveys as a method; these usually reflect certain difficulties in formulating the right questions, and the responses' sensibility to question wording. Considering the high cost of conducting opinion polls, they are not widely used to formulate state-wide policies, such as in Illinois (Herbst, 1998, 2002). However, it is definitely worth noting that policy makers often equate public opinion with interest groups. This poses the question of whether interest groups (also) represent the general public or any part thereof, and what the relationship is between opinion and action.

The public(s) on the way from opinion to action

When trying to find a theoretical definition of the public, we realise there are certain difficulties; instead of a single, homogeneous public, it would be better to speak of a multitude of different publics. This is the result of refusing to define the public as something measured by opinion polls. Using the discursive approach and the definition that the public is formed 'in the course of discussion surrounding an issue' (Price, 1992, p 29), the resulting image of the public is far more plastic and dynamic, and gives a better indication of the way the public may be involved in decision making. Price (1992) claims that, since he sees the formation of the public as a process, both the size and the structure of the public may change over time.

   Based on these two criteria, there are several possible definitions of the public. The *general public* is essentially represented by opinion polls, and therefore comes closest to an aggregated approach to the population. The *voting public* represents the electorate – that is, those citizens qualified to participate in elections. The *attentive public* is people interested in public affairs and the *active public* is that part of the population that is directly involved in political events (Price, 1992, pp 35-41). Obviously, the size of these publics decreases gradually from the general to the active public. However, the entire concept of public involvement gains a new dynamic if we realise that the public is constituted around certain issues. This suggests the existence of *issue publics* (Price, 1992, 2008), which further rally both the attentive and active citizens around a certain issue. Considering the plurality of such publics, an individual may simultaneously be part of both an active and passive part of the population (Price, 2008, p 21); however, most people belong to a single or a few issue publics (Krosnick, 1990).

   Foote and Hart (1953, pp 310-316) present a theoretical model showing the way the public opinion formation process is transformed into group action. The model identifies five stages of the entire cycle. First comes the *problem phase*, during which the public defines a certain problem, and then defines itself in relation to this problem. The public and the problem therefore appear simultaneously. The *proposal phase* follows, defined by the growing feeling that something needs to be done about the problem, and by proposing various alternatives, albeit not necessarily well-developed ones. Then comes the *policy phase*, during which the public finally forms a group rallying around certain well-articulated alternatives. This is the time of negotiations, defining positions and unifying attitudes. It is followed by the *programme phase*, in which specific group action is taken - that is, public opinion comes into an efficient mode. Groups are clearly organised, group members are assigned specific tasks and work toward implementing a certain programme. The programme undergoes continuous revisions, and its outcomes are constantly pitted against expectations. At this stage, the problem may again be redefined and the entire cycle thus repeats itself. Usually, however, this only happens after the last, *appraisal phase*, which represents the culmination of the current efforts.

The previously mentioned process is repeated for each issue around which a public is constituted. Over time, issues may evolve and the respective publics may be transformed accordingly: they may expand or diminish depending on the importance of the issue at hand. If the publics are therefore defined dynamically, this raises the question of which quality of public opinion the polls as an aggregation actually measure.

The capacity of public opinion

Public opinion had been criticised for lack of competence even before the emergence of empirical surveys (Lippmann, [1922] 1997; see also Price, 1992). If people are to present competent opinions, they need to show an interest in political events and keep themselves well informed. However, as indicated earlier, only a part of the general public shows an interest in any issues, and most people only focus on very few issues or even a single one. It does not therefore come as a surprise that not only may people have firmly fixed attitudes and opinions, they may also have none.

During the individual stages of a panel analysis, Converse (1964) noticed that instead of displaying consistent liberal or conservative opinions, a large part of the population chose a liberal approach for one issue and a conservative approach for another, but they also changed their opinions from one wave to another almost at random. This led him to the conclusion that a survey can hardly measure fully crystallised attitudes, and in some cases these can be described, for various reasons, rather as 'non-attitudes'. His conclusions were later opposed with the claim that measurement error is to blame for opinion instability (for example Achen, 1975). However, Converse's finding was later developed to claim that a certain part of opinions within an opinion poll is formed depending on the immediate context, and a respondent is sampling from various alternatives (Zaller, 1992). Considering that the non-attitudes hypothesis significantly disputes the role of public opinion as a crucial element in a democracy, as well as the possibility of involving citizens in the decision-making process, this spurred a still ongoing debate (for a summary of the debate, see Saris, 2004; Van der Veld and Saris, 2004).

Interactions of public opinion and public policy in theories

So far, we have attempted to define the interaction between public opinion and public policy based on various conceptualisations and definitions. However, this section will attempt to present theories dealing with the mutual influence and dynamic of the two concepts. The first of these theories is agenda setting. It tries to explain the way various issues attract the attention of the public, mass media or policy makers, or, more generally, whether they result in social change or retaining the status quo (Dearing and Rogers, 1996, pp 1-2). The agenda-setting process currently works with three different agendas: the media agenda, public agenda and policy agenda. However, researchers have so far failed to formulate as comprehensive a theory as could be expected. Historically, research in this area has followed two (Kalvas, 2008) or possibly three (Dearing and Rogers, 1996) parallel traditions. The first school focuses on the formation of the public agenda, studying the influence of mass communication on public opinion, and its origins can be traced back to an article by McCombs and Shaw (1972). The second tradition focuses on policy agenda setting, in which the primary focus is the way a problem becomes a public policy issue (Cobb and Elder, [1972] 1983; Kingdon, 1984). The third line of thought, albeit a minor one, focuses on the actual construction of the media agenda (see Dearing and Rogers, 1996). Agendas are defined as 'a set of issues' arranged hierarchically and visible or communicable at a given moment in time (Dearing and Rogers, 1996, p 2). A key element within the agenda-setting process is the dynamic over time and within the actual agenda, but also the dynamic between different agendas and their possible mutual influence. Issues are entered into or dropped from an agenda with varying intensity and may not be present in all agendas simultaneously. The changing presence of various issues within different agendas may indicate the influence of the mass media or public opinion on public policy, and vice versa. The main discovery of the agenda-setting theory is the fact that each issue has a different position within the hierarchy - that is, a different salience - but they also develop differently throughout the entire process.

Another example of a theory regarding the mutual influence of public opinion and public policy is the so-called 'thermostatic' model of democracy (Wlezien, 1995; Soroka and Wlezien, 2010). The fundamental proposition in this model is that for a representative democracy to function properly, the government must respond to public opinion, and public preferences must be reflected in its policies. Such an opinion-policy relationship is reciprocal, meaning that the citizens' preferences and government activities react to each other. The public plays the role of a thermostat. If there is a discrepancy between a given policy and the citizens' preferences, the public voices the desire for a change, and the government will adjust its policies as much as possible to conform to the desired outcome. Such a reciprocal process takes place within a certain context; therefore, the model also includes political institutions, and especially issue salience (Soroka and Wlezien, 2010). As Soroka and Wlezien (2010) have shown in their analyses, the more salient an issue, the better the model functions - that is, policies are adjusted to reflect citizens' preferences. Where the public pays attention, policy makers are more likely to represent their interests.

In their model, Soroka and Wlezien (2010) had to address the aforementioned misgivings regarding the competence of citizens' opinions, and the varying sizes of different publics. According to them, citizens need not have detailed insight into a specific policy; all they need is a simple opinion on whether the policy is set correctly. Similarly, the model does not require that all citizens pay attention constantly; it is sufficient if a significant number of them monitor policies and respond to any changes. The model may not therefore emerge for all policies; on the contrary, it does not expect a great deal of public responsiveness in the case of minor issues.

The influence of public opinion on public policy: a normative approach versus an analytical approach and the problem of measurement

The thermostatic model is one of the examples of studying the influence of public opinion on public policy. As mentioned at the beginning of this chapter, there are essentially two aspects to this relationship: the first is the *normative* approach - that is, whether there should be an influence and how large it should be; and the second is an *analytical* aspect - that is what influence actually exists and whether it is measurable. The quality of a democracy is often defined by the degree of influence the citizens and/or the public are able to exert over their government's decisions - to what degree their preferences are reflected in the decision-making process, and how responsive the government is to them. In short, the greater the public's influence, the better the democracy (Burstein, 2006, 2014; Soroka and Wlezien, 2010). Not all researchers agree with this conclusion, however. As far as the normative approach to the opinion-policy relationship is concerned, it is debated whether the availability of public opinion through opinion polls actually diminishes the quality of democracy and governance, since it leads to a constant monitoring of the public's moods, and subsequent changes in policies or inaction. Moreover, politicians are concerned with their re-election, which results in them abandoning policy making and reverting to a 'permanent campaign' (Manza et al, 2002, p 4).

As far as the actual influence of public opinion on public policy is concerned, existing research is not in agreement. Some researchers assign public opinion a great deal of importance, others only minor importance. The third approach maintains that influence may differ depending on a specific situation, from strong influence to minor (Manza and Cook, 2002). For quite a long time, the overwhelming consensus was that public opinion plays a fairly major role, but gradually opinions emerged claiming that the influence may actually be overestimated (Page, 2002; Burstein, 2006, 2014). As Burstein (2006, 2014) points out, sampling bias is the greatest problem in many studies. Studies often focus on a single specific policy, sometimes several, but these are usually salient issues where a greater degree of public attention can be expected, and consequently public opinion's influence on public policy may appear fairly significant. When less salient issues are included, though, the influence is no longer as substantial. However, even if all policies over a given time period were identified and a random selection was made, the overall influence could still not be assessed, due to the incomplete data regarding public opinion. Opinion polls do not capture opinions on all existing policies, but only those that, as defined by the agenda-setting theory, transcend the policy agenda to the public and/or media agenda. The overall influence of public opinion on public policy should therefore ideally include even those policies on which there is no known public opinion.

Burstein (2014) emphasises another reason why it is impossible to draw a clear conclusion from existing studies: they have a different approach to defining public opinion and public policy as concepts. Public opinion is constituted by data from opinion polls, which, however, as explained earlier, have their limitations and deficiencies. Moreover, they are seldom specific enough to refer to specific policies or proposals. The available data are usually more general, concerning various issues and their hierarchy, measured by the MIP (most important problem) question or closed-ended questions (for more on the issue of questions regarding important or problematic issues, see Červenka, 2008; Wlezien, 2005). However, more general measures, such as 'policy moods', are also utilised, monitoring the degree of people's liberal or conservative attitudes in extremely widely defined areas: such attitudes are taken to represent a general response to the government's actions (Stimson, 1999; Erikson et al, 2002).

Policy concepts also vary. As Burstein (2014) highlights, some studies define policies as laws, others as government expenditures on various areas. Burstein himself defines a policy based on Kingdon's *policy proposal*, which means 'a particular proposed solution to a policy problem, one out of possibly many alternatives that might be considered by a legislature' (Burstein, 2014, p 28). In this view, policy is therefore not only a single specific bill, but all proposals concerning the problem at hand, which are identical or very similar, and are therefore linked to a single solution – that is, represent a single policy (Burstein, 2014, p 28).

As we can see, researchers are not uniform in their conclusions regarding the influence of public opinion on public policy. Moreover, such conclusions depend on the chosen method of measurement and operational definitions of the measured concepts.

The case of the Czech Republic

History of public opinion research

This section focuses on the relationship between public opinion and public policy in the Czech Republic. But first we briefly outline the current situation regarding public opinion surveys, so that it is clear which period the available data cover, and how long and systematic a time series we may therefore expect.

Public opinion research has a fairly long tradition in the Czech Republic, albeit often interrupted due to restrictions imposed by the former communist regime. The first research institution was established in 1946, shortly after World War II, inspired by the British organisation Mass Observation, as well as by George Gallup and his methods of studying public opinion in the United States. The Czechoslovak Institute for Public Opinion Research (ÚVVM) was a state institution, formally subordinated to the Ministry of Information. Even though the official title included the word 'Czechoslovak', research was only conducted in the Czech lands and cooperation with a similar institution in Slovakia was never established. The Institute had fairly high aspirations, as regards both research independence and implementation, striving to use state-of-the-art methodology and statistical analyses (Adamec, 1998; Šamanová, 2006). Unfortunately, its outside contacts, such as participation in conferences or membership in international public opinion research organisations, were soon curtailed. Following the communist putsch in February 1948, restrictions also affected the ÚVVM. After a purge of its staff, the Institute was no longer allowed to focus on political issues, and pre-election polls for the elections in May 1948 were never compiled or published. Opinion polls subsequently focused on such issues as skirt hemlines or refuse collection, and in 1950 the Institute was eventually dissolved (Adamec, 1998; Šamanová, 2006).

The second stage of public opinion research in Czechoslovakia came in the 1960s, at a time of gradual social and political liberalisation, even if the regime remained non-democratic. In 1965, the presidium of the Central Committee of the Czechoslovak Communist Party approved the establishment of the Institute for Public Opinion Research under the Czechoslovak Academy of Sciences. Again, researchers had high aspirations; the Institute initiated cooperation with Hadley Cantril, and invited Elisabeth Noelle-Neumann for a visit. The Institute expanded its activities to Slovakia, where it conducted data collection.[1] The first opinion poll was conducted in 1967, and subsequent polls even dared to address political questions such as the degree of freedom of speech, or the Communist Party's ability to ensure the advancement of socialism and democracy (Šamanová, 2006; see also Škodová, 2007). Unfortunately, the invasion of the armies of the Warsaw Pact in August 1968, and the subsequent occupation of Czechoslovakia,

---

[1]   Data collection in Slovakia was to be performed by ÚVVM successors until the split of the Federation at the end of 1992.

instigated a major turn in society which had a profound impact on public opinion research. Witnesses recall that not only was the publication of poll results restricted, but citizens were much less willing to respond to such polls (Bečvář, 1996). Polls no longer concerned political events. The Institute was dissolved in 1972, and a new organisation, the Cabinet for Public Opinion Research, was subordinated to the Statistical Office - that is, a state organisation. In 1978, it adopted its original name, but its agenda remained the same: it researched topics prescribed by the Communist Party and under its supervision, and results were presented to Party officials, not to the public. Research results were either never published or were published only in part (Šamanová, 2006).

Another major turning point in the area of Czech public opinion research was the revolution in 1989, and the subsequent transition to a democratic regime. Freedom of speech brought the opportunity to conduct research with no regard to the current political representation, and the public opinion research field was gradually transformed into a structure common in other democratic countries - that is, there are a number of predominantly private entities conducting research on various topics and for different clients (universities, research organisations, governmental bodies or private companies).

The ÚVVM was renamed the Public Opinion Research Institute and continued to work under the auspices of the Czech Statistical Office until 2001; then it changed its name to the Public Opinion Research Centre (CVVM), and was incorporated into the Academy of Sciences of the Czech Republic. Since the 1990s the Institute/Centre has conducted regular monthly polls on various issues, such as the public service, and publishes the results through press releases.[2]

As far as private institutions are concerned, there are a number of both domestic and foreign companies specialising in public opinion research in the Czech Republic, including for example GFK Czech, Ipsos, Median, Mediaresearch, Millward Brown Czech Republic, NMS Market Research, PPM Factum Research, STEM/MARK and TNS Aisa. All of these companies are members of the Association of Agencies for Market and Public Opinion Research (SIMAR), which is an ESOMAR representative (European Society for Opinion and Market Research – nowadays in fact a worldwide association for market, social and opinion researchers). Membership in the association binds them to conduct their research in accordance with quality standards and an ethical code.[3]

As regards the perception of public opinion by the policy makers themselves, there has unfortunately been no research in the Czech Republic similar to that conducted by Susan Herbst in the US (1998, 2002). We may expect, however, that in-depth interviews would reveal similar patterns of argumentation. It is safe to assume that when thinking about public opinion, the mass media would hold a prominent position, as both an indication of the citizens' attitudes and an immediate source of feedback. However, the extent to which public opinion

---

[2] http://cvvm.soc.cas.cz/en/about-us/about-us

[3] www.simar.cz/

would be represented by interest groups and opinion polls in the eyes of Czech policy makers is not as clear-cut. Differences may be expected in the field of utilising surveys for creating or adjusting policies, taking into account that this concerns policy making on a nationwide level. Even though scepticism toward opinion polls is occasionally expressed in the Czech Republic, it is usually limited to politicians' doubts regarding party preferences, politicians' popularity and trust (see, for example, Janík et al, 2013; Martinek, 2014). No such reservations have been expressed regarding issue polls; however, it remains unclear whether such data are subsequently utilised in policy making. On the one hand, conducting surveys is a fairly costly undertaking; however, various governmental bodies in the Czech Republic have their own research facilities that commission opinion polls or monitor publicly available data from different research companies. Such analyses may then serve as a basis for decision making regarding specific policies.

Governmental bodies such as the Ministry of Agriculture, Ministry of Environment, Ministry of Foreign Affairs, Ministry of Education, Youth and Sports, and the Ministry of Labour and Social Affairs have their own research institutions that conduct research based on their specific needs. In particular, institutions affiliated to the Ministry of Labour and Social Affairs, such as the Occupational Safety Research Institute or the Research Institute for Labour and Social Affairs, partly conduct their analyses using data from social research and/or public opinion research performed by a polling company at their behest. Similarly, the Czech National Monitoring Centre for Drugs and Drug Addiction, a part of the Office of the Government of the Czech Republic, is charged with collecting, analysing and providing data and information in the form of annual reports concerning drug use.[4] It utilises both data gathered in special surveys commissioned from polling companies, as well as publicly available data from public opinion research (see for instance its 2012 annual report[5]). Similarly, the Ministry of Environment publishes a Statistical Environmental Yearbook of the Czech Republic, which provides room for public opinion, using both Eurobarometer data and freely available data from other opinion polls (CVVM) (see for example the 2011 Statistical Environmental Yearbook of the Czech Republic[6]). Since both documents serve as sources in the government's decision-making processes, this implies that public opinion is important to certain governmental bodies and their policies, at least on a formal level.

---

[4]   See www.drogy-info.cz/index.php/english/mission/national_monitoring_centre_for_drugs_ and_drug_addiction_national_focal_point_short

[5]   www.drogy-info.cz/index.php/english/annual_reports_and_other_main_resources/annual_ report_the_czech_republic_drug_situation_2012

[6]   www.mzp.cz/en/statistical_environmental_yearbooks_documents

Interest in politics and issue salience

The theoretical section has discussed both the weaknesses and strengths of opinion polls; taking into account these strengths, public opinion will actually be represented in this section by opinion polls. Firstly, building upon the discussion about citizens' capacity to pay attention to and be engaged in public affairs, we will discuss the data on interest in politics and involvement in solving public issues. In this section, to demonstrate whether public opinion and public policies correspond in the same time frame, public opinion is defined as issue salience in the public agenda and is measured by a closed-ended question on the urgency of dealing with selected areas of public life. Policies are defined as the annual state budget expenditures on selected, fairly generally defined areas. At the end of the chapter, we will demonstrate the relationship between public opinion and public policy using the example of building an anti-missile radar base in the Czech Republic.

As regards the possibility of public opinion to influence public policy, doubts are usually expressed regarding citizens' ability to understand public affairs, and their overall interest in politics and policies. During the last decade, approximately half of the Czech population has declared a general interest in politics. From a geographical standpoint, people are far more interested in national politics than political events in the world and within the European Union. Approximately three-fifths of the population pays attention to domestic political affairs. From approximately two-thirds in the years 2005–08, attention dropped slightly in 2009 to the current level. About one-third of the population consistently pays attention to affairs within the EU; however, interest in world politics has dropped in the last ten years, from approximately half of the population to less than two-fifths (see Figure 11.1). As we can see, a major part of the population openly declares a lack of interest in public affairs, and the number has even been slightly increasing.

When focusing on specifically defined activities in public life instead of a declared general interest, it turns out that these activities include predominantly passive ones, such as monitoring political information in the media (63% of people do that often or sometimes), or debates with friends (39% of people do that often or sometimes). On the contrary, active involvement in a political party, participation at public meetings or meetings with politicians are very rare. Inaction is also predominant in public and political activities – that is, solving public issues. About half of the people never engage in such activities, another third only very rarely. We have therefore about 14% of the population that may be said to participate occasionally in solving public issues, and only 2% of the population do this often (see Figure 11.2).

Whereas certain activities, such as work for a political party or persuading friends to vote for a certain party and/or candidate, have remained fairly constant over time, others, such as political discussions, as well as involvement in solving public issues or meeting with politicians, have suffered a certain decrease compared to

Figure 11.1: Interest in politics, comparison over time (percentage)

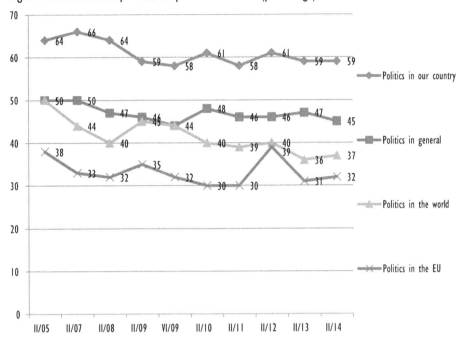

Note: Sum of responses 'very' and 'somewhat interested'; recalculation to 100 percent includes 'somewhat uninterested', 'not at all interested' and 'do not know' responses

Source: the data are from CVVM The Institute of Sociology of the Czech Academy of Sciences of the Czech Republic, Our Society Project; see also Nováková (2014)

the year 2002. In general, none of the activities have increased in frequency, but have been stagnating or slightly decreasing in most cases (see Figure 11.3).

A substantial part of the population therefore shows no interest in politics, and only a limited number of those declaring their interest participate in public affairs in ways other than monitoring information in the media. Using Lippmann's metaphor (Price, 1992, p 31), the public is divided into *actors* and *spectators*.

The degree of importance that citizens assign to specific issues was measured by a closed-ended question regarding the difficulties in each area, and therefore the urgency of finding adequate solutions (see Table 11.1).

Citizens usually assign priority to social issues, such as unemployment, social security or the standard of living, but also healthcare, a functioning economy and tackling economic and general crime (that is, people's security). Problems which are viewed as not that pressing include culture, the military, foreign relations and transport services.

The increased urgency of social and economic issues is directly related to the world economic crisis. Decreased importance has been noted in the areas of citizens' security (crime), the environment, and also research and development and transport services (see Figures 11.4–11.16). As far as state expenditures are concerned (see Figures 11.4–11.16), the majority of funds are allocated to social issues, represented primarily by the Ministry of Labour and Social Affairs, followed

Figure 11.2: How often do you...? (percentage, 2/2014)

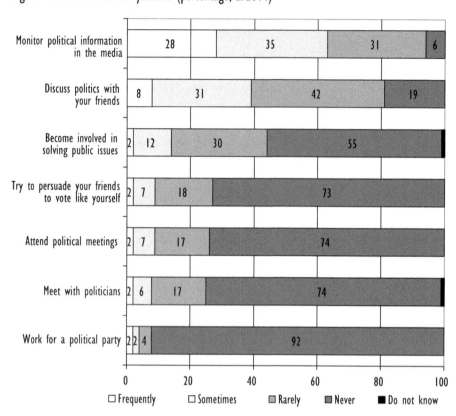

Source: the data are from CVVM The Institute of Sociology of the Czech Academy of Sciences of the Czech Republic, Our Society Project 3-10 February 2014, 1,081 respondents over the age of 15; see also Nováková (2014).

closely by education. On the other hand, we may track a more substantial decrease in the funds allocated to defence and transportation.

Even though the operationalisation of public opinion based on a single question regarding the complex area of public policy might face some of the methodological and interpretation problems discussed in the theoretical section, still this comparison can bring useful insight into the opinion–policy dynamics. It cannot, of course, be used to infer the degree of direct influence of public opinion on currently approved policies, but it is possible that correlation in certain areas might be indicative of the (opinion) framework within which the government and parliament operate and to which they must respond. Such a comparison may also be impaired by excessive aggregation (see the objections against studies: for example Stimson, 1999); however, it essentially provides an overview of the diversity of public preferences, and offers the government possible avenues of response.

As shown in Figures 11.4–11.16 and especially Table 11.2, between the years 2004 and 2012, there was a very weak correlation between opinions on the urgency of solving problems in various public areas and resources that were spent on them; the foreign affairs issue might be considered as an exception. It is important to note that the sample is relatively small and the period is relatively short. Perhaps with a longer time span, the pattern of dynamics between opinions on the urgency of solving problems and state budget expenditures might be more apparent.

Figure 11.3: How often do you...? (%, comparison over time)

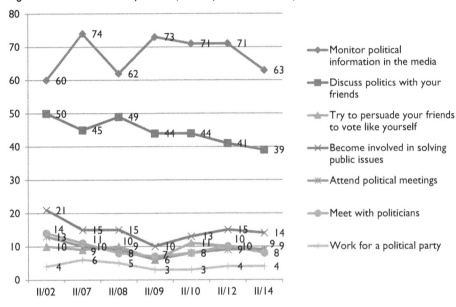

Source: the data are from CVVM The Institute of Sociology of the Czech Academy of Sciences of the Czech Republic, Our Society Project 3-10 February 2014, 1,081 respondents over the age of 15; see also Nováková (2014).

The case of building an anti-missile radar base in the Czech Republic

A very specific example of comparing public policy and public opinion is the issue of building an anti-missile radar base in the Czech Republic. News of the Czech Republic's possible involvement in the American missile defence system appeared in 2006, and in January 2007 the US government officially requested permission to build the base in the Brdy mountain range (aktuálně.cz, 2007; Červenka, 2007). This spurred an intense public debate, which did not abate even when the Czech-American negotiations culminated in signing an agreement on placing the radar in Czech territory in July 2008; another agreement was then signed in September of the same year (Roškot, 2008; oL and ČTK, 2008). At the end of 2008, both agreements were ratified by the upper chamber of the Parliament, but they still had to await ratification by the lower chamber and the President (oL and ČTK, 2008). However, in September 2009 President Barack Obama decided to end the American initiative to build the base as a part of the American anti-missile shield in Central Europe (Wirnitzer, 2009).

Table 11.1: Urgency of dealing with selected areas of public life (percentage, 2/2014)

	Very urgent	Quite urgent	It is not urgent	Do not know
Unemployment	80	16	4	0
Economic crime	70	23	5	2
Social security	67	26	7	0
Economy	64	30	5	1
Healthcare	53	36	10	1
Security of citizens	49	39	11	1
Standard of living	48	39	12	1
Agriculture	39	42	15	4
Justice	33	44	17	6
Legal environment	32	47	16	5
Education	28	46	22	4
Environment	26	49	23	2
Security situation of the CR	20	39	33	8
Research and development	17	44	31	8
Transport services	14	42	40	4
The CR relations with foreign countries	12	40	40	8
Situation in the army	9	32	47	12
Culture	7	29	60	4

Note: Row percentages. Items in descending order, depending on the 'very urgent' score.
Source: the data are from CVVM The Institute of Sociology of the Czech Academy of Sciences of the Czech Republic, Our Society Project 3-10 February 2014, 1,081 respondents over the age of 15; see also Červenka (2014).

From the very beginning, debates concerning the radar base in the Czech Republic were fairly intense. The building of the military base was opposed by local municipalities, which had established a League of Mayors against the Radar (iDNES.cz et al, 2007), and by such civic initiatives as Ne základnám, Hnutí nenásilí and Greenpeace (Mezinárodní humanistická organizace – Česká republika, 2009; Greenpeace, 2009). On the other hand, the government had established the office of Coordinator of Government Communications Regarding the Anti-missile Defence Programme in May 2007 (Vláda České republiky, 2007), and even though it claimed that the office should play a mainly informative, not a persuasive role (Vláda České republiky, 2008), it was not very convincing in its arguments.

Public opinion was fairly sceptical about the building of the radar base from the start. As shown in CVVM opinion polls, disagreement over support predominated throughout the debates, with approximately two-thirds of the people constantly opposing the base and about one-quarter of respondents over the age of 15 expressing their support (see Figure 11.17).

Figure 11.4-11.16: Comparison of opinions on the urgency of dealing with selected areas of public life and state budget expenditures

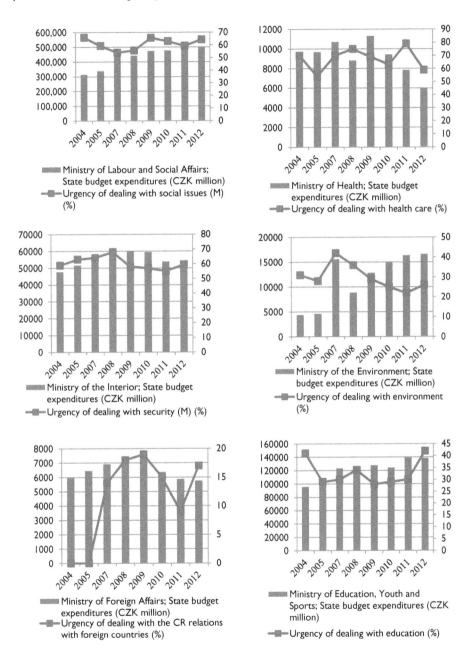

Figure 11.4-11.16 continued: Comparison of opinions on the urgency of dealing with selected areas of public life and state budget expenditures

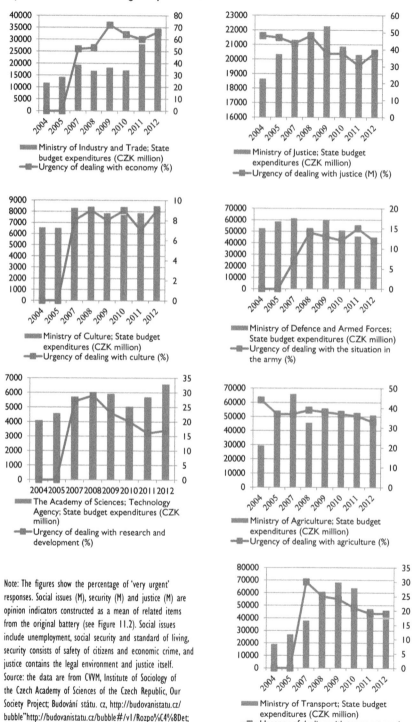

Ministry of Industry and Trade; State budget expenditures (CZK million)
Urgency of dealing with economy (%)

Ministry of Justice; State budget expenditures (CZK million)
Urgency of dealing with justice (M) (%)

Ministry of Culture; State budget expenditures (CZK million)
Urgency of dealing with culture (%)

Ministry of Defence and Armed Forces; State budget expenditures (CZK million)
Urgency of dealing with the situation in the army (%)

The Academy of Sciences; Technology Agency; State budget expenditures (CZK million)
Urgency of dealing with research and development (%)

Ministry of Agriculture; State budget expenditures (CZK million)
Urgency of dealing with agriculture (%)

Ministry of Transport; State budget expenditures (CZK million)
Urgency of dealing with transport services (%)

Note: The figures show the percentage of 'very urgent' responses. Social issues (M), security (M) and justice (M) are opinion indicators constructed as a mean of related items from the original battery (see Figure 11.2). Social issues include unemployment, social security and standard of living, security consists of safety of citizens and economic crime, and justice contains the legal environment and justice itself.
Source: the data are from CVVM, Institute of Sociology of the Czech Academy of Sciences of the Czech Republic, Our Society Project; Budování státu. cz, http://budovanistatu.cz/ bubble"http://budovanistatu.cz/bubble#/v1/Rozpo%C4%8Det; Own calculations

Table 11.2: Cross-correlations of opinions about the urgency of dealing with issues and state budget expenditures in particular areas (ministries)

	Kendall's tau-b
Social issues (M)	0.036
Environment	-0.286
Security issues (M)	0.143
Health	-0.182
Education	-0.148
Foreign affairs	0.467
Economy	0.200
Culture	0.078
Situation in the army	-0.276
Justice (M)	-0.148
Agriculture	-0.265
Research and development	-0.200
Transport services	0.000

Source: The data are from CVVM The Institute of Sociology of the Czech Academy of Sciences of the Czech Republic, Our Society Project; Budování státu.cz.
http://budovanistatu.cz/bubble#/v1/Rozpo%C4%8Det; Own calculations

Considering that at the time of the first opinion poll - that is before the official US request in January 2007 - it was not completely clear what kind of facility it would be, the question asked was about building an anti-missile defence base in general. In autumn 2007, it was further specified that it was to be a radar base, and this led to the assumption that the public might find it more acceptable than an anti-missile base; however, the data show that no such thing happened (see also Červenka, 2007). Although the public maintained a constant discordant opinion, the government carried on the negotiations and signed official agreements with the US.

It might therefore seem that public opinion had no influence on the government's decisions whatsoever; that would, however, be an oversimplification. Looking at the course of events (see for instance oL and ČTK, 2008), we can see several important changes. First, the government strove to emphasise that the facility in the Czech Republic would be a radar base only, not a full anti-missile base, which was planned to be built in Poland. The government also tried to emphasise that the base would not be built as a result of Czech–US cooperation, but would pool the capacities of the entire North Atlantic Treaty Organization (NATO), which was supposed to improve the public's perception of the facility. Negotiations also focused on the interests of Czech companies and scientific projects. Last but not least, the Office of Coordinator of Government Communications Regarding the Anti-missile Defence Programme had commissioned public opinion polls. In this

Figure 11.17: Opinions on building an anti-missile radar base in the Czech Republic (percentage

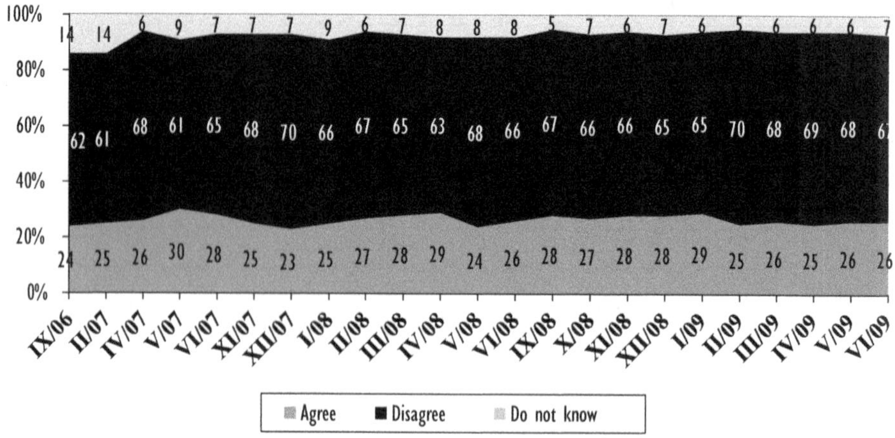

Note: The figure combines 'strongly' and 'somewhat agree' and 'strongly' and 'somewhat disagree' responses.
Source: The data are from CVVM The Institute of Sociology of the Czech Academy of Sciences of the Czech Republic,
Our Society Project; see also Červenka (2009b).

regard, Morávek (2011) points out that the framing of the question influences the distribution of responses. When the question frame stressed the security issue as an important element, the level of agreement increased. In the end, paradoxically, the government came to a similar conclusion. In documents it admitted that if the Czech Republic's security was emphasised, people would tend to offer a more positive response; however, if the question frame focused more on US security, support was not as great (Vláda České republiky, 2008).

The question posed by CVVM presented neither of the earlier frames. However, research indicates that people indeed perceived the radar base as important for Czech–US and Czech–NATO relations, not as a response to a threat to the Czech Republic's security or sovereignty (Červenka, 2009a). Throughout the debates that took place from 2006 to 2009, the public consistently called for a referendum on the building of the radar base (almost three-quarters constantly supported the referendum, approximately one-quarter was against it) (Červenka, 2009b); 80% of the population then expressed their satisfaction over President Obama's decision to abandon the plan to build a radar base in the Czech Republic (Červenka, 2009c). This example illustrates that the influence of public opinion on public policy may not be quick or straightforward. Public opinion represented by opinion polls and discussed in the media, however, helps create the overall context in which other actors operate. As shown in the previous paragraphs, the government tried to adapt to this context, both rhetorically and even by postponing the decision. This is also a good example of the symbolic use of opinion polls in the decision-making process.

Conclusions

The relationship between public opinion and public policy is multi-layered and definitely not straightforward. As has been shown in the case of an anti-missile radar base in the Czech Republic, public opinion has become an indispensable part of both politics and policy making, at least on a symbolic level, since it creates a framework for policy makers' activities. However, its true influence on specific policies is far more difficult to determine, as the analysis examining the link between public opinion and public policies in different areas demonstrated. The difficulties stem from differing theoretical concepts of public opinion, as well as from the capacity of the general public to understand specific policy proposals; but are also caused by the availability of data (or lack thereof), which usually reflect the public's general opinion on a specific issue, rather than evaluating its attitudes towards individual policy measures.

Considering that public opinion's influence on public policy changes over time and depends on the salience of a specific issue, there are still fairly large opportunities for the activities of political parties and various interest groups, which may carry certain weight. Also, since public opinion is very important on a symbolic level, it influences the policy makers' activities in areas where it is available. On one hand, this leads to poll-driven policy making; on the other, some actors may raise concerns about the manipulation of public opinion if policy makers try to utilise the public discourse to their advantage in their communication strategies (Manza et al, 2002). Soroka and Wlezien (2010, p 182) end their study by claiming that 'democracy works'; and, as Burstein (2014, p 68) points out, 'politics is not necessarily zero-sum'. If actors other than public opinion play a part in policy making, it does not therefore mean that the people and democracy have lost. In many areas, the public may not have formed clear opinions and interest groups might even strengthen the relationship between the public and policy makers.

What is therefore the value and role of aggregated citizens' opinions in the policy-making process? We could say that while substantial on the symbolic level, in practical application it is rather unclear. While we cannot expect the public to pay attention to, develop an opinion on, or approve every single specific policy, it certainly forms an opinion on the overall work of the government in various areas. Such opinions then create a social climate whose projected changes may influence other actors. If formed and available, public opinion may therefore become a strong formative force.

Acknowledgement
This research was supported by a GAČR grant 'Understanding of Intergroup Differences in the Discursive Processes of Public Opinion' to the Institute of Sociology of the Academy of Sciences of the Czech Republic (GAČR/13-10320S).

References

Achen, C.H. (1975) 'Mass political attitudes and the survey response', *American Political Science Review*, 69(4): 1218-31.

Adamec, Č. (1998) 'K počátkům výzkumu veřejného mínění' [The origins of public opinion research], in J. Šubrt, Č. Adamec, J. Buriánek, J. Dubský, I. Gillernová, S. Hampl, J. Herzmann, P. Průšová, J. Slavíková, A. Surynek, I. Tomek and Z. Zbořil, *Kapitoly ze sociologie veřejného mínění: teorie a výzkum* [The chapters on the sociology of public opinion: theory and research], Praha: Karolinum, pp 75-94.

Aktuálně.cz (2007) 'Fakta: Vše kolem amerického radaru' [Facts: all about the US radar], *Aktuálně.cz* [online], 19 September. Available from http://zpravy. aktualne.cz/fakta-vse-kolem-americkeho-radaru/r~i:article:340686

Bečvář, J. (1996) *Ústav pro výzkum veřejného mínění ČSAV 1967-1972* [Institute for Public Opinion Research under the Czechoslovak Academy of Sciences 1967-1972], Praha: Ústav pro soudobé dějiny Akademie věd České republiky.

Blumer, H. (1948) 'Public opinion and public opinion polling', *American Sociological Review*, 13(5): 542-49.

Bourdieu, P. (1979) 'Public opinion does not exist', in A. Mattelart and S. Siegelaub (eds) *Communication and Class Struggle*, 1, New York: International General, pp 124-30.

Burstein, P. (2006) 'Why estimates of the impact of public opinion on public policy are too high: empirical and theoretical implications', *Social Forces*, 84(4): 2273-89.

Burstein, P. (2014) *American Public Opinion, Advocacy, and Policy in Congress: What the Public Wants and What It Gets*, Cambridge: Cambridge University Press.

Cobb, R.W. and Elder, C.D. [1972] (1983) *Participation in American Politics: The Dynamics of Agenda-Building* (2nd edn), Baltimore and London: Johns Hopkins University Press.

Cochran, C.E., Meyer, L.C., Carr, T.R. and Cayer, N.J. (2009) *American Public Policy: An Introduction* (9th edn), Boston: Wadsworth Cengage Learning.

Converse, P.E. (1964) 'The nature of belief systems in mass publics', in D.E. Apter (ed) *Ideology and Discontent*, New York: Free Press, pp 206-61.

Crespi, I. (1997) *The Public Opinion Process: How the People Speak*, Mahwah, NJ: Lawrence Erlbaum Associates.

Červenka, J. (2007) 'Americké protiraketové základny v ČR a Polsku z pohledu domácí veřejnosti' [US anti-missile bases in the Czech Republic and Poland in the view of native public], *Naše společnost*, 5(1): 3-9.

Červenka, J. (2008) 'Veřejná agenda' [Public agenda], in M. Škodová, J. Červenka, V. Nečas, F. Kalvas, P. Tabery and T. Trampota (eds) *Agenda-setting: teoretické přístupy* [Agenda-setting: theoretical approaches], Praha: Sociologický ústav AV ČR, pp 48-62.

Červenka, J. (2009a) 'Občané o americké radarové základně v ČR – leden 2009' [Citizens on a US anti-missile radar base in the Czech Republic - January 2009], *Tisková zpráva CVVM Sociologického ústavu AV ČR* [online], 11 February, Praha: Sociologický ústav AV ČR. Available from http://cvvm.soc.cas.cz/media/com_form2content/documents/c1/a3593/f3/100869s_pm90211a.pdf

Červenka, J. (2009b) 'Občané o americké radarové základně v ČR – červen 2009' [Citizens on a US anti-missile radar base in the Czech Republic - June 2009], *Tisková zpráva CVVM Sociologického ústavu AV ČR* [online], 13 July, Praha: Sociologický ústav AV ČR. Available from http://cvvm.soc.cas.cz/media/com_form2content/documents/c1/a3662/f3/100938s_pm90713.pdf

Červenka, J. (2009c) 'Jak občané hodnotí rozhodnutí vlády USA odstoupit od plánu na vybudování protiraketové radarové základny v ČR?' [How does Czech public evaluate the US government's decision to cancel the planned installation of a US anti-missile radar in the Czech Republic?], *Tisková zpráva CVVM Sociologického ústavu AV ČR* [online], 30 November, Praha: Sociologický ústav AV ČR. Available from http://cvvm.soc.cas.cz/media/com_form2content/documents/c1/a3695/f3/100971s_pm91130a.pdf

Červenka, J. (2014) 'Naléhavost zabývání se oblastmi veřejného života – únor 2014' [Urgency of some problems in the view of public opinion - February 2014], *Tisková zpráva CVVM Sociologického ústavu AV ČR* [online], 20 March, Praha: Sociologický ústav AV ČR. Available from http://cvvm.soc.cas.cz/media/com_form2content/documents/c1/a7200/f3/po140320.pdf

Davison, W.P. (1958) 'The public opinion process', *Public Opinion Quarterly*, 22(2): 91-106.

Dearing, J.W. and Rogers, E.M. (1996) *Agenda-Setting*, Thousand Oaks: SAGE.

Donsbach, W. and Traugott, M.W. (2008) 'Introduction', in W. Donsbach and M.W. Traugott (eds) *The Sage Handbook of Public Opinion Research*, London: SAGE, pp 1-5.

Erikson, R.S., MacKuen, M.B. and Stimson, J.A. (2002) 'Public opinion and policy: causal flow in a macro system model', in J. Manza, F.L. Cook and B.J. Page (eds) *Navigating Public Opinion: Polls, Policy, and the Future of American Democracy*, New York: Oxford University Press, pp 33-53.

Foote, N.N. and Hart, C.W. (1953) 'Public opinion and collective behavior', in M. Sherif and M.O. Wilson (eds) *Group Relations at the Crossroads*, New York: Harper & Brothers, pp 308-31.

Glynn, C.J., Herbst, S., O'Keefe, G.J., Shapiro, R.Y. and Lindeman, M. (2004) *Public Opinion*, Boulder, CO: Westview Press.

Greenpeace (2009) 'Rozum zvítězil. Radar zastaven!' [Sense has prevailed. Radar stopped!], *Tisková zpráva Greenpeace* [online], 17 September. Available from www.greenpeace.org/czech/cz/news/rozum-vyhral-radar-zastaven

Herbst, S. (1993) *Numbered Voices: How Opinion Polling Has Shaped American Politics*, Chicago: University of Chicago Press.

Herbst, S. (1998) *Reading Public Opinion: How Political Actors View the Democratic Process*, Chicago: University of Chicago Press.

Herbst, S. (2002) 'How state-level policy managers "read" public opinion', in J. Manza, F.L. Cook and B.J. Page (eds) *Navigating Public Opinion: Polls, Policy, and the Future of American Democracy*, New York: Oxford University Press, pp 171-83.

iDNES.cz, ČTK and mia (2007) 'Starostové z Brd vyrazili do boje proti radaru' [Mayors from Brdy went into battle against the radar], *idnes.cz* [online], 29 August. Available from http://zpravy.idnes.cz/starostove-z-brd-vyrazili-do-boje-proti-radaru-fl3-/domaci.aspx?c=A070829_222927_domaci_mia

Janík, M., Kabátová, Š. and Kálal, J. (2013) 'Průzkum: Levice chystá drtivé vítězství, ODS by paběrkovala' [Survey: the left is preparing a landslide victory, the ODS would glean], *Lidové noviny* [online], 22 February. Available from www.lidovky.cz/pruzkum-levice-chysta-drtive-vitezstvi-ods-by-paberkovala-por-/zpravy-domov.aspx?c=A130221_202419_ln_domov_sk

Jann, W. and Wegrich, K. (2007) 'Theories of the policy cycle', in F. Fischer, G.J. Miller and M.S. Sidney (eds) *Handbook of Public Policy Analysis: Theory, Politics, and Methods*, Boca Raton: CRC Press, Taylor & Francis Group, pp 43-62.

Kalvas, F. (2008) 'Politická agenda' [Policy agenda], in M. Škodová, J. Červenka, V. Nečas, F. Kalvas, P. Tabery and T. Trampota (eds), *Agenda-setting: teoretické přístupy* [Agenda-setting: theoretical approaches], Praha: Sociologický ústav AV ČR, pp 63-73.

Kingdon, J.W. (1984) *Agendas, Alternatives, and Public Policies*, New York: Harper Collins.

Klein, R. and Marmor, T.R. (2006) 'Reflections on policy analysis: putting it together again', in M. Moran, M. Rein and R.E. Goodin (eds) *The Oxford Handbook of Public Policy*, Oxford: Oxford University Press, pp 892-912.

Krosnick, J.A. (1990) 'Government policy and citizen passion: a study of issue publics in contemporary America', *Political Behavior*, 12(1): 59-92.

Lippmann, W. (1922 (1997)) *Public Opinion*, New York: Free Press Paperbacks.

Mancini, P. (1999) 'New frontiers in political professionalism', *Political Communication*, 16(3): 231-45.

Manza, J., and Brooks, C. (2012) 'How sociology lost public opinion: a genealogy of a missing concept in the study of the political', *Sociological Theory*, 30(2): 89-113.

Manza, J. and Cook, F.L. (2002) 'The impact of public opinion on public policy: the state of the debate', in J. Manza, F.L. Cook and B.J. Page (eds) *Navigating Public Opinion: Polls, Policy, and the Future of American Democracy*, New York: Oxford University Press, pp 17-32.

Manza, J., Cook, F.L. and Page, B.I. (2002) 'Navigating public opinion: an introduction', in J. Manza, F.L. Cook and B.J. Page (eds) *Navigating Public Opinion: Polls, Policy, and the Future of American Democracy*, New York: Oxford University Press, pp 3-14.

Martinek, J. (2014) 'Zeman: Koalici jsem mohl škrtem pera vyhodit do povětří' [Zeman: I could blow up a coalition by a stroke of a pen], *Právo* [online], 8 February. Available from www.novinky.cz/domaci/327069-zeman-koalici-jsem-mohl-skrtem-pera-vyhodit-do-povetri.html

---

McCombs, M.E. and Shaw, D.L. (1972) 'The agenda-setting function of mass media', *Public Opinion Quarterly*, 36(2): 176-87.

Mezinárodní humanistická organizace – Česká republika (2009) *Kampaň proti radaru* [The campaign against the radar] [online]. Available from www.svetbezvalek.cz/cs/kampan-proti-radaru

Morávek, J. (2011) 'Analýza rámců' [Frame analysis], in M. Nekola, H. Geissler and M. Mouralová (eds) *Současné metodologické otázky veřejné politiky* [Current methodological issues of public policy], Praha: Karolinum, pp 105-35.

Noelle-Neumann, E. (1993) *The Spiral of Silence: Public Opinion – Our Social Skin* (2nd edn), Chicago: University of Chicago Press.

Nováková, J. (2014) 'Angažovanost občanů a zájem o politiku – únor 2014' [Interest of Czech citizens in political events - February 2014], *Tisková zpráva CVVM Sociologického ústavu AV ČR* [online], 12 March, Praha: Sociologický ústav AV ČR. Available from http://cvvm.soc.cas.cz/media/com_form2content/documents/c1/a7194/f3/pd140312.pdf

oL and ČTK (2008) 'Senát schválil smlouvy o radaru. Teď jsou na tahu sněmovna a prezident' [The Senate approved treaties on a radar. Now is the turn of deputies and President], *ihned.cz* [online], 27 November. Available from http://zpravy.ihned.cz/c1-30891170-senat-schvalil-smlouvy-o-radaru-ted-jsou-na-tahu-snemovna-a-prezident

Page, B.J. (2002) 'The semi-sovereign public', in J. Manza, F.L. Cook and B.J. Page (eds) *Navigating Public Opinion: Polls, Policy, and the Future of American Democracy*, New York: Oxford University Press, pp 325-44.

Peters, J.D. (1995) 'Historical tensions in the concept of public opinion', in T.L. Glasser and C.T. Salmon (eds) *Public Opinion and the Communication of Consent*, New York: Guilford Press, pp 3-32.

Price, V. (1992) *Public Opinion*, Newbury Park, CA: SAGE.

Price, V. (2008) 'The public and public opinion in political theories', in W. Donsbach and M.W. Traugott (eds) *The Sage Handbook of Public Opinion Research*, London: SAGE, pp 11-24.

Price, V. and Roberts, D.F. (1987) 'Public opinion processes', in C.R. Berger and S.H. Chaffee (eds) *Handbook of Communication Science*, Newbury Park, CA: SAGE, pp 781-816.

Roškot, J. (2008) 'V Londýně podepsána smlouva SOFA o radaru' [SOFA agreement on a radar signed in London], *Právo*, 20 September, p 1.

Saris, W.E. (2004) 'Different judgment models for policy questions: competing or complementary?', in W.E. Saris and P.M. Sniderman (eds) *Studies in Public Opinion: Attitudes, Nonattitudes, Measurement Error, and Change*, Princeton, NJ: Princeton University Press, pp 17-36.

Soroka, S.N. and Wlezien, C. (2010) *Degrees of Democracy: Politics, Public Opinion, and Policy*, Cambridge: Cambridge University Press.

Stanyer, J. (2007) *Modern Political Communication*, Cambridge: Polity Press.

Stimson, J.A. (1999) *Public Opinion in America: Moods, Cycles, and Swings* (2nd edn), Boulder, CO: Westview Press.

Šamanová, G. (2006) '(Kvazi)demokratická období výzkumu veřejného mínění před rokem 1989' [(Quasi) democratic periods of public opinion research before 1989], *Naše společnost*, 4(1): 19-21.

Škodová, M. (2007) 'Výzkum nemůže existovat bez zpětné vazby a svobody projevu' [Research cannot exist without feedback and freedom of expression], *Naše společnost*, 5(1): 31-35.

Van der Veld, W. and Saris, W.E. (2004) 'Separation of error, method effects, instability and attitude strength', in W.E. Saris and P.M. Sniderman (eds) *Studies in Public Opinion: Attitudes, Nonattitudes, Measurement Error, and Change*, Princeton, NJ: Princeton University Press, pp 37-59.

Vláda České republiky (2007) 'Vládním mluvčím pro radar se stane Tomáš Klvaňa' [Tomáš Klvaňa becomes the government spokesperson for a radar issue], *Tisková zpráva, V*láda České republiky [online], 28 May. Available from www.vlada. cz/cz/media-centrum/aktualne/vladnim-mluvcim-pro-radar-se-stane-tomas-klvana-23010/

Vláda České republiky (2008) 'Tomáš Klvaňa: Vláda si nepřeje přesvědčovací kampaň pro radar' [Tomáš Klvaňa: government does not want a persuasive campaign for a radar], *Vláda České republiky* [online], 23 January. Available from www.vlada.cz/cz/media-centrum/aktualne/tomas-klvana-vlada-si-nepreje-presvedcovaci-kampan-pro-radar-30151/

Weisberg, H.F. (2008) 'The methodological strengths and weaknesses of survey research', in W. Donsbach and M.W. Traugott (eds) *The Sage Handbook of Public Opinion Research*, London: SAGE, pp 223-31.

Wirnitzer, J. (2009) 'PŘEHLEDNĚ: USA "zamázly" radar v Brdech, Češi litují i oslavují' [CLEARLY: USA stopped the radar in Brdy, Czechs regret and celebrate], *idnes.cz* [online], 17 September. Available from http://zpravy.idnes. cz/prehledne-usa-zamazly-radar-v-brdech-cesi-lituji-i-oslavuji-po6-/domaci. aspx?c=A090917_121519_domaci_jw

Wlezien, C. (1995) 'The public as thermostat: dynamics of preferences for spending', *American Journal of Political Science*, 39(4): 981-1000.

Wlezien, C. (2005) 'On the salience of political issues: the problem with "most important problem"', *Electoral Studies*, 24(4): 555-79.

Zaller, J.R. (1992) *The Nature and Origins of Mass Opinion*, Cambridge: Cambridge University Press.

TWELVE

Policy analysis outsourcing

Vojtěch Sedláček, Arnošt Veselý

Introduction

It has been suggested by many authors (for example Boston, 1994; Dunleavy, 1995; Peters, 1996) that external sources of expertise might be displacing the advisory processes and capacities inside government. This hypothesis has been recently labelled as the 'externalization thesis' (Veselý, 2013). By *externalisation* is meant the relocation of advisory activities previously performed inside government organisations to places outside of government. Externalisation can take different forms and have different causes and consequences.

One particular form of externalisation is outsourcing, which can also be understood as replacing internal policy advice with external advice on the basis of a contract with an actor outside government (usually a private consulting company or individual advisors). In this respect, Peters (1996, p 2) argued that

> in addition to the changing role definitions of the senior public service, the internal resources available for career officials to fulfil their role as policy advisors also appear to have diminished significantly. There has been a 'lost generation' of young policy analysts who have not been hired by government in most industrialised democracies.

Peters, however, makes it clear that 'it is difficult to quantify the extent of this malaise in the public sector', and acknowledges that this claim is based upon anecdotal evidence (of which there is, according to Peters, a good deal).

Contracted consultancies are also well established as significant actors in the Czech Republic. This chapter deals with outsourcing of policy advice in the Czech Republic. First, we attempt to quantify the extent of outsourcing in the Czech ministries as the most important institutions of the central public administration. Then we describe the types and roles of different commercial providers of policy advice. This is followed by a discussion of why outsourcing happens and its possible consequences. Apart from statistical data, in this chapter we draw upon more than ten years' experience both consuming and providing outsourced policy analysis in the Czech central state administration as well as interviews from representatives of both the demand and supply sides.

The extent of policy advice outsourcing

Let us first attempt to quantify the extent of outsourcing. Although outsourcing concerns all types of public institutions, in this section we focus upon the expenditures of 14 ministries on consulting and advisory services. We use data from two national publicly available registers, ARIS (Automatizovaný rozpočtový informační system [Automated budget information system]) and ÚFIS (Prezentační systém finančních a účetních informací státu [System of financial and accounting informations of the state]). These registers contain data on public expenditures classified according to Ministry of Finance Decree Number 323/2002 Collection, on the budget structure. The expenditures and revenues are classified according to several classification schemes, including ministerial 'chapters' (for example the Ministry of Finance) and the type of expenditures/revenues. Under the latter classification is item 5166 entitled 'Consulting, advisory and legal services'. These are defined as: 'Expenditures for the contractual acquisition of information which does not have the status of property' This information includes consulting, advice, analyses, reports, legal services or other information that the organisation uses for decision making and is not explicitly legally bound to deliver according to law (the provisioning of information which the organisation is obliged to provide according to specific legal norms is classified under item 5169).

As for the time period, we have been limited by the availability of ARIS and ÚFIS data. These datasets for our analysis covered the period from 2001 to 2011, providing us with only a ten-year time series. The covered period, however, is very interesting. It includes both right-wing and left-wing governments; periods of economic boom, economic recession and the global economic crisis in 2008, followed by immense cuts in public budgets. Also worth mentioning is the EU accession in 2004 as well as changes to the regulatory rules on public contracts (the amendment to the Act on Public Contracts), which directly influences the outsourcing of advisory and consulting services.

The first question is what is the proportion of external expenditures for policy advice in the overall current costs and how does this proportion change over time. To look for the answers to this question it was necessary to acquire data on expenditures for the outsourcing of policy advice and data on the amount of the overall current costs of the state budget (Table 12.1).

It is clear from Table 12.1 that the proportion of outsourcing of policy advice (item 5166) is relatively small when compared to the overall current costs of the state budget. It is also clear, however, that the proportion increased up to the year 2006. The later development is more random and cannot be judged to be a longer-term trend. Various factors might explain this, most importantly the entry into the EU in 2004 (which arguably led to a demand for new expertise and skills) and the economic crisis that started in 2008. Our analysis revealed that there is no linear trend over time. For instance, it is not possible to explain the proportion of expenditures using macroeconomic variables in the form of real changes in the GDP (Veselý et al, 2015). Similarly, though several interviewees

Table 12.1: The proportion of total external expenditures for policy advice (item 5166) in the overall current costs; total for all ministries, in 2012 values

	A External costs for policy advice (in thousands CZK)	B Total current costs (in thousands CZK)	Proportion A/B (%)
2001	693,493	179,728,996	0.386
2002	1,267,468	194,138,676	0.653
2003	980,311	147,662,974	0.664
2004	1,048,995	147,650,795	0.710
2005	1,231,640	156,090,237	0.789
2006	1,485,035	161,698,557	0.918
2007	1,378,950	164,767,011	0.837
2008	1,480,989	169,357,234	0.874
2009	1,128,155	162,478,471	0.694
2010	1,077,129	177,289,437	0.608
2011	1,277,010	169,226,250	0.755

Source: State's closing accounts, state budget. Own calculations.

claimed that the level of involvement of external consultants in policy making has grown steadily since the arrival of the Structural Funds after the Czech Republic's EU accession in 2004, our data cannot confirm such a hypothesis.[1]

It seems that internal, rather than external factors might better explain the results. It is clear from the analysis that a certain turning point occurred in 2006. This turning point might have been caused by the fact that a new version of the Act on Public Contracts was passed on 14 March 2006 and that, among other things, significantly changed the limits for assigning public contracts. These were also reflected in the area of policy advisory services. According to the version of the Act on Public Contracts from 2006, the limits for small contracts were decreased. This led to two reactions on the part of contracting authorities. Whereas before small contracts did not have to be tendered, authorities now had to announce tenders for policy advice taking into account the limit of CZK3 million for the expected value of the public contract. At the same time it occurred in practice that the contracting authorities broke up larger public contracts into several smaller contracts (contrary to the law) in order to be below the limit for small contracts, thus avoiding having to announce a 'classic' tender.

The interviews with contracting authorities signalled another possible impact of this amendment on the growth of the proportion of external expenditures

---

[1] However, it is possible that policy advice related to EU structural funds is formally posted under a different budget chapter and thus did not appear in our data.

for policy advice within overall current costs. The contracting authorities stated that each change (amendment) to the Act on Public Contracts means a risk when they make decisions. New procurement conditions and a lack of objective experience with the new and amended procurement procedures led the contracting authorities (as mentioned in their own statements) to 'stock up' (see the turning point in 2006), or 'postpone' the need for public contracts to a later time when the 'given amendment to the Act on Public Contracts will be sufficiently verified'. Thus the contracting authorities act like rational decision makers, who want to minimise the risks of their decisions. This hypothesis, however, would require further verification.

There is another important internal factor that could have an effect upon the consulting statistics. This is Resolution Number 146 by the Government of the Czech Republic from 7 March 2012 which states that if a ministry or other administrative authority concludes a contract for the delivery of consulting, advisory or legal services for more than CZK1 million from one supplier during a calendar year, the proposal for the conclusion of such a contract is subject to the government's approval. The ministries probably reacted rationally to this fact by moving part of the expenditures for consulting and advisory services (item 5166) to a different item (5169), which is designated as 'purchases of other services'. But it is also possible that they indeed reduced their expenditures on consulting because this decree caused another administrative burden.

Another question is whether a larger number of employees at a ministry leads to lower expenditures on the outsourcing of policy advisory services. In other words, do larger ministries have greater capacities to perform policy advisory services? Our analysis found a slight positive correlation between the number of employees and the costs of outsourcing. In other words, larger ministries (measured by the number of employees) have, on average for the entire period, a lower quota of external expenditures. There are, however, differences among ministries. For instance, the correlation coefficient between the external expenditures and the number of employees at the Ministry of Transport is highly positive while it is highly negative at the Ministry for Regional Development, even though both ministries belong to the same size group (small). This might be caused by the fact that levels of externalisation may vary in different policy domains (Bakvis, 2000). A closer look at the data, however, shows that at many ministries the proportion of outsourcing changes significantly over time. This suggests that the level of outsourcing is strongly influenced by ad hoc – probably mostly political – factors rather than by 'objective' needs for expertise.

Commercial providers of policy analysis in the Czech Republic

In general, policy analysis might be contracted out from the public administration to three basic types of institutions: universities, think tanks and commercial providers, ranging from 'one man and a dog' companies to local representatives of well-established international management consulting firms. Leaving academic and think tank institutions aside (see Chapters Sixteen and Seventeen), in this chapter we focus on commercial providers, notably consulting companies.

There are many ways consulting firms might be classified. The basic dimensions for classification include internal organisation and business model, industry coverage and geographical presence. In this respect, Cheng (2012) differentiates six major types of consultancies: strategy consulting, accounting firms, IT specialists, boutique consulting, internal consultants and independent consultants.

Strategy consulting firms, as the title suggests, provide consulting and advice on strategic issues. In the business world their mission is related to a company's overall strategy, business transformation, divesting or acquisition, and so on. According to Cheng, strategy consultancies 'must tackle high-dollar questions at a CEO- or senior executive-level in order to make the hefty strategy consulting price tag (often over $500,000 a month for a team of five) a reasonable investment'. As Gross, Poor and Roberson (2004) point out, after the fall of the communist regimes in 1989, Central and Eastern Europe, with its need for fundamental transformation in countless social and economic areas, was flooded with consulting opportunities. Large-scale privatisation led to the entry of many foreign investors and this was accompanied by the consulting services they were using. Not only the private sector, but also public institutions were eager for advice: 'Ministries had to be reorganized, regulation had to be revised and reinterpreted, and the relationship between policymakers and private-sector leaders had to be rebuilt' (Gross et al, 2004, p 35). As a result, most of the top tier international strategy consulting firms such as McKinsey & Company, AT Kerney and the Boston Consulting Group are now present in the Czech Republic.

The second type, accounting firms, include large international audit and accounting firms such as PricewaterhouseCoopers (PwC), KPMG, Ernst & Young (EY) and Deloitte, which usually also have strong consulting practices. Given their foundation in accounting and audit, this type of company usually provides services in the areas of process optimisation, compliance, operational effectiveness and so on. Just like the strategy consulting firms, most of the accounting firms opened offices in the Czech Republic relatively shortly after 1989, following their international clients and the opportunities related to the transformation of the economy.

With the growing importance and complexity of information and communication technologies in the everyday life of both private and public institutions, ICT-related (Information and Communication Technologies) consulting established itself as a specific category in the past two decades. The presence of ICT consulting companies in the public sector has two distinctive aspects: advising on the internal IT (information technology) matters of government offices and transforming the way the government interacts with citizens through the various tools of eGovernment. With the arrival and growing significance of eGovernment, IT consultancies have gained considerable know-how on government's key processes and functions in general. As a result, some of them engage in non-IT assignments such as overall process analysis and optimisation. Consulting is usually added to the larger portfolio of services provided by IT companies. We can find consulting practices within companies such as IBM, CSC or Microsoft. On the other hand, many IT consulting-centred firms such as Accenture or CapGemini also implement or integrate IT solutions as such. The presence of IT consulting companies in the Czech Republic is appropriate to the size of the Czech IT market, with most major players having their offices in Prague or Brno.

The fourth type, boutique consulting, also referred as to as niche consultancies, provides advice in highly specialised areas or to specific industries. Boutique consulting companies are usually of a smaller size, compared to consulting practices associated with audit and accounting firms. Since few companies labelled as boutique consulting have a global presence, most boutique consultancies have instead a local or regional reach. In the general categorisation, companies focused mainly on providing policy analysis to government agencies fall under this category.

As for the fifth type, internal consultants, many corporations have adopted a practice of having an internal team that provides the same kind of advice and services as external consultant firms. Such teams usually work close to senior executives, keeping a relatively high degree of autonomy. A parallel might be drawn between in-house corporate consultants and internal advisors to government.

Last but not least, there are independent consultants. According to Cheng (2012) many consultants 'don't even operate under the banner of a major company. These entrepreneurial souls often work by themselves or in a very small team of two to six people total'. Naturally, independent consultants usually have deep knowledge in a limited number of subjects.

All of these types are present in the Czech Republic; their significance in providing policy advice differs, however. With the lack of any reliable data, it is impossible to quantify the impact these private providers of policy advice have on policy making in the Czech Republic. Based upon our experience, we can, however, formulate some tentative conclusions. As for strategy consulting firms, their impact does not seem to be very significant. Despite the fact that government is the traditional target customer of strategic consultancies, their role in advising the Czech central state administration seems to be rather limited.[2] This might be due to several reasons. First, it might be that public administration, being predominantly 'fire-fighting', does not demand strategic advice. It is, of course, also possible that this is mainly due to the high price of such advice, which public institutions cannot legitimately afford. In this respect it is worth mentioning that there are notable examples of the real significance of strategy consulting firms. The most prominent example is an unsolicited (that is, strictly speaking, not contracted out) report by the Czech division of McKinsey & Company called

---

[2]   McKinsey & Company in their Czech web presentation claims to be 'the trusted advisor to the world's leading businesses, governments, and institutions' and BCG's Czech website has an exhaustive list of services provided to the public sector.

Decreasing Results of Czech Primary and Secondary Education: Facts and Solutions (McKinsey & Company, 2010). This report, funded exclusively by McKinsey & Company, had a huge impact upon preparation of the strategic documents of the Ministry of Education, Youth and Sport.

In any event, in comparison to strategy consulting firms, large auditing and accounting firms, such as PwC or EY, seem to have a bigger impact. The activities of these firms include the creation of methodology for preparation of public strategies, analysis and design of tax collection process improvement, and background analysis for preparation of new operational programmes from the European structural funds. The fact that the core business of these companies centres around audit gives their consulting services extra credibility. Some politicians and officials intentionally stress that the analysis was performed by an international auditing firm, despite the fact that the provided services had nothing to do with audit procedures and standards.

The role of IT consulting companies was heavily influenced by eGovernment initiatives in the second half of the 2000s. Since some of the eGovernment programmes in the Czech Republic fundamentally changed the way public administration is organised and the way it operates, the IT companies had to acquire considerable know-how on public institutions and policies as such. Consequently, they also started to engage with public administration on non-IT topics including policy analysis. This trend has been enhanced by the fact that with the advancing digitisation of public administration more and more public policies are somehow related to IT systems. Both accounting firms and IT consultancies are traditionally strong in project and programme management, which also makes them the preferred choice if advice on project management is needed.

Boutique consultancies, on the other hand, are more likely to provide expertise on particular subjects such as water treatment, waste management or engineering (such as, for example Mott MacDonald in the Czech Republic). It is also relatively common that larger multinational consultancies subcontract smaller, more expert-oriented companies in order to cover both the project management and subject matter expertise aspects of policy analysis. A specific segment of consulting services concerns the use of the EU funds. Many companies that focus upon grant advising offer evaluation of the interventions' impact as well as producing background studies and problem analyses on various social and economic issues in order to help set the direction of future interventions.

There are also a lot of independent consultants. Their role and impact is, however, even more obscure than the role of private companies. There have been number of cases discovered by the mass media of hugely overpriced advice to the public administration (especially to ministries). It has been shown that the choice of advisors depends more on personal ties than the actual skills and competencies of the consultants. As a consequence, for many people individual advising to ministries is associated with corruption.

Possible explanations of policy analysis outsourcing

Why is policy advice outsourced? What reasons lead government to search (and pay) for external advice? Several hypotheses of why externalisation happens have been formulated (Perl and White, 2002; Veselý, 2013). They can be divided into three broad types of factors (Veselý, 2013). The first set of factors relates to a lack of internal capacity. The second set concerns the political factors which lead the government to prefer external advice over internal. The third set refers to the context in which the policy advice is provided. These factors, of course, are not mutually exclusive.

First, it is possible to explain outsourcing by an incapacity and lack of competencies and skills in the public administration to provide relevant policy advice. This lack of competence can mean both lack of subject matter expertise and lack of the ability to manage the proper production of an analysis or strategy. With the growing complexity and specialisation, no one can expect the public administration to hire and permanently retain experts covering the full range of competencies. For instance, for the Ministry of Trade it might be unreasonable to *permanently* employ nano-tech or bio-tech experts, despite the fact that such expertise might be useful for, say, writing the competitiveness strategy. In the case of niche expertise, outsourcing policy analysis comes as a natural choice. While there might be subject matter experts present and available within the organisation, crafting complex analysis, not to mention strategy, demands a specific set of skills on top of the subject matter expertise.

Similarly, sometimes internal expertise cannot be created and mobilised in a sufficient time frame. The demand for policy analysis might emerge quickly with an urgent deadline. Moreover, the boundaries of analysed problems are often blurred or fuzzy. It happens very often during an analysis that new needs for data, research, expert opinions appear, or simply a need for more manpower to get the task done. While for the ministry it might be difficult if not impossible to get additional capacities on board quickly, mainly due to staff and wage limitations and complex hiring processes, a professional consultancy can scale the delivery team up without much effort.

In addition, new factors, especially joining the EU, have brought new demands on the quality and structure of required analysis. To give an example, in the 2007-13 EU programming period, the Structural Funds allowed the public administration to gain a significant amount of resources to improve its overall performance. The absorption of funds is project-based, requiring a defined set of documentation when applying for funding. One of the documents required for certain types of interventions was a cost-benefit analysis. At the time of the first projects back in 2006/07, there were very few civil servants who were actually able to produce cost-benefit analyses. As a result most of the cost-benefit analyses were outsourced to commercial consultancies.

Less obvious, however, is why this practice has remained to the present day. It seems that in general public administration institutions have made little effort to *internalise* expertise and skills in areas they permanently need (such as evaluation, cost-benefit analysis and so on). A simple look at the ministerial organisational charts tells us that units or departments related to policy analysis and evaluation are very rare, with policy analysis being usually part of the job description of departments focusing on a particular subject matter. With the current absence of a civil service act (which remains the case even 25 years after the fall of the communist regime) the capacity as well as commitment of the administration to attract, train and retain professional policy analysts remains in doubt. Experience also shows examples of talented civil servants being head-hunted by management consulting companies after successful delivery of a high-profile policy analysis or strategy paper.

In this respect Veselý (2012) suggested that a more important factor influencing the internal capacity is workforce competition by the private sector in particular domains as well as different prices of policy advice among sectors. We can hypothesise that the competencies of the workforce in domains where the private sector cannot provide higher remuneration, such as culture, sport, defence or social work, are better than in sectors like finance, energy and the environment. As a consequence, the departments responsible for these domains do not have to ask for external advice, and if they have to do so, they can obtain it relatively inexpensively. Available data for the Czech Republic indeed seems to give some support to this hypothesis. For instance, the Ministry of Culture shows the lowest externalisation.

Interestingly, outsourcing might also have some advantage in terms of pressure on the content and quality of advice. One of our interviewers stated that as a customer of a contracted consultancy, the public institution has better control over the quality of produced analysis because there are formal acceptance procedures that the contractor must comply with. He argued that often it is much easier to push an external consultancy to rework the output or 'run an extra mile' than it was with internal staff, who in many cases 'didn't sparkle with enthusiasm'.[3]

The second set of explanations concerns the political factors which lead the government to prefer external advice over internal. The public administration might outsource to be able to claim 'independence and a high profile'. Smith (1977) pointed out independence as a key success factor in any policy analysis, reminding readers that 'some observers go so far as to infer that an independent non-governmental organization is the only, or at least the most likely, in which truly creative policy analysis can be performed'. While such a statement is highly

---

[3] However, it does not follow that contracted analysis is necessarily of high quality. Public contractors are often unable to recognise a good analysis, and as a result the contracted companies are able to sell documents of very low quality (see conclusions). To confront the authors' observations with other opinions, in September 2014 we arranged two exploratory interviews. One was with an experienced 'consumer' of outsourced policy analysis (a former deputy minister and a former director of advisors to the prime minister). The second was with an experienced provider of outsourced policy analysis working in a very influential consulting company.

controversial, and was marked as such even by Smith himself, the truth remains that engaging a recognised well-branded consultancy might give the impression of high priority given to the subject. Outsourcing to a top tier management consultancy might be a good strategy for claiming independence and quality.

It is, however, also a good strategy for passing the responsibility outside the public administration. In other words it might fulfil the need for having someone to blame, when the policy fails. Adopting a political decision is always associated with a risk that you will make a wrong call and outsourcing might be an interesting risk mitigation strategy. It might come in handy to have an opportunity to claim that that the decision was wrong because it was based on incorrect analysis. If the analysis was produced by internal staff, the responsible decision maker will still take the largest portion of blame, as it was 'his or her' people who failed. But when the analysis was produced by an external provider, a significant part of the blame might be externalised to the provider.

Besides low internal competence and political factors, which are more or less general and apply not only to the Czech Republic, there are also other more specific and contextual explanations of contracting out. The first concerns the trust deficit. Trust is a crucial element in policy analysis, especially in the period after elections when the political representatives are replaced. It is also good to mention that there have been frequent changes of government in the Czech Republic in recent years. With the absence of a professional civil service rooted in the system by appropriate legislation, it is common that the new political representation brings 'its own people', not only for top management positions, but also for mid-management and expert staff. It has been witnessed several times that until 'trusted' people are installed in critical positions, reliance on the current civil servants might be uncertain. When decision makers responsible for delivering policy analysis do not trust internal staff, they will probably decide to outsource.

Another factor relates to the mode of financing. Czech ministries use a historical approach to budgeting. That means that the ministerial spending of the current year is taken as the baseline for the next year's budget. The same applies to particular ministerial sections and departments. Savings are *dangerous* as they can cause your budget to be cut more next year. This also applies to funds for external services, including policy advice. Simply put, to spend money on *any* analysis might be a good strategy to get the same money again for next year. In our experience, we may say that it is not exceptional to hear from public officials as the end of the fiscal year approaches: 'we have some money left, it might be good to ask for some analysis'.

Last but not least, we have to repeat that the outsourcing of policy analysis is sometimes associated with corruption. This is because the cost of 'advice' is often hard to calculate. If the price of advice is criticised as too high, the advisors often respond that thanks to their good advice the state saved a lot of money. It is also usually very difficult to judge what is and is not good advice. As a consequence, funds in the budget allocated to analysis are one of the easiest targets for diversion of public finance.

Conclusion

Outsourcing of policy advice in the Czech Republic is a highly understudied phenomenon. The evidence we have is still largely incomplete. Yet there is no doubt that it is a crucial and widespread phenomenon. Very recently, in the last two or three years, both the mass media and politicians' speeches have started to pay attention to the outsourcing of policy advice. It has been argued that the amount of public funds invested in outsourced policy analysis is simply too high and that policy advice should be generated mostly within the public administration to save the public money.

While the aspect of efficiency is no doubt very important, the discussion tends to overlook other, arguably even more important aspects, especially the quality of advice and effects of outsourcing upon public administration. Indeed, it is interesting to note how little attention is paid to the quality of policy advice, be it internal or outsourced. It is usually assumed that the quality of outsourced advice is higher, because the providers are experts with special skills, not available in the public sector. Nevertheless, this cannot always be, and perhaps quite often is not, the case. This is because the bidding process, based upon the current public procurement law, clearly favours the criterion of *price* over all other criteria. As a result, the winner is usually the one with the lowest cost, regardless of the quality of the applicant as well as the proposal. In practice, we quite often hear complaints from public officials on the quality of advice they get from the private companies. When asked why they have chosen this company, they respond that they did not have any other real choice, despite knowing it would not produce high quality policy advice.

Another usually overlooked consequence of outsourcing is the further decline in internal capacity. If contracting out is criticised it is because it is too costly. The 'internalisation' of policy advice is associated with a reduction in public expenditures. Yet good policy advice will always be expensive, be it outside or inside government. To get and maintain people who are able to provide useful advice presumes creating good conditions for them. This includes not only salary but also opportunities for further growth. Outsourcing in the Czech Republic is almost always discussed in isolation, without any link to the quality of the public services. But these are certainly two sides of the same coin.

Last but not least, the overall approach of government to contracting is unclear and often populist. As mentioned earlier, outsourcing has sometimes, especially during the last two years, been described as an unequivocal evil, inefficiently consuming public funds. Yet there is no doubt that some forms of outsourcing can be effective and useful. If so, the public administration must be *able* to contract out. Our experience and the evidence we have clearly shown that the current Czech public administration has very little capacity to specify requirements on externally provided analysis or to recognise its real quality and value. In fact, calls for analysis are often something like 'we want to know everything about everything'. However, without strengthening the capacity to contract out, the effect of contracting is not likely to be very positive.

Acknowledgement

The chapter was written with the financial support of PRVOUK programme P17 'Sciences of Society, Politics, and Media under the Challenge of the Times'.

References

Bakvis, H. (2000) 'Rebuilding policy capacity in the era of the fiscal dividend: a report from Canada', *Governance*, 13(1): 71-103.

Boston, J. (1994) 'Purchasing policy advice: the limits to contracting out', *Governance*, 7(1): 1-30.

Cheng, V. (2012) *What is Management Consulting?* [online], Fast Forward Media, Inc. Available from www.caseinterview.com/management-consulting

Dunleavy, P. (1995) 'Policy disasters: explaining the UK's record', *Public Policy and Administration*, 10(2): 52-70.

Gross, A., Poor, J. and Roberson, M.T. (2004) 'Consulting in Central Europe', *Consulting to Management*; 15(1): 33-39.

McKinsey & Company (2010) *Klesající výsledky českého základního a středního školství: fakta a řešení* [Decreasing results of Czech primary and secondary education: facts and solutions], Praha: McKinsey & Company.

Perl, A. and Donald J.W. (2002) 'The changing role of consultants in Canadian policy analysis', *Policy and Society*, 21(1): 49-73.

Peters, B.G. (1996) *The Policy Capacity of Government, Research Paper no. 18*, Ottawa: Canadian Centre for Management Development.

Smith, Bruce (1977) 'The non-governmental policy analysis organizations', *Public Administration Review*, May/June: 253-58.

Veselý, A. (2012) 'Policy advisory system in the Czech Republic: from state monopoly to hollowing out?', Paper presented at the XXIInd World Congress of Political Science in Madrid, Madrid.

Veselý, A. (2013) 'Externalization of policy advice: theory, methodology and evidence', *Policy and Society*, 32(3): 199-209.

Veselý, A., Ochrana, F. and Klazar, S. (2015) 'An analysis of expenses for the outsourcing of policy advice on the level of the ministries of the Czech Republic', *Prague Economic Papers*, 24(5): 581-601.

Part IV

Parties and interest group-based policy analysis

Czech political parties and policy analysis in the perspective of policy advisory systems

Vilém Novotný, Martin Polášek, Michel Perottino

Introduction

Political parties represent one of the pillars of liberal democracy and play an important, although often unheeded role in the process of policy making. Parties not only aggregate and formulate demands arising from civil society, they also hold a privileged position in delegating their representatives to central policy-formulating and decision-making posts in the legislature and the executive; consequently, they can have a significant influence on the policy-making process. Czech political parties have faced many challenges and problems related for example to the formation of the Czech state after 1993, the economic transformation of the 1990s, accession to the EU, and the world economic crisis in 2008. This difficult position has been made even more uncertain in recent years with the advent of escalated apolitical discourse that stresses professionalism and apolitical (depoliticised) politics.

This leads us to the logical question: what expert policy capacities do Czech political parties have in order to influence the process of policy making in the direction that they have determined for themselves? We study the parties' formal mechanisms and organisational structures in the form of policy advisory systems, which are necessary for the elaboration of the required policy expertise. We are interested in finding out what kind of organisational and expert capacities in the form of policy advisory systems exist in political parties (similarly Craft and Howlett, 2012b).

Our main goal is to present the structure of the advisory systems of the main Czech political parties. Arrangements of policy advisory systems are considered the main determinant of the policy (analytical) capacity of individual organisations (see for example Howlett and Oliphant, 2010), which Czech political parties need for the successful fulfilment of their role in the political system.[1] This topic is new

---

[1] Here we apply Howlett's conception of relations among policy capacity (the broader ability of an organisation to successfully enter into policy making), policy analytical capacity (a narrower concept related to the capability of an organisation to perform policy analysis and research), and policy advisory system (see Howlett, 2009; Howlett and Oliphant, 2010). For applications of these concepts outside public administration, see Howlett and Oliphant (2010), and Evans and Wellstead (2013).

and not sufficiently studied in the Czech environment,[2] because the majority of Czech political science research concentrates on the party system itself and not on the structure and functioning of parties. That is why our study will have above all an exploratory character. In its conceptualisation we are inspired by texts focusing on political party organisation (particularly Katz and Mair, 1995 and the tradition of cartel party theory, and Harmel and Janda, 1994 and their theory of party change) as well as by texts studying the notion of policy work (Colebatch, 2006; and especially Howlett, 2009) and primarily by texts studying advisory systems in the sphere of public administration (for example Halligan, 1995; Craft and Howlett 2012a; Hustedt, 2013). For this purpose we have based our research mainly on the study of party organisation documents (such as party regulations, organisation systems, statutes of constituent party bodies) and the observation of intra-party life (party congresses, the work of expert committees). This is complemented by semi-structured and informal interviews.[3]

We will pay substantial attention to the Social Democrats (ČSSD) and the Civic Democratic Party (ODS) which up until 2013 embodied the two basic pillars of the Czech party system. These parties represent the two 'poles' of possible government coalitions; to be precise they have taken part in every political government since 1992. For this reason, we assume that their policy capacity substantially influenced and affected government policy activities. We will try to follow their development from 1992 to the present, but the focus of our research lies mainly between 2010 and 2013.

In the following text we first briefly introduce the assumptions and the theoretical framework of the issue of policy advisory systems. Then we apply the location theory of policy advisory systems to the political parties. And finally, we present several conclusions regarding the advisory systems and the policy capacities of Czech political parties.

Theoretical framework

Our exploration of party advisory systems combines the approaches to political party organisation research with the approaches to policy analysis, or rather policy work analysis as a newer and broader approach to analysis oriented more at the issue of public administration. Stressing the organisational and not the ideological perspective of political party research, the issue of organisation seems to us a suitable interconnection between the two broad currents of research. We assume that political parties are essentially modern complex organisations in the form of organised anarchies (Cohen et al, 1972; Wiesendahl, 1984; Zahariadis, 2007), as are public administration organisations. Since we believe there is no significant difference between a political party as an organisation and the government as an

---

[2] For Czech public administration, see for example Veselý (2013).

[3] This area, of course, deserves further and deeper scientific inquiry. For description of one particular research design, see Polášek et al (2014).

organisation, it is possible, in general, to use the same approaches and concepts for research on political party organisations that are used for the study of public administration organisations. However, it is necessary to respect the specific organisational arrangements of political parties, which differ from those of public administration.

For this reason, we use here the theory of party development – which is elaborated in the cartel party theory (Katz and Mair, 1995) and in the integrated theory of party goals and party change (Harmel and Janda, 1994) – as it best epitomises the logic of party organisation structure. In particular, the concept of the three 'faces' of a party[4] is well suited to capture both the organisational structure and the power constellations within the party. Another presupposition we share with cartel party theory and the integrated theory of party goals and party change is that party organisation develops in reaction to external forces as well as internal ones.

In terms of policy analysis this implies that with regard to internal and external pressure, political parties should develop their organisational arrangements so that they may produce the required policy expertise. In this respect we consider the concept of political party orientation in accordance with its primary goal[5] (see Strøm, 1990; Harmel and Janda, 1994; Wolinetz, 2002) very helpful. A political party always follows several different goals, but none of them are permanent since they change according to the power configuration within the party. What is assumed here is the ability to react in various ways to external and internal pressures,[6] which can provide a suitable explanation of the organisational operation of the party and the focus of its activities.

On the other hand, we work primarily with research and concepts developed as part of the study of policy work. This is a newer and broader approach to policy analysis (Colebatch, 2006), which in our opinion captures the diversity of partisan policy work better than the traditional narrow American concept of analysis focused mainly on analytical work.[7] In policy work research, our research perspective is closest to Howlett's (2009) conception. Here we are interested in studying what kinds of institutional arrangements and analytical capacities exist

---

[4]   These are the party on the ground, the party in the central office and the party in public office (see for example Katz and Mair, 1992; Mair, 1994).

[5]   Vote seeking, policy seeking, office seeking, democracy seeking and so on.

[6]   For instance, globalisation, demographic development, economic crisis, party system competition, elections, personal dissent or opposition within the party, type of intraparty organisation and so on.

[7]   In view of other research we expect a relatively low level of policy analytical capacity of political parties (compare Cross, 2007; Grunden, 2013), thus it would not make sense for us to focus only on a narrow approach to analysis which could significantly distort our perception of political parties' ability to generate the necessary expertise.

in political parties.[8] Howlett sets out from Fellegi's (1196, p 1) definition of policy capacity as covering issues associated with 'government's arrangements to review, formulate and implement policies within its jurisdiction'. Over time he has reworked this concept and now considers policy capacity to be a multifaceted concept which can be scrutinised on three levels: the level of the subsystem (macro), the organisational level (meso) and the micro-level as the behaviour of 'policy workers' (for example Craft and Howlett, 2012b).

Since we do not suppose a strong policy analytical capacity within political parties, the policy advisory system will be a key analytical concept focusing our work here. According to Howlett and Oliphant (2010, p 19), the policy advisory system is also a critical determinant of the policy capacity along with the policy analytical capacity in a given field or a specific problem area. Policy advisory systems represent the configuration of organisations concerned with policy research or policy analysis.[9] With regard to the exploratory character of our research, we have decided to base our study on the traditional 'location' model of policy advisory systems, which differentiates between the internal and external organisation (Halligan, 1995).

Intra-party arrangements

Within the intra-party arrangement it is suitable to distinguish between organisations of employees and organisations of party members. The first type represents the professional party administration, the party bureaucracy that is organised according to a classical 'top-down' hierarchy. Organisations belonging to the second type are on the contrary built 'bottom-up'. This distinction primarily plays a role in analysis, because in practice there are personnel links between the two structures – that is, party members are often simultaneously employees of a party (for example, secretaries of expert committees and so on). It means that in compliance with Halligan's model we can for our purposes distinguish between party bureaucracy and broader, interior, intra-party arrangements.

Party bureaucracy

Party bureaucracy means the professional administration responsible for a party's administrative work; in essence it is close to public administration. It is the professional administration concentrated around the central party office that seems to be the most significant when it comes to policy capacity, as the majority of the party bureaucracy, especially on the regional and local levels,

---

[8] It is also necessary to stress here that our research focuses on policy expertise and for this reason we do not work with marketing and elections expertise which represents another important sum of expert knowledge related to political parties

[9] Although Howlett later formulated a more sophisticated analysis of policy advisory systems (for example Craft and Howlett, 2012a), it will be sufficient for the purposes of the present study to work with its more general definition.

deal with generalist operational administrative work. On the other hand, party headquarters concentrate specialised employees who do policy work and who can be considered 'policy workers'. The party bureaucracy is thus one of the most important bearers of expertise in any given party. In general, the scope of authority and the organisational arrangement of a party's bureaucratic bodies are determined by party regulations. The key document for their organisational structure and the delimitation of mutual relations is the organisational rules of individual parties. It is usually possible to identify three bodies within the party's central office that provide policy expertise.

Analytical bodies

When it comes to expert capacity, it is the analytical bodies in a party's central office that are most important, for example in the form of the 'Political and Analytical Department' in the ČSSD or the 'Political Department' in the ODS. These units represent the fundamental internal professional analytical capacity of the party and they are strategic policy units. Usually these are relatively small and generally employ approximately 3-6 employees, often in part-time positions. In some parties these can be hired professionals, non-members of the party, or people from academia; in others they can be members of youth organisations or party members complying with all these criteria. The subject content of their work is usually divided according to individual policies. On account of the small number of staff, one official usually deals with several topic areas. These units also process various ad hoc analyses for intra-party discussion, they often mediate information from commissioned sociological surveys and to a large extent they participate in the coordination and finalisation of election materials.

These analytical units are linked both to other units of party expert capacities and to the party's political bodies. The head of this unit plays the key role here as he or she is often authorised to coordinate the work related to the party's expert capacities, harmonising their output, mainly for election purposes, and is present at meetings of the party's political bodies. Staff in these units can participate in the work of other expert units in various forms, for example as secretaries of central expert committees (ODS) or as ad hoc guests.

Administrative support of expert bodies

Another important element, particularly of a procedural character, of the expert analytical capacity of a party is the organisational support of party expert bodies (providing premises for meetings, minutes, correspondence and so on). This can be a separate unit of the party's central office, such as the Department for Expertise and Archives that contains the Shadow Cabinet Unit and Expert Commissions Unit (ČSSD), or this support can be provided by the main analytical unit, as was the case in the ODS. Secretaries of these bodies play the key role here. They organise the administration and running of the given body and they usually fulfil this role for several units. These procedural experts[10] are recruited in various ways. They are either older, well-established employees of the party administration or employees of analytical units who are responsible for a particular policy.

Other auxiliary bodies

Apart from these units explicitly designated as providing party expert capacity, we must not overlook other constituents of the professional administration that participate, often ad hoc due to their specialisation in other tasks in this capacity. These are primarily those units of the central office which are responsible for contact with the media, such as the PR and Marketing Department in the ČSSD and the Media Department in the ODS. These units primarily provide source data for politicians' speeches in the form of general surveys from the press, internet and so on. This ad hoc auxiliary work is not organised according to individual policy areas, but according to the type of media.

Internal to the party

This means primarily the organisation which includes members in the wider context of the party in contrast to the narrower notion of employees of the party's central office. To investigate the configuration of party policy expert bodies, we can apply the analytical distinction of the three 'faces' of a party (for example Katz and Mair, 1992). This distinction reveals very well the configuration of the organisational and power arrangements of an individual party and the interaction of these three 'faces' determines the resulting suggestions of policies, or rather the party's policy capacity.

The party on the ground

Policy expert bodies at the level of the membership base, that is mainly at the local and regional levels, are not very well developed. In some cases, even those that are not in our focus, this could be explained by the relatively small membership base,[11] which does not provide sufficient resources to cover all the required positions.

At the local level we presume that probably all those interested in public office participate either through the standard party organisation or through the

---

[10] For a salient distinction of policy experts on substantial, procedural and decisional criteria see Colebatch et al, 2010, p 13. For political parties we would add specialised politicians as the fourth type (see Polášek et al, 2014).

[11] The membership of Czech political parties ranges from several thousand in smaller parties such as TOP 09 (Tradition, Responsibility, Prosperity 2009), the Green Party, ANO 2011 (Action of Dissatisfied Citizens 2011) and so on up to about 50,000 members in the Communist Party of Bohemia and Moravia (KSČM); the ČSSD, the Christian and Democratic Union – Czechoslovak People's Party (KDU-ČSL) and the ODS had approximately 20-25,000 members in 2013.

formal advisory structures of a given municipal council and office. The regional level is more interesting than the local level, because regions represent a very strong autonomous pillar in the Czech Republic with their own authority and resources.[12] This statutory organisation of power is reflected in the stratarchical arrangement of most parties where regions represent an autonomous and very strong element within a party, which is highlighted even more as a result of the formation of regional autonomy in 2000. It is, thus, remarkable that only the Social Democrats have established regional expert committees since 1996. However, it is necessary to add that regional representatives are often members of central expert committees.

The party in central office

When we study the intra-party policy consultation system on the level of the party's central office, it is necessary to distinguish between the arrangement as part of the party bureaucracy – that is, the organisational units of a party's headquarters, which are staffed by party employees, and central expert bodies, which are occupied by party members who are usually not employees of the party.

Permanent bodies of policy expertise

The first of these are the traditional bodies of policy expertise; these are usually the central expert committees. The number as well as the subject fields of these committees change over time, but the basic organisational logic is based on specific policy sectors. Another characteristic feature is also the fact that the head of a committee and the main party expert are often one and the same person. However, it is not the only organisational model. For example in the ČSSD there was a certain duality between the head of the expert committee and its guarantor, who was the highest political authority in the party on a given issue. He or she also represents a link with the political leadership of the party. Central expert committees are the basic pillars of expert capacities in political parties, because their task is to provide expert data for a selected issue, formulate a party position on a particular policy, serve as a consultative body for representatives of the party in public office and so on. What is accentuated most, however, is their input into the process of elaboration of the party election manifesto, which we can see for example in the creation and use of Orange Books from 2009 and 2012 in the ČSSD and the Agenda 2014 in the ODS.

The second traditional body is generally the shadow cabinet, which expresses the ambitions of opposition parties to capture ministerial offices in the next government. This body has been typical mainly for the ODS. For a relatively

---

[12] Constitutional Act Number 347/1997 Collection of Laws on the Creation of Higher Territorial Self-Governing Units.

long period (2002–10)[13] the Civic Democrats preferred this more personified model that consisted of a designated shadow minister or party speaker and his/her team of experts. This party formulated individual expert position materials, such as the Blue Chance from 2003 to 2004 and Vision 2020.

Over time, parties started to broaden the range of their permanent expert bodies so that they fostered bodies that had not previously played a very important role and that complemented the dominant ones. The reason why parties have broadened this portfolio is not only a reaction to the growing importance of the personification of politics and the necessity for quick responses to political developments; it is also an effort to centralise the party organisation. For example, after the Social Democrats went into opposition in 2006,[14] they decided to emphasise their opposition activity with a clearly personified shadow cabinet. The shadow minister was usually a guarantor responsible for the central expert committee, but at the same time he or she formed a small, dedicated team of advisors in consultation with whom he or she was able to react faster to political developments. On the other hand, the ODS added the central expert committees instead. They were formed in 1997, but worked only until 2002 when they were replaced by the shadow cabinet system. However, the Civic Democrats returned to central expert committees in 2010/2011 and their output was Agenda 2014.

One-off events (manifesto conferences)

This model has traditionally been used in the Civic Democratic Party, where these 'idea' conferences usually related to one topic have existed since 1999. The Czech Social Democratic Party also started to use this tool in 2000 for the party's manifesto discussion but it was broadened in 2010; their concept is more pluralistic in the form of manifesto conferences on fundamental manifesto issues.

Other expert bodies

Apart from these bodies we can also find other expert bodies. In the ČSSD these are for example the chairman's advisors.[15]

---

[13] The first shadow cabinet of the ODS was established by Vaclav Klaus after the party lost the parliamentary elections in 1998, when the Civic Democrats became the largest opposition party.

[14] The Social Democrats formed their first shadow cabinet led by Miloš Zeman in 1996 when they became the strongest opposition party.

[15] Department of the Central Office of the ČSSD Chairman and Advisors, Organisation Rules Part XVII.

The party in public office

In respect of the representation of the party in public office, we can distinguish between organisations that associate representatives of the party in the executive and the legislature. Being in public office is important for two reasons: first, it places the party's own experts, primarily functional experts, in the government; second, it is also a contact to rich sources of expertise outside of the party in the legislature and the executive.

The legislature

Within the legislature, the most important are the representatives' clubs that are formed in all authorities at all levels of governance. At the local or regional levels, there are representatives' clubs, at the traditional national level parliamentary and senate clubs and at the supranational level there are party groups in the European Parliament.

The executive

Government ministers are usually linked with the general political bodies of the party and expert bodies at the level of the central office, primarily the central expert committees. We have found no formal organisation of this small, but important group. On the other hand, regional and local levels do not form these groups. At the regional level, there is for example in the ODS the so-called Shadow Association of the Regions of the Czech Republic. It was established in 2013 as a result of the party's failure in regional elections in 2012 when the Civic Democrats did not succeed in winning office in a single region for the second time. The situation is more consolidated at the local level, as there are official formal groups within parties that link their mayors, for example the Mayors' Club for the ČSSD and the Mayors' Conference in the ODS.

Extra-party arrangements

We believe that for the study of political parties it is necessary to adapt Halligan's (1995) model for the specific organisation of political parties along the lines of Kuhne's typology of extra-party sources of policy consultation (Kuhne, 2008). Kuhne's typology is based on the idea of an advisory system location model; however, it is analytically more detailed than Halligan's original idea, and for this reason we consider it a good starting point. Kuhne describes a wide range of consultation systems and differentiates between three main sources of external policy-formulating expertise: academic (science based), lobbying (interest based) and professional (consultancy based).

Scientific political advising

Universities

The nature of cooperation between political parties and scholars in the Czech Republic is unique. There are several structural barriers - reactions to the former communist regime - that prevent greater involvement of universities and individual scholars in acting as consultants to political parties on public policies. The fact that the legislation on universities explicitly prohibits formal activities of political parties and movements at university premises represents the first barrier.[16] The second barrier is tied to the sensitivity of Czech scholars (and of the Czech public) to direct political intrusions in the university environment. The academic community seems to nurture its independence in everyday politics, which was gained as a result of the leading role of academia in the Velvet Revolution in 1989. For all these reasons, it is rare for scholars to openly cooperate with political parties or act as party consultants or advisory body members. It is much more common for academics to direct their efforts at public administration.

However, this does not mean that the academic and the political communities are completely disconnected. Quasi-independent groups and think tanks established by political parties usually fund or hold events for scholars and thus facilitate interaction between academics and politicians. But there seems to be no formal institutional cooperation between public universities and political organisations in the Czech Republic. The situation is slightly different with private colleges. The CEVRO Institute, established by the CEVRO think tank of the Civic Democratic Party in 2006, is the most successful party-related education project so far (it educates the party's cadres and promotes right-wing politics in general).

Still, the involvement of political parties with the Czech academic world is primarily limited to the personal initiative of individual scholars. These scholars are sometimes party members or, more frequently, they are party supporters and policy entrepreneurs seeking to win support for the public policy solutions they believe in. Jan Keller (Technical University of Ostrava), Martin Potůček (Charles University/think tank Centre for Social Market Economy and Open Democracy - CESTA) and Jiří Pehe (New York University Prague/think tank CESTA), for example, represent scholars involved in promoting the left-wing policies of the ČSSD. On the other end of the political spectrum, the ODS has collaborated with academics such as Petr Fiala (Masaryk University/Centre for the Study of Democracy and Culture (CDK)), Ladislav Mrklas (CEVRO), Miroslav Ševčík (University of Economics (VŠE)/Liberal Institute (LI)) and others.

The cooperation between these scholars and parties usually takes the shape of participation in ideological conferences. Sometimes scholars also sit on party advisory bodies. It is important to distinguish between scholars, party members, party supporters and political entrepreneurs looking for support of their ideas.

---

[16] The Higher Education Act Number 111/1998 Coll., Part 2, Section 10.

Yet scholars who act as expert advisors or consultants usually do so for public administration bodies or for nongovernmental organisations (NGOs) and through this role they cooperate with political parties via their elected officials.

Personal friendships between political leaders and intellectuals may also play an important role in facilitating contact. For example, the former Prime Minister Petr Nečas helped his friend Petr Fiala, the former rector of Masaryk University, assume the position of Head Advisor on Science and Research in Nečas's administration and that of the 'independent' Minister of Education. Fiala later became a member of the Parliament and the party leader for the Civic Democrats in 2014.

Academic think tanks

In the context of the abovementioned barriers, joint projects of political parties and academic think tanks are also rare. Think tanks typically establish partnerships with public administration bodies. If there is any evidence of cooperation between political parties and academic think tanks, it would generally be initiated by a specific scholar who is a think tank employee. These scholars would probably fall into the category of policy entrepreneurs who promote their favourite policy solutions (compare Zittoun, 2001). For example, the former MP for the Freedom Union (Unie Svobody) Petr Matějů, who founded the Institute for Social and Economic Analyses (ISEA), cooperated with the ODS on their position paper 'Blue Chance for Education' in 2003 (Novotný et al, 2012).

Advocacy think tanks

Cooperation between political parties and advocacy think tanks is less problematic and much more common (see also Chapter Seventeen). The right-wing parties in the Czech Republic rely on quite a wide choice of think tanks promoting different interests. The left-wing parties, especially the ČSSD, cooperate instead with party-based foundations sharing their interests. This imbalance might be related to the political atmosphere in the country which favours right-wing ideologies, or to the fact that right-wing parties try to appeal to liberal as well as conservative voters. Liberal and conservative think tanks producing right-wing policy research are plentiful in the Czech Republic. They range from the Liberal Institute, the Civic Institute, the Centre for the Study of Democracy and Culture to the Centre for Economics and Politics, eStat.cz and so on. In general these organisations receive funding and organisational support from two German party-based foundations, the Konrad-Adenauer-Stiftung (KAS) and Hanns-Seidel-Stiftung (HSS).

Left-wing parties, on the other hand, ask for expertise from think tanks which cooperate on the basis of shared interests. The majority of political parties have their own (quasi) think tanks to find and supply relevant research and first of all to educate party leaders. The most successful think tank of this kind is the CEVRO (linked to the ODS), which replaced the Centre for Economics and Politics (CEP

– founded by Václav Klaus) after a conflict between the leaders. The ČSSD uses the Masaryk Democratic Academy (MDA)[17] for similar purposes. Since 2011, the MDA, Fridrich-Ebert-Stiftung (FES) and the Slovak DIRECTION - Social Democracy (SMER-SD) have been running the Academy for Social Democracy in order to educate their leaders. However, despite its ongoing effort to transform into a real think tank, the MDA has not been able to become one, so other left-wing projects such as CESTA competed for attention.

Political foundations

Political foundations play an important role especially in the area of funding and knowledge building.[18] The policy analysis performed by the political foundations cooperating with the ČSSD make up for the absence of interest-oriented think tanks promoting social democratic values. German party-based foundations and foundations supported by different party groups of European Parliament members also play a crucial role.

As we have mentioned, cooperation with German party-based foundations is vital for the ČSSD, which has been partnering with the Prague office of the FES since 1990. The Prague branch of this foundation is not only an important source of funding for policy-consulting and knowledge-building activities but it also provides expertise directly through its own team of researchers. Similarly, the ODS has worked closely with the KAS and the HSS, both of which established branches in Prague as early as 1991. These two foundations provide funding for research, but they do not employ researchers or analysts. In recent years, the cooperation between the ODS and these foundations has reduced due to conflicting views on the European Union and both foundations are prioritising their partnerships with the pro-European TOP 09. Other German political foundations support other Czech parties. For example, the Heinrich-Böll-Stiftung funds the Green Party and the Rosa-Luxembourg-Stiftung supports initiatives promoting policies which resonate with the Communist Party.

Foundations funded by the European Parliament party groups and European party families represent another indirect source of policy knowledge. Czech political parties access these sources with the help of their representatives in the European Parliament and via party membership in European political associations. The ČSSD is a member of the Party of European Socialists which has been operating its own Foundation for European Progressive Studies since 2008. Similarly, The ODS is a member of the Alliance of European Conservatives and

---

[17] Until 2009, the official name was Masaryk Workers' Academy (1896-1948, re-established 1991).

[18] It is important to note that political foundations cannot directly finance the activities of political parties. Their support is usually channelled through cooperation with quasi-autonomous party think tanks and organisations.

Reformists which started a foundation called New Direction – the Foundation for European Reform in 2010.

Analytical bodies of the executive and legislature

The analytical institutions of the executive and the legislature represent an important non-partisan source of policy capacity. Political parties can access this capacity through their representatives in public office.

The legislature

The analytical institutions of legislative bodies include the Parliamentary Institute (PI) at the national level and the European Parliament Directorate-General for Parliamentary Research Service (until 2013 the Directorate-Generals for Internal and External Policies) at the European level. It is important to note that funding for expert consultants is also available to Czech senators, MPs and MEPs, who are free to use this flat subsidy as they see fit. For this reason, the expertise they receive with the help of this resource can be considered a part of the greater party-based system of policy expertise and knowledge production.

The executive

The use of the public administration policy capacities fits the cartel party theory. The expert bodies incorporated into the public administration system include policy analysis teams operating either under individual authorities or in the form of directly managed research organisations in different policy departments.[19] Looking at the situation from the perspective of parties, we have also noted that some political representatives of the state executive set up special advisory bodies. At the level of regions, these include the Economic Council of the Association of Regions headed by Jan Švejnar and founded by Michal Hašek (ČSSD) in 2011. At the level of the government, a prime example of a special advisory body was the government's National Economic Council, which worked closely with the ODS-led administrations, the cabinets of Prime Ministers Mirek Topolánek (2009) and Petr Nečas (2010-13).

---

[19] The Czech civil service law was amended to separate the civil service and politics till 2015. Thus, parties in the government could easily install their members in positions of power in the state administration and public corporations.

Lobbying

Quasi-independent party-based organisations

Quasi-independent party-based organisations set up as independent bodies despite their close ties to political parties represent an addition to Kuhne's typology. We can see these entities as relics of the organisational structure of mass political parties which used to create a wide range of organisations for its members to join. On the other hand, there are advantages to this model from the perspective of policy capacity. Their formally independent status may be attractive for important external actors and thus enable cooperation with partners such as German political foundations or policy scholars whose environment is extremely sensitive to direct political engagement. For these reasons, quasi-independent party-based organisations can serve as hubs for knowledge sharing among experts while there need not be any direct interaction with the respective political parties.

Traditional parties with a history of mass party organisation, such as the ČSSD, the Communist Party and the KDU-ČSL, would typically create a range of party organisations. The ČSSD, for instance, relies on a number of supporting organisations, some of which operate very closely with the party: for example, Social Democratic Women, the Senior Club, Social Democrats in Exile. Other supporting organisations might be established as independent organisations: the Young Social Democrats, the Masaryk Democratic Academy and the Czech Union of Workers' Athletic Clubs. What's more, the Social Democratic Party fosters additional quasi-autonomous organisations which bring together party supporters such as the Friends of Social Democracy (since 2010), the environmental group Zvonečník (Phyteuma orbiculare) (since 2008), a religion-based association called the Social Christian Platform of the Social Democratic Party (since 2009) and the women's group the Orange Club (since 2012). The links among the membership of all these groups are noteworthy. The current party leader, Bohuslav Sobotka, is a member of practically all these groups.

The contrast with the right-wing could not be starker; Czech right-wing parties tend to lack any links to supporting organisations. The ODS is a case in point: the Blue Team of ODS Supporters was not founded until 2009 and an exclusive contract of cooperation with the youth group Young Conservatives was only signed in 2011. This lack of a network of supporters may be a result of the party's short history.

Unions and lobbying groups

Political parties maintain relationships with traditional interest groups which might help them access useful knowledge and information. Traditional interest groups tend to be narrowly focused organisations advocating for a single interest. The ČSSD, for example, cooperates with the Czech Patient Union headed by Luboš Olejár and with the Czech Renters Association, long represented by the party member Stanislav Křeček, a former MP and currently the deputy of the Ombudsman. Cooperation between the NGO sector and the ODS is minimal; the only noteworthy ODS partner group is the Confederation of Political Prisoners founded in 1990.

Professional associations, on the other hand, are powerful actors in the Czech political scene and represent important partners for political parties. These associations also usually have professional analysts at their disposal who supply them with quality data for policy making. Left-wing parties continue to cooperate with labour unions, particularly the ČSSD. The party's most important partner is the Union Headquarters of the Bohemian-Moravian Confederation of Trade Unions, whose network of professional advisors is possibly the most robust in the Czech civil society. Besides the highly prized macroeconomic analysis supplied by the research team of Mr Martin Fassmann, the Union possesses the capacity (and legal expertise) to comment on draft laws in tripartite negotiations and to send its own representatives to participate in policy working groups. Moreover, the former union leaders Richard Falbr, Milan Štěch and Jaroslav Zavadil have become prominent public office holders elected on the ballots of the ČSSD.

Right-wing parties traditionally defend the interests of employers and thus build coalitions with employer associations, which also have researchers and experts on board. The two most important groups in this area are the Confederation of Industry of the Czech Republic and the Chamber of Commerce.

The extensive autonomy afforded to regional and municipal governments in the Czech Republic also lends cities and regions the status of important political actors. Their representatives often form associations and have a policy capacity to comment on draft legislation. The umbrella organisation the Association of Regions of the Czech Republic has set up committees, such as the Economic Council which operates under the auspices of Jan Švejnar. Municipal governments have formed the Union of Towns and Municipalities of the Czech Republic. Political parties influence these organisations and associations through their members who are elected to mayoral or governor offices.

Civil society, pressure groups and new social movements have also been gaining political influence. So far, left-wing parties have been more successful in building civil society allies. The ČSSD, for example, formed partnership with the leaders of the ProAlt movement – the Initiative for Critique of Reform Measures and Supporting Alternatives, which drove the anti-government protests in 2011 and 2012.

Representatives of large corporations

Forming partnerships with big businesses and their representatives does not seem to be a priority for Czech political parties. Contacts with the representatives of large corporations are usually mediated by employer unions (for instance Škoda Auto). Connections with large public enterprises such as the power utility ČEZ Group, the state-run forestry company Lesy ČR and Prague Public Transit

Company are built through party nominees for boards of directors and other decision-making bodies. In the Czech discourse, however, any relations between politicians and businesses are viewed with suspicion about their potential for corruption. Yet, despite the negative connotations evoked by the overlap of business and politics, it is hard to separate the two arenas in reality. It has been illustrated by the enormous success of the industry tycoon Andrej Babiš for ANO 2011 in the 2013 election or by the great popularity of the politician, landowner and prince Karel Schwarzenberg (TOP 09) among Czech voters.

Professional political consultation

Professional political consultation is mainly linked with the capital-intensive management of political parties. This is typical of the 'business firm' model of party organisation described by Hopkin and Paolucci (1999). Generally speaking, professional political advising fits into context of the externalisation and privatisation introduced by 'New Public Management'. It also necessarily influenced the functioning of political parties. According to Kuhne (2008), professional political advising provides expertise in several areas. First, there are the public opinion research institutes. Opinion polls have become an integral part of the functioning of Czech political parties, particularly in preparing electoral campaigns (especially in the case of Jiří Paroubek, ČSSD leader from 2006 to 2010).

The second source of expertise is PR agencies and agencies for political communication and marketing. Their services are mainly used for elections and electoral campaigns. This area does not fall under policy analysis, but it is useful to mention it here, because the services of these agencies consume large amounts of the party budgets (see for example Polášek, 2012; Perottino and Polášek, 2012), and thus they indicate a dominant orientation of the parties towards elections. The Social Democrats can be considered pioneers in this area, because they started using the services of a public relations company as early as 2004. By 2006 they had multiplied cooperation with Czech (for example VIP Christian) and foreign (for example Crane Consulting, Euro RSCG Worldwide, Penn Schoen Berland Associates,[20] Greenberg Carville Schrum) agencies (see Polášek, 2012). With some delay the ODS started to use foreign companies as well (for example, Arthur Finkelstein for the 2009-10 campaign). This kind of consulting is well established in the observed parties and large amounts of their budgets are spent on it. This supports the assumption that the observed parties aim mainly at winning votes.

The last source of expertise is professional consultancies of the McKinsey type. Within the examined parties this type has been found only in a limited form concerning the annual financial audits required by law. This is surprising, because

---

[20] The same agency stood behind the successful campaign of the ANO 2011 party in the 2013 election.

supranational audit firms such as Ernst&Young, Delloitte and PwC have been winning valuable contracts in Czech public administration.[21] Thus we could expect that they would try to get similar contracts with parties because their activities are known to party members in public offices.

Conclusion

We have seen that political parties in the Czech Republic have developed policy advisory systems and that there are more or less formal mechanisms of generating expertise within a party. Closer examination has shown that the parties' internal organisation concentrates on obtaining information and on harmonisation of attitudes for public presentation. In the party sector, we mostly find policy analysis in its broader sense of 'policy work'. Policy analysis in the parties is institutionally anchored and there are actual policy units as well as mechanisms for policy generation, but it is restrained as parties focus on electoral competition. Analytical capacity is primarily provided by external sources. These are intermediated through party representatives in public office, through contacts with both science-based policy advice organisations and with civil society organisations such as traditional interest groups, new social movements and pressure groups.

The examined political parties, having represented the two main poles of the Czech party system, have focused primarily on the interests of civil society towards the state (representativeness) and, consequently, on winning the most votes in the elections (vote seeking). Therefore it is not surprising that their policy advisory systems concentrate mainly on the elaboration of electoral programmes and elections as such.[22] Another important aspect supporting this dominant orientation is the contamination of the Czech political environment with frequent elections. For these reasons, there remains little capacity for policy analysis within Czech political parties. There are certain formal units, which could serve as hubs for policy analysis, but these spend most of their time preparing expertise for manifesto discussions and manifestos themselves.[23]

Acknowledgement
This chapter was supported by the Czech Science Foundation (GACR) under Grant number 13-20962S 'Policy-Related Expertise in Czech Political Parties'.

---

[21] We found only one case in this area. The ODS adopted the Deloitte pension reform analysis that was produced for the Ministry of Social Affairs under Petr Nečas.

[22] This dominant orientation towards elections can be illustrated by one example from the ČSSD. In 2009-10, in cooperation with the Free University in Brussels, a series of round tables was prepared, with invited Western academicians, aiming to foster the expert capacities of the party. However, the party did not use this effort for its own policy capacity building, as was intended, but rather for the party's presentation to voters.

[23] Of course these findings are limited by the scope of the examined parties.

References

Cohen, M., March, J. and Olsen, J. (1972) 'A garbage can model of organizational choice', *Administrative Science Quarterly*, 17(1): 1–25.

Colebatch, H. K. (2006) 'What work makes policy?', *Policy Sciences*, 39(4): 309–321.

Colebatch, H. K., Hoppe, R. and Noordegraaf, M. (2010) 'Understanding policy work', in H. Colebatch, R. Hoppe and M. Noordegraaf (eds) *Working for Policy*, Amsterdam: Amsterdam University Press, pp 11–25.

Craft, J. and Howlett, M. (2012a) 'Policy formulation, governance shift and policy influence: location and content in policy advisory systems', *Journal of Public Policy*, 32(2): 79–98.

Craft, J. and Howlett, M. (2012b) 'Subsystem structures, shifting mandates and policy capacity: assessing Canada's ability to adapt to climate change', *Canadian Political Science Review*, 6(1): 3–14.

Cross, W. (2007) 'Policy study and development in Canada's political parties', in L. Dobuzinskis, M. Howlett and D. Laycock (eds) *Policy Analysis in Canada: The State of the Art*, Toronto: University of Toronto Press, pp 610–35.

Evans, B. and Wellstead, A. (2013) 'Policy dialogue and engagement between nongovernment organisations and government', *Central European Journal of Public Policy*, 7(1): 60–87.

Fellegi, I. (1996) *Strengthening our Policy Capacity: Report of the Deputy Minister's Task Force*, Ottawa: Supply and Services Canada.

Grunden, T. (2013) 'From hand to mouth: parties and policy-making in Germany', in S. Blum and K. Schubert (eds) *Policy Analysis in Germany*, Bristol: Policy Press, pp 181–95.

Halligan, J. (1995) 'Policy advice and the public sector', in B. Guy Peters and D.T. Savoie (eds) *Governance in a Changing Environment*, Montreal: McGill-Queen's University Press, pp 138–72.

Harmel, R. and Janda, K. (1994) 'An integrated theory of party goals and party change', *Journal of Theoretical Politics*, 6(3): 259-87.

Hopkin, J. and Paolucci, C. (1999) 'The business firm model of party organisation: Cases from Spain and Italy', *European Journal of Political Research*, 35: 307-339.

Howlett, M. (2009) 'Policy analytical capacity and evidence-based policy-making: lessons from Canada', *Canadian Public Administration*, 52(2): 153–73.

Howlett, M. and Oliphant, S. (2010) 'Environmental research organizations and climate change policy analytical capacity: an assessment of the Canadian case', *Canadian Political Science Review*, 4(2–3): 18–35.

Hustedt, T. (2013) 'Analyzing policy advice: the case of climate policy in Germany', *Central European Journal of Public Policy*, 7(1): 88–111.

Katz, R. and Mair, P. (1992) 'Introduction: the cross-national study of party organizations', in R. Katz and P. Mair (eds) *Party Organizations: A Data Handbook on Party Organizations in Western Democracies 1960–90*, London: Sage, pp 1-20.

Katz, R.S. and Mair, P. (1995) 'Changing models of party organization and party democracy: the emergence of the cartel party', *Party Politics*, 1(1): 5–27.

Kuhne, C. (2008) *Politikberatung für Parteien: Akteure, Formen, Bedarfsfaktoren* [Political advising for political parties: actors, forms, and demand factors]. Wiesbaden: VS Verlag für Sozialwissenschaften.

Mair, P. (1994) 'Party organization: from civil society to the state', in R. Katz and P. Mair (eds) *How Parties Organize: Change and Adaptation in Party Organizations in Western Democracies*, London: Sage, pp 1–22.

Novotný, V., Merklová, K. and Buben, R. (2012) 'ČSSD v perspektivě teorie tří proudů: reformy české vysokoškolské politiky jako případ interakce politické strany a veřejné politiky' [ČSSD in perspective of the multi-stream theory: Czech higher education reforms as a case of interaction between political party and policy], in M. Polášek, V. Novotný, M. Perottino, R. Buben, K. Merklová and J. Koubek. *Mezi masovou a kartelovou stranou: Možnosti teorie při výkladu vývoje ČSSD a KSČM v letech 2000–2010* [Mass and Cartel Parties: Sources of Theory for Interpreting the Development of ČSSD and KSČM in 2000–2010]. Praha: SLON, pp 129–47.

Perottino, M. and Polášek, M. (2012) 'KSČM v perspektivě stranickoorganizační' [KSČM: An organizational perspective], in M. Polášek, V. Novotný, M. Perottino, R. Buben, K. Merklová and J. Koubek. *Mezi masovou a kartelovou stranou: Možnosti teorie při výkladu vývoje ČSSD a KSČM v letech 2000–2010* [Mass and cartel parties: sources of theory for interpreting the development of ČSSD and KSČM in 2000–2010]. Praha: SLON, pp 110–28.

Polášek, M. (2012) 'ČSSD v perspektivě stranickoorganizační' [ČSSD: an organizational perspective], in M. Polášek, V. Novotný, M. Perottino, R. Buben, K. Merklová and J. Koubek. *Mezi masovou a kartelovou stranou: Možnosti teorie při výkladu vývoje ČSSD a KSČM v letech 2000–2010* [Mass and cartel parties: sources of theory for interpreting the development of ČSSD and KSČM in 2000–2010]. Praha: SLON, pp 70–109.

Polášek, M., Perottino, M. and Novotný, V. (2014) 'Expertiza v politických stranách: téma a jeho teoretické uchopení' [Policy-related expertise in political parties: a theoretical foundation], *Politologická revue*, 20(1): 147–66.

Strøm, K. (1990) 'A behavioral theory of competitive political parties', *American Journal of Political Science*, 34(2): 565–98.

Veselý, A. (2013) 'Externalization of policy advice: theory, methodology and evidence', *Policy and Society*, 32(3): 199–209.

Wiesendahl, E. (1984) 'Wie politisch sind politische Parteien? Zu einigen vernachlässigten Aspekten der Organisationswirklichkeit politischer Parteien' [How political are political parties? Some neglected aspects of organisational reality of political parties], in J. Falter, C. Fenner and M. Greven (eds) *Politische Willensbildung und Interessenvermittlung*, Opladen: Vs Verlag für Sozialwissenschaften, pp 78–88.

Wolinetz, S. (2002) 'Beyond the catch-all party: approaches to the study of parties and party organization in contemporary democracies', in R. Gunther, J. Montero and J. Linz (eds) *Political Parties: Old Concepts and New Challenges*, Oxford: Oxford University Press, pp 136–65.

Zahariadis, N. (2007) 'The multiple streams framework: structure, limitations, prospects', in P. Sabatier (ed) *Theories of the Policy Process* (2nd edn), Boulder, CO: Westview Press, pp 65–92.

Zittoun, P. (2001) 'Partis politiques et politiques du logement, échange de ressources entre dons et dettes politiques' [Political parties and housing policy: exchange between political gifts and debts], *Revue Française de Science Politique*, 51(5): 683–706.

FOURTEEN

Policy analysis and the voluntary sector

Karel Čada, Kateřina Ptáčková

Current opportunities for change

'I did not expect the NGOs to gain such a powerful position in our country and in the supranational world, and to lead such an irreconcilable fight with parliamentary democracy. It is a fight that they are winning more and more as time goes by', said former Czech President Václav Klaus regarding 20 years of post-communist transformation. Whereas for Václav Klaus nongovernmental organisations (NGOs) represent a threat to democracy, his predecessor, Václav Havel, saw them as a cornerstone of his conception of 'non-political politics', based more upon civil society than political parties.

Either way, debates about the role of NGOs in politics have mirrored broader discussions about the nature of modern governance. Pierre and Peters (2000, p 29) describe a tendency to discuss the apparently increased influence of nongovernmental actors in governance in the context of new forms of decentralisation and diffusion of power, a reconceptualisation of the public sector where state-centred hierarchies have been replaced by a complex mix of hierarchies, networks and markets and where governmental policy workers are forced to steer different flows of policies with respect to the competencies of other actors rather than stream their own programmes forward. NGOs, with their increasing degree of professionalisation, produce policy-making innovations as forums for developing and testing knowledge, setting standards and steering behaviour (Dunleavy and O'Leary, 1987, p 302).

Laforest and Orsini (2005) argue that the shift towards governance and greater reliance on third parties in policy making has created new pressures to ensure that policies are designed and delivered in a consistent and effective manner. As a result, the evidence-based policy approach has substituted the opinion-based one, with knowledge and research becoming key assets in the production of policy.

> As voluntary sector organizations begin to assume a greater role in policy-making, they can contribute significantly through the gathering and sharing of information, and can act as the go-between for transmitting this valuable body of knowledge/information to citizens. (Laforest and Orsini, 2009, p 486)

The shift has had particular impacts on countries with a historical tradition of advocacy-based NGOs representing their members' or supporters' interests. Laforest and Orsini identified four significant changes which the new emphasis on evidence and knowledge have brought to the NGO sector: (1) organisations have developed new sets of skills, including research, to influence policy; (2) organisations predominantly assert claims which can be supported by research; (3) the sector's involvement in policy is being depoliticised, and tailored to fit into pre-existing bureaucratic patterns of decision making; (4) conflicts exist between organisations with the necessary resources to influence policy and those underprivileged due to ideological opposition or lack of research capacity.

With respect to these changes, Phillips (2007) identified three elements of a new policy style of NGOs: (1) they are under pressure to produce research and analysis that is evidence-based; (2) they are involved in trust-based networks as the central institutional form in the new governance; and (3) they function in a multi-level way. Subsequently, she distinguished three capacities which are cultivated by NGOs: (1) policy capacity as the ability to provide policy analysis and advice; (2) network capacity in terms of the resources and practices for building and sustaining partnerships; and (3) project and programme capacity as the production of services, programmes or projects supporting an organisation's mission and its sustainability. In terms of the capacity of NGOs, Osborne (2008) also speaks about innovative capacity as the potential to change the paradigm of their services or their skills base. The described capacities of NGOs can be viewed as evidence of a new form of collaborative policy making (Innes and Booher, 2003), collaborative governance (Ansell and Gash, 2008; O'Flynn and Wanna, 2008; Donahue and Zeckhauser, 2011) or interactive governance (Torfing et al, 2012).

Even though policy analysts from NGOs have increasingly been cooperating with those in the public service, one can see profound differences reflecting the different realities in each sector. For example, Wellstead and Evans (2013) found that NGOs' policy analysts have a much greater degree of conviction and commitment to the cause than their public service counterparts. Keen (2006) lists specific activities which can be associated with NGOs' policy work: (1) monitoring government; (2) researching issues relevant to a policy field; (3) making pre-budget submissions; (4) preparing submissions in response to government inquiries; (5) liaising with political representatives and their staff; (6) being available for consultation; (7) sitting on government committees and task forces; (8) influencing legislation; (9) networking with relevant policy communities; (10) disseminating information; (11) ensuring the visibility, credibility and legitimacy of the organisation; and (12) encouraging public debate.

However, the collaborative work represents just one side of the coin of NGOs' policy work. Čada and Ptáčková (2014) place critical policy capacity in contrast to collaborative policy capacity. Critical policy capacity refers to the potential of NGOs to explicate a dominant meaning in policy content and process and uncover suppressed or marginalised meanings. Unlike the outcomes-oriented collaborative policy work, critical policy work challenges procedural issues in favour of active engagement of citizens. They organise public meetings, mobilise the public through the media and organise blockades and protests.

In this chapter, we look at the specific position of the Czech NGO sector within the public policy-making process. We discuss the structure of the formal opportunities Czech NGOs have for participation in designing and implementing public policies, the capacities they have for gathering information and producing policy analysis, and finally the strategies they have developed to exert their influence over public policies. We focus on the NGOs and informal activist groups that strive to influence public policies and/or public discourses, without distinguishing whether this is their ultimate goal or they are primarily focused on different issues and seek to influence the policies simply as a means to achieve other goals or make the achievement of these goals easier.

NGOs as policy actors

In common Czech practice, NGOs are understood as private law entities existing for some other purpose than profit making. Representatives of the civic sector usually use a narrow definition of NGOs that covers the legal forms of civil associations, foundations, foundation funds, public benefit corporations, churches and religious societies. Overall, there are more than 100,000 NGOs registered; however, this number does not indicate much about the actual functioning of these organisations, as they are not required to report inactivity or termination.

The activities of the vast majority of NGOs focus on sports, hobbies, leisure and recreation. Many of these organisations are rooted in the period before 1989 (sporting clubs, hunting associations, beekeepers, voluntary firemen and so on) and have broad membership (Frič, 2005). These NGOs have minimal or no overt interest in public policies, except efforts to guarantee their funding, and this chapter does not analyse their policy work in detail. We mainly focus on both institutional and grassroots organisations that participate in policy processes seeking to influence public policies beyond their own funding agenda or exercise control over government and administration. Based on their area of interest, available capacities and strategies applied, we distinguish several types of NGOs: participatory activists, transactional activists, umbrella organisations, radical political groups and service providers. Alongside formalised organisations, however, there is a significant emerging scene of individuals and rather informal community-based activist groups influencing both local and central policies. Their effects are mostly episodic and fluid, turning from one particular issue to another; some of them gradually become professional and formal NGOs. There are important transfers of personnel and know-how between these groups and transactional activists.

The first group of advocacy-oriented NGOs relies on 'participatory activism' (Císař, 2013), with relatively wide individual participation and mostly formalised and conventional interactions with the political system. We distinguish two subgroups of participatory activism. 'Trade union participatory activists' assert rather materialistic claims (for example, employees' wages, benefits), they are institutionally incorporated into the decision-making process and enjoy a highly privileged position compared to other NGOs (Pinková, 2011). The 'other participatory activists' make rather non-materialistic claims. They include quite influential associations and unions joining together thousands of disabled people, representing their interests and providing them with services, and many other less influential initiatives and NGOs representing the interests of neighbourhoods or groups - people with common interests (cultural, social and so on).

The second group of advocacy-oriented NGOs can be identified with 'transactional activism'. According to Císař, transactional activism is 'not primarily concerned with mobilizing individuals, but is instead focused on the development of capacities that would enable organizations to shape public debates and influence various publics via the media' (Císař, 2010, p 740). These organisations are particularly significant and specific to the post-socialist context (Petrova and Tarrow, 2007). Without having a massive membership base, these NGOs are able to engage themselves and other relevant actors in democratic processes and participate in public policy making. They are mostly formalised and professionalised, employing expert knowledge and focusing on the advocacy of post-materialistic values. In the Czech context transactional activism is mainly represented by environmental and human rights organisations, recently complemented more visibly by organisations dealing with good governance and anti-corruption issues.

Third, somewhere in between 'transactional activism' and 'participatory activism', there are umbrella organisations representing the interests of their NGOs members on a sectoral or regional basis. Most of them are primarily focused on horizontal policies affecting the financial and legal environment for NGOs. Some also support the efforts of their members in a particular sector (such as environmental policy or social policy) (Pospíšilová, 2005).

Fourth, there are radical political groups, both left-wing and right-wing, that are characterised by their advocacy-oriented activities, detachment from the current political and social system and ultimate goal of changing the dominant hegemony (Císař et al, 2011). The scope of allies they are willing and able to mobilise is very limited. Their structures are informal and argumentation is based more on moral values than on rational expertise. In the 1990s and early 2000s, their protests focused mostly on international and supranational economic and political organisations; currently they mainly focus on economic and social issues of national or local relevance (Navrátil and Císař, 2013).

Fifth, social and healthcare organisations are not usually discussed with regard to political activism and policy analysis, as they are primarily providers of social services, not vehicles of policy change. However, they remain crucial actors in social policy processes and key partners of local, regional and central governments in social policy implementation. They also participate in policy making at the stage of policy formulation, mainly through participation in advisory bodies and planning processes. In addition, some of them enjoy premium access to news media and to political representatives. Social and healthcare NGOs are usually highly formalised, employ expert knowledge, and follow professional standards of work. Few operate with a broad membership base; their clients are usually not their members.

Alongside formalised organisations, there is a significant emerging scene of individuals and rather informal community-based activist groups influencing both local and central policies. Their effects are mostly episodic and fluid, turning from one particular issue to another; some of them have gradually become professional and formal NGOs. There are important transfers of personnel and know-how between these groups and transactional activists.

Structure of NGOs' policy opportunities

In contrast to some other European states, the Czech Republic has no general legal standards and binding rules for public participation in decision making (Vajdová, 2004). The NGOs' current legal position in the political process is a result of several historical processes. First, quite a generous and liberal legal framework was established in the post-revolution era, including a very low threshold for establishing a civic association that prevailed until 2013. There was only a limited set of restrictions on their activities and almost no transparency obligations, while all were eligible for tax credits and other benefits. The low threshold and financial resources from Western agencies in the early 1990s led to massive institutionalisation of civil society in the form of civic associations (Frič, 2005).[1] However, a much more comprehensive regulation entered into force in 2014. Second, NGOs' policy opportunities expanded significantly with the integration of the Czech Republic into the EU, primarily thanks to the implementation of several assessment procedures (for example, Environmental Impact Assessment, Strategic Environmental Assessment or Regulatory Impact Assessment). Third, despite the strong institutional framework, experience with and confidence in participative methods of decision making have remained limited both among the general public and in public administration and government. Thus the structure of the political opportunities of NGOs is highly dependent on the current attitudes of political representatives towards NGOs, with the most fluctuation in the position of transactional activists. The initial supportive attitude was replaced by hostility under Prime Minister Václav Klaus in the 1990s, when all activists except the representatives of employers and employees were treated as enemies (Císař et al, 2011). However, even during this period, the position of the Czech government was balanced by the process of accession to the EU. Later, the positions of individual single government departments became more and more diverse and often dependent on the attitude of a particular person in

---

[1] As of 1 January 2012, there were 100,728 civic associations and organisational units thereof, while all the other forms of NGOs comprised fewer than 8000.

their top management. In 2007, the perception of the openness of the policy process to transactional activists changed as the Green Party, which was strongly interlinked with NGOs, won seats in the parliament and government (Císař et al, 2011). In particular, NGOs 'captured' the Ministry of the Environment, led by a representative of the Green Party, and obtained exceptional access to the policy process and the minister himself. Without any significant institutional change, the position of NGOs changed dramatically after the Green Party left the government. Almost all ministerial contacts were interrupted and the advocacy activities of NGOs moved to the members of parliament and other significant actors.

Currently, the most important formalised institutional mechanism for NGOs to influence policy at the national level lies in the processes of drafting new pieces of legislation and strategic documents. They formulate their comments in the so-called 'comment procedure' and participate in the governmental or departmental advisory bodies that discuss not only laws but also broader policies.[2] The logic of both types of participation is different. While the comment procedure is one-off, one-way and episodic and usually comes at the very end of the legislative procedure, participation in advisory bodies opens the legislative process from its beginning, helping NGOs to access information, interact with other actors and develop their strategies based on the current situation (Pinková, 2011).

The comment procedure is governed by the Government Legislative Rules. Comments must always be sought from several NGOs – labour unions and employers' representatives, in particular. In addition, every department may ask other institutions for comments, and even those not asked by the department can provide their comments on drafts of legislative materials. In both cases, the decision about how to deal with the NGO's comments rests entirely on the department; this part of the procedure is not legally defined. The approaches of the departments differ significantly. To enhance their influence many NGOs 'go public' with their comments – they write press releases or media articles to push the departments to take their positions into consideration.

At the preparation stage, the possibilities for providing comments on legislative proposals are limited by the MPs' legislative initiatives. Government proposals are often changed significantly during the legislative procedure in the parliament without any possibility of people outside parliament influencing them. This practice is often criticised by NGOs as detrimental in terms of transparency, public and expert debate, and a conceptual approach to policy making. At the same time, some NGOs push their own proposals via allied MPs to influence policy.

Besides commenting on legislative proposals within the 'comment procedure', NGOs are entitled to provide comments within the procedures of environmental impact assessments, strategic environmental assessments and regulatory impact assessments. These procedures were implemented in the Czech legislation during the process of Europeanisation as 'ready-made' tools. So far they have been used in

---

[2] Besides this, some of the departments invite NGO representatives into the committees distributing public funding to NGOs.

a highly formalised manner and have resulted in a rather low rate of consultations with the public.

NGOs' influence on governmental advisory bodies is limited. They are either not present at all or form only a minority of the members. However, there are several exceptions. First and foremost, since the revolution, the Council of Economic and Social Agreement has been the main tool for collective bargaining between the government, trade unions and employer and industrial associations, giving trade unions privileged access to the policy process. Since 1998, there has been the Government Council for NGOs, which collates, discusses and submits materials relating to NGOs to the government, mostly on their financial and legislative environment. At least half of its members consist of experts on NGO issues, typically from large foundations, NGO associations and so on. The council not only discusses and prepares legislative proposals but actively lobbies for them to be passed as well.

Finally, there are several issue-specific NGO access points to the policy process. In the social sphere, NGOs can participate in the community planning of social services. Community planning is based on the participation of local users, providers and purchasers of social services. In fact, users and providers are often represented by the same NGOs. Involved organisations, based upon their expertise, interpret the generalised experience of their clients. Relying on various methods of planning and analysis, both partners in the process (the public administration and NGOs) draw significantly on the experience of their Western counterparts. In the environmental area, all the civic association are entitled to ask state administrative bodies to get information about all intended interventions and initiated administrative proceedings in the interest of nature protection. They are also entitled to participate in administrative proceedings. In addition, environmental NGOs are able to participate in several special administrative proceedings, for example with regard to building, nuclear power, GMOs (genetically modified organisms). These quite generous competencies of NGOs may be considered the heritage of the post-revolutionary spirit as they are based on the law which has been in force since 1990.

The post-revolutionary spirit of the 1990s combined with the EU's push for participative methods led to relatively generous formal possibilities for NGOs to take legal action against administrative and court decisions. However, national politicians are typically reluctant to allow participative tools, and the public administration is unable to involve NGOs at the early stages of policy planning, in negotiating and in seeking consensus. This leads to protracted decision-making processes and a lot of frustration on all sides. Moreover, public administration officials often operate in a kind of schizophrenic position, juggling responsibility for the involvement of NGOs in the policy process with specific political orders regarding the outcomes.

NGOs' policy capacity

To consider the resources NGOs have at their disposal to influence the policy process and about their decisions on how to allocate these resources, we have to focus mainly on specific issue-related know-how (contributory expertise); procedural know-how as an ability to provide the specific know-how in a form acceptable to other policy actors (interactional expertise); and the partnership and relations they build with other actors to enhance these capacities. This is what Susan Phillips (2007) calls 'network capacity'. Finally, we also have to look at the material resources that enable NGOs to fulfil their missions, implement their programmes and exert influence over policy development.

In the Czech Republic, a representative of a civic association or another NGO is not 'automatically considered to be a representative of the public by other political actors' (Synková, 2011, p 62). The legitimacy of many NGOs, mainly transactional activists and social services providers, results rather from the epistemic sources of their knowledge, their scientific expertise and experience than from the membership they represent. (O'Neill, 2001) This is why these sources are of crucial importance for them. The ways NGOs gain their expertise are basically threefold.

NGOs' subcontracting, co-production and production of expertise

In order to build their expert claims, NGOs can (1) use externally produced expertise, (2) produce expertise in cooperation with academia or (3) produce their own expertise. Each of these possibilities is associated with different epistemic, social and material resources. Behind this typology, one can see a dilemma between independent and needs-targeted expertise. In the first case, NGOs can get independent expertise at the expense of direct participation in the research process. In the second case, NGOs can participate in the research process, which could therefore better respond to their needs, but the final expertise loses its status of impartiality and may thus have a lower impact on public policy and public debate.

In a situation of unlimited resources, dealing with research outcomes produced by an external actor would be preferred by many NGOs over their own research production, as subcontracted research outcomes 'provide the NGOs with the much needed "view from the outside"' (Stöckelová, 2012, p 155). Externally produced expertise is often understood as more legitimate than that produced by NGOs themselves. However, there is a significant shortage of resources available for subcontracting expertise. Most NGOs' funding comes from national, regional or local public sources, followed by private foundations, typically on a short-term, yearly project basis, with little space for outsourcing research.[3] Once the organisation manages to get some resources for research, they are usually part of a larger grant. These resources are considered then to be part of the organisation's common budget and using them internally is preferred to outsourcing research (Stöckelová, 2012). Even if the expertise is produced outside, the NGOs do not utilise it mechanically but rather creatively (Čada and Ptáčková, 2013). They adapt the knowledge to the context of their operations and goals, both in fulfilling programme responsibilities and in influencing public policies.

In the case of cooperation with academia, NGOs are more active than previously. They participate in defining the research agenda, in collecting and processing data and in the creative implementation of the results in practice. A study analysing the current situation of cooperation between NGOs and academia in the Czech Republic (Čada and Ptáčková, 2013) revealed two sets of factors, structural and non-structural. The structural factors result mainly from science funding schemes, science evaluation criteria and the values that dominate the scientific field. The authors argue that current structural conditions are generally not in favour of the development of NGO-science networks. There are for example no special programmes enhancing this kind of cooperation; there is also, similarly to the German case, no strong tradition of donating to alternative science, as can be seen in the US (Strunck, 2013). EU structural funds may be considered one of the rare institutional tools for supporting NGOs' participation in research and innovation processes. Thus, the development of collaborative networks between science and NGOs relies mainly on non-structural, situational and individual factors and motivations of single actors from NGOs and academia. The study revealed a number of connections and collaborations between NGOs and science, including many academic research projects in which people from NGOs participate. These partnerships are motivated mainly by the previous experience of the involved actors. Stöckelová analysed the migration of people between NGOs and academia arguing that these migrants, recognised and reputable in both worlds, may be understood as 'the boundary persons', similar to 'boundary objects' introduced by Star and Griesemer (1989). Stöckelová's research revealed that the mobility of persons between academia and NGOs exists and seems crucial for possible collaboration and meaningful utilisation of scientific knowledge. NGOs and academia cooperate most often in the areas where researchers must rely more on the assistance of practitioners in the field, and in the areas where one can identify 'scientific dissidents' whose arguments are not entirely accepted by the scientific community, such as environmental science (for example GMOs or nuclear power) or medical science (for example vaccinations or home births).

Third, NGOs can produce knowledge and expertise on their own. In-house expertise is most often produced and used in the policy process, even though

---

[3]   The situation is different in the case of sports associations, churches and other organisations with a strong membership base, which obtain a large share of funding from membership fees (especially labour unions) and private philanthropy (especially churches).

NGOs have relatively limited opportunities to fund their own research activities.[4] Typically, NGOs conduct analysis aimed at public policies and legislation. These analyses are carried out both by formally qualified social scientists, economists or lawyers and by members of NGOs without the necessary education. This kind of expertise is hardly ever subcontracted from policy analysts outside the NGO and is primarily focused on gaining the arguments for policy process participation and influence. The methods employed mainly include various types of comparative case studies and secondary analyses of existing reports. Studies of compliance of national laws with EU norms are produced as well. On the other hand, NGOs' self-production of scientific research is rather rare. It is generally more common in the social sciences than in the natural sciences or technology and even if it is primarily evidence-based, it usually includes policy recommendations as well. NGOs are more often involved in research projects in cooperation with academia or in utilisation of available scientific expertise produced without their involvement.

Contributory vs interactional expertise

Inspired by Collins and Evans' (2002) typology of contributory and interactional expertise, we distinguish four main types of both scientific and experience-based expertise produced and used by NGOs in the policy process (see Table 15.1). Certainly, these categories are rather analytical and the boundaries between them are blurred (Jasanoff, 2003).

Table 15.1: Four main types of expertise

Expertise	Contributory	Interactional
Scientific	Based on a degree or other formal qualification, contributes to the science of the field being analysed	Based on a degree or other formal qualification, contributes to the understanding of the interactions between various participants of the policy process
Experience-based	Stemming from experience that is not recognised in the form of degrees or other formal qualifications that contributes to the science of the field being analysed	Stemming from experience that is not recognised in the form of degrees or other formal qualifications, to interact constructively with other participants in the policy process

NGOs' production and co-production of *scientific/contributory expertise* may include cases in which an environmental NGO carries out research aimed at the impact of tourism on the population in Šumava National Park, a development NGO gathers and analyses statistically representative data on ICT skills, access and usage by the main immigrant groups, or an environmental NGO cooperates with academics in

---

[4] In 2012 CZK26.6 billion from public budgets was invested in science and research, NGOs received CZK0.047 billion.

monitoring local air pollution and measuring its effects on health. Because of their academic and research expertise, some NGOs are hired to conduct research for the public administration. For example, the majority of research studies commissioned by the governmental Agency for Social Inclusion have been conducted by NGOs, even though they have to fulfil requirements of formal qualifications and research experience.

NGOs working with clients (for example social services providers) or speaking in the name of their members (for example patients' associations) often draw *experience-based expertise* from their own programme activities and use it for 'experience-based advocacy'. 'Much of what they advocate, lobby and campaign on uses detail drawn from their own projects' (Slim, 2002). Rather than original research, these micro-studies consist of 'systematisation of experience acquired through practical engagements of NGO employees', as an employee of one of the biggest Czech NGOs put it (Stöckelová, 2012). Room for this kind of expertise mainly exists in social services planning. According to Slim (2002), this micro case study approach is then added to the more macro-analysis produced by academic and policy researchers to produce an advocacy discourse of personalised facts which claim to illustrate trends.

Gathered and reflected experience is the most common source of *interactional expertise*. Basic understanding of the policy process, insight into different types of procedures, terms, required forms of comments and so on are based on knowledge of legislation. NGOs with a primary focus on public policies either employ lawyers or outsource law expertise (for example, ad hoc consultations, studies of literature, attendance at seminars) to understand their formal possibilities for participating in the policy process. Seminars and lectures in advocacy (what advocacy is; how an NGO can exercise advocacy; how the legislative process works and how to monitor it; how to decide on advocacy priorities) are given and books published (Kopečný, 2008; Šedivý and Mendlíková, 2012) by some umbrella organisations, foundations and associations. However, NGOs' lobbying practices, know-how, advocacy strategies and particular tactical decisions are mainly based on previous experience. In the Czech Republic, the entire system of public and social services is in constant flux. 'With any new political representation, the system is reorganized (often dramatically) – new institutions are created while others are abolished, and the competencies and responsibilities of the organizations are often changed too' (Veselý, 2013, p 321). In this environment, being close to the particular public officials responsible for a policy may be valued less than the expertise and know-how in building relations in general or the ability to keep up with the liquid and changing institutional rules.

To monitor the legislative procedures, NGOs use both publicly available sources, most often the internet, and internal sources covering stakeholders, politicians and department officials: these are approached both formally and informally by four out of five NGOs seeking to influence public policy on the national level (Fórum dárců, 2007). 90% of these NGOs monitor the legislative process at least once a month. The study revealed that most of the NGOs do not feel weaknesses in terms of their ability to follow the legislative process, while half of them stressed the lack of time. Monitoring services are often provided by umbrella organisations.

Networking

The policy activities of the Czech third sector horizontal community (umbrella organisations) are, unlike their Western counterparts, mostly concentrated on internal affairs (the legislative environment for NGOs, funding) and not on societal problems and the role of NGOs in their solution (Frič, 2005). In addition, there are several well-functioning regional and sectoral coalitions, typically based around a certain field of activity, for example environmental issues, children and youth, social issues, women's rights, or within some regional or local areas. The estimated total is about 80 umbrella organisations and associations (Vajdová, 2004). They are often successful both on the level of local projects and on the national legislative level. This is currently also the case of anti-corruption activities, as we discuss in more detail hereafter. The umbrella organisation provides the members with various services, mostly focusing on information and experience sharing. However, the central topic for most of the umbrella organisations is to represent and advocate the interests of their members in relation to the public administration and government (Pospíšilová, 2005). Umbrella organisations enable the NGOs to find common interests, share specific contributory expertise and extend the legitimacy of their arguments within the policy process.

To enhance their expertise and advocacy capacities, both NGOs and informal groups also focus on networking with other societal partners besides NGOs. In many cases, the networking capacity of the NGO is personalised rather than institutionalised, and access to important unofficial networks can easily be lost when a certain individual leaves the organisation (Synková, 2011). An analysis of transactional capacity revealed that transactional activists pay more attention to establishing relationships, coalitions and networks than participatory activists (for example labour unions) (Císař et al, 2011, p 157). However, Navrátil and Císař (2013) show that in reaction to the strategies of the government during the economic crises, even the traditionally self-contained, hierarchical and highly structured trade unions were forced to change their orientation towards more intensive cooperation with other non-state actors.

Presence of NGOs in the policy process

Since there are no comprehensive data on the NGOs' overall effects on public policy based on their policy analysis, we provide two brief case studies to illustrate the current presence of NGOs and their expertise in the policy process.

The anti-corruption agenda

In 2008, the initiative 'Inventory of Democracy' (*Inventura demokracie*) was founded by university students in relation to the forthcoming 20th anniversary of the Velvet Revolution. The initiative asked politicians to give the citizens 'a present' in the form of four new legislative acts, aimed at the regulation of lobbying, parliamentary privilege, public procurement and control of the public media. When the anniversary passed and nothing changed, the students continued approaching the politicians and pushing them to take action. Gradually they changed their working methods, broadened their scope of interest in favour of general support of public participation in decision making and started cooperating with other initiatives.

In 2010, the 'Anti-Corruption Endowment' (*Nadační fond proti korupci*) was established to support the activities of NGOs, grassroots initiatives and active individuals. Most of its support goes to policy analysis, case studies on legislation, public budgets, election campaigns and public contracts. Those analyses are to back up organisations' or individuals' efforts to change public policies on the national and local level. In 2011, the 'Open Society Fund' established another foundation aimed at supporting watchdogs, promoting participative democracy and fighting corruption. All of these activities significantly contributed to the NGOs' expert and networking capacities for fighting corruption.

In 2011, the government reacted to the strengthening anti-corruption discourse by establishing 'The Government Anti-Corruption Committee' and the 'Fight against Corruption' working group of the government's National Economic Council, inviting experts from anti-corruption NGOs to both of these bodies. Links to NGOs' campaigns can even be found on the government's official website. NGO representatives became publicly recognised experts and regular guests on TV political discussion programmes.

The anti-corruption efforts culminated in the launch of the 'Reconstruction of the State' (*Rekonstrukce státu*) in 2013. The campaign is presented as a 'joint programme of MPs, senators, a number of renowned experts, businesses, chambers of commerce and associations, anti-corruption organisations and local supporters'.[5] The aim of the project is to push through nine original legislative proposals that are believed to have the capacity to significantly reduce corruption Among the most frequently used tools are legal analyses; common meetings, discussions and round tables organised both to produce expertise and to create a sense of community among experts; formal and informal meetings with politicians and public servants at the central and local levels; and intensive media work. Interestingly, the representatives of various NGOs were willing to give up their original organisational identities in favour of the common public identity of the 'Reconstruction of the State'.

The legitimacy of the initiative is derived from the expertise and practical legal experience of its proponents. It relies minimally on the university and academic experts. Its official team consists of ten lawyers, nine analysts, four economists, two political scientists, one architect, one sociologist and one statistician. Only one member is affiliated to a university, and all the others to various NGOs. The campaign does not primarily seek active public support; citizens are not called to action in terms of participation in demonstrations or changing their everyday

---

[5]   www.rekonstrukcestatu.cz

behaviour. However, their support is mobilised through the media and they are encouraged to follow the campaign's recommendations in the elections (not to vote for those candidates who do not support the campaign's proposals).

The 'Reconstruction of the State' has met with unprecedented success. The ready-to-use legislative proposals were successfully advocated in a strictly apolitical way as tools to prevent and fight against corruption. The idea of 'who does not support these proposals supports corruption' was broadly accepted. The campaign took full advantage of the issue-specific window of opportunity.

Corruption is considered to be one of the distinctive 'valence issues', as defined by Stoke (1963) in opposition to 'position issues'. Position issues 'are issues on which candidates are free to select from a range of alternative positions and about which voters have varying views' (Enelow and Hinich, 1982, p 117). On the contrary, candidates in an election do not select a position towards valence issues because all the voters have the same point of view. In the discourse on corruption as the most serious public problem, a party cannot simply adopt a pro-corruption position. In this situation the parties' competition is the result of 'differing perceptions by the voters of the extent to which the candidates possess a public good (or bad) such as trustworthiness, honesty, incompetence, and the like' (Enelow and Hinich, 1982, p 117). In gaining support for their proposals, the 'Reconstruction of the State' employed a combination of expert capacity with the moral authority of civil society discourse. In the pre-election period of 2013, the parties respected the expertise-based and apolitical solutions offered by the 'Reconstruction of the State' and incorporated them into the tangible and specific content of the otherwise vague and indefinite anti-corruption rhetoric. Finally, the initiative was dubbed by the news media as the 'true election winner', as two-thirds of new MPs had publicly endorsed its proposals before the election.

Social inclusion policies

In the Czech national context, social inclusion policies are basically epitomised by the so-called Roma issue. As of today, approximately 80,000 socially excluded people live in the Czech Republic, three-quarters of whom are Roma (GAC, 2006). The problem of the social exclusion of the Roma is deeply rooted in history and became even more serious after 1989 when, for various reasons, a majority of the Roma population lost their jobs and many of them also housing in the process of privatisation (Čada, 2012).

The social inclusion agenda belongs to the area where the Czech state shares its responsibilities and competences with both supranational and local actors. Even if the social exclusion of the Roma population is a nationwide problem, its consequences are mainly handled by local municipalities. Since 1989, NGOs have become another crucial actor in this sphere. They are mostly focused on social services provision in line with standards set by the Ministry of Labour and Social Affairs. Since the beginning of the 1990s, there has been a strong push for standardisation and professionalisation. Some successful organisations have even significantly influenced the final form of the quality standards (Synková, 2011). As a result, small, local voluntary NGOs have been gradually displaced by the organisations able to follow the applicable standards and succeed in funding competitions.

NGOs currently engage in policy making and policy implementation mainly through interactions with local authorities and NGOs in a relatively institutionalised framework of knowledge sharing and joint definitions and solutions to emerging problems and challenges. NGOs are deeply involved in social services planning procedures, sit on various advisory and expert committees, and share responsibilities with public administration. Since the early 1990s, NGOs have been broadly believed to be more effective in policy implementation (social services provision) than the state and its agencies. Studies and analyses carried out by NGOs have been used by the public administration as the basis for its decision making.

As Synková (2011, p 21) argues:

> NGOs are increasingly important for the study of Romani (or any other) topics not only because they are present in the field and work with people, but because they produce a huge amount of texts about the situation of these people that are widely accessible on the Internet. Other kinds of materials produced by (and for) NGOs in large quantities belong to the genre of so-called 'grey literature', which is used to draft policies and develop institutional procedures. NGOs themselves are thus important actors not only through their projects. They also influence the image of their 'target groups' through their rhetoric, representation of reality and way of functioning.

As the opportunities for participation in the policy process have increased, NGOs' ability to broker knowledge about communities, other actors and policy issues has become a highly valued asset as well.

This cooperative approach towards public policies can be illustrated by one of the biggest Czech NGOs, 'People in Need' (*Člověk v tísni*), a well-established organisation with more than 300 employees. They focus on social work (housing, children's education, employment, debt), conduct expert studies for governmental bodies, provide expert comments, and advocate legislative changes on the national level. They refuse the ethnic basis of social inclusion policies and argue for a primary focus on vulnerable, excluded and marginalised people, not on the Roma people. There has always been tension on the organisational, academic and even governmental level over the ethnicisation and de-ethnicisation of the social exclusion problem that, as Synková (2011, p 74) pointed out, 'obviously discloses much deeper issues concerning power struggles between different camps, and questions of access and control'. However, the 'ethnic-blind' discourse arguing for not using the ethnic label to avoid stereotypes and not to obscure the social mechanisms that create 'ghettos' was dominant in the 2000s.

The situation has changed in the last couple of years, possibly due to several factors. First of all, the economic crisis after 2008 steeply increased unemployment, hitting the group of less educated workers and unskilled occupations the most. The population of underdeveloped and economically weak regions was desperate and turned its anger against their socially excluded Roma neighbours. The right-wing neo-Nazi extremists reacted upon these sentiments by organising demonstrations and marches in several Czech towns where socially excluded Roma were located. Some of those demonstrations were met with local people's support. The municipalities in general were not able to react to this situation appropriately and some of them even supported the public events organised by extremists. Established NGOs that provide services in some of the impoverished areas did not speak out against these events and encouraged the Roma inhabitants to stay rather passive. However, several new initiatives started to call for the political mobilisation of Roma people, activation of 'civil society of the socially excluded' (Brož, 2012) and a clear affirmation that the public marches were the manifestation of racism, were unacceptable and should be actively blocked.[6]

In 2011, the initiative 'Hate is Not a Solution' entered the public discourse, stressing the necessity to actively fight against hatred, racism and neo-Nazism. Members of this initiative consider the roots of social exclusion to be structural and significantly influenced by the Czech majority's racism. They find the current social inclusion policy (including social services provision) extremely paternalistic. In their opposition to the prevailing discourse they stressed the importance of the ethnic base of social exclusion. This initiative was followed by the 'Housing for All' initiative, which originated in response to two local social housing crises, and the 'Konexe' operating in Ústí nad Labem, one of the most deprived Czech cities. Volunteers gathered behind these initiatives, accusing the governing system of incompetence and failures. Established NGOs are considered to be a part of this establishment and as such are held responsible for the current situation.

These initiatives provide the impoverished Roma people with periodic consultations and support. They derive their legitimacy from community-based knowledge, questioning the relevance of scientific expertise and policy analysis and considering 'apolitical expert advice' as a different form of ideology (Čada and Ptáčková, 2014). They also refuse traditional institutionalised involvement in the policy process, for example participation in advisory bodies or social services planning. In contrast to the established NGOs, they emphasise the mobilisation of public attention through intensive media work.

Conclusions

Similarly to other CEE countries, the global ideas of New Public Management (NPM) resonated strongly in the Czech Republic, especially as the country

---

6   The local protests aimed at protecting 'our city and our neighborhood' from fascism and racism were fed by radical lefts who shifted from global/glocal issues to local ones. Navrátil and Císař argue that this shift was enabled by 'relatively shallow social embeddedness of the radical left in Czech society' (Navrátil and Císař, 2013, p 29).

was run by mostly right-wing or centrist government coalitions inspired by the free market and minimal state ideology (Veselý, 2012). However, while in many industrial countries NPM forced NGOs to ground their activities and interventions in depoliticised knowledge and policy analysis at the expense of traditional members' interests, the Czech NGO sector was born directly into the NPM era. Many NGOs actively participating in the policy process (transactional activists) have never derived their legitimacy from active membership or representation of members' interests. Since the early 1990s, the newly emerging NGOs have built their legitimacy on epistemic sources, scientific knowledge, expertise and so on. As a result, NGOs have become crucial actors in the implementation part of the policy process, employing widely diverse forms of expertise and evidence-based policy making. However, in many areas the government has remained rather detached and reluctant to accept NGOs as equally relevant actors in the initial stages of the policy process.

With regard to limited resources and increasing their legitimacy in the public policy discourse, re-using available scientific contributory expertise produced by other actors is generally preferred by the NGOs over original production and outsourcing. However, the situation is different with respect to sectoral public policies, where many NGOs produce their own studies and papers. Law, economics and the social sciences are the disciplines most often employed. The analyses are focused on obtaining arguments for the policy discussion. Both publicly available and newly produced data are analysed using various methods (comparative case studies, SWOT analyses and so on), which are often employed intuitively and not in a rigid scientific way. The NGOs' interactional knowledge, that is their expertise to interact constructively with other participants in the policy process, stems mainly from experience and mutual learning. Umbrella organisations, which enhance both the member NGOs' advocacy know-how and networking capacity, play a key role. For NGOs with limited membership, building coalitions is crucial to legitimising their arguments and demonstrating experts' consensual opinions on their positions.

The recent economic crisis has been accompanied by declining trust in democracy and growing dissatisfaction with politicians' performance. During the period of 2008-12 the right-wing governments in power introduced many budgetary cuts and austerity policies that had significant impacts not only on NGOs' funding but also on their strategies, policy agendas and networking (Navrátil and Císař, 2013). Eventually, they also led to the emergence of several new forms of NGOs, activist groups and coalitions. Grassroots NGOs and both local and nationwide activist groups tested new attitudes towards the policy process and policy analysis while opposing the traditional institutionalised involvement of established NGOs in the policy process ('captured in partnership'), questioning the relevance of scientific expertise ('ideology of its kind') and focusing on empowering disadvantaged citizens and communities. New coalitions integrating transactional expertise-based activism with public mobilisation through the social media met with unprecedented success in influencing the public discourse and public policies. However, the discourse related to NGOs' professionalisation, institutionalised participation in the policy process and formal partnership between NGOs and the government remains influential.

Acknowledgements

The chapter was produced with the financial support of Specific University Research SVV 2014 260112. Karel Čada's work on this publication was done under the research project supported by Czech Science Foundation 'Social Dynamics Acceleration: Uncertainty, Hierarchical/Flat Governance Structures, and History Interiorization' (grant no. P404/11/2098).

References

Ansell, C. and Gash, A. (2008) 'Collaborative governance in theory and practice', *Journal of Public Administration Research and Theory*, 18(4): 543-71.

Brož, M. (2012) 'Open letter to PIN (Otevřený dopis organizaci Člověk v tísni k situaci v Předlickém ghettu)', *Deník referendum*, 6 November.

Čada, K. (2012) 'Social exclusion of the Roma and the Czech society', in M. Stewart (ed) *The Gypsy Menace: Populism and the New Anti-Gypsy Politics*, London: C. Hurst & Co.

Čada, K. and Ptáčková, K. (2013) 'Possibilities and limits of collaboration between science and NGOs in the Czech Republic', *Journal of Cleaner Production*, 49(15): 25-34.

Čada, K. and Ptáčková, K. (2014). 'Between clients and bureaucrats: an ambivalent position of NGOs in the social inclusion agenda in Czech statutory cities', *Policy and Society*, 33(2): 129-39.

Císař, O. (2010) 'Externally sponsored contention: the channelling of environmental movement organisations in the Czech Republic after the fall of communism', *Environmental Politics*, 19(5): 736-55.

Císař, O. (2013) 'Post-communism and social movements', in D. Snow, D. della Porta, B. Klandermans and D. McAdam (eds) *Encyclopedia of Social and Political Movements* (vol 3), London: Blackwell, pp 994-99.

Císař, O., Vráblíková, K. and Navrátil, J. (2011) 'Staří, noví, radikální: politický aktivismus v České republice očima teorie sociálních hnutí' [Old, new, radical: political activism in the Czech Republic through the prism of social movement theory], *Sociologický časopis/Czech Sociological Review*, 47(1): 137-67.

Collins, H.M. and Evans, R. (2002) 'The third wave of science studies: studies of expertise and experience', *Social Studies of Science*, 32(2): 235-96.

Donahue, J.D. and Zeckhauser, R.J. (2011) *Collaborative Governance: Private Roles for Public Goals in Turbulent Times*, Princeton, NJ: Princeton University Press.

Dunleavy, P. and O'Leary, B. (1987) *Theories of the State: The Politics of Liberal Democracy*, London: Macmillan Education.

Enelow, J.M. and Hinich, M. . (1982) 'Nonspatial candidate characteristics and electoral competition', *Journal of Politics*, 44(1): 115-30.

Fórum dárců (2007) *Analýza participace neziskových organizací na legislativním procesu v České republice* [The analysis of the NGOs' participation in the legislative process in the Czech Republic] [online]. Available from http://aa.ecn.cz/img_uploa d/65636e2e6e6e6f2e2e2e2e2e2e2e2e2e/Analyza_participace_NNO_CR.pdf

Frič, P. (2005) 'The third sector and the policy process in the Czech Republic', *Third Sector European Policy Working Paper No. 6*, London: London School of Economics and Political Science.

GAC (2006) *Analýza sociálně vyloučených romských lokalit a absorpční kapacity subjektů působících v této oblasti* [Analysis of socially excluded Roma localities and communities and the absorption capacity of subjects operating in the field], Praha: MPSV.

Innes, J.E. and Booher, D.E. (2003) 'Collaborative policymaking: governance through dialogue', in M. Hajer and H. Wagenar (eds) *Deliberative Policy Analysis: Understanding Governance in the Network Society*, Cambridge: Cambridge University Press, pp 33-59.

Jasanoff, S. (2003) 'Breaking the waves in science studies: comment on H.M. Collins and Robert Evans, 'The Third Wave of Science Studies', *Social Studies of Science*, 33(3): 389–400.

Keen, S. (2006) 'Non-government organizations in policy', in H.K. Colebatch (ed) *Beyond the Policy Cycle*, Sydney: Allen & Unwin, pp 27-41.

Kopečný, O. (2008) *Jak ovlivnit politiku v České republice a Evropské unii, Manuál pro nevládní neziskové organizace* [How to influence policies in the Czech Republic, manual for the NGOs], Praha: Glopolis.

Laforest, R. and Orsini, M. (2005). 'Evidence-based engagement in the voluntary sector: lessons from Canada', *Social Policy & Administration*, 39(5): 481-97.

Navrátil, J. and Císař, O. (2013). 'Towards "local justice movement(s)"? Two paths to re-scaling the austerity protest in the Czech Republic', *Working paper WP KVE 12/2013*.

O'Flynn, J. and Wanna, J. (eds) (2008) *Collaborative Governance: A New Era of Public Policy in Australia?*, Canberra: ANU E Press.

O'Neill, J. (2001) 'Representing people, representing nature, representing the world', *Environment and Planning C*, 19(4): 483-500.

Osborne, S.P. (ed) (2008) *The Third Sector in Europe: Prospects and Challenges*, London and New York: Routledge.

Petrova, T. and Tarrow, S. (2007) 'Transactional and participatory activism in the emerging European polity the puzzle of East-Central Europe', *Comparative Political Studies*, 40(1): 74-94.

Phillips, S.D. (2007) 'Policy analysis and the voluntary sector: Evolving policy styles', in L. Dobuzinskis, M. Howlett and D. Laycock (eds) *Policy Analysis in Canada: The State of the Art*, Toronto: University of Toronto Press, pp 272-84.

Pierre, J. and Peters, B. (2000) *Governance, Politics and the State*, New York: Palgrave MacMillan.

Pinková, A. (2011) *Zaměstnavatelské a podnikatelské organizace v ČR: prosazování organizovaných zájmů* [Employers' and entrepreneurs' organisations in the Czech Republic: interest groups' lobbying], Brno: Centrum pro studium demokracie a kultury.

Pospíšilová, T. (2005) *Oborové zastřešující organizace v občanském sektoru ČR 2005. Zpráva z výzkumu* [Specialised umbrella organisations in the civic sector in the Czech Republic 2005. Research report], Praha: Nadace rozvoje občanské společnosti a Fakulta humanitních studií Univerzity Karlovy v Praze.

Slim, H. (2002) 'By what authority? The legitimacy and accountability of non-governmental organizations', Paper presented at International Meeting on Global Trends and Human Rights before and after September 11, International Council on Human Rights Policy, Geneva.

Star, S.L. and Griesemer, J.R. (1989) 'Institutional ecology, translations' and boundary objects: amateurs and professionals in Berkeley's Museum of Vertebrate Zoology, 1907-39', *Social Studies of Science*, 19(3): 387-420.

Stoke, D.E. (1963) 'Spatial models of party competition', *American Political Science Review*, 57(2): 368-77.

Stöckelová, T. (2012) 'Social technology transfer? Movement of social science knowledge beyond the academy', *Theory & Psychology*, 22(2): 148-61.

Strünck, C. (2013) 'Public interest groups and policy analysis: a push for evidence-based policy-making?', in S. Blum and K. Schubert (eds) *Policy Analysis in Germany*, Bristol: Policy Press, pp 217-31.

Synková, H. (2011) *Legitimation and Professionalization of a Romani NGO in the Czech Republic*, PhD thesis, Praha: Univerzita Karlova v Praze.

Šedivý, M. and Medlíková, O. (2012) *Public relations, fundraising a lobbing: pro neziskové organizace* [Public relations, fundraising and lobbying for non-profit organizations], Praha: Grada Publishing, a.s.

Torfing, J., Peters, B.G., Pierre, J. and Sorenson, E. (2012) *Interactive Governance: Advancing the Paradigm*, Oxford: Oxford University Press.

Vajdová, T. (2004) *Zpráva o neziskovém sektoru v České republice* [The report on NGOs sector in the Czech Republic], Praha: Rada vlády pro nestátní neziskové organizace.

Veselý, A. (2012) 'Policy advisory system in the Czech Republic: from state monopoly to hollowing out?', Paper presented at XXII Congress of Political Science Conference, Madrid, 8–12 July.

Veselý, A. (2013) 'Accountability in Central and Eastern Europe: concept and reality', *International Review of Administrative Sciences*, 79(2): 310-30.

Wellstead, A. and Evans, B.M. (2013) 'Policy dialogue and engagement between non-governmental organizations and government: a survey of processes and instruments of Canadian policy workers', *Central European Journal of Public Policy*, 7(1): 60–87.

Part V

Academic and advocacy-based policy analysis

FIFTEEN

The news media and decision making

Vlastimil Nečas, Tomáš Trampota

Introduction

The growing interest in investigating the links between the media and politics in the first half of the last century led to the gradual formation of a specific academic discipline generally referred to as political communication and defined as: 'the role of communication in the political process' (Chaffee, 1975, p 15). Its origins are linked to the development of communication studies and mass communication theory in the United States in the first half of the last century (Blumler and Gurevitch, 2001). The research into political communication originally focused on analysing the influence that the media have on voters' behaviour (Lippmann, 1922) and on propaganda (Lasswell, 1971). The historic milestones include the establishment of the Princeton Center for Radio Research in 1937, where P.F. Lazarsfeld conducted his influential research focusing on the news media's influence on voters' decision making, mainly in *The People's Choice* (Lazarsfeld et al, [1944] 1968) and later *Personal Influence* (Katz and Lazarsfeld, 1955).

The history and the present state of political communication research is characterised by a broad range of interests, diversity of approaches and interdisciplinary nature drawing on the theories and analytical procedures of several disciplines from the field of social sciences. Currently, one can identify three main areas of political communication research: studying the media's effects on the public and politics; political marketing and content analyses of the media's coverage of politics; analyses of media systems and the role of the news media in the processes of political decision making. The rather heterogeneous approaches as well as the broad scope in the fields of research are linked in agenda-setting theory as the prevailing interpretation framework for the theoretical, conceptual and methodological bases of research in political communication (Dearing and Rogers, 1996; Kaid, 2004; McCombs, 2004). The theoretical bases and methodological tools of the 'Western' research on political communication were largely drawn upon in the investigations into the media and politics in the new democratic environment of Czechoslovakia and later in the Czech Republic, where researchers sought inspiration mainly in the English-speaking world and, to a lesser extent, in German-speaking countries. In this way, the continuous links to the limited research before the revolution were interrupted and a new tradition largely inspired by the situation on the Western side of the Iron Curtain began to unwind.

The media system in the Czech Republic

The role of the news media in political decision making was transformed in the Czech Republic in relation to the overall change in the social system and related changes in the media system after the Velvet Revolution in 1989. The media underwent a crucial transformation of their political function; the layout of the Czech media landscape changed and so did the news media. The following are the key contours of the changes within the democratisation of the media system:

- privatisation of the daily press and the founding of new dailies;
- removal of the broadcasting media from state control and ownership and the setting up of a dual system;
- new media legislation pursuant to democratic principles;
- new models of public service media regulation;
- emergence of an advertising market.

The transition of the media system from the totalitarian system of media, linked to the state and to the political system stemming from the constitutionally secured position of a single party, the Communist Party of Czechoslovakia, to a democratic system of free, privatised media was accompanied by an intensive metamorphosis of the news media. This applied mainly in the area of normative demands, journalistic culture and the perceptions of the final recipients.

Until 1989 the Czech media system was owned and controlled by the state and strongly centralised, the printed media were linked to the state's bodies (parties comprising the National Front, political and interest groups such as the Socialist Youth Association, and ministries such as the Ministry of Agriculture). The system manifested a high level of organisational political parallelism (Hallin and Mancini, 2004) as the political organisations published the daily press and controlled what was published. Radio and TV news coverage was provided by state institutions, funded directly by the state's budget. The system of the news media featured control over information. The censorship was neither direct nor in advance – on the contrary, it was consequential censorship based on fear of subsequent punishment and strengthening editors' self-censorship and their senior workers' control.

The year 1989 and the developments which followed put an end to the organisational political parallelism in the Czech Republic and caused a decentralisation of information flows. The only exception still retaining the organisational link between the media and politics in the area of the daily press was *Haló noviny* (The Hello News), published directly by the Communist Party. Other dailies were privatised, often under dubious circumstances, and fell into private hands (*Mladá fronta Dnes*, *Právo*); were transformed from illegal samizdat to official papers (*Lidové noviny*); or emerged as brand new dailies. The new dailies' front pages began to advertise their independence in the new democratic environment and their content was increasingly governed by the laws of the market and their efforts to appeal to the relevant target group (Benda, 2007). A new image of journalistic practice developed gradually. Especially in the first half of the 1990s one can hardly speak about objective journalism in the true sense of the term, since the negation of the previous regime resulted in an inclination towards right-wing ideology and championing the new regime instead of real objectiveness. However, the political role of the media in the 1990s still awaits a thorough analysis.

The 1990s were, in the domain of news media, characterised by the onset of commercial television, emergence of tabloids and arrival of foreign investors. The fact that most Czech dailies (except for *Právo*) were transferred into the hands of foreign owners in the 1990s also met with a negative reception from the professional public. Bořivoj Čelovský (2002) published his *Konec českého tisku* (The End of Czech Press) and expressed a concern that the foreign owners might use their dailies to assert their political interests. In February 1994 Nova TV became the first commercial nationwide television broadcaster and was financed by the CME Group: it became the most popular TV station within two months and entirely transformed the nature of TV news. It brought news based on a tabloid search for scandals, full of human interest stories and depoliticised content. The narration of the news stories manifested the spirit of the tabloid media: revelations about celebrities' private lives, simplified dramatisation rooted in negative messages and conflict. The onset of the tabloid media was enhanced by the launch of the new tabloid daily, *Blesk* (The Flash), by the Ringier publishing house in 1992; it soon assumed the position of the most widely read daily in the Czech Republic and retained that position since. Unlike the tabloids published in Germany or the UK, *Blesk* is depoliticised and focuses on celebrities and consumer issues. Political news focuses solely on politicians' scandals, revelations about their private lives or corruption (Trampota and Končelík, 2011). The leading position of the tabloid media in the television and press market resulted in other media assuming tabloid features and transformed the media representation of politics in the Czech Republic generally.

Research on political communication in the Czech Republic

This excursion research into political communication in the Czech Republic uses the model established by James Dearing and Everett Rogers, who describe the processes of political communication from the perspective of agenda-setting theory. As we have already mentioned, the examination of political communication is a rather heterogeneous and interdisciplinary field and agenda-setting theory is currently one of the main tools whereby the research on political communication can be anchored (Dearing and Rogers, 1996; Kaid, 2004; McCombs, 2004; Rogers, 2004).

We will briefly introduce agenda-setting theory in order to put it in context. The original concept of agenda setting stems from a search for the relationship between the setting of media content and the public's preferences; initial studies on agenda setting focused on correlation analyses of the media and the public agenda – that is, on the media's capacity to determine the public's priorities (McCombs and Shaw, 1972). The scope of the research gradually shifted from the relationship between the thematic agenda of the media and the public's preferences towards analysing other relationships such as the influence of political agendas on mass media's content or the relationship of the media agenda to realities outside of the media (Funkhouser, 1973; Shoemaker, 1989).

At present, the agenda-setting approach integrates a number of research areas from cognitive psychology, for example examining intra-personal processes of decision making (Scheufele, 2000) and analyses of political institutions (Walgrave et al, 2008) down to comprehensive analyses of media contents (de Vreese, 2005), bias in news (Nečas, 2008) and media organisations (Shoemaker and Vos, 2009). A key moment in the development of agenda-setting research can be seen in the integration of qualitative analytical methods (Weaver, 1984 Entman, 1993; McCombs, 2004). In the course of the 1980s and 1990s the direction of the research shifted from focusing solely on issue salience in the agenda towards an interest in the ways in which issues are framed and contextualised. The framing research has gradually proven that the public not only responds to explicitly exposed media issues, but also to the ways, contexts and implicitly present interpretation schemes within which the issues are presented by the media (de Vreese, 2005; Kaid, 2004). The media determine not only *what* we are supposed to think about, but also *how* to think about it and, as a consequence, what to think (McCombs and Shaw, 1993). The historical roots of framing theory are linked (Entman, 1993; Reese et al, 2001; de Vreese, 2005) to Ervin Goffman (1974) and the concept belongs to the central notions of agenda setting. The definitions of the framing notion are ample; however, the one most frequently used in the context of agenda setting is that by Robert Entmann: 'To select some aspects of a perceived reality and make them more salient in a communicating text, in such a way to promote a particular problem definition, causal interpretation, more evaluation, and/or treatment recommendation' (Entman, 1993, p 52).

As is clear from this concise outline, the development of the investigation into agenda-setting processes has gone through several stages and spread into copious areas of research. James Dearing and Everett Rogers (1996) identify three basic areas of interest in political communication research: analyses of the media agenda, investigations into the public agenda and the political agenda. A separate area consists of comparative analyses of the relations between the individual agendas caused by external factors (see Figure 15.1).

Given the limited scope of this text and the emphasis on the role of the media in political communication, we will focus on two of the areas mentioned previously. Firstly, we will deal with the Czech media's coverage of politics and the external influences on the appearance and building of the media agenda. Secondly, we will deal with the available information about the agenda-setting processes in the Czech Republic.

Figure 15.1: Three main components of the agenda-setting process

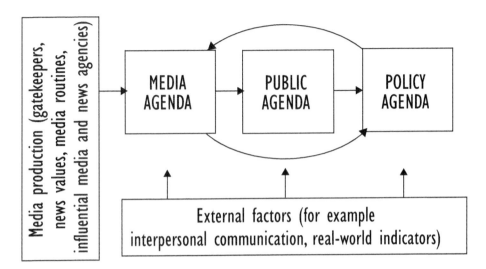

Source: Adapted from Rogers and Dearing (1988).

Coverage of politics in the Czech media

Analyses of the media's coverage of political events and agents comprise a significant part of the Czech research on political communication. The scope of analyses of the news media's content ranges from purely descriptive frequency analyses, to combinations of quantitative and qualitative approaches focusing on analyses of frames and narrative structures present in the news media to solely qualitative text analyses employing the methods of grounded theory or discourse analyses. The analyses of the Czech political news focus mainly on the characteristics linked to balance of issues and relevant agents, bias or partisanship of the media coverage and framing of politics. The results of the analyses illustrate some similar characteristics of the Czech news media's political coverage, which can be divided into three groups: 'horse-race' rhetoric of election coverage, personalisation and 'domestication' of events and emotionalisation of the coverage.

'Horse-race' rhetoric of election coverage

In the Czech news media, elections are depicted as a competition of a certain kind – that is, a 'horse race'. The conception of elections as a competition or race is enhanced by the thematic focus of the coverage emphasising the technology of voters' decision making and the prediction of results. The coverage emphasises issues such as voter turnout, party preferences and the potential post–election distribution of power in representative bodies. The content aspect of elections, such as the parties' and candidates' political standpoints and priorities, remain in the background. The narration of the political struggle as a clash between two rivals is one of the traditional strategies of the Czech media's representation of pre-election politics. This was apparent, for example, before the elections to the House of Representatives in 2010, which were narrated as a fight between the leaders of the two strongest parties, namely Petr Nečas, the chair of the Civic Democrats (ODS), and Jiří Paroubek, the leader of the Social Democrats (ČSSD). Narration based on dramatisation through two contrasting rivals was also employed before the presidential election in 2013, when some news media tended to focus on those favourite candidates who were expected to progress to the second round of the election.

Personalisation and domestication of events

The Czech media's political coverage appears to be strongly personalised and dominated by Czech political agents whereas non-politicians or foreign persons are granted only limited access to the media. Personalisation also means that political events are reduced to politicians' personal animosities or interests. For instance, international events are presented as tools whereby individuals or small groups (political parties or their fractions) assert their interests. The communication of politics in the news media tends to incline away from focusing on systemic and decision-making processes towards an interest in individual political agents. Politics is presented through the prism of disputes between individuals or political parties; the coverage is strongly polarised and described with metaphorical language, negativity and conflict.

For instance, analyses of the coverage of the process of ratifying the Lisbon Treaty point out the fact that it focused almost entirely on Czech political agents. International actors entered the debate only rarely and they did not initiate any new issues or subsequent discussions. The situation is practically the same in the case of the actors from the EU bodies. The Czech debate about the form of the 'Euroconstitution' may seem strictly polarised between the left and the right, as well as reduced to the disputes between the two main political entities, the ODS and ČSSD (Nečas, 2007).

The term 'domestication' refers to a conspicuous effort by the news media to present important international events to the domestic public through specific framing which stresses the key role or crucial importance to the Czech Republic. Regular analyses of foreign event coverage in the Czech media indicate the frequency, intensity and markedness of such framing of foreign political events. One of the manifestations of the domestication of foreign news in the Czech media is the usage of specific metaphors and references to the historic events whose impact upon the country was traumatic (for example references to symbolic years ending in 'eight' – 1848, 1938, 1948, 1968). The media use these tools, and so do politicians, who themselves often articulate these historical parallels and other metaphors; these are then reproduced by the media and maintained as a part of the agenda. Allusions to historical injustice, war, infringement of national sovereignty or abuse of political power enhance the negative tone of the media coverage of foreign political events.

Emotionalisation

In addition to personalisation, there is also a strong tendency towards emotionalisation of the form and content of media messages. The elements of the overall emotionalisation of the political discourse in the media hint at the absence of rational, argument-based debate on political issues. There is a clear tendency to present politics in conflicting and emotional ways (politicians'/partisan interests, historic threats, metaphorical discourses).

It is usual to present emotive allusions to historic events, to which current affairs are likened and which are depicted as the country's fatal moments – which can be repeated. The content tends to link Czech politics to one strong ally, on the grounds of the persistent bipolar model of the division of the world between Russia and the US; these ties are presented, usually in a highly emotional form, as crucial for the country's destiny. The content typically lacks a clear informational context that enables the recipients to form their own opinions on the given event. On the contrary, its presentation encourages them to adopt a personal standpoint on the grounds of sympathy or antipathy towards individual actors.

It may also be interesting to point out the perceived contradiction between the overall emotionalisation of the political discourse in the media (eschewing arguments, inclination towards metaphor, historical parallels, threats, conflicts and so on) on the one hand, and the journalists' explicit requirement for expert decision making on certain issues, such as foreign policy. Frequently the media prefer expert opinions to those of political decision makers, referring to the latter as populist and overly emphasising the 'voice of the street' and presenting the political discourse as detached from expert decision making.

External influences and the building of the media agenda

Regarding political communication in the Czech Republic, it is essential to distinguish between the broadcast media and the press, having different types of regulation. The broadcast media traditionally present politics as objectivised in the spirit of so-called internal pluralism, striving to give equal room to representatives of all relevant political parties in news and current affairs programmes. They are required to do so by the Radio and Television Broadcasting Act (Act 231/2001 Collection of Laws). The broadcast media are subjected to a higher level of regulation than the press, as far as the presentation of politics is concerned. The access of representatives of political parties to the broadcast media's programmes usually adheres to the balance of political powers in the Czech Republic's parliament. The broadcasters employ a different pattern of representing politics before elections, when they select politicians for the programmes based on public opinion polls.

Generally speaking, as far as normative theories are concerned the journalistic culture in the Czech Republic has tended to favour the procedures of German or British objective journalism attempting objective and openly unbiased political journalism. Despite sceptical evaluations of the first decade of the development of the democratic media system, which described it as Italianisation of the media (Sparks and Reading, 1994) – that is, covert clientelistic links between the media and politicians – in the regulation of the broadcast media this was more apparent in the method of nominating and electing members of supervisory boards (the Radio and Television Broadcasting Board, the Czech Radio Board and the Czech Television Board) than in other areas.

The democratic task of the media to provide a deliberative space where diverse political beliefs and ideologies are presented and compete is normatively different according to the type of the media, genre and period, for example the pre-election period. The responsibility for the form, course and content of the pre-election public debate in the broadest sense of the word is not distributed evenly among the existing media: The print media are factually and formally exempted from this obligation, as neither society nor the law expect the print media and their internet derivatives and substitutes to be impartial. However, the situation is different in the broadcast media. In the national context, they are required by law to adhere to some qualitative conditions linked to the democratic task of the media and especially their role in the process of opinion formation. Although this requirement applies to all broadcasters (both public service and private ones), in practice it is ascribed mainly to the public service media: Czech Radio and Czech Television.

Regarding the role of the news media in the decision-making process, the key issue is one of access to content – that is, who is allowed to contribute their voice and interpretation of reality to the media agenda. Of course, this issue is normatively regulated in its relation to political communication and related to the concept of pluralism. The Czech Republic, like most European countries, applies a different conception of plurality to broadcast and print media. Electronic media are connected to internal plurality – that is, the concept that each individual medium should evenly cover all relevant ideological streams present in the society. The print media are linked to external plurality – that is, the plurality of the newsstand, whereby consumers acknowledge that each individual media product may incline to a certain level of bias and support some of the ideologies or political streams; however, the entire range of the print media – the 'newsstand', metaphorically speaking - provides for the full offer (Hallin and Mancini, 2004).

The diverse roles different media types play in the political process were apparent in the first direct presidential elections in the Czech Republic, which took place in early 2013. The second round of the elections, with two candidates, offered the possibility to hold a television duel, inspired by American TV debates - a concept later adopted in other Western countries, and whose history dates back to the first debate between Richard Nixon and John Kennedy in 1960. A more politically biased role was evident for the print media. On the first election day, the best-selling quality paper, *Mladá fronta Dnes* (Youth Front Today), commended Karel Schwarzenberg, one of the candidates: 'He has exceptional international experience. He has the ability to assert our country's interests in a dignified and yet clear way. And he offers voters an amazing life story'. On the other hand, the daily published a negative view of the other candidate: 'Even over the last few days, his transparent account has been receiving anonymous donations'. The bias of the right-wing *Lidové noviny daily* (The People's Paper) was even more pronounced, as it continued to support Karel Schwarzenberg on the first election day and devoted a front page story to him entitled 'Black horse of the election', and accompanied by his photograph. The main text on the front page opened with praise of Karel Schwarzenberg: 'He is the only presidential candidate who has managed to win over his original rivals backed by a substantial voter base'. The front page also presented the chief editor Dalibor Balšínek's support for the candidate:

> There is an alternative that may disrupt the vision of the gloomy finale. He may become an original the Czech Republic's people do not have be ashamed of. An educated person with a responsibility towards history, which is binding for the future; and the fact that he sometimes falls asleep is of minor importance.

The political position and preferences of the dailies are often revealed on the day following the election. After the first round of the presidential election *Mladá fronta Dnes* proclaimed it a 'Good vote' and emphasised the surprising result for Karel Schwarzenberg and his unexpected qualification for the second round; this was accompanied by a victorious and cheerful image of him. The daily's positive response to the results of the first round was enhanced by chief editor Robert Čásenský's comment published on the front page under the headline 'Czechs can vote. The final round will be the way it should be'. *Lidové noviny* was even more upbeat about Karel Schwazernberg's result. The chief editor's comment, entitled 'Victorious campaign', was openly adoring and began 'The black horse of the election did not fail'. The text continues: 'Voters can also be considered winners. This is because the decisive second round of the presidential contest offers the possibility for a vote instead of no vote'.

Two days before the decisive final round of the presidential election *Lidové noviny* carried on backing Karel Schwarzenberg and the main article on the front page was a negative one devoted to the rival candidate: 'Zeman's campaign. Lies and more lies', with a sub-headline '5 slanders that influenced the candidates' competition before the second round of the presidential election'. *Lidové noviny* set out to show how Zeman made use of false information in order to defame his opponent. *Mladá fronta Dnes* joined in this evaluation of Zeman's campaign a mere day before the election and published a front-page article 'Election nonsense', with the sub-headline 'Zeman and his team publish untrue and rude slander about his opponent and his family. Schwarzenberg's team was unable to prepare the minister for the debates'. The second sentence of the sub-headline gives the impression of an effort to objectivise the material and a strategy to find something negative about the other candidate so that the overall message will be viewed as balanced.

The presidential election showed that the Czech print media had begun to engage in politics. The transformation of the printed media's deliberative task into promotion and its biased role over the last two years has been enhanced by the transformation of the ownership structure of the media with new Czech owners (Jaromír Soukup, Andrej Babiš, Zdeněk Bakala). The core of their business is linked to other industrial areas and they often pursue their own political interests and in some cases have begun to assert them in the media. Thus, a new form of political parallelism is emerging and resembles the organisational political parallelism present before 1989 and discussed previously. This trend reached its climax in 2013, when a new political party, *ANO* (YES), was set up, led by the controversial billionaire Andrej Babiš, suspected of pre-revolution collaboration with the communist secret police; approximately three months before the elections to the House of Representatives he acquired one of the country's largest publishing houses, Mafra, which publishes two of the country's main quality papers. The success of Babiš' party ANO, which won nearly a quarter of the mandates to the parliament resulted in his influence on the parliamentary media commission, which influences the election of members of the public service media regulatory boards (Czech Television, Czech Radio and the Radio and Television Broadcasting Board). The arrangement suggest that the influence that politicians exert on the media is growing and that the Italianisation of the Czech media typical of the early stage of the transformation of the media system may soon be replaced by Berlusconisation (that is, interconnection of media and political powers and instrumentalisation of media for political purposes)

Although the political positioning of the broadcast media towards political parties is rather neutral, Czech daily newspapers follow the preferences of their readers and the content is biased in terms of editorial policy - for example, selection of issues and frequency of explicit references to respective politicians. The left-leaning daily *Právo* (The Law) has historically inclined toward the Czech Social Democratic Party. During pre-election periods *Právo* often highlights the campaigns of the Czech Social Democratic Party. On the other side, the rather right- leaning dailies such as *Hospodářské noviny* (The Economic News) and *Lidové noviny* (The People's News) are open to the agendas of Czech right-wing parties and personalities. These aspects of the Czech media landscape have become a part of policy-making processes and affect the communication strategies of political actors.

Agenda-setting research

As we outlined earlier, the research on agenda setting stems from the search for a relationship between the thematic structure of media content and the public's preferences or an examination of the media's capacity to influence public opinion by defining the salience of issues which are then acknowledged as important by the public. The only extensive empirical research focusing on testing this relationship took place in 2008 in cooperation between the Faculty of Social Sciences at Charles University in Prague and the Centre for Public Opinion Research of the Academy of Sciences of the Czech Republic. The collection of panel data for the analysis of the public agenda took place from April to July in 12 weekly observations. The research on the media agenda was based on detailed quantitative content analysis of three television channels, two radio stations and five dailies from March to July. The dataset of nearly 30,000 items makes this survey the most detailed analysis of the agenda of the Czech news media ever conducted in the Czech Republic.

This study confirmed the original agenda-setting hypothesis on both a general and individual level. From a general perspective, the correlation analysis of the media and the public agenda confirmed the original hypothesis of McCombs and Shaw (1972). The findings of the Czech study also followed the original hypothesis on an individual level, as the agenda-setting effect of the mass media varied from one issue to the next. The key factor related to the transfer of salience from the media to the public involves the relationship between a given issue and the respondent. The agenda-setting effect of the mass media is stronger for issues on which respondents do not have personal experience. In other words, the strength of the agenda-setting effect is reduced in cases where the mass media are not the exclusive source of information for a given respondent (Škodová and Nečas, 2009). The focus on agenda-setting processes within Czech social studies is rather marginal and predominantly influenced by the early works of Maxwell McCombs and Donald Shaw (1972). This influence also concerns terminology, as terms for specific parts of the agenda-setting process have been adopted and this terminology thus has become part of the Czech academic discourse. The few studies in place up to now focus on in-depth analysis of the relationship between the media and the public agenda and on further research of the media agenda, which also includes works dealing with intermedia influences (Váně et al, 2012; Nečas, 2013)

Conclusions

The relationship between the media and politics in the Czech social sciences is included in three disciplines: media studies, sociology and political science. These disciplines pursue their own separate and rather detached research on political communication. In sociology, political communication appears mainly in connection with the results of public opinion surveys, voters' behaviour and the Czech public's political preferences. Political studies touch upon political communication within election studies, mainly in relation to rational choice theories and partially in the area of political marketing. This disciplinary distinctiveness seems to be a strong limiting factor in Czech political communication research. As we outlined earlier, research on political communication should be based on an interdisciplinary approach using the theoretical and methodological apparatuses of several social science disciplines. The current Czech research on political communication is anchored within specific disciplines and often focuses on its own discipline-relevant segment within the mass media–public–politics triad. The Czech Republic's research on political communication is broken down into three separate areas with their own theoretical, terminological and methodological backgrounds which are not linked.

Acknowledgement

The chapter was written with the financial support of PRVOUK programme P17 'Sciences of Society, Politics, and Media under the Challenge of the Times'.

References

Benda, J. (2007) *Vlastnictví periodického tisku v ČR v letech 1989–2006* [The ownership of the periodical press in the Czech Republic 1989–2006], Praha: Karolinum.

Blumler, J., Gurevitch, M (2001) '"Americanization" reconsidered: U.K.–U.S. campaign communication comparisons across time', in W. Bennett and R. Entman (eds) *Mediated Politics: Communication in the Future of Democracy*, Cambridge: Cambridge University Press.

Chaffee, S.H. (ed) (1975) *Political Communication*, Beverly Hills, CA: SAGE.

Čelovský, B. (2002) *Konec českého tisku* [The end of the Czech press], Ostrava: Tilia.

De Vreese, C. (2005) *Framing Europe: Television News and European Integration*, Amsterdam: Het Spinhuis.

Dearing, J. and Rogers, E. (1996) *Agenda-Setting*, Thousand Oaks, CA: SAGE.

Entman, R. (1993) 'Framing: toward clarification of a fractured paradigm', *Journal of Communication*, 43(4): 51-58.

Funkhouser, G. (1973) 'The Issues of the sixties: an exploratory study in the dynamics of public opinion', *The Public Opinion Quarterly*, 37: 62-75

Goffman, E. (1974) *Frame Analysis: An Essay on the Organization of Experience*, Cambridge: Harper Row.

Hallin, D. and Mancini, P. (2004) *Comparing Media Systems: Three Models of Media and Politics*, Cambridge: Cambridge University Press.

Kaid, L. (ed) (2004) *Handbook of Political Communication Research*, Mahwah, NJ: Lawrence Erlbaum Associates.

Katz, E. and Lazarsfeld, P. (1955) *Personal Influence: The Part Played by People in the Flow of Mass Communication*, New York: Free Press.

Lasswell, H. (1971) *Propaganda Techniques in the First World War*, Cambridge, MA: MIT Press.

Lazarsfeld, P., Berelson, B. and Gaudet, H. (1968) *The People's Choice: How the Voter Makes Up His Mind in a Presidential Campaign*, New York: Columbia University Press.

Lippmann, W. (1922) *Public Opinion*, New York, NY: Harcourt, Brace.

McCombs, M. (2004) *Setting the Agenda: The Mass Media and Public Opinion*, Cambridge: Polity Press.

McCombs, M.E. and Shaw, D.L. (1972) 'The agenda-setting function of the mass media', *Public Opinion Quarterly*, (36): 176-87.

McCombs, M. and Shaw, D. (1993) 'The evolution of agenda-setting research: twenty-five years in the marketplace of ideas', *Journal of Communication*, 43(2): 58-67.

Nečas, V. (2007) 'Constitutional debate in the Czech Republic', *Prague Social Science Studies, Media Series MED – 011*, Prague: Faculty of Social Sciences, Charles University.

Nečas, V. (2008) 'Research of bias in selected journals: a meta-analysis', *Bodhi*, 2(1): 117-35.

Nečas, V. (2013) *Koncept nastolování agendy v kontextu českých mediálních studií* [Agenda-setting theory in the context of Czech media studies], PhD thesis, Prague: Faculty of Social Sciences, Charles University.

Reese, S., Gandy, O. and Grant, A. (2001) *Framing Public Life: Perspectives on Media and Our Understanding of the Social World*, Mahwah, NJ: Lawrence Erlbaum Associates.

Rogers, E.M. (2004) 'Theoretical diversity in political communication', in L. Kaid (ed) *Handbook of Political Communication Research*, Mahwah, NJ: Lawrence Erlbaum Associates, pp 3-16.

Rogers, E.M. and Dearing, J.W. (1988) 'Agenda-setting research: where has it been? Where is it going?', in J.A. Anderson (ed) *Communication Yearbook 11*, Newbury Park, CA: Sage.

Scheufele, D. (2000) 'Agenda-setting, priming, and framing revisited: another look at cognitive effects of political communication', *Mass Communication and Society*, 3(2–3): 297-316.

Shoemaker, P. (1989) *Communication Campaigns about Drugs: Government, Media, and the Public*, Hillsdale, NJ: Lawrence Erlbaum Associates.

Shoemaker, P. and Vos, T. (2009) *Gatekeeping Theory*, London: Routledge.

Sparks, C. and Reading, A. (1994) 'Understanding media change in Eastern Central Europe', *Media Culture and Society*, 16(2): 243-70.

Škodová, M. and Nečas, V. (2009) *Veřejná a mediální agenda: komparativní analýza tematizace veřejné sféry* [The public and the media agenda: comparative analysis of issues in the public sphere], Praha: Professional Publishing.

Trampota, T. and Končelík, J. (2011) 'The tabloidisation of the Czech daily press', in B. Dobek-Ostrowska and M. Glowacki (eds) *Making Democracy in Twenty Years*, Wroclaw: University of Wroclaw Press.

Váně, J., Štípková, M., Kreidl, M. and Kalvas, F. (2012) 'Framing and agenda-setting: two parallel processes in interaction', *Czech Sociological Review*, 48(1): 3-38.

Walgrave, S., Soroka, S. and Nuytemans, M. (2008) 'The mass media's political agenda-setting power: a longitudinal analysis of media, parliament, and government in Belgium (1993 to 2000)', *Comparative Political Studies*, 41(6): 814–36.

Weaver, D. (1984) 'Media agenda-setting and public opinion: is there a link?', in R. Bostrom and B. Westley (eds) *Communication Yearbook 8*, Beverly Hills, CA: Sage.

SIXTEEN

Think tanks and policy discourses

Ondřej Císař, Milan Hrubeš

Introduction

Although think tanks are probably most developed in the US, as is their scholarly analysis, they and various other policy-oriented research institutions have played a significant role in the political systems of many established democracies (see for example McGann and Weaver, 2000; McGann, 2009). Likewise, they have become an important part of EU politics. In general, think tanks research public policies and produce different types of both evidence-based and ideologically driven expertise, opinions and recommendations which serve several types of audiences, mostly policy makers and the media. In a developed political system, one can find different types of think tanks working in the framework of various policy discourses. In this chapter we focus on think tanks and policy discourses in the Czech Republic.

Drawing on available information, the aim of this chapter is to map out and analytically describe Czech think tanks. First we define think tanks and present their established typology; second, we introduce discursive institutionalism and define policy discourses. Further, we differentiate Czech think tanks on the basis of their belonging to these discourses, summarise the basic characteristics of the most important Czech think tanks, and pay particular attention to their connectedness to other actors in the field. Do they establish connections within their particular discourse, or do they link up across the discourses? Consequently, are they able to serve as integrative agents in the public sphere, or do they seem to contribute to the building of rather autonomous ideological currents in the Czech Republic? Which of these currents is the most developed?

Think tanks and policy discourses

Think tanks form a special type of civil society organisation or NGO, whose purpose is the production of policy-relevant expert knowledge typically offered to public institutions, state officials and the media. According to McGann (2009, p 9):

> Think tanks or public policy research, analysis, and engagement institutions are organizations that generate policy oriented research, analysis, and advice on domestic and international issues that enable

policymakers and the public to make informed decisions about public policy issues.

In general, think tanks research issues relevant to public policies and formulate policy recommendations. Four basic types, namely academic, contractual, advocacy and party-affiliated think tanks, can be distinguished (here and in the next two paragraphs we draw on McGann and Weaver, 2000, pp 1–36; see also Table 16.1).

Table 16.1: Types of think tanks

	Employees	Funding	Who decides on the goals and work plan?	End products
Academic think tanks (universities without students)	High academic qualifications without ideological orientation	Foundations, private sector, individuals	Researchers and donors	Academic monographs and scientific articles
Contractual think tanks	High academic qualifications without ideological orientation	Public institutions	Public institutions asking for analyses	Research reports (impartial style)
Advocacy think tanks	Ideological and/or political orientation	Foundations, private sector, individuals	Heads of organisations	Policy papers
Party-affiliated think tanks	Party membership and loyalty	State and party subsidies	Party	Various

Source: McGann and Weaver (2000, p 10, modified).

The first two types share the stress they put on highly educated employees, often holding PhDs, rigorous methods of scientific research and overall self-presentation as nonpartisan organisations. They differ in the way they are financed, how they formulate their priorities and the types of their outputs. The goals and priorities of academic think tanks are usually decided internally, although their donors also may have a say in them. They primarily focus on producing academic publications. On the other hand, as a result of their dependency on mostly public contracts, contractual think tanks pursue agendas defined by their sources of funding. These think tanks produce research reports and background documents for many purposes of public administration.

There are also several characteristics common for advocacy and party-affiliated think tanks. Advocacy think tanks are formally independent, but at the same time they advocate a certain ideologically defined position or social interest. Instead of nonpartisan research these organisations aim at persuading policy makers, opinion leaders, the media, and ultimately the public about their interpretation of the world. They are usually rooted in some belief and/or value system or ideology. In their research they often rely on information and resources provided by those whose interests they advocate, such as trade unions or private firms. Their employees are often based in these interest groups rather than at the universities. Party-affiliated think tanks are even more oriented towards partisanship than advocacy think tanks, since they are affiliated to political parties whose values and programme they maintain and advocate in public debate.

Of course, these are ideal types. Several of them can be used for the description of a specific case. Even more so if we want to apply this typology in the context of a post-communist country, since think tanks played multiple roles in the context of post-communist transformation:

> Central and Eastern Europe provides numerous examples of new think tank models that were introduced to the think tank landscape in Europe. These were often hybrids that produced quality work, mobilised the public, compensated for a disintegrating state bureaucracy, and filled gaps in the nascent civil society. (McGann, 2009, p 28)

The presented typology differentiates among functionally different types of think tanks. However, based on their definition, think tanks are not only functionally different, but are also part of and help produce wider policy discourses in a particular society. In line with the premises of discursive institutionalism, we define policy discourses as 'both the policy ideas that speak to the soundness and appropriateness of policy programmes and the interactive processes of policy formulation and communication that serve to generate and disseminate those policy ideas' (Schmidt and Radaelli, 2004, p 193). In the perspective of discursive institutionalism (see also Schmidt, 2010; for a somewhat different application in the Czech context see Potůček, 2012), the concept of policy discourse not only takes the power of ideas and ideologies seriously, but also links them to actors and their institutional surroundings; in other words, the concept of policy discourse embraces ideas, actors and institutional settings. By focusing on think tanks as the primary promoters of policy ideas, we particularly aim at mapping the former two, namely ideas and actors (and their relations). In this chapter, we take into account a wider institutional setting in which think tanks interact only if they themselves identify its components as parts of their interaction network.

Policy discourse is at the same time a set of ideas and a field of their interactions (see Schmidt and Radaelli, 2004, pp 194-197; we draw on these pages in our further definition). First, policy discourses can be defined as more or less coherent sets of values, identities, norms and collective memories; second, and at the same time, they are formed by institutional interactions of policy-oriented organisations, be they think tanks, other NGOs, political parties or the media. In this paper we focus on think tanks, but also model their declared interactions with other types of actors. In this respect, we focus on the interactional or transactional dimension of policy discourse, on how organisations interact (see for example Císař, 2013; Císař and Navrátil, 2015).

Based on previous work on the political and ideological landscape of the Czech Republic (Dvořáková, 2002; Gjuričová et al, 2012; Potůček, 2012) and our research on NGOs and social movements (for example Císař, 2013; Císař and Navrátil, 2015), we differentiate among four major policy discourses:

- Liberal-conservative discourse (often labelled neoliberal or in the Czech context Klausian after Václav Klaus, the first Prime Minister of the Czech Republic and its second President): This discourse puts particular stress on the values of classical liberalism (liberty, or economic freedom) in the economic dimension and on traditional values in the cultural one (heterosexual families, the church's involvement in public life, nationalism).
- Support for democracy discourse (in the Czech context often labelled Havelian after Václav Havel, pre-1989 dissident leader who became the first President after the fall of communism): This discourse values liberal democracy, putting stress on civil society and social pluralism. It does not primarily view citizenship in terms of liberty - that is, private autonomy; it also acknowledges its other layers, especially stressing its public dimension - democratic involvement in public life - and diversity of ways of life in a pluralistic society.
- Social democratic discourse: This puts stress on social justice and social citizenship, aiming at an effective defence of the welfare state against neoliberal policies.
- International and foreign policy discourse: This largely relates to the accession of the Czech Republic to the European Union (EU) and the role the country plays (and should play) in international relations, international cooperative structures and development.

If we combine the typology of think tanks (Table 16.1) with the four discourses, the result is a new typology (see Table 16.2), which categorises Czech think tanks according to their functional type (academic, contractual, advocacy, party-affiliated) and discursive membership.

Data

Identifying think tanks in the Czech Republic is not an easy task. There is neither a database nor an official list of think tanks. Moreover, in line with McGann's (2009) general diagnosis, think tanks are largely not well-established institutions with a clear definition and understanding in the Czech public discourse. Therefore, to identify relevant think tanks, we combined several sources. First, we searched the Internet for the query think tank site:cz. Second, we used the Anopress TI database, which monitors the Czech media to search for think tanks influencing Czech public discourse. Anopress TI covers national news daily as well as regional newspapers, journals, magazines, radio and TV programmes. Third, we also drew on the 2013 Global Go to Think Tank Index (GGTTI) provided by the Think Tanks and Civil Societies Program (TTCSP) at the University of Pennsylvania.

Table 16.2: Think tanks in Czech policy discourses

Discourse	Liberal-conservative		Support for democracy	Social democratic	International and foreign policy
Academic			Institute for Democracy and Economic Analysis (IDEA)		Institute of International Relations (IIR) Association for International Affairs (AMO)
Contractual think tanks	Centre for the Study of Democracy and Culture (CDK)				
					Prague Security Studies Institute (PSSI)
Advocacy					European Values EUROPEUM
	CEVRO – Liberal Conservative Academy	Liberal Institute Civic Institute Centre for Economics and Politics (CEP)	Václav Havel Library Aspen Institute	Centre for Social Market Economy and Open Democracy (CESTA) Masaryk Democratic Academy	Glopolis
Party think tanks					

The criterion for including a think tank on our list was that it was recorded in at least two of the three sources we searched. Based on this search, we identified 16 of the most important think tanks in the Czech Republic (see Table 16.2 and the next section for the list and their description). Academic and university-related institutions such as Center for Economic Research and Graduate Education (CERGE) and Center for Social and Economic Strategies (CESES) (see other chapters of this book) are not included; they primarily present themselves as institutions of research and education.

The analysis of respective policy discourses and their representatives (think tanks) draws on data we collected from our survey and publicly available sources – the annual reports of the researched think tanks and their websites. The survey was conducted between September 2013 and January 2014. We used an online questionnaire that consisted of both open and closed-ended questions concerning important factors related to think tanks' organisation, personnel, finance and cooperation. The questionnaire was completed by 14 out of the 16 approached think tanks.

Both the survey and publicly available data were used for the network analysis later in the paper. A tie (see Figure 16.1) represents declared cooperation with other organisations mentioned in the questionnaire (the question was: What are the organisations you cooperate with?) and cooperation mentioned in the annual reports by the studied think tanks. There was no limit on partners they could declare themselves to be cooperating with; they were only asked to declare partners, not to evaluate the intensity of the cooperation. The network is asymmetrical and binary (cooperate/not cooperate). Organisations mentioned at least twice either in the questionnaire or in the annual reports of the studied think tanks were included in the analysis. In order to measure network centrality, we relied on the in-degree centrality measure, to represent the incoming ties, since it is a suitable measure of an organisation's prominence in the network (for more see Hanneman and Riddle, 2005; Císař and Navrátil, 2015).

Think tanks in the Czech Republic after 1989

Civil society has played an important role in post-communist democratisation in Central and Eastern Europe. The experience of anti-communist regime opposition helped the concept to gain in influence after the regimes were successfully toppled. It seemed that civil society was indeed an effective political force; now there was a need to build up a new civil society compatible with a slowly developing democracy. After the fall of the communist regime, this was linked with another important influence, coming especially from the US, its political practice, traditions and academic research. They all seemed to converge in the conclusion that a functioning democracy needs developed networks of both associations in which individuals can meet and cultivate social capital and organisations producing novel policy ideas (Carothers, 1999). The general perception was that the former would help produce capable citizens and the latter ideas for these citizens to use in the new political situation. According to this view, there were no utilisable policy discourses available in the immediate period after the collapse of communism.

As a result, these new organisations began to be supported by many international agencies, which wanted to contribute to democratic consolidation in post-communist countries. In general, these civil society-building programmes supported various types of NGOs (nongovernmental organisations), including (certain types of) think tanks. In addition to US donors, such as National Endowment for Democracy (NED) and International Republican Institute (IRI), German political foundations also became important in this respect. Originally, they mostly focused on support for what they understood as missing in post-communist political culture, namely liberal and conservative values, leaving a lasting imprint on the landscape of Czech think tanks. Indeed, our research shows that the average age of liberal-conservative think tanks far exceeds their counterparts in different ideological camps, which started to catch up with liberal and conservative organisations only later on (for Czech think tanks see Table 16.2).

At the same time, we do not want to say that these think tanks were implanted from abroad only; these ideas clearly prevailed in the post-communist period as a readily available reaction to the failure of the communist regime (Szacki, 1995).

Liberal-conservative discourse

The liberal-conservative think tanks in this study are very small, with an average of four employees; only some of them stress ideological orientation as a condition for recruitment. In terms of resources, they mostly rely on foundations, the EU and private donors. The last five-year annual budget averaged £143,000. The topics mostly covered concern politics, culture and religion, and the preferred targets include politicians, experts and the public. Accordingly, these organisations disseminate their outputs primarily through commentaries in newspapers, opinion pieces and internet channels (websites, Facebook and others). Here we focus on the CDK, the Liberal Institute, the Civic Institute, the CEVRO and the CEP.

CDK

The Centre for the Study of Democracy and Culture (CDK, Centrum pro studium demokracie a kultury) is an independent association established in 1993. The CDK can be categorised as an academic, contractual as well as an advocacy think tank. It aims to contribute to the development of democratic political culture, to stress the irreplaceability of Christian values. The CDK claims a liberal-conservative position and an ecumenical position in questions of faith.

The CDK is comprised of three units; two of them are institutes – the Institute for Politics and Culture (IPC) and Institute for Christian Studies (ICS) - and the third is a publishing house. Both institutions closely cooperate and carry out research projects on the relations between politics, religion, history and culture. The IPC's activities consist of research and managing various projects mainly on supporting democratisation as well as on other current political and social issues. The ICS conducts research, mostly focused on religion and history. Besides these activities both institutions hold seminars and conferences where they present research outputs and inform the wider public about current events.

The CDK focuses on translating and publishing books. It also publishes the journal *Contexts* (*Kontexty*) which typically offers various articles concerning philosophical, cultural and literary issues. The CDK also publishes two more journals. Within the IPC, the journal *Politics Review* (*Revue Politika*) and within the ICS the journal *The History of the Church* (*Církevní dějiny*).

The Liberal Institute

The Liberal Institute (LI, Liberální institut) is an independent association established in 1990. It is an advocacy think tank. Its main goal is to spread, develop and apply classical liberal ideas as well as to promote programmes based on the principles of classical liberalism.

To fulfil its stated goals, the LI organises a number of activities. Firstly it conducts research that focuses mainly on Czech macroeconomic transition and similar processes in transforming countries as well as on microeconomic aspects of post-centrally planned economies. The LI also concentrates on economic policy and state efficiency. Besides this focus, the LI studies current economic strategies and the Czech government's policies. Secondly the LI organises educational activities that are focused on students and the public. Thirdly the LI strives to disseminate classical liberal ideas mainly via organising discussion forums and events, for example connected to Tax Freedom Day.

The LI publishes the journal *Terra Libera* (via the company Terra Libera, which is associated with the LI) every two months and also focuses on translating books concerning classical liberalism.

The Civic Institute

The advocacy think tank the Civic Institute (OI, Občanský institut) was founded in 1990. It is an independent association originally focused on promoting a free market economy. Since the mid-1990s the OI has moved to a more conservative position, stressing cultural and social issues, mainly moral, religious and the pre-political foundations of what the organisation understands as a free society: first of all, the traditional family. Its goal is developing and disseminating conservative and Christian ideas and values.

Although interconnected, the OI's activities can be divided into three main fields: (1) education and raising public awareness, (2) publishing and (3) providing public library services and operating a reading room. Within the first field the OI organises summer schools, lectures, seminars and conferences that are mainly aimed at secondary school and university students. Its educational programmes also aim at members of parliament, government officials, public policy specialists, media editors and members of diplomatic corps.

The OI publishes a monthly bulletin which consists of essays, policy studies and papers on political philosophy and public policy as well as on themes concerning international relations. Besides periodicals, the OI focuses on publishing books by conservative thinkers.

CEVRO

CEVRO – The Liberal Conservative Academy (CEVRO – Liberálně-konzervativní akademie) is an association founded in 1999. It is an advocacy and party-affiliated think tank (affiliated to the Civic Democratic Party, the ODS). Its main goals are popularisation of liberal-conservative ideas, providing political education, democracy and right-wing politics promotion. The CEVRO also strives to enhance Czech political culture and wide discussion on current political and social issues.

The CEVRO's core activity is education. The first programme is political education and is mostly based on the long-term and systematic education of the members of the ODS on all levels. The party members, be they candidates or elected politicians, are trained in communication and management as well as educated in political science, economics, international relations and law. The second programme is education provided by the private college CEVRO Institute College (Vysoká škola CEVRO Institut) established by the CEVRO in 2006. The college offers bachelor's and master's degree programmes in the social sciences. The third programme is focused on democracy promotion. The CEVRO strives to transfer Czech judicial, economic as well as political experience gained during the years of transformation via various lectures, trainings and exchange programmes.

The CEVRO publishes two weeklies: *The Week in European Politics* (*Týden v Evropské politice*), which reports on the past week's events in European politics, and *The Week in Czech Politics* (*Týden v České politice*), which provides information about the past week's events in Czech politics. It also publishes a fortnightly, called *Fortnightly* (*Čtrnáctideník*), which provides basic information to parliament members about current issues discussed in the Parliament, and the monthly magazine *CEVRO Revue,* which serves as the main communication instrument with the wider public.

CEP

The advocacy think tank the Centre for Economics and Politics (CEP, Centrum pro ekonomiku a politiku) was founded as a nonpartisan association in 1998. It has been seen as an institutional umbrella for associates and followers of Václav Klaus. The CEP's main goal is to promote the principles of a free market economy, limited government and individual freedom and to formulate and further public policies based on these principles.

The CEP's core activity is research on key policy issues, political and economic themes. Its outputs are primarily intended for policymakers, the media and the academic and policy communities. It mostly consists of various contributions that criticise any political or economic acts that according to the CEP are in contradiction to the principles of a free market economy, limited government, individual freedom and state sovereignty. The CEP opposes the European Union, the global governance concept, progressive political ideologies such as multiculturalism and environmentalism and human rights promotion. The CEP closely cooperates with the Václav Klaus Institute (Institut Václava Klause, IVK), which declares the same goals. Many of the CEP's activities are carried out together with the IVK.

The CEP publishes its own research outputs and commentaries in anthologies and articles. It also publishes a newsletter on current political issues.

Support for discourse on democracy

Václav Havel, who promoted the ideas of democratic citizenship and civil society, symbolised a vision different from the previously mentioned camp. Although Havel put stress on civil society, this has not translated very much into the sphere of think tanks. Instead, his ideas have been diffused throughout society through a number of independent public intellectuals. Still, we can find three visible think tanks which carry his intellectual heritage, with a general stress on support to principles of democracy.

These organisations have been established only recently; they are rather small, with an average of 6.5 employees; and they largely put stress on a university education for their employees. In terms of resources, they rely mostly on foundations, but also on public and private sectors and individuals. Their average annual budget over the last five years was £314,000. The portfolio of topics covered is highly varied, ranging from democracy to public policies and culture. In their communication they mostly rely on the internet, and they also produce academic publications and opinion pieces. Their primary target groups are experts, public administration and the public. Here we focus on IDEA, the Václav Havel Library and the Aspen Institute.

IDEA

The Institute for Democracy and Economic Analysis (IDEA, Institut pro demokracii a ekonomickou analýzu) was established as an autonomous academic and contractual think tank within the Economics Institute of the Academy of Sciences of the Czech Republic in 2009. It is a politically independent organisation aimed at improving the quality of the Czech democracy and economy by developing and supporting broad-based and rigorous discussions of the important issues, mainly economic and social reforms, environmental and energy policies, the functioning of government and the European Union.

The IDEA's activities cover (1) advising and consulting with governmental institutions and parliamentary members on various policy documents and providing its own ideas for policies, (2) formulating and participating in the creation of a national vision and strategy for the future development of the Czech Republic, and (3) informing citizens and encouraging them to actively participate in public life and in holding elected politicians accountable to the public interest.

The IDEA organises and participates in round tables, workshops, conferences and parliamentary hearings, publishes policy briefs and position papers, opens up to citizens on various occasions and provides information about its activities and proposals.

The Václav Havel Library

The Václav Havel Library (KVH, Knihovna Václava Havla) is a public benefit company established in 2004. Although its primary task is to organise research, documentary and library activities connected to the first President of the Czech Republic, Václav Havel, KVH focuses also on educating and informing the public on human rights as well as building a civil society.

The KVH is involved in a number of diverse activities ranging from archiving, running the library, organising exhibitions, educating and publishing to conducting research and organising debates, seminars and conferences. These activities have in common the personality of Václav Havel, his work and his opinions on politics and society; however, we can identify two main fields here. The first is Václav Havel himself. The KVH has opened a permanent exhibition about him and makes Havel's dramatic and literary work available to the public. The second concerns current and important issues of politics and society.

The KVH publishes a quarterly called *Václav Havel Library Notebooks*. The library's researchers and associates regularly present their archival and research work there.

The Aspen Institute

The Aspen Institute Prague (AIP) is a public benefit company established in 2012 as a Central European partner of the Aspen Institute. It focuses on policy innovation and inclusive dialogue, declaring that its goal is to contribute to the development of an open society and values-based leadership. The AIP declares itself to be a non-ideological organisation with no political party affiliation.

The AIP's educational and policy-based activities are divided into three areas: the first includes fostering leadership. Programmes within this area are devoted to young leaders across various professions and their training in personal and professional skills. The second area concerns policy. The policy programme is based on forums for experts. The media and public are excluded. The third area covers activities dedicated to the public. Within this programme the AIP organises conferences and public debates.

The AIP also publishes a quarterly journal which is designed for the wider public.

Social democratic discourse

Only later on and in relation to the general renewal of social democracy did social democratic discourse start to emerge. Compared to the previous discourses, the social democratic one is organisationally much weaker, its average number of employees is only 1.5 and its five-year average annual budget approaches £29,000. These organisations require their employees to have a university education. They very much rely on individual contributions, also receiving foundation and public money. In terms of issues, they focus solely on politics and public policies and mostly rely on internet-based communication channels. They primarily target policy makers and the public. Here we focus on the Masaryk Democratic Academy and CESTA.

The Masaryk Democratic Academy

The Masaryk Democratic Academy (MDA, Masarykova demokratická akademie) is an association that was founded in 1896, and after the communist ban it was re-established in 1991. It is a social democratic educational institution with the main goal to conduct research activities, educate and raise public awareness of social democratic values and ideas. The Masaryk Democratic Academy is associated with the Czech Social Democratic Party (ČSSD).

The MDA concentrates on three principal activities. First of all, the MDA participates in diverse educational programmes that are intended for the wider public as well as for ČSSD members. Research and cooperation on ČSSD programme development is the second principal activity. The MDA also closely participates in developing other ČSSD documents, be they long-term strategies or policy papers. The third activity comprises raising public awareness of social democratic values and ideas.

The MDA publishes a journal; it also publishes various reports from conferences, seminars and workshops.

CESTA

The Centre for Social Market Economy and Open Democracy (CESTA, Centrum pro sociálně-tržní ekonomiku a otevřenou demokracii) is an association founded in 2011 by representatives of the political centre and democratic left. The CESTA's main goal is to enter into and participate in the substantial debate about the recent and future role of the democratic state in changing economic and political conditions. Within this goal the CESTA strives to challenge the neoliberal views on the role of state.

The CESTA's activities are divided into three projects. The first focuses on economic and social issues such as pensions, tax and healthcare reforms as well as fighting corruption. Here CESTA provides feedback on ČSSD's proposals and programme documents on these social issues and also helps formulate various policy documents. The second project is called the Diagnosis of the Current Situation (Diagnóza doby) and comprises internal workgroup discussions. Political party funding is the theme of the third project. Here the CESTA aims to bring this problem to the closer attention of politicians and the wider public.

The CESTA publishes various documents, mainly policy briefs, policy papers and research papers. However, its activities have recently been phased out.

International and foreign policy discourse

On average, and compared to the previously discussed discourses, the organisations dealing with international and foreign policy issues form the second oldest and the most resource-endowed network of think tanks. Their average number of employees is more than 10 and their average five-year annual budget approaches

£343,000. They stress university education as a condition for employment and financially rely mostly on foundations and public funds, including the EU. In terms of topics covered, they concentrate on international relations, the EU and security. Their most common output is policy papers, but they also produce opinion pieces, research reports for institutions and internet-based communications. Their primary targets are politicians, experts and public administration. We focus on the Institute of International Relations, the Association for International Affairs, the Prague Security Studies Institute, European Values, EUROPEUM and Glopolis.

IIR

The IIR, Institute of International Relations (ÚMV, Ústav mezinárodních vztahů), originally set up by the Ministry of Foreign Affairs of the Czech Republic, was basically re-established after 1989, although it already existed before the end of communism. As a result of its transformation into a public research organisation, it increased its institutional independence in 2007. The goal of the institute is to conduct research in the field of international relations, assist with Czech foreign policy formulation and inform professionals as well as the public about current problems in international relations.

The IIR's core activity is basic and applied research which is concentrated mainly on the following three areas: (1) European integration and the Czech Republic's role in it, (2) security policy - that is, fostering the Czech Republic's sensitivity to security challenges, and (3) developments in particular countries and regions of the world. Outcomes of the research are presented at round tables, seminar discussions and conferences, and published in scholarly journals and books. The IIR also organises educational programmes such as student internships and a doctoral programme and provides public library services. Recently, the institute has put particular stress on its high academic profile.

The IIR publishes three journals: the web-based *International Politics* (*Mezinárodní politika*), the printed *International Relations* (*Mezinárodní vztahy*) in Czech and *New Perspectives* in English. It also publishes books on international relations and foreign policy.

AMO

The Association for International Affairs (AMO, Asociace pro mezinárodní otázky) was officially established in 1997, although its first educational activities were already realised in 1995. It is an independent association whose goal is to promote education and research in the field of international relations to promote and improve mutual understanding and tolerance among people.

The AMO's activities are concentrated in three main domains. The first is research especially on Czech foreign policy, the EU, the Euro-Atlantic area, Eastern Europe, the Middle East and the Far East. The second core activity of the AMO is education. In this area the AMO organises various educational programmes mostly intended for secondary and university students. The third activity concerns international projects. Within this activity the AMO tries to communicate the Czech transformation experience from the period of the 1990s to support civil society development in countries which are presently undergoing transformation.

The AMO publishes the European Union External Affairs Review dedicated to all aspects and dimensions of the European Union's external relations.

PSSI

The Prague Security Studies Institute (PSSI) was founded in 2002. It declares itself to be a non-profit nongovernmental organisation, which focuses on security-related dimensions of governance in the Czech Republic and other post-communist states. The PSSI strives to contribute to the development of democratic institutions and values via educating policy practitioners in Central and Eastern Europe.

The PSSI's core activity is education and research in the field of security studies. Within this field, the PSSI runs several educational programmes. These programmes aim at fostering and improving education as well as conducting research on current security issues. In addition to academically oriented programmes, the PSSI focuses on public policy, identifying and analysing relevant foreign policy and security-related issues that affect the transatlantic community, and provides training on the construction of a free democratic society. This training comprises seminars and workshops led by policy practitioners and experts.

The PSSI publishes a newsletter which informs readers about current PSSI activities and events. It also publishes books as well as policy papers and briefs.

European Values

The advocacy think tank European Values (EH, Evropské hodnoty) is an association founded in 2005. Its main objective is to actively encourage the public to take an interest in common European values. For this organisation, European values are defined as personal freedom, human dignity, solidarity, active civil society, market economy, democracy and rule of law.

The EH devotes its attention to five areas: (1) European integration, (2) the transatlantic alliance and international relations, (3) the dynamic economy, (4) internal security and (5) accountable governance – the quality of democracy. These five themes are connected with the European aspect - that is, the EH considers them as the most important for the Czech Republic and its position in the European Union and the world.

The EH organises both public and non-public lectures, discussions, seminars and conferences as well as publishing various documents ranging from policy papers, and analyses to opinion articles in newspapers.

EUROPEUM

The advocacy think tank EUROPEUM, Institute for European Policy (EUROPEUM, Institut pro evropskou politiku) is an independent association founded in 1998. It focuses on European integration with the goal of contributing to democracy, security, freedom and solidarity and to the Czech Republic's active involvement in the EU.

There are six core themes that EUROPEUM is interested in. These issues cover internal as well as external EU affairs with regard to the Czech and Visegrad countries' visions vis-à-vis the EU and vice versa. Specifically EUROPEUM organises round tables, seminars and conferences and publishes a wide range of documents, such as policy briefs, policy papers, various articles and analyses. EUROPEUM also concentrates on research activities meant to formulate new visions, ideas and opinions on the EU and Czech policy making. An important part of EUROPEUM's work is also education.

EUROPEUM publishes the *V4 Revue – Visegrad Revue* and a newsletter in which it provides information on its activities.

Glopolis

The advocacy organisation Glopolis is an independent think tank, officially recognised as a public benefit company, founded in 2004. It focuses on global development and the Czech Republic and EU's responses to their challenges, with the goal of implementing smart and responsible economic, energy and food systems as well as improving political culture. Although it is independent, it is close to the standing of the Green Party.

Most of Glopolis' activities concern five core themes. The first is economy and finance. Within this theme Glopolis aims at the transformation of economic systems towards responsible production, consumption and effective distribution of human well-being. Climate and energy is the content of the second core theme. Glopolis strives for better and more effective management of energy policies that will help essential climate change adaptation. Food security is the third theme. Glopolis aims at changing current food systems towards sustainable productive capacities and functioning markets, especially in poor countries. The fourth theme concerns the future of the Czech Republic. The Czech Republic and its position in the EU is the fifth core theme.

Glopolis organises various meetings, consultations, conferences and workshops to present its analyses, proposals and visions, engaging not only with the public, but mainly with opinion, decision and policy makers. It also used to publish a *Globalization and Development Policy* newsletter.

Discursive networks

In order to map out interorganisational relations and the prominence of the studied think tanks, we look at their centrality within the network of ties. Since we suppose that their standing depends on their recognition by other network members, we measure their prominence by the number of incoming ties a particular organisation receives from others (so-called in-degree, see Hanneman and Riddle, 2005).

Figure 16.1 demonstrates that, with the exception of organisations in the support for democracy category, the think tanks we studied in the Czech Republic form discursive clusters; in other words, they connect most intensively with the organisations belonging to the same discourse, instead of reaching out to organisations in other discourses. Comparatively, in terms of the number of organisations with which they declare cooperation, the liberal-conservative discourse is most developed; it is numerous and dense. Konrad Adenauer Stiftung (KAS) forms the biggest node in this part of the network, since it largely provides funding for its members. Similarly to other civil society organisations in the Czech Republic (see for example Císař and Vráblíková, 2013), think tanks seem to follow money.

Figure 16.1: Network of Czech think tanks

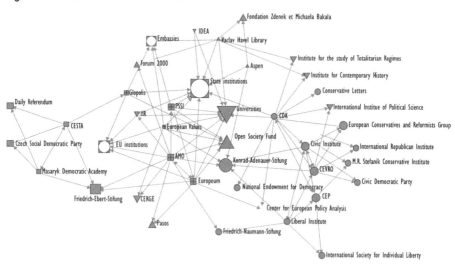

Note: A circle denotes liberal-conservative organisations; an upward triangle: support for democracy organisations; a square: social democratic organisations; a box: international and foreign policy organisations; a downward triangle: other research institutions; a circle in a box: public institutions.

In addition to the surveyed organisations, this discursive sub-network is formed by a number of other declared partners. Among those we find domestic organisations such a political party (ODS), a university-based institute (MPÚ, International Institute of Political Science affiliated to Masaryk University in Brno) as well as a number of international funding and political agencies. This network is densely connected not only domestically, but also transnationally; as mentioned earlier, these organisations have traditionally been supported from abroad through programmes of civil society assistance.

This help, together with the general discursive conditions conducive to liberal and conservative values and non-conducive to the values of the political left after 1989 (see Gjuričová et al, 2012; Císař, 2013) seem to account for the disproportionate robustness of different policy discourses. Expectedly, the least developed is the social democratic network. These organisations are positioned at the periphery of the network, declaring almost no cooperation with organisations outside of their small subfield. Compared to the liberal-conservative network, the declared relations of these organisations are neither numerous nor reciprocated.

In the network, two other policy discourses can be recognised, although the support for democracy organisations does not seem to form a cluster similar to the other categories. On the contrary, international and foreign policy think tanks form a very dense sub-network of organisations with the Open Society Fund, their funding source, as the very prominent actor.

All in all, state and other public institutions, universities and funding agencies are the most prominent actors in the network, since their decision-making power, financial and cultural capital make them targets of organisations from different camps. In fact, they are the only organisations linked to different discourses. In general, rather than establishing ties across the public sphere Czech think tanks create relatively separate discursive spaces independent of others. The liberal-conservative organisations are most numerous and have clearly developed the densest network of declared cooperation.

Conclusions

This chapter intended to map out the landscape of Czech think tanks. In order to do so, it was based on two types of literature: empirical studies of think tanks and discursive institutionalism. Drawing on think tank studies, we categorised Czech think tanks as academic, contractual, advocacy and party affiliated. Drawing on discursive institutionalism, we differentiated among four major policy discourses in the Czech Republic: liberal-conservative, social democratic, support for democracy, and international and foreign policy discourses.

According to our data, the liberal-conservative discourse is most inter-organisationally developed; these organisations declare cooperation with a number of partners. International and foreign policy-oriented organisations as well as think tanks belonging to the category of support for democracy follow suit; although they do not declare as many partners as liberal-conservative think tanks do, they are more resource-endowed. On average, they have more employees and bigger budgets than their liberal-conservative counterparts. Out of these three, international and foreign policy think tanks are the most resource endowed. Social democratic organisations present the exact opposite of the previous categories in all respects: probably owing to the general ideological and funding context, they are poorly resource endowed, not numerous and not densely connected.

In general, the paper demonstrates that think tanks orient themselves toward decision-making institutions and funding sources; in other words, they follow influence and money. Since they also seek cooperation with universities, they follow knowledge too. Seeking influence, money and knowledge constitute the basic trio of think tanks' functioning.

Acknowledgement

The chapter was written with the financial support of PRVOUK programme P17 'Sciences of Society, Politics, and Media under the Challenge of the Times'.

References

Carothers, T. (1999) *Aiding Democracy Abroad: The Learning Curve*, Washington, DC: Carnegie Endowment for International Peace.

Císař, O. (2013) 'Post-communism and social movements', in D. Snow, D. della Porta, B. Klandermans and D. McAdam (eds) *Encyclopedia of Social and Political Movements* (vol. 3), London: Blackwell, pp 994-99.

Císař, O. and Navrátil, J. (2015) 'Promoting competition or cooperation? The impact of EU funding on Czech advocacy organizations', *Democratization*: 22(3): 536-59.

Císař, O. and Vráblíková, K. (2013) 'Transnational activism of social movement organizations: the effect of European Union funding on local groups in the Czech Republic', *European Union Politics*, 14(1): 140-60.

Dvořáková, V. (2002) 'Civil society in the Czech Republic', in P. Kopecký and C. Mudde (eds) *Uncivil Society. Contentious Politics in Post-Communist Europe*, London and New York: Routledge, pp 134-56.

Gjuričová, A., Kopeček, M., Roubal, P., Suk, J. and Zahradníček, T. (2012) *Rozděleni minulostí. Vytváření politických identit v České republice po roce 1989* [Divided by the past. Formation of political identities in the Czech Republic after 1989], Praha: Ústav pro soudobé dějiny AV ČR.

Hanneman, R.A. and Riddle, M. (2005) *Introduction to Social Network Methods*, Riverside, CA: University of California.

McGann, J. (2009) *European Think Tanks: Regional and Trans-Atlantic Trends*, Philadelphia: Think Tank and Civil Society Program.

McGann, J. and Weaver, K. (eds) (2000) *Think Tanks and Civil Societies. Catalyst for Ideas and Action*, New Brunswick, NJ and London: Transaction Publishers.

Potůček, M. (2012) 'Discourses on social rights in the Czech Republic', in A. Evers and A. Guillemard (eds) *Social Policy and Citizenship: The Changing Landscape*, Oxford: Oxford University Press, pp 335-56.

Schmidt, V.A. (2010) 'Taking ideas and discourse seriously: explaining change through discursive institutionalism as the fourth "new institutionalism"', *European Political Science Review*, 2(1): 1-25.

Schmidt, V.A. and Radaelli, C.M. (2004) 'Policy change and discourse in Europe: conceptual and methodological issues', *West European Politics*, 27(2): 183-210.

Szacki, J. (1995) *Liberalism after Communism*, Budapest: Central University Press.

SEVENTEEN

Science policy implications for policy knowledge generated in academia

Tereza Stöckelová

The science policy framework of knowledge production

As in other European countries, the professional lives of academics in the Czech Republic are becoming increasingly tightly governed through research assessment (Strathern, 2000; Shore, 2008; Felt, 2009). Academics are expected to account for public funding in the form of auditable, rather strictly defined outputs. Having a rather direct bearing on the funding of universities and research institutions, as well as individual research teams, these expectations influence knowledge practices in a significant way. They shape research themes, research focus, and publication and communication strategies. The science policy reforms started after 2001 were declared to promote excellence, internationalisation and perhaps most significantly the societal utility of science (Stöckelová and Linková, 2009). As this chapter will show, the effects of the reform measures have however been rather ambiguous with regard to increasing the public and policy relevance of academic knowledge.

Key elements of Czech science policy

The reforms started in 2001 set up several new trends in Czech research. Firstly, while the public funding for research remains relatively limited (in 2012 it was about €1 billion, that is 0.7% of GDP), it is increasingly distributed on a competitive basis: through (individual and team) research grants from the Czech Science Foundation. Also, the institutional funding of research organisations is dependent on their annual research performance. Secondly, as corporate actors, represented by associations such as the Confederation of Industry of the Czech Republic and the Association of Innovative Entrepreneurship Czech Republic, have gained a stronger voice in the governmental Research and Development Council and thus in defining public research value and legitimacy, there has been a shift in emphasis from basic research to applied research and innovation. Also the priority is on science, technology and medicine, as compared to social sciences and humanities. Thirdly, the two trends crossbred in the introduction of a research assessment methodology in 2004.

Though the methodology has been changing slightly over the years, the fundamental classification of relevant research outputs remains stable. They are divided into two main groups: basic and applied research. While both categories have to be considered in relation to the production of policy-relevant knowledge – and this will be done later in the chapter – the outputs of applied research are of primary relevance. While in the technical and natural sciences, applied outputs primarily include patents, prototypes and other commercially valuable products, in the social sciences, according to this research assessment methodology, the core of the applied outputs is policy-relevant knowledge. The current methodology includes the following relevant types of outputs considered as policy-relevant knowledge: results reflected in legislation and norms; results reflected in directives and regulations of a non-legislative nature that are binding within the competence of the given provider; certified methodologies and practices; the heritage procedure;[1] specialised maps with expert content; software; and research reports containing classified information (Úřad vlády ČR, 2013, pp 35-41).

Effects of the research evaluation methodology and public funding schemes

In order to understand how the methodology shapes academic knowledge practices it is crucial to pay attention in detail to the definition of the respective outputs. All of the outputs have to be somehow adopted or approved by a public, regional or transnational administrative body (such as a ministry). Only these users are recognised as giving value to researchers' results from the point of view of the methodology. Moreover, the results have to be adopted rather mechanically by the public bodies: in the case of results reflected in legislation and norms or directives and regulations of a non-legislative nature, the contents of the result must be incorporated into a regulation or part of a regulation without changes to the core of the proposal, which do not include for example technical legislative adjustments (Úřad vlády ČR, 2013, p 42). Similarly, only those results integrated into strategic policy documents that were created as part of a given public tender are counted. A research report counts only if it contains classified information and cannot be published (Úřad vlády ČR, 2013, p 62). This narrow definition of recognised applied outputs has resulted in three types of reactions on the part of the Czech academic community in social sciences and humanities.

Firstly, some academics have concentrated exclusively on basic research. As it has become increasingly difficult to fit in with the narrow definition of the outputs, even those researchers who previously cultivated links to the policy-making process have started to reorient their efforts to basic research outputs. Even though they might previously have been collaborating with various non-academic users of their research results, these do not fit the current narrow evaluation framework (Stöckelová, 2009, 2012a).

---

[1] The evaluation methodology defines the heritage procedure as 'a procedure, which consists of a set of activities, and in some cases even materials and technologies, verified in the applied research of national and cultural identity, which leads to the preservation and improvement of objects of cultural heritage. The condition for the heritage procedure is proven practical testing' (Úřad vlády ČR, 2013, p 44).

Secondly, other academics have decided to adjust to the defined criteria and engage in projects funded by the Technology Agency of the Czech Republic. The agency was created in 2009 to replace research programmes run previously by individual ministries, where the funds were supposedly not distributed in very accountable ways.[2] Two funding streams are most relevant for knowledge related to policy making. In the first programme scheme, 'beta', selected public administrative bodies can announce tenders for research institutions. This concerns varied topics from technical infrastructure to environmental and social policies. Funding of at least 200 projects is envisioned for the period of 2012-16 with CZK640 million, roughly €24 million. The main objective of the second programme, 'omega', is 'to strengthen research activities in the area of applied social sciences and apply the results of these activities to increase the competitiveness of the Czech Republic, enhance the quality of life of its inhabitants and balance socio-economic development'.[3] The programme will run during 2012-17 with a budget of roughly €11 million; so far, 48 projects have been supported starting in 2012 and 82 projects starting in 2013.[4] In both cases the funding is conditioned by a promise on the part of the research teams to deliver applied outputs corresponding with the research assessment methodology and on the part of the selected public administration body (such as a ministry) to certify and use the outputs produced. Only those projects that deliver such expected outputs are considered successful, which appears to limit the funded projects in terms of potential critiques of dominant political and policy approaches.

Thirdly, academics continue to engage in applied and potentially policy-relevant research beyond the official assessment criteria as and when they can gather other types of profit from such activities. They may offer consultation work to private companies on a commercial basis, motivated by financial remuneration, as is often the case with economists (Stöckelová, 2012b, pp 22-23). They may collaborate with nongovernmental organisations (NGOs) or social movements concerned with issues of public and policy concern. This, for example, is the case of the controversy over the management of the National Park Šumava in which environmental NGOs and academic scientists, mostly biologists, form a robust and long-tern coalition (see Stöckelová, 2004); or the case of social sciences academics' collaboration with NGOs on furthering gender equality policies. Recently academics have been trying to influence policy making in the area of research and higher education policy through their civic activities such as

---

[2] It has to be noted however that some ministries (such as the Ministry of Industry and Trade or the Ministry of Health) were still able to keep a substantial budget for research, development and innovation (R&D&I) alongside that (compare www.vyzkum.cz/FrontClanek.aspx?idsekce =70456 8). Yet other ministries may also use EU Structural Funds to commission research.

[3] www.tacr.cz/index.php/en/programmes/omega-programme.html

[4] www.tacr.cz/dokums_raw/vysledky_1_verejne_souteze_program_omega_projekty_ doporucene_k_podpore_1.pdf; www.tacr.cz/sites/default/files/shared/omega/podporene. pdf.

the 'Science is Alive Forum!', formed by junior researchers primarily from the Academy of Sciences of the Czech Republic. Academics can also serve on public advisory bodies concerned with policy making, motivated by access to otherwise inaccessible data or symbolic and political capital related to their participation. And finally, they may be active in professional bodies concerned with policy making in a given area of their disciplinary interest (such as, for example, the Chamber of Tax Advisors of the Czech Republic).

Finally, academic knowledge influences policy making through an increasing number of students in the fields of social sciences and humanities who may work during or after their masters or doctoral studies at policy-relevant institutions (the public administration or NGOs). Currently in the Czech Republic this trend is strongly articulated in policy dealing with social exclusion and inclusion. The Agency for Social Inclusion, which is a department of the Office of the Government of the Czech Republic, employs a number of social science students and graduates as analysts, fieldworkers and contract researchers. Also, the NGO Platform for Social Housing[5] that led the 2013 campaign against the proposed law on social housing and contributed to some extent to stopping it is closely and personally linked to academia. The engagement of academics with the policy-making processes thus takes multiple forms, though often indirect and individualised (rather than formally mediated through academic institutions and official procedures).

Academics' engagement in research and higher education policy making

It is interesting to note that research and higher education policies themselves are definitely among the public policy areas of academics' special interest. Since the 1990s academics have strived to influence these policies in various ways: through official consultation and advisory bodies (for example the Council of Higher Education Institutions of the Czech Republic and the Council for Research, Development and Innovation) in which academic institutions have their representatives; through the public media and events in public spaces (including demonstrations); or by assuming executive posts such as Minister of Education (for example, in f 2012-13 two successive ministers were university professors of political science and biochemistry respectively).

The academic community has shared no common interests and goals in these efforts. On the contrary, it has often struggled within the academic field (Bourdieu, 1990) between disciplines or between different types of institutions (the Academy of Sciences of the Czech Republic versus universities; metropolitan versus regional universities), articulated in discussions and tensions over national research and higher education policies. As Linková and Stöckelová (2012) showed, the initial impulse for quantitative, 'impact factor'-based research evaluation was formulated and driven by a group of natural scientists who saw it as a tool to eliminate what

---

[5]   www.socialnibydleni.org

was, in their view, mediocre research being funded from the public budget. It was only later that they lost control over the evaluation methodology in favour of bureaucrats, industrial lobbyists and other groups of academics. Similarly, during the negotiating over cuts in the research, development and innovation budget in 2010, the Academy of Sciences of the Czech Republic and most of the university representatives stood in sharp opposition to each other (Linková and Stöckelová, 2012, p 627).

It is apparent that the forms and content of academics' engagement in policy-making processes depend on a number of factors including their discipline, institutional affiliation and position within the academic field. Engagement in public policy always lies in the intersection between expertise and (academic) politics. It can never be disinterested and purely rational as if the 'public good' were apolitical and the means of its attainment could be disconnected from its very articulation. It is in this context that the privileged position of one academic discipline in public policy formation, which will be discussed in the following section, may raise questions.

Economists as agents of public policy formation

The vocabulary of efficiency, financial accountability and New Public Management are, unsurprisingly, dominant in the Czech political and policy discourse in many areas. While the multiple contexts and repercussions of this situation are discussed in other chapters of this volume, from the point of view of the present chapter it is important in relation to the priority it gives to economists as experts in most of the policy areas. The instrumental knowledge and the impression of quantitative objectivity (Porter, 1995) economists are able and willing to deliver makes them favourite counterparts of politicians and policy makers. This part of the chapter will therefore focus specifically on academic economists and their engagement in the policy process.

The establishment of economic expertise in the policy space after 1989

It is no coincidence that many key figures of the 1989 change of the political regime (for example, Václav Klaus, Valter Komárek, Vladimír Dlouhý) and the first three Prime Ministers of the Czech Republic after the split of the country in 1992 (Václav Klaus, 1993-97; Tošovský, 1997-98; Miloš Zeman, 1998-2002) were economists, and a number of them even academic economists in their former professions. It could be argued that the primacy of the 'economic transformation' agenda (in terms of both time and significance) apparently called for economists to occupy the leading executive position in the country. However, the primacy cannot be taken for granted; it was installed and coevolved with the shaping of the new political elite after 1989. It was a result of the specific framing of the public and political space.

As Bockman and Eyal persuasively show, this framing process started long before 1989. In their study 'Eastern Europe as a Laboratory for Economic Knowledge: The Transnational Roots of Neoliberalism' they argue that the countries of the former Soviet bloc, including Czechoslovakia, were an economic laboratory for Western, especially American economists since the 1960s. In particular, the then minority libertarians fighting Keynesianism were interested in demonstrating the perverted effects of economic planning on Central and Eastern Europe. The authors trace rather close ties between economists from the two 'blocs', through personal meetings as well as specialised literature, to argue that economic liberalism did not come to the Czech Republic from outside after 1989 but had been growing domestically. According to them, it was precisely this network of economists engaged with Western monetarist theory before 1989 (for example, Václav Klaus, Tomáš Ježek, Dušan Tříska, Karel Dyba and Josef Zieleniec) that successfully occupied executive positions in the 1990s and started to draft and enact policy reforms, such as the voucher privatisation[6] of state-owned enterprises (Bockman and Eyal, 2002). Since the beginning of the 1990s, academic economists (and political scientists) have also been substantially though indirectly influencing policy making through their daily presence in the public media, thus forming and framing the political discourse in which policy debates take place.

Another factor related to the robust economic framing of public and social policy in the Czech Republic has surely been the move mentioned earlier to New Public Management in European countries in general (Pollitt and Bouckaert, 2004; for Central and Eastern European countries see Veselý, 2013). With this approach, economic expertise ceases being one among others and the efficiency and financial perspective become superior across policy areas. The 2008 economic crisis only strengthened this framing, with the emphasis on the supposed necessity for cuts and austerity measures. In this context, the National Economic Council was appointed as the primary, most influential and most publicly visible expert body of the government.

The case of the National Economic Council

The National Economic Council (NERV) was first formed in January 2009 by Prime Minister Mirek Topolánek and later renewed in 2010 by the subsequent Prime Minister Petr Nečas; its operation was suspended in August 2013 in relation to the resignation of the Nečas government and the instalment of the caretaker government. NERV's key mission was to analyse the 2008 economic crisis and its effects on the country and suggest possible measures for restarting economic growth. Importantly, however, by advising on public finances it also took a stance on policy reforms in areas as diverse as pensions, healthcare and education.

It consisted of business and academic economists. In 2010 seven out of its 15 members declared academic engagement at public or private higher education

---

[6] See https://ec.europa.eu/europeaid/privatisation-state-owned-enterprises-czech-republic_en

institutions or public research institutes, and the council claimed intensive collaboration in the wider academic sphere (the Institute of Economic Studies of the Faculty of Social Sciences, Charles University; Center for Economic Research and Graduate Education – Economics Institute (CERGE-EI); and the University of Economics, Prague). While Chapter Four of this volume discusses NERV's operation and the substance of the expertise produced, the academic linkage is the focus of this chapter. How did it play out in the operation and presentation of the body? What motivated academics to participate in such a body and how did they link their academic and council work?

It was repeatedly stressed in the official presentation of the council that 'NERV members are not state employees; activities within NERV are realized in their free time'.[7] Direct financial remuneration thus could not have motivated academics' participation since they were not paid for their work in NERV. Also, as discussed in the first part of the chapter, work for NERV would not be counted as part of academic work in the current research evaluation framework. The published reports do not correspond to any outputs recognised by the methodology. Participation in the body thus could not be translated in any straightforward way into officially recognised academic capital of the involved economists.

In spite of that, the members of the council linked their academic and expert engagements in various ways. At least one of the council's reports claimed to be supported by university institutional funding and academic research grants, and university students apparently participated in its preparation, sometimes as sole authors.[8] Another NERV report was launched on the campus of one of the universities, where some of the council's members teach.[9] These linkages may be interpreted as an attempt to convey to NERV, and the proposed governmental policies, the image of academic rigour and independence and to 'depoliticise' the debate on the policies and future developments of the country in the name of 'unavoidable necessities' and 'global competitiveness' (Stöckelová, 2010). On the other hand, what NERV membership might have offered to academics was the public visibility and symbolic capital stemming from participation. All the public media outputs of the council members were placed on the council's governmental website: by 20 January 2014 there were 1069 articles placed on the website. It also can be presumed that the council members gained access to restricted or otherwise barely accessible data which they could also use for their academic work.

Although the 2011-12 governmental policies were hugely unpopular and provoked some of the biggest union and civil society protests in the country since 1989, participation in this governmental body did not seem to compromise the

---

[7]   www.vlada.cz/en/ppov/ekonomicka-rada/national-economic-council-51372

[8]   www.vlada.cz/assets/ppov/ekonomicka-rada/aktualne/Ramec_strategie_
      konkurenceschopnosti.pdf

[9]   www.vlada.cz/assets/ppov/ekonomicka-rada/dokumenty/NERV-Boj-proti-korupci--
      sbornik.pdf

academics. This is an effect of the high prestige scientists and university teachers maintain with the Czech public (Public Opinion Research Centre, 2013) and the status of expertise as supposedly value free and the opposite of politics, characteristic of the Czech political and public culture (Konopásek et al, 2008).

Academics in professional bodies

The other type of engagement of academic economists with public policies worth attention is their participation in professional bodies. The case of a university economics department where I carried out qualitative research on educational and academic practices between 2010 and 2012 may be a paradigm for this.[10] Influencing public policies takes place in less spectacular but still rather significant ways.

The department concerned is oriented towards professional (not academic) education and the majority of its alumni aim to 'practise'. A significant part of department members also have double (and sometimes triple) employment: they teach at the university while working as practitioners in private companies and also serve as executive members of various professional bodies active in the field of study. In the latter capacity they participated significantly in the post-1989 transformations and changes in the field. Through collaboration with the Ministry of Finance, they participated in formulation of legislation (involving the translation but also 'domestication' of European legislation), and through professional bodies they continue to establish 'best practices' and influence the interpretation of the legislation in practice. They serve as editors and publish in journals of the professional bodies, which are widely disseminated in the community.

Most of the department members perceive their double or even triple engagements as mutually advantageous and even unavoidable for quality teaching in the professional study programme. They draw upon their direct experience from 'practice' in their teaching and they draw upon academic expertise in their professional practice. The latter is also often claimed as a reason for a successful professional to 'return' to the department for doctoral studies later in their professional life. The multiple engagements of teaching staff, researchers and doctoral students are perceived in the department as a sign of success and competence, while confinement to academic work only is rather looked down upon. Last but not least, the professional work of academics also compensates for the relatively low university salaries of teaching staff (which may often be below the average salary in the country) (Dvořáčková et al, 2014).

From the point of view of research assessment on the national and institutional level, the situation is however more complicated. The expert and applied work of the department members stays mostly unrecognised by the official methodology (for both 'basic' and 'applied' research outputs). Articles in professional non-

---

[10] Giving the name of the university would compromise the anonymity promised to research participants.

academic journals do not get recognition in the assessment relevant for university and department funding or for the academic promotion of individuals (to professorship or associated professorship). Expert consultation work does not get recognition either, unless it fits the strictly defined categories of output for applied research (as described in the first section of the chapter).

This creates frustration and indignation at the department in relation to the assessment rules. Researchers question the very notion of 'impact' in this light. 'I lead a research group supported by the Czech Science Foundation and after two years we did not manage to produce an article in an impact factor journal[11] but we managed to change a paragraph in a law. So tell me what an impact is?', asks a senior researcher in an interview with us. And her colleague adds:

> The notion of impact often seems comic to me as most of the [impact factor] articles have zero influence on the professional public because the majority of people do not read them at all. If I publish an article in a professional journal with an edition size of 5000 issues and it is distributed to all professionals, then I appreciate the impact of such an article on the professional public as higher [than an 'impact factor' journal article]. But I get completely a nothing for it for my qualification [in terms of academic career].

Given its emphasis on the application and impact of research, it is paradoxical that the current Czech science policy not only does not support, but also effectively discourages the existing expert involvement of academics in policy making and professional practice. The efforts of science policy to make involvement with practice accountable in the form of strictly defined quantitative indicators may apparently result in creating a hiatus between the previously interwoven academic and professional parts of academics' work and identity.

Conclusion

The involvement of academics in Czech politics and policy making has a strong history. Not only were the first two presidents of the independent Czechoslovak Republic, Tomáš Garrigue Masaryk and Edvard Beneš, former university professors of sociology, but an important part of the new political elite constituted after 1989 was also formed in academic circles, in this case predominantly economists from the Economic Institute of the Czechoslovak Academy of Sciences. Until today, scientists and university teachers continue to have high prestige among the Czech public. There are however a number of recent trends that complicate the picture.

---

[11] The category of impact factor journals includes those indexed in the Web of Science database of the Thomson Reuters Company, see http://wokinfo.com/essays/impact-factor; http://wokinfo.com/products_tools/analytical/jcr. Articles published in these journals are highly valued by the research evaluation methodology (Úřad vlády ČR, 2013, pp 34-36).

Firstly, with the rise of New Public Management approaches in policy making, economics has sometimes become the sole expertise sought after and utilised by policy makers in an increasing number of policy areas. Secondly, the current form of research assessment employing a narrow definition of recognised 'applied outputs' requires expertise to respond to very concrete expectations of policy makers not only regarding the form of knowledge but also its contents (the outputs have to be 'certified' by public administrations or adopted in legal and conceptual documents without changes). Both of these trends raise concerns regarding the plurality of expertise reaching the policy-making processes. Thirdly, from the point of view of academics, the current research assessment methodology often puts them in the uncomfortable position of 'choosing', especially in social sciences and humanities, between an orientation on 'academic impact' (manifested through impact factor publications and citations) and social impacts (including applied research, policy-relevant expertise and also various engagements in the public debate and public media) (see Čada et al, 2009). This forced choice may interfere with the existing policy-relevant engagements of academics. Moreover, an orientation on social impact may, in some disciplines, weaken the chances for the academic careers of individuals.

The pressing current issues related to academics' involvement in policy making today are, on the one hand, the diversity of expertise invited into the policy process, and on the other, the possibility to embed the production of policy-relevant expertise in individual academic careers.

Acknowledgement

This chapter has been completed with institutional support RVO: 68378025.

References

Bockman, J. and Eyal, G. (2002) 'Eastern Europe as a laboratory for economic knowledge: the transnational roots of neoliberalism', *American Journal of Sociology*, 108(2): 310-52.

Bourdieu, P. (1990) *Homo Academicus*, Cambridge: Polity Press.

Čada, K., Ptáčková, K. and Stöckelová, T. (2009) *Věda a nevládní organizace: zkušenosti, možnosti, inspirace* [Science and nongovernmental organisations: experience, potentials, inspirations], Praha: Zelený kruh.

Dvořáčková, J., Pabian, P., Smith, S. Stöckelová, T., Šima, K. and Virtová, T. (2014) *Politika a každodennost na českých vysokých školách: Etnografické pohledy na vzdělávání a výzkum* [Politics and everyday life at Czech universities: ethnographic views on education and research], Praha: Sociologické nakladatelství.

Felt, U. (ed) (2009) *Knowing and Living in Academic Research: Convergence and Heterogeneity in Research Cultures in the European Context*, Prague: Institute of Sociology of the Academy of Sciences of the Czech Republic.

Konopásek, Z., Stöckelová, T. and Zamykalová, L. (2008) 'Making pure science and pure politics: On the expertise of bypass and the bypass of expertise', *Science, Technology & Human Values*, 33(4): 529-53.

Linková, M. and Stöckelová, T. (2012) 'Public accountability and the politicization of science: the peculiar journey of Czech research assessment', *Science & Public Policy*, 39(5): 618-29.

Pollitt, Ch. and Bouckaert, G. (2004) *Public Management Reform: A Comparative Analysis*, Oxford: Oxford University Press.

Porter, T. (1995) *Trust in Numbers: The Pursuit of Objectivity in Science and Public Life*, Princeton, NJ: Princeton University Press.

Public Opinion Research Centre (2013) *Prestiž povolání – červen 2013* [Prestige of professions – June 2013], Prague: Institute of Sociology, Public Opinion Research Centre.

Shore, C. (2008) 'Audit culture and illiberal governance: universities and the politics of accountability', *Anthropological Theory*, 8(3): 278-98.

Stöckelová, T. (2004) 'Příroda v národním parku Šumava: Příroda nezačíná tam, kde končí lidská intervence' [Nature in the Sumava national park: nature does not start where human intervention stops], *Vesmír* 83: 86-95.

Stöckelová, T. (2009) 'Politická a morální ekonomie vědy' [Political and moral economy of science], in T. Stöckelová (ed) *Akademické poznávání, vykazování a podnikání: Etnografie měnící se české vědy* [Czech science in flux: ethnography of making, administering and enterprising knowledge in the academy], Praha: Sociologické nakladatelství, pp 38-72.

Stöckelová, T. (2010) 'Spočítej a panuj: De/politika kalkulace' [Count and rule: de/politics of calculation], in P. Barša (ed) *Kritika depolitizovaného rozumu: Úvahy (nejen) o nové normalizaci* [Critique of depoliticised reason: reflections (not only) on new neonormalisation], Všeň: Grimmus, pp 61-76.

Stöckelová, T. (2012a) 'Immutable mobiles derailed: STS and the epistemic geopolitics of research assessment', *Science, Technology & Human Values*, 37(2): 286-311.

Stöckelová, T. (2012b) *Nebezpečné známosti: O vztahu sociálních věd a společnosti.* [Dangerous liaisons: on the relation of social sciences and society], Praha: Sociologické nakladatelství.

Stöckelová, T. and Linková, M. (2009) 'Uvedení k výzkumu: Problematizace vědy a genderu' [Introduction: problematisation of science and gender], in T. Stöckelová (ed) *Akademické poznávání, vykazování a podnikání: Etnografie měnící se české vědy* [Czech science in flux: ethnography of making, administering and enterprising knowledge in the academy], Praha: Sociologické nakladatelství, pp 12-36.

Strathern, M. (ed) (2000) *Audit Cultures: Anthropological Studies in Accountability, Ethics and the Academy*, London: Routledge.

Úřad vlády ČR (2013) *Metodika hodnocení výsledků výzkumných organizací a hodnocení výsledků ukončených programů (platná pro léta 2013 až 2015)* [Methodology of evaluation of research organisations and evaluation of finished programmes (valid for the years 2013-2015)] [online]. Available from www.vyzkum.cz/FrontClanek.aspx?idsekce=695512

Veselý, A. (2013) 'Accountability in Central and Eastern Europe: concept and reality', *International Review of Administrative Sciences*, 79(2): 310-30.

EIGHTEEN

Czech public policy programmes and policy analysis education

Arnošt Veselý, Eva M. Hejzlarová, Anna Zelinková

Introduction

The first public policy schools and programmes were created in the US in the late 1960s (Ellwood and Smolensky, 2001). Gradually, policy programmes have expanded to most other developed countries (Geva-May, 2006; Geva-May and Maslove, 2007; Cloete and Rabie, 2008; Fritzen, 2008; Geva-May et al, 2008; Wu et al, 2012; Reiter and Töller, 2013). After the fall of communism in 1989, policy programmes began to be created in Central European countries such as Hungary, the Czech Republic and Slovakia. However, with the exception of analyses of public administration programmes in Central and Eastern European countries (Hajnal and Jenei, 2008; Hajnal, 2003, 2014; Hajnal and Jenei, 2008), virtually nothing is known about such programmes in these countries.

This chapter seeks to describe Czech public policy programmes and the role of policy analysis in them. To do so, we focus upon programmes carried out in universities and accredited by the Ministry of Education, Youth and Sport that provides bachelor's, master's or doctoral degrees. This is because there is no evidence on non-academic programmes, and to the best of our knowledge professional and continuing education courses on public policy/policy analysis are virtually non-existent in the Czech Republic.

First, we briefly describe the higher education system in the Czech Republic and provide an overview of the programmes that are related to public policy. Second, we focus upon public policy programmes in the Czech Republic. Then we describe the role and nature of the policy analysis courses offered in these programmes. This is followed by a quantitative analysis of diploma theses in the three most important programmes, which sheds light on their orientation. We conclude with some more general remarks on the idiosyncratic features of public policy education in the country.

The chapter is based mostly on analysis of the publicly available list of study programmes accredited by the Ministry of Education, Youth and Sport, an internet search, email correspondence with public policy and policy analysis instructors, syllabus analyses as well as a quantitative analysis of master's theses in the three main public policy programmes.

Study programmes and study fields in Czech higher education

Higher education in the Czech Republic is governed by Act Number 111 (the so-called Higher Education Act). Higher education consists of three cycles: bachelor's degree programmes (usually three years); master's degree programmes (usually two years) and doctoral degree programmes (lasting three or four years). Higher education institutions are public, state and private. Under the Higher Education Act, they are classified as universities (24 public, two state and three private), which offer study programmes at all three levels of higher education, and non-universities (two public and 43 private), which offer mainly bachelor's programmes but may also provide master's programmes. Higher education institutions differ greatly in size and number of students. The public ones usually have many more students than the private ones, which often have a very small number of students in given programmes. With a few exceptions, when compared to private higher education institutions, public universities are more research-focused and usually are also more prestigious.

Students have to follow a study plan within an accredited degree programme. Accreditation is awarded by the Ministry of Education, Youth and Sports on the basis of a recommendation by the Accreditation Commission (*Akreditační komise*). The creation and provision of study programmes is one of the recognised academic rights and freedoms of higher education institutions, so their number and prevailing orientation have changed over the years. The number and content of programmes depend on the particular institution. In practice, accreditation depends more on the assumed quality of the guarantor of the programme (who must be a professor or associate professor in a given field) and the qualifications of other instructors than on the proposed curriculum. In fact, the actual curriculum is almost exclusively in the hands of the guarantor of the programme and is not determined by any external standards. As a result, programmes with the same labels might differ substantially in their content and scope. According to the law, there are three modes of study: on-site, distance or a combination of these (combined studies).

Study programmes at higher education institutions cover almost all areas of science and the arts. Study programmes (*studijní programy*) are usually subdivided into 'fields' of study (*studijní obory*).[1] Sometimes, a field of study might have the same name as a study programme. At other times, however, a broad range of heterogeneous fields of study is included under one study programme. Students usually identify themselves more with the field of study than the general study programme under which it falls, especially if the field of study is highly specialised and distinctive.[2] Sometimes the connection between the field of study and the study programme under which it is included in the accreditation is hard to find.

---

[1] Sometimes studijní obory is also translated as 'branches of study'.

[2] Students speak of the field of study and often are even unaware that formally it falls under a more general study programme.

Consequently, for any analysis of education it is important to analyse particular fields of study, and not study programmes. However, information about the programme under which the field of study falls can reveal the institutional and disciplinary roots of the concrete field. This is because particular study programmes are usually organised only by one higher education unit (usually a department). As a result, a field of study often shares the same instructors, some courses and usually also the same paradigms and methodological approaches with other fields of study under the programme. For instance, the 'Public Policy and Human Resources' field of study at Masaryk University in Brno falls under the study programme 'Social Policy and Social Work'. This is organised by the Department of Social Policy and Social Work. Thus it might be correctly assumed that while the field of study is generally autonomous and distinct from others, it is embedded in social policy and social work paradigms and methodology.

Public policy programmes in the Czech Republic

Now we can focus more specifically on the programmes and study fields related to public policy. Our analysis is based on the official list of all study programmes and fields of study accredited by the Ministry of Education, Youth and Sport, and published on the ministry's website. The list contains 9144 fields of study in total. We have searched particularly for fields of study that have 'policy' in their titles. Because fields of study with a strong public policy focus might be hidden under different labels (for example, political science or economics), we also used an internet search to identify other relevant study programmes and fields of study. We have, of course, also utilised our familiarity with the current situation in the field and personal contacts we have, because all the relevant information is not always publicly available.

Table 18.1 shows the results of our search of accredited study programmes and fields of study. It reveals that there are only three institutions that provide accredited fields of study with a primary focus on public policy: the Faculty of Social Sciences, Charles University in Prague; the Faculty of Social Studies, Masaryk University in Brno; and the Anglo-American University in Prague. The first two are public universities (and also the two largest in the Czech Republic) and the third is a private university.

First and foremost, public policy can be studied at the Faculty of Social Sciences, Charles University in Prague. As described in Chapter Two, the Department of Public and Social Policy was established in 1993 under the newly founded Institute of Sociological Studies.[3] The first students in the two-year master's programme Public and Social Policy (in Czech) were enrolled in the 1993/94 academic year.

Gradually, other types of Public and Social Policy fields of study have been accredited and opened by the department. In the 1996/97 academic year, the

---

3   To date, the institute has two departments: the Department of Public and Social Policy and the Department of Sociology.

doctoral programme on Public and Social Policy (in Czech) was established, which enabled more research in the field. In the 2007/08 academic year, a master's study programme for professionals (in the so-called 'combined study' mode, see above) was introduced. The English version of the master's field of study in Public and Social Policy was accredited in 2013/14 (the English version of the doctoral programme was accredited one year earlier).

Currently, the Department of Public and Social Policy thus organises fields of study in public policy in different modes (both on-site and combined), languages (both Czech and English) and levels (master's and doctoral).[4] The curricula in these fields of study differ somewhat (that is, it is a bit different in the on-site versus combined and the Czech versus English fields of study). The overall instructional philosophy is, however, essentially the same. All the fields of study include courses in public policy, policy analysis, public administration, social policy and public economics. In addition, students are supposed to specialise in one or several policy domains (particularly health, education or social policy). In the on-site mode, one semester of practice in the public sector is compulsory.

All of these fields of study are officially subsumed under the study programme of Sociology. From the very beginning, many if not most students have come to the fields of study organised by the Department of Public and Social Policy (DPSP) after graduation from the bachelor's field of study in Sociology and Social Policy organised jointly by the Department of Sociology and the DPSP. As a result, most students in these fields of study have a strong background in sociology. However, the bachelor's programme in Sociology and Social Policy is not exclusively sociological. It contains compulsory courses in public policy and other fields such as economics. The distinctiveness of the 'Prague public policy school' is, however, its strong methodological focus.

Moreover, students from other fields and universities are also admitted to the master's and doctoral fields of study organised by the DPSP. While the DPSP fields of study are strongly embedded in sociology, links to other fields have also been gradually established. After a long period of preparation, a new bachelor's field of study called 'Political Science and Public Policy' was accredited in 2014 and offered from 2015. This will be organised jointly by the DPSP and the Institute of Political Sciences at the same faculty. For the first time, it will formally come under the 'Political Science' study programme.

Second, since 2009 public policy has been studied at Masaryk University in the Faculty of Social Studies. Public policy can be studied in the 'Public Policy and Human Resources' field of the study programme 'Social Policy and Social Work'. This field of study is organised on different levels (bachelor's and master's). The bachelor's level must be a double subject course of study (in combination with another study field: Social Work, Psychology, Sociology, Political Science, Media Studies and Journalism, Social Anthropology, Gender Studies, Environmental

---

[4]   There are currently about 500 graduates of the masters field of study in Public and Social Policy (both on-site and combined) and 40 graduates of the doctoral programme.

Studies, European Studies, Education or Economic Policy). The bachelor's level is on-site and taught in Czech. The master's level is organised in different modes (both on-site and combined) and languages (both Czech and English). Students who study on-site can choose among three specialisations: 'labour market, employment policy and human resources', 'personnel management and organisational development' and 'social policy'. Students in the combined mode can study the specialisations 'personnel management and organisational development' or 'social policy'. There is not an accredited study programme at the doctoral level on public policy, only 'Social Policy and Social Work' (in both Czech and English, both on-site mode and combined). The fields of study in public policy are organised by the Department of Social Policy and Social Work. There is also an Institute of Public Policy and Social Work which is a part of the faculty and focuses on research.

Third, public policy is studied at the Anglo-American University. The Anglo-American University was founded in 1990 and is the oldest private university in the Czech Republic. The master's in 'Public Policy' study programme (and field of study) at the School of Humanities and Social Sciences has been accredited since 2007.[5] This field of study is organised in on-site mode and taught only in English. There are far fewer graduates compared with the public universities.

Though there are only three institutions providing study programmes/fields directly focusing upon public policy, there are many other programmes that involve some courses in public policy or policy analysis.[6] These can be divided into two groups. The first consists of 'general' disciplines closely related to public policy that involve some elements of public policy in their curricula, such as political science, public administration, social policy and social work, regional studies or (public) economics (see Table 18.2). The second group consists of fields of study focusing upon particular policy domains such as economic policy, EU policy or education policy (see Table 18.3). Usually, however, the policy aspect is not in the label of the field of study, even though it is clearly present in the curriculum (for example in domains such as gender, civic sector studies or the environment).

---

[5] The master's study programme (and study field) Applied Sociology and Public Policy is accredited at the Anglo-American University, but it was not available in 2014.

[6] Interestingly, there is also an example of an institution with public policy in its title that does not provide any programmes or even courses related to public policy (that is, the School of Public Policies in Opava).

Table 18.1: Accredited public policy programmes

HE institution	Faculty/ Schools	Study programme	Study field	Type of study (bachelor's, master's, PhD)	Language	Selected subjects (courses) related to policy analysis
Charles University in Prague	Faculty of Social Sciences	Sociology	Sociology and Social Policy	Bachelor's	CZ	Introduction to Public Policy Problems of Czech Society and Public Policy Social Problems
			Public and Social Policy	Master's, PhD	CZ, EN	Public Policy Methods of Policy Analysis Policy Design Methods Political Aspects of Policy-making The Policy-Making Process Regulatory Impact Assessment: Theory and Practice Managerial Methods in Public and Social Policy Evaluation of Public Policies and Programmes
		Political Science	Political Science and Public Policy	Bachelor's	CZ	Introduction to Public Policy Political Aspects of Policy-making
Masaryk University	Faculty of Social Studies	Social Policy and Social Work	Public Policy and Human Resources	Bachelor's	CZ	Introduction to Public Policy European Union Public Policy Public Policy Analysis
		Social Policy and Social Work	Public Policy and Human Resources	Master's	CZ, EN	Implementation of Public Programmes Decision-making in Public Policy
Anglo-American University	School of Humanities and Social Sciences	Applied Sociology and Public Policy	Applied Sociology and Public Policy	Master's	EN	Study programme was not opened in 2014.
		Public Policy	Public Policy	Master's	EN	Public Policy in Knowledge Based Societies Public Policy as a Discipline Comparative European Public Policies Methods of Policy Analysis and Design

Source: Authors. Based upon the list of programmes and fields accredited by the Ministry of Education, Youth and Sport and the web pages of the given institutions.

Table 18.2: Other study programmes and fields of study related to public policy and policy analysis (public administration, political science, social policy and social work and public economics)

HE institution	Faculty/ Schools	Study programme	Study field	Type of study (bachelor's, master's, PhD)	Language	Selected subjects (courses) related to policy analysis
Charles University in Prague	Faculty of Arts	Social Policy and Social Work	Social Work	Bachelor's, master's	CZ	Introduction to Public Policy and Public Administration I, II
Masaryk University	Faculty of Social Studies	Social Policy and Social Work	Social Policy and Social Work	Bachelor's, master's, PhD	CZ (PhD – CZ + EN)	Public Policy Analysis Decision Making in Public Policy Implementation of Social Policy
		Social Policy and Social Work	Social Work	Bachelor's, master's	CZ	Public Policy Analysis Decision Making in Public Policy Public Policy Psychology and Public Policy
		Political Science	Political Science	Master's	CZ	Policy Analysis Decision Making in Public Policy Public Policy Analysis
	Faculty of Economics and Administration	Economic Policy and Administration	Public Economics and Administration	Master's	CZ, EN	Governance and Public Policy European Union Public Policy Public Policy - Design and Implementation Public and Social Policy
		Economic Policy and Administration	Public Economics	Master's	CZ, EN	Governance and Public Policy
		Economic Policy and Administration	Public Administration (L'Administration publique)	Master's	CZ	Public Policy - Design and Implementation
University of West Bohemia	Faculty of Philosophy and Arts	Political Science	Political Science	Bachelor's, master's, PhD	CZ	Policy Analysis
Silesian University in Opava	Faculty of Public Policies in Opava	Social Policy and Social Work	Public Administration and Regional Policy	Bachelor's	CZ	Public Policy

continued

Table 18.2 continued

HE institution	Faculty/ Schools	Study programme	Study field	Type of study (bachelor's, master's, PhD)	Language	Selected subjects (courses) related to policy analysis
		Social Policy and Social Work	Public Administration and Social Policy	Master's	CZ	Public Policy
Technical University of Ostrava	Faculty of Economics	Economic Policy and Administration	Public Economics and Administration	Bachelor's, master's, PhD	CZ	Public Policy
University of Economics, Prague				Master's	CZ	Public Policy
University of Finance and Administration	Faculty of Social Studies	Social Policy and Social Work	Social Policy	Bachelor's	CZ	Public Policies
		Political Science	Political Science	Bachelor's	CZ	Decision Making and Policy Analysis

Table 18.3: Other study programmes and study fields related to public policy and policy analysis (various policy domains)

HE Institution	Faculty/ Schools	Study programme	Study field	Type of study (bachelor's, master's, PhD)	Language	Selected subjects (courses) related to policy analysis
Charles University in Prague	Faculty of Humanities	Humanities	Civil Sector Studies	Master's PhD	CZ, EN	Public Policy
Masaryk University	Faculty of Social Studies	Environmental Humanities	Environmental Studies	Bachelor's, master's	CZ	Public Policy Analysis
		Sociology	Gender Studies	Bachelor's	CZ	Public Policy Analysis
	Faculty of Economics and Administration	Economic Policy and Administration	Non-profit-making Organisation Economy and Management	Bachelor's	CZ	Public Policy and Creation of Programmes
University of International and Public Relations	-	International and Public Relations	European Studies and Public Administration	Master's	CZ	Analysis and Decision Making in Policy

Policy analysis courses

In this section we will focus on policy analysis courses. Not surprisingly, the most courses on policy analysis can be found at the Faculty of Social Sciences in Prague. From the introduction of the master's programme in Public and Social Policy in 1993, policy analysis has played a key role in the curriculum. Two connected courses have been taught: *Metody analýzy politiky* (Methods of Policy Analysis) followed by *Metody tvorby politik* (Methods of Policy Design). Though the substance of these two courses has changed over time, the basic features have existed for more than two decades. The courses have been based upon students' group work concentrated on a *real* policy problem and have always had a substantial time allocation (four instruction hours per week per course). The choice of problem has been, and still is, for the students to make, though the instructors help the students to find and formulate problems that are manageable within the one-year period. Instead of teaching (and testing) academic knowledge, these two courses have always been based upon the *application* of various policy analysis methods and heuristics when analysing policy problems.

At Masaryk University two courses are taught in the Faculty of Social Studies which are more professional than academic: *Analýza veřejných politik* and *Analýza policy*. The course *Analýza veřejných politik* (Public Policy Analysis) is organised by the Department of Environmental Studies and the course content is focused on environmental issues. Students working in groups apply theoretical knowledge to concrete cases in environmental policy (for example, the promotion of renewable energy sources, discussion of the Šumava National Park or breaking mining limits). The course *Analýza policy* (Policy Analysis) is organised by the Department of Political Science. The teaching methods include lectures by policy experts, consultations with policy experts, student team work and student presentations. The student teams are required to submit a 10-page policy paper focused on a particular policy area. The policy papers are evaluated by the respective experts.

Most other courses at the Czech universities are more theoretically (academically) oriented, for example at Masaryk University the courses in the Faculty of Social Studies, *Tvorba a implementace veřejné politiky* (Public Policy), and in the Faculty of Economics and Administration, *Tvorba a implementace veřejné politiky a hodnocení veřejných projektů* (Public Policy – Design and Implementation), and *Veřejná politika a tvorba programů* (Policy and Creation of Programmes) (see Table 18.4).

Table 18.4: Policy analysis courses in the Czech Republic curriculum

HE institution	Faculty/ Schools	Study field	Course name	Instructor(s)	Basic literature
Charles University in Prague	Faculty of Social Sciences	Public and Social Policy (on-site, in Czech)	Metody analýzy politik (Methods of Policy Analysis)	Martin Nekola	Veselý, A., Nekola, M. (2007) *Analýza a tvorba veřejných politik. Principy, metody a praxe* Nekola, M, Geissler, H., Mouralová, M. (2011) *Současné metodologické otázky veřejné politiky*
			Metody tvorby politik (Methods of Policy Design)	Arnošt Veselý	Bardach, E. (2000) *A Practical Guide for Policy Analysis* Dunn, W.N. (2003) *Public Policy Analysis: An Introduction* Nekola, M, Geissler, H., Mouralová, M. (2011) *Současné metodologické otázky veřejné politiky* Patton, C.V., Sawicki, D.S. (1993) *Basic Methods of Policy Analysis and Planning* Potůček, M. (2006) *Manuál prognostických metod* Veselý, A., Nekola, M. (2007) *Analýza a tvorba veřejných politik. Principy, metody a praxe* Veselý, A. (2009) *Vymezení a strukturace problému ve veřejné politice*
		Public and Social Policy (combined, in Czech)	Metody analýzy a tvorby politik I (Methods of Policy Analysis and Policy Design I)	Arnošt Veselý	Veselý, A., Nekola, M. (2007) *Analýza a tvorba veřejných politik: přístupy, metody a praxe* Veselý, A. (2009) *Vymezení a strukturace problému ve veřejné politice*
			Metody analýzy a tvorby politik II (Methods of Policy Analysis and Policy Design II)	Arnošt Veselý	Veselý, A., Nekola, M. (2007) *Analýza a tvorba veřejných politik: přístupy, metody a praxe*
		Public and Social Policy (on-site, in English)	Policy Analysis	Arnošt Veselý, Martin Nekola	Bardach, E. (2000) *A Practical Guide for Policy Analysis* Dunn, W.N. (2003) *Public Policy Analysis: An Introduction* Patton, C.V., Sawicki, D.S. (1993) *Basic Methods of Policy Analysis and Planning*

HE institution	Faculty/ Schools	Study field	Course name	Instructor(s)	Basic literature
Masaryk University	Faculty of Social Studies	Public Policy and Human Resources Social Policy and Social Work Social work Political Science Environmental Studies Gender Studies	Analýza veřejných politik (Public Policy Analysis)	Karel Čada, Bohuslav Binka	Veselý, A., Nekola, M. (2007) *Analýza a tvorba veřejných politik: přístupy, metody a praxe* Lijphart, A. (2012) *Patterns of Democracy* Howlett, M., Ramesh, M. (2003) *Studying Public Policy: Policy Cycles and Policy Subsystems* Kingdon, J. (1995) *Agendas, Alternatives and Public Policies* Moran, M., Rein, M., Goodin, R.E. (2006) *The Oxford Handbook of Public Policy* Lenschow, A. (2010) *Environmental Policy: Contending Dynamics of Policy Change* Hill, M.J. (2005) *The Public Policy Process* Mankiw, G.N. (2009) *Principles of Economy* Bovens, M., 't Hart, P., Kuipers, S. (2006) *The Politics of Policy Evaluation* Dryzek, J. (2010) *Foundation and Frontiers of Deliberative Governance*
		Political Science	Analýza policy (Policy Analysis)	Stanislav Balík, Ondřej Krutílek	Peters, G., Pierre, J. (2006) *Handbook of Public Policy* McGann, J.G., Johnson, E.C. (2005) *Comparative Think Tanks, Politics, and Public Policy* Fiala, P., Schubert, K. (2000) *Moderní analýza politiky* John, P. (1998) *Analysing Public Policy*
		Social Work	Tvorba a implementace veřejné politiky (Public Policy)	Jiří Winkler, Imrich Vašečka	Winkler, J. (2002) *Implementace institucionální hledisko analýzy veřejných programů* Winkler, J. (2007) *Teorie rozhodování a dynamika sociální politiky* Parsons, W. (1995) *Public Policy* Hill, M. (1997) *The Policy Process in the Modern State* Howlett, M., Ramesh, M. (2003) *Studying Public Policy: Policy Cycles and Policy Subsystems*

continued

Table 18.4 continued

HE institution	Faculty/ Schools	Study field	Course name	Instructor(s)	Basic literature
	Faculty of Economics and Administration	Public Economics and Administration Public Administration	Tvorba a implementace veřejné politiky a hodnocení veřejných projektů (Public Policy – Design and Implementation)	Alain Darre, Ivan Malý, Marek Pavlík, Jiří Špalek	Potůček, M. (2005) *Veřejná politika* Jabłoński, A. (2006) *Politický marketing: úvod do teorie a praxe* Potůček, M. (1997) *Nejen trh: role trhu, státu a občanského sektoru v proměnách české společnosti* Malý, I., Pavlík, M. (2007) *Tvorba a realizace programů veřejné politiky*
		Non-profit Organization Economy and Management	Veřejná politika a tvorba programů (Public Policy and Creation of Programmes)	Marek Pavlík	Malý, I., Pavlík, M. (2007) *Tvorba a realizace programů veřejné politiky* Malý, I., Pavlík, M. (2004) *Tvorba a implementace veřejné politiky*
University of West Bohemia			Policy analýza (Policy Analysis)	Petr Jurek	Veselý, A., Nekola, M. (2007) *Analýza a tvorba veřejných politik: přístupy, metody a praxe* Potůček, M. (2005) *Veřejná politika* Fiala, P., Schubert, K. (2000) *Moderní analýza politiky* Patton, C.V., Sawicki, D.S. (1993) *Basic Methods of Policy Analysis and Planning* Weimer, D.L., Vining, A.R. (2005) *Policy Analysis: Concepts and Practice* Hogwood, B., Gunn, L. (1984) *Policy Analysis for the Real World* Dunn, W.N. (2003) *Public Policy Analysis: An Introduction*
Anglo-American University	School of Humanities and Social Sciences	Public Policy	Methods of Policy Analysis and Design		Bardach, E. (2000) *A Practical Guide for Policy Analysis* Dunn, W.N. (2003) *Public Policy Analysis: An Introduction* Lazareviciute, I. (2003) *Manual for Trainers: How to Be a Better Policy Advisor?* Patton, C.V., Sawicki, D.S. (1993) *Basic Methods of Policy Analysis and Planning* Proctor, T. (2005) *Creative Problem Solving for Managers: Developing Skills for Decision Making and Innovation* Staroňová, K. (2002) *Techniques and Methods of Policy Analysis* Start, D., Holand, I. (2004) *Tools for Policy Impact: A Handbook for Researchers* Weimer, D.L., Vining, A.R. (2005) *Policy Analysis: Concepts and Practice*

continued

Table 18.4 continued

HE institution	Faculty/ Schools	Study field	Course name	Instructor(s)	Basic literature
University of International and Public Relations	-	European Studies and Public Administration	Rozhodování a analýza v politice (Analysis and Decision Making in Policy)	Pavel Prokop	Prokop, V. (2012) *Rozhodování a analýza v politice* Fiala, P., Schubert, K. (2000) *Moderní analýza politiky*

Analysis shows that there are two Czech textbooks mainly used. The first is *Analýza a tvorba veřejných politik: Principy, metody a praxe* (Methods of Policy Analysis and Design) edited by Arnošt Veselý and Martin Nekola. This book was originally inspired by Dunn's *Public Policy Analysis*, and is similarly structured. Nevertheless, it is greatly modified for the Czech context and also supplemented by other chapters and methods not covered in Dunn's book. The second book is *Moderní analýza politiky: uvedení do teorií a metod policy analysis* (Modern Policy Analysis: Introduction to the Theories and Methods of Policy Analysis) by Petr Fiala and Klaus Schubert (2000). As for the foreign books, the most widely used is Dunn's *Public Policy Analysis*. It is evident that the instructors prefer 'classical' policy analysis textbooks over interpretive ones.

Diploma theses in public policy programmes

In order to describe various facets of policy analysis instruction, we decided to focus on the outputs of the educational process – diploma theses. The analysis of diploma theses contained in this chapter is a part of a broader research project (Mouralová et al, 2015). In this section, we first discuss methodological issues, second we give brief portraits of the diploma theses and at the end we describe the findings of the analysis.

Methodology

Three study programmes at three universities were included in our research: Public and Social Policy at Charles University in Prague, Public Policy and Human Resources at Masaryk University in Brno and Public Policy at the Anglo-American University in Prague. These programmes were selected as they explicitly refer to public policy - that is, the words 'public policy' occur in their names (either in Czech or in English), which also refers to policy analysis issues. We analysed diploma theses defended in full-time master's study programmes. The focus on full-time courses was driven by both practical reasons (the longer history and the possibility of comparison) and symbolic reasons (it is the 'basic' form of study programme and therefore the 'norm'). We analysed 109 diploma theses defended under these programmes in 2011-13 (61 from the Public and Social Policy programme, 43 from the Public Policy and Human Resources programme and five from the Public Policy Programme[7]).

We used content analysis (for example, Babbie, 2012) to examine the diploma theses and focused on the following aspects: the specific policy area (that is, educational policy, family policy and so on), theoretical background, methodological background and embedding in local and/or international sources. In the theses, we focused on the declarative dimension (for example, whether the student declared using the Advocacy Coalition Framework [ACF]) and did not examine to what extent the student applied the declared theories or methods. There could be cases where declared theories or methods are not actually applied; on the other hand, some theses could use concepts implicitly without naming them specifically. Nevertheless, the declaration is a crucial dimension from the perspective of identity and follows the social constructivist point of view. It relates to the way the programme is constituted, what language is used, what is supposed to be included in the thesis and what it is supposed to look like.

Diploma theses for the Public and Social Policy programme (Charles University, Prague)

Diploma theses in the Public and Social Policy programme are the most numerous and diverse, covering a wide range of subject areas. The diversity of topics is at least partly due to the custom of not restricting students in their interests. The personal preferences of students are supported and instructors do not push them to choose from a list of suggested topics. Nevertheless, strong representation of several subject areas, such as social policy, family policy, educational policy and healthcare policy, shows that the effect of instructors' specialisations is also obvious.

A typical diploma thesis has approximately 90 pages and does not pay much attention to the general methodological background of the thesis; on the other hand, it refers to a wide variety of data, methods and heuristics which evoke an applied policy analysis approach rather than a 'pure' policy research approach. The majority of students performed their own surveys, which mostly consisted of semi-structured interviews. However, expert interviews were also a widespread research strategy, used as a source of information rather than as data for analysis. The methodology chapter is on average rather short and constitutes about 6% of the whole text. There are big differences between individual theses in the features of the chapter.

A typical diploma thesis refers to various theories and concepts, both general ones focusing on policy processes and mechanisms and specific ones related to a concrete subject field (family, education, labour market, security and so on). With regard to the number, we can question to what extent the theories are

---

[7] Due to the low number of diploma theses in the programme and also due to their diversity, we were not able to subject them to analysis.

really used and to what extent their role is rather ornamental. The references of a typical diploma thesis consist of 85 units of literature or other sources, and 15 of these are in foreign languages.

Public Policy and Human Resources programme (Masaryk University, Brno)

Diploma theses in the Public Policy and Human Resources programme are more homogenous; they show many common features and strict management of diploma theses is apparent. The topics of the diploma theses are more specific than those at Charles University and the thematic scope of the school is also narrower. The majority of the theses focus on labour market and social policy, but education is also covered.

The narrower scope of the diploma theses is also evident in a lower average (and median) number of pages (72) and fewer sources (50 resources per thesis, including around seven foreign). Apart from that, the theoretical background is not robust; most of the theses (37 of the 43 analysed) have a background only in specific theories relating to the subject field (for example the family or labour market). In a large number of theses, the chapter serves more to introduce the reader to the context of the topic rather than presenting theories in order to explain certain phenomena.[8] Only a small number of diploma theses (the remaining six) contain a combination of a specific theory with a general theory. The general theories presented in the theses do not indicate any preferred theoretical stream. The diversity implies instead that the use of theory is influenced by students' individual preferences.[9]

A strong emphasis on methodology is typical for the diploma theses of the Public Policy and Human Resources programme. The methodology chapter typically has six pages and on average makes up more than 8% of the thesis. The methodology chapters are very similar across theses: considerable attention is paid to the general methodological background of the thesis; data and their collection are described afterwards. On the other hand, almost no attention is paid to the methods of data analysis and there are very few specific methods of policy research and policy analysis. A typical diploma thesis consists of 50 units of literature or other sources and seven of these are in foreign languages.

---

[8] Significantly, the title of the chapter is 'The context and legitimacy of the problem' – the theoretical chapter should provide the reader with some explanation of the phenomena but is more often focused on explaining why the subject is considered a problem. A similar phenomenon was typical for the Public and Social Policy programme in the early years 1997 to 1999. The situation cannot be explained simply by a possible delay but also by requirements for the diploma theses.

[9] Namely, in the theoretical background the concepts of welfare state, New Public Management, rational choice, policy cycle and one of the policy process theories (ACF) are mentioned.

Findings

We can conclude that there are differences in the pedagogical approaches and study outputs of the Public and Social Policy programme and the Public Policy and Human Resources programme (the thematic range of the diploma theses, the background in literature and so on). At the same time, there are also similarities. The most remarkable is that in both programmes methodological issues are more important in the diploma theses than the theoretical background. In both programmes, methodology is a regular part of the thesis: in the Public and Social Policy programme, the stress is put on the variety of applied methods and data used and resembles applied policy analysis, in the Public Policy and Human Resources programme the focus is put on the general methodological background and data collection. There are some gaps, such as data analysis, which is typically lacking, but as a whole, students writing diploma theses are less ignorant about methodological issues than theoretical ones (see earlier). This may be influenced by the specific development of public policy as an academic discipline in the Czech Republic, where it is much easier to adopt methodologies from related disciplines than to transfer the knowledge of theories and theoretical thinking as such.

Conclusions

The landscape of public policy instruction in the Czech Republic is highly fragmented. A policy aspect is present in many study programmes and fields of study; however, public policy is systematically studied only in three institutions. Our analysis has revealed that with one exception (the Anglo-American University), there is no study *programme* on public policy, policy studies or policy analysis. Thus the *field* of study of public policy always falls under a study programme related to a different discipline. As mentioned previously, in Brno it is Social Policy and Social Work and in the Faculty of Social Sciences in Prague it is Sociology. This suggests that in the Czech Republic public policy is still not recognised as an autonomous discipline, and it still 'stands on the shoulders of other disciplines'. This is not, however, exceptional. Public policy has different roots and different connections in different countries. In Germany, a country which has a lot in common with the Czech Republic in terms of history and culture, public policy and policy analysis is predominantly associated with political science (Reiter and Töller, 2013).

Because of the hegemonic position of the Faculty of Social Sciences in the provision of public policy instruction in the country, the field is heavily influenced by the 'Prague school's' orientation. Most importantly, this is visible in the emphasis upon methodology (mostly, though not exclusively, quantitative) and strong sociological affiliation. From the very beginning the Prague school has also had a strong professional orientation – that is, it seeks to provide students with skills useful in practice rather than (only) academic knowledge. It is difficult, however, to generalise about public policy instruction in the Czech Republic.

There are similarities (such as a strong emphasis upon methodology both in Prague and Brno), but also differences and not all other institutions follow the Prague school orientation. Moreover, the Prague school is reorienting itself with the new generation of scholars who place more emphasis upon post-positivist methodology.

Acknowledgement

The chapter was written with the financial support of PRVOUK programme P17 'Sciences of Society, Politics, and Media under the Challenge of the Times'.

References

Babbie, E. (2012) *The Practice of Social Research*, Wadsworth: Cengage Learning.

Bardach, E. (2000) *A Practical Guide for Policy Analysis*, New York: Chatham House Publishers.

Bovens, M., 't Hart, P. and Kuipers, S. (2006) 'The politics of policy evaluation', in M. Moran, M. Rein and R.E. Goodin (eds) *Handbook of Public Policy*, Oxford: Oxford University Press, pp 319-35.

Cloete, F. and Rabie, B. (2008) 'Overview of tertiary public policy training in South Africa', *Africanus* 38(2): 55-76.

Dryzek, J. (2010) *Foundation and Frontiers of Deliberative Governance*, Oxford: Oxford University Press.

Dunn, W.N. (2003) *Public Policy Analysis: An Introduction* (3rd edn), Upper Saddle River, NJ: Prentice Hall.

Ellwood, J.W. and Smolensky, E. (2001) 'Public policy schools', in N.J. Smelser and P.B. Baltes (ed) *International Encyclopedia of the Social and Behavioral Sciences*, Amsterdam: Elsevier, pp 12563-67.

Fiala, P. and Schubert, K. (2000) *Moderní analýza politiky* [Modern policy analysis: introduction to the theories and methods of policy analysis]. Brno: Barrister & Principal.

Fritzen, S.A. (2008) 'Public policy education goes global: a multi-dimensional challenge', *Journal of Policy Analysis and Management*, 27(1): 205-14.

Geva-May, I. (2006) 'Canadian public policy analysis and public policy programs: a comparative perspective', *Journal of Public Affairs Education*, 12: 232-46.

Geva-May, I. and Maslove, A. (2007) 'In between trends: developments of policy analysis instruction in Canada, the United States, and the European Union', in L. Dobuzinskis, M. Howlett and D. Laycock (eds) *Policy Analysis in Canada: The State of the Art*, Toronto: Toronto University Press, pp 185-217.

Geva-May, I., Nasi, G., Turrini, A. and Scott, C. (2008) 'MPP programs emerging around the world 19', *Journal of Policy Analysis and Management*, 27(1): 187-204.

Hajnal, G. (2003) 'Diversity and convergence: a quantitative analysis of European public administration education programs', *Journal of Public Affairs Education*, 9(4): 245-58.

Hajnal, G. (2014) 'Public administration education in Europe: continuity or reorientation?', *Teaching Public Administration*, 11: 1-20.

Hajnal, G. and Jenei, G. (2008) 'The study of public management in Hungary: management and the transition to democratic Rechtsstaat', in W. Kickert (ed) *The Study of Public Management in Europe and the US: A Comparative Analysis of National Distinctiveness*, London: Routledge, pp 209-32.

Hill, M.J. (1997) *The Policy Process in the Modern State* (3rd edn), London: Prentice Hall.

Hill, M.J. (2005) *The Public Policy Process* (4th edn), New York: Pearson Longman.

Hogwood, B. and Gunn, L. (1984) *Policy Analysis for the Real World*, London: Oxford University Press.

Howlett, M. and Ramesh, M. (2003) *Studying Public Policy: Policy Cycles and Policy Subsystems* (2nd edn), Oxford: Oxford University Press.

Jabłoński, A. (2006) *Politický marketing: Úvod do teorie a praxe* [Political marketing: introduction to theory and practice] (1st edn), Brno: Barrister & Principal.

John, P. (1998) *Analysing Public Policy*, London: Continuum.

Kingdon, J. (1995) *Agendas, Alternatives and Public Policies*, New York: Longman.

Lazareviciute, I. (2003) *Manual for Trainers: How to Be a Better Policy Advisor?* [online]. Bratislava: NISPAcee. Available from www.nispa.sk/_portal/publication_details.php?p_id=71&style=eb

Lenschow, A. (2010) 'Environmental policy: contending dynamics of policy change', in H. Wallace, M.A. Pollack and A.R. Young (eds) *Policy-Making in the European Union*, Oxford: Oxford University Press.

Lijphart, A. (2012) *Patterns of Democracy* (2nd edn), New Haven, CT: Yale University Press.

Malý, I. and Pavlík, M. (2007) *Tvorba a realizace programů veřejné politiky* [Design and implementation of public policy programmes], Brno: Masarykova univerzita.

McGann, J.G. and Johnson, E.C. (2005) *Comparative Think Tanks, Politics, and Public Policy*, Northampton, MA: Edward Elgar.

Malý, I. and Pavlík, M. (2004) *Tvorba a implementace veřejné politiky* [Design and implementation of public policy], Brno: Masarykova Univerzita.

Mankiw, G.N. (2009) *Principles of Economy*, Mason: Cangave Learning.

Moran, M., Rein, M. and Goodin, R.E. (eds) (2006) *The Oxford Handbook of Public Policy*, New York: Oxford University Press.

Mouralová, M., Hejzlarová, E., Holík, R., Hubáček, M. and Jeřábková, A. (2015) 'What do diploma theses unveil about academic public policy in the Czech Republic?', *Central European Journal of Public Policy*, 9(2): 164-89.

Nekola, M., Geissler, H. and Mouralová, M. (eds) (2011) *Současné metodologické otázky veřejné politiky* [Current methodological issues in public policy], Praha: Karolinum.

Parsons, W. (1995) *Public Policy*, London: Prentice Hall.

Patton, C.V. and Sawicki, D.S. (1993) *Basic Methods of Policy Analysis and Planning* (2nd edn), Upper Saddle River, NJ: Prentice Hall.

Peters, G., Pierre, J. (eds) (2006) *Handbook of Public Policy*, Thousand Oaks, CA: Sage Publications.

Potůček, M. (ed) (1997) *Nejen trh: role trhu, státu a občanského sektoru v proměnách české společnosti* [Not only market: the role of the market, government, and the civic sector in the development of public policy], Praha: Sociologické nakladatelství.

Potůček, M. (ed) (2005) *Veřejná politika* [Public policy], Praha: Sociologické nakladatelství.

Potůček, M. (ed) (2006) *Manuál prognostických metod* [Handbook of future study methods], Praha: Sociologické nakladatelství.

Proctor, T. (2005) *Creative Problem Solving for Managers: Developing Skills for Decision Making and Innovation*, New York: Routledge.

Prokop, V. (2012) *Rozhodování a analýza v politice* [Decision-making and analysis in public policy], Praha: Grada.

Reiter, R. and Töller, A.E. (2013) 'The role of policy analysis in teaching political science at German universities', in S. Blum and K. Schubert (eds) *Policy Analysis in Germany*, Bristol: Policy Press, pp 265-77.

Staroňová, K. (2002) 'Techniques and methods of policy analysis', in M. Grochowski and M. Ben-Gera (eds) *Manual for Advisor: How to Be a Better Policy Advisor?*, Bratislava: NISPAcee, pp 89-126.

Start, D. and Holand, I. (2004) *Tools for Policy Impact: A Handbook for Researchers* [online], London: Overseas Development Institute. Available from www.odi.org.uk/RAPID/Publications/Documents/Tools_handbook_final_web.pdf

Veselý, A. (2009) *Vymezení a strukturace problému ve veřejné politice* [Public policy problems delimitation and structuring], Praha: Karolinum.

Veselý, A. and Nekola, M. (eds) (2007) *Analýza a tvorba veřejných politik: Principy, metody a praxe* [Methods of policy analysis and design], Praha: Sociologické nakladatelství.

Weimer, D.L. and Vining, A.R. (2005) *Policy Analysis: Concepts and Practice* (4th edn), Upper Saddle River, NJ: Prentice Hall.

Winkler, J. (2002) *Implementace: Institucionální hledisko analýzy veřejných programů* [Implementation: public programmes from the institutional perspective], Brno: Masarykova univerzita.

Winkler, J. (2007) *Teorie rozhodování a dynamika sociální politiky* [Theories of decision-making and dynamics of social policy], Brno: Masarykova univerzita, Fakulta sociálních studií.

Wu, X., Lai, A.Y.H. and Choi, D.L. (2012) 'Teaching public policy in East Asia: aspirations, potentials and challenges', *Journal of Comparative Policy Analysis*, 14(5): 376-90.

NINETEEN

Conclusions: the present and future of policy analysis in the Czech Republic

Arnošt Veselý, Martin Nekola

Introduction

In this concluding chapter we put together findings from all the chapters of the book and elaborate on them. This is meant not as a mere summary of particular chapters but as a 'meta-view' on the findings. We, as editors, did our best to include authors from different backgrounds, worldviews and experience. We have provided them with the basic idea, purpose and structure of the book. They were, however, completely free in developing and elaborating their personal views.

Honestly, we were a bit afraid of getting too many disconnected and contradicting ideas with no general message. To our relief and surprise, that did not happen. Though there are certainly points where different authors disagree, we were astonished by several recurrent topics and ideas that different authors felt were important to stress. For instance, without any prompting from us, several authors chose to either describe or analyse the government's National Economic Council (NERV). This is not because it is the dominant and most powerful advisory institution. Instead, for many, it is the quintessence of the prevailing mode of policy advice, emphasising efficiency, economic rationality and a technocratic approach.

Another recurring topic was the traditional *personal* link between academia and policy. Several authors stressed that many influential politicians, and almost all historically important figures, had their origins in academia. From T.G. Masaryk, E. Beneš, A. Rašín to V. Havel, V. Klaus, M. Zeman and P. Fiala. All of them were or have been established scholars and/or intellectuals who decided to enter politics at a particular point in their lives.

This concluding chapter is structured as follows. First, we summarise the distinctive features of Czech policy analysis as compared to other countries, especially Germany (as a European country with a distinctive policy analysis tradition and our neighbour) and the United States (as a cradle of traditional policy analysis). Second, we discuss how different factors, including the polity and institutions, might explain the idiosyncrasies of Czech policy analysis. We conclude with possible prospects of policy analysis in the country.

The distinctive nature of Czech policy analysis

Similar to other countries, interest in public policy in general and policy analysis in particular can be related to the political and socioeconomic conditions and development of social sciences in the second half of the twentieth century. However, in contrast to Germany or the United States, demand for science-based policy-related knowledge led to the establishment of different types of policy research represented mainly by centralised sectoral research institutes (*resortní ústavy*). Despite the fact that, like Western Europe, the application of scientific knowledge through methods of rational management and planning had failed, the communist regime's nature and the dominance of the Marxist-Leninist ideology of scientific communism did not allow for full development of theoretical thinking about public policy processes and reasons for policy advice failure. Contemporary public policy and policy analysis thus 'inherited' a traditional emphasis on methodology (especially the positivist paradigm cultivated within sociology) and rather weak theoretical thinking relying on import of theories from Anglo-Saxon or (to a lesser extent) continental policy studies (Germany, France, the Netherlands). This may be one of the reasons for the rather low integration of policy analysis into the mainstream of Czech political science. While policy analysis is an integral part of political science in Germany or even its central approach (Fiala and Schubert, 2000, p 34), it is on its periphery in the Czech Republic.

A distinctive feature of traditional policy analysis in the US is a close connection between the discipline and practice in the process of problem solving given by its orientation towards specific clients' needs and inputs. Moreover, not only have public sector clients demanded policy analysis, but also a variety of both for-profit and non-profit organisations from the private sector have either developed or contracted policy advisory capacities. Contrary to the US situation, Czech policy analysis seems to be firmly anchored within the academic sphere, having less overlap with policy-making practice and policy advocacy/lobbying. In the Czech Republic, a specific intersection of both traditions in a sort of *personal union* of academics, policy bureaucrats and politicians can be observed. Quite a lot of (former) academics are involved in the policy-making process as middle and top level officials in the central public administration or even as political leaders. The most prominent and influential political figures have often been professors or academics (for example Masaryk, Klaus, Zeman, Fiala).

This, however, does not mean that there is an easy and direct link between power and knowledge. The public administration appears to be a hegemonic 'client' that demands policy advice, however is not able to formulate its needs and policy ideas clearly and precisely enough, or to utilise available policy-relevant knowledge, both internal and external. Indeed, this is not only the problem on the side of the public administration. But it shows that even a personal interconnection between academia and policy/politics does not guarantee a truly functioning link between knowledge and practice. Despite relatively high mobility across sectors – from academia to policy making (see Chapter Three), from academia to nongovernmental organisations (NGOs) (see Chapter Fourteen) and from academia to public administration (see Chapters Seven and Eight) – utilisation of policy analysis is rather a matter of sporadic islets of positive deviation, be they within particular public administration organisations, policy sectors or policy tasks (for example, formulation, implementation and evaluation).

The issue of (non)utilisation is also related to the location of policy analysis capacities, which are situated mostly in academia and sectoral research institutes. The public administration's dominance on the demand side of the policy advice system is not balanced out by demand from other client-stakeholders such as advocacy groups, trade unions, political parties and NGOs. These stakeholders do not dispose of sufficient internal analytical capacities and at the same time do not create demand for external policy advice (see for example Chapter Thirteen on political parties which invest significantly more resources into PR than to developing analytical capacities or external policy advice).

Another significant feature of contemporary policy work is the emphasis on 'rational expert advice' on both the demand and supply sides. Policy advice is seen as a transfer of (objective) scientific knowledge for instrumental use in government. As such, it is reserved for experts/professionals, especially economists, who in searching for optimal problem solutions utilise a 'toolkit' comprising microeconomic analysis, quantitative methods (such as cost-utility analyses) and organisational analysis. Critical discussion based upon argumentation is not really supported and valued; instead a strong bias towards economics can be identified (see Chapter Seventeen) and the tradition of open and explicit treatment of values in policy work is missing (see Chapter Thirteen). Interpretive policy analysis has slowly been established in the Czech Republic as a legitimate academic approach for investigation of the role of values and ideas in political processes. However, its use in practice in deliberation and management of controversies not solvable by traditional rational approaches is very rare in the Czech Republic (see Chapter Four).

We can conclude that policy work has many forms in the Czech Republic and these differ to a greater or lesser extent not only from the textbook approaches known from the US but also from policy analysis as practised in Germany or other European countries. A lack of analytical capacities leading among other things to less specialisation of those who are supposed to actually do policy analysis is also distinctive. We can see this in the 'policy patchwork' of local mayors (Chapter Nine), in the multitasking of policy bureaucrats (Chapters Seven and Eight), in 'policy minimalism' towards the EU (Chapter Six) and in the 're-using' of expertise by NGOs (Chapter Fourteen).

System of governance as a determinant of Czech policy analysis

The particular nature of Czech policy analysis and its difference from policy analysis in other countries can be at least partially explained by a different system of governance (polity).

Policy analysis, as it is known from the textbooks of Bardach (2000) or Weimer and Vining (1999), is typically an American phenomenon. It has been developed in a particular political context (polity) which is quite different from the European one. Typical US governance features relevant for policy analysis include decentralisation, an emphasis on individual responsibility, subsidiarity, pluralism and a market orientation. There has always been great reluctance towards large-scale intervention from the central government, and too much regulation. As a result, policy making has usually been more incremental and piecemeal than has been the case in Continental Europe.

In sharp contrast to the US, as several authors throughout the book stressed, the Czech Republic has a long tradition of proactive public policies. For a long time, it has been taken for granted that the state is responsible for solving social problems. Because the governance structure has always been substantially more centralised than in the US, it has been mainly the central government, embodied in ministries and other parts of the central administration, that has been expected to come up with the solutions. For a long time, too *little* intervention has been considered a bigger problem than too much regulation. Consequently, most areas of life have been subject to detailed laws and regulation. The proactive role of the state has also been advocated by the country's 'founding fathers' – T.G. Masaryk and E. Beneš.

Of course, the general picture of the context previously portrayed is a bit of a simplification. There have been countertrends, especially during recent decades. The Czech Republic governance system has been highly decentralised during the last decade, almost to the point that in some policy domains (such as education) the central government has been nearly 'hollowed out' in terms of direct executive power. Similarly, there has been much debate on overregulation and especially immediately after 1989 there has been strong opposition to large-scale policy making, which has been seen by many as a continuation of communist planning.

Nevertheless, a high level of overall regulation and an expectation that the central government should take responsibility in solving public problems is deeply embedded in the Czech culture and this has not changed despite strong right–wing rhetoric after 1989. As a result, even small-scale problems are naturally connected to bigger ones.

We can take kindergartens as an example. While kindergartens are founded by municipalities which are fully responsible for their availability, quality and financing (with the exception of personnel costs), they are subject to country-wide laws and other provisions set mostly by the Ministry of Education, Youth and Sport, Ministry of Health and other central public administration institutions. These determine, for instance, hygienic norms, maximum of children per class and so on. Similarly, although kindergartens are generally free in how they structure their curricula, they have to adhere to so-called Framework Educational Programmes set by the ministry, and controlled by Czech school inspection. Thus, although they are in many respects highly autonomous and are *not* governed by the ministry, both kindergartens and municipalities have to work in a highly regulated environment which substantially constrains their space for decision making. As a result, any discussion on how to improve kindergartens in any municipality inevitably leads to discussion on how to improve *higher order* public policies (that is at the national level). Any policy analysis is, by definition, determined by the tools the decision makers have at their disposal for designing the policy. If at the local level these tools are limited, or are perceived as limited, then there is a natural tendency to look for solutions at a higher level, such as the region or the whole country.[1]

Given this polity context, it is not surprising that in the Czech Republic there has been a long tradition of looking for general, systemic and holistic solutions to public problems, rather than small and incremental ones. For many people, small-scale policies do not seem to solve the substance of the problem, and they try to look for more systematic and large-scale solutions to the perceived problem. Consequently, the genre of small-scale, 'quick and dirty' policy analysis is rather rare. This is also the reason why the original intention to import US policy analysis as it is depicted in the main textbooks was not successful and US textbooks had to be substantially adapted to the Czech context (see Chapters One and Eighteen).

Thus instead of small-scale analyses, the Czech Republic is rather a country of 'strategies' (*strategie*), 'conceptions' (*koncepce*), 'plans' (*plán*), 'action plans' (*akční plány*) and 'implementation plans' (*implementační plány*). These documents usually try to describe the problem or topic (such as 'sustainable development', 'research and development', 'care for children from socially disadvantaged environments') in a holistic way. Such documents are usually less analytical (in terms of data and depth of information analysis), and more normative and prescriptive. There is also often a surplus of them. For instance, currently there are about 19 'strategic' documents covering the topic of education which are registered by the Ministry of Education, Youth and Sports. These strategies set goals and main policy directions, but often rather generally and vaguely. As a result, many, if not most of these strategies are toothless and have little impact upon real policy making.

The overproduction of 'strategies' of various sorts at the expense of small-scale policy analyses is clearly the result of a traditionally centralised and proactive government, looking for systemic solutions. The strategic documents are mostly about structuring problems, setting goals and formulating solutions. Other policy analysis 'steps' (see Bardach, 2000) fit less with the 'strategic genre'. For instance, at the macro and general level, it is difficult to formulate *variants* of policies. At

---

[1]   This is further encouraged by the huge fragmentation of municipalities. They are often very small and do not have capacities for analysis (see Chapter Nine).

the macro level, different policy tools (for example financing and legislation) are supposed to work together rather than alone. Similarly, evaluation of options is possible only when you face several concrete and mutually exclusive (disjunctive) possibilities. This is not the case for strategic documents, in which usually rather broad 'strategic directions' are set. This polity context influences the frequency of policy-related activities (see Chapters Seven and Eight).

The future of Czech policy analysis

In Chapter Two, Potůček argues that Czech public policy has entered early adulthood. It has grown and matured, and has gradually changed from both within and outside. As for external influences, Czech policy analysis has inevitably changed with changes in the polity (governance) and institutions. For instance, substantial decentralisation implemented in the last decade led to changes in competencies and policy capacities. As in other countries, policy making was considered to be an 'official preserve' of the state where outsiders were able to propose advice on public policies, but only authoritative leaders were entitled to decide and to 'make policy' (Colebatch et al, 2010, p 19). Nowadays, a much broader array of actors call for taking part in policy making, and among other things base this claim upon their expertise and knowledge. The central government is no longer the only provider and user of policy analysis. Multiple actors lead to multiple sources of expertise and analysis – often conflicting.

Consequently, more and more people (including politicians and officials) are aware of the limits of simply producing strategic documents.[2] In fact, decision makers, officials and practitioners are challenging the usefulness of *any* documents for improving policy making. They argue that they have little impact on improving practice. This opens space for other types of policy work rather than writing policy documents, especially for communication, mediation, facilitation and so on.

At the time of this writing, public policy and policy analysis in the Czech Republic are also changing from within. Or, to put it more bluntly, the discipline is changing its identity. For a long time, it has been a *part* of other disciplines (especially sociology). The field of study of public and social policy has been institutionalised under the broader study programme 'sociology' and it has been part of the Institute of Sociological Studies. Most people identified themselves as 'applied sociologists'. While acknowledging a *specialisation* in public policy, most people involved in public policy grounded their professional prestige in

---

[2]   In this respect, the role of the EU is very interesting. Several authors throughout the book have suggested that the direct impact of EU policy documents on practice is rather low. We should not, however, underestimate the indirect effect on the nature of policy work. The EU for instance strongly stresses the importance of evaluation, which in turn has led more and more people to specialise in evaluation and cultivate their skills in it. On the other hand, the EU also demands 'strategic documents' which are often written for the sake of 'just being written'. As Šlosarčík suggests in Chapter Six, the EU serves more as an exporter of norms and rules rather than ideas.

---

other fields rather than public policy, mostly sociology, economics or public administration. This has been supported by the fact that in the Czech Republic, traditional disciplines with a long history have always been preferred, while new interdisciplinary fields have always been looked at suspiciously. But recently a new, more autonomous identity is being formed. It seems that we are approaching the point of a 'critical mass' of policy researchers and the boundaries of traditional disciplines are too restricting for them. Their identity is being formed around the public policy and policy analysis fields and is further supported by increasing participation in significant events such as the International Public Policy Conference and international networks of policy scholars.

Acknowledgement

The chapter was written with the financial support of PRVOUK programme P17 'Sciences of Society, Politics, and Media under the Challenge of the Times'.

References

Bardach, E. (2000) *A Practical Guide for Policy Analysis*, New York: Chatham House.

Colebatch, H., Hoppe, R. and Noordegraaf, M. (2010) 'Understanding policy work', in H. Colebatch, R. Hoppe and M. Noordegraaf (eds) *Working for Policy*, Amsterdam: Amsterdam University Press.

Fiala, P. and Schubert, K. (2000) *Moderní analýza politiky* [Modern policy analysis], Brno: Barrister & Principal.

Weimer, D. and Vining, A.R. (1999) *Policy Analysis: Concepts and Practice*, Upper Saddle River, NJ: Prentice Hall.

Index

References to boxes, tables, figures are in *italics*